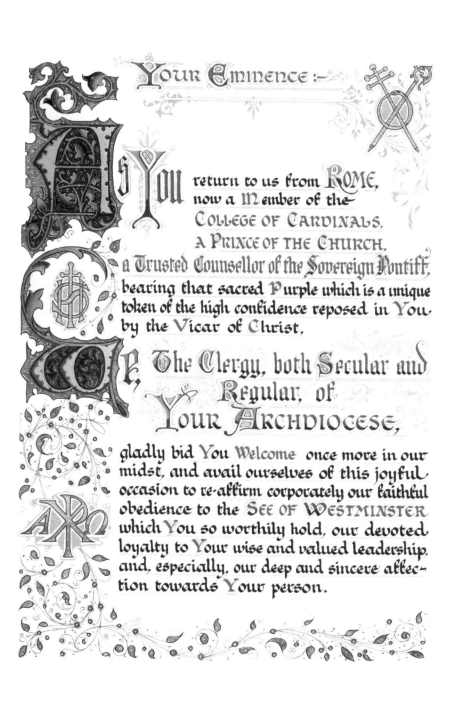

YOUR EMINENCE :-

AS YOU return to us from ROME, now a Member of the COLLEGE OF CARDINALS, A PRINCE OF THE CHURCH, a Trusted Counsellor of the Sovereign Pontiff, bearing that sacred Purple which is a unique token of the high confidence reposed in You by the Vicar of Christ,

WE, The Clergy, both Secular and Regular, of YOUR ARCHDIOCESE, gladly bid You Welcome once more in our midst, and avail ourselves of this joyful occasion to re-affirm corporately our faithful obedience to the SEE OF WESTMINSTER which You so worthily hold, our devoted loyalty to Your wise and valued leadership, and, especially, our deep and sincere affection towards Your person.

CARDINAL HINSLEY

Priest and Patriot

James Hagerty

CARDINAL HINSLEY
Priest and Patriot

*Ecce sacerdos magnus, qui in diebus suis placuit Deo,
et inventus est iustus.*

*See the great priest, who in his time pleased God,
and was found righteous.*

The Liturgy of the Hours

FAMILY PUBLICATIONS

ISBN 9781871217865

Cover Picture: Cardinal Hinsley by Simon Elwes

Frontispiece: The first page of the address made to Cardinal Hinsley, on the occasion of his elevation to the Sacred College, by the Provost of the Westminster Cathedral Chapter.

published by
Family Publications, Denis Riches House,
66 Sandford Lane, Oxford OX1 5RP, UK
www.familypublications.co.uk

Printed in England by
Cromwell Press, Trowbridge, Wilts.

Contents

CONTENTS

FOREWORD

Arthur Hinsley was a remarkable priest, born of working-class parents in a small East Yorkshire village and ordained for the Diocese of Leeds, he became the fifth Cardinal Archbishop of Westminster and a Prince of the Roman Catholic Church.

Hinsley's fifty-year ministry was full and varied but never entirely without controversy. In succession a professor, curate, headmaster, parish priest, seminary rector, papal diplomat and ultimately cardinal-archbishop, Hinsley's actions were imbued with the love of God, devotion to the Holy See, and loyalty to his country. Though his direct, uncompromising and occasionally maladroit approach may have attracted criticism it was more than offset by the warmth of his personality, his pastoral zeal, and his deep affection for the Church which he served so earnestly.

After six gruelling years in Africa, Hinsley had earned a peaceful retirement but his appointment to Westminster marked a new phase in his career. It was during this final phase that he established his reputation as a churchman of great significance in the history of twentieth-century British Christianity. In the Second World War Cardinal Hinsley became a Church leader of international renown with his vociferous condemnation of European fascism. It was during this period that he fought strongly for the rights of Catholics at home and abroad, and reached out to other Christians through the ground-breaking 'Sword of the Spirit' movement.

Using much new evidence from a wide variety of archival sources, and drawing skilfully upon the research and findings of others, Dr Hagerty's timely and excellent work examines Cardinal Hinsley's life in great detail and there emerges the picture of a diligent and prayerful priest who never compromised either his faith, or his patriotism.

This is a very welcome book and a most valuable contribution to the history of English and Welsh Catholicism and also the history of the Catholic Church in Africa.

Rt Rev Arthur Roche STB STL, Bishop of Leeds

ACKNOWLEDGEMENTS

Simply putting names on a page does not adequately convey my gratitude for the encouragement, assistance and advice which I have received during the preparation of this biography of Cardinal Hinsley. During the past seven years I have relied heavily on the knowledge, skill and erudition of so many people who have willingly and generously given of their time and professional expertise. Through their many kindnesses I have been able to complete a work which I began over twenty years ago.

I am especially grateful to:

Bishop Arthur Roche, Bishop of Leeds, for writing the Foreword, for his unfailing encouragement, and for his letters of introduction to archive repositories in Rome and Valladolid.

Mgr Nicholas Hudson, Rector of the Venerable English College, Rome; the Trustees of the English College, Rome; Mgr Michael Kujacz, Rector of the Royal English College, Valladolid; the Trustees of the Royal English College, Valladolid; Mgr Liam Bergin, Rector of the Pontifical Irish College, Rome; the Trustees of the Pontifical Irish College, Rome; Abbot Aidan Bellenger OSB; the Trustees of Downside Abbey; and the Trustees of St Bede's Grammar School, Bradford.

Dr Marco Grilli, Archivio Segreto Vaticano; Rev Dr John Sharp and Fr Petroc Howell, Diocese of Birmingham; Fr Stewart Foster, Diocese of Brentwood; Robin Gard (RIP), Diocese of Hexham and Newcastle; Mgr George Bradley (RIP) and Robert Finnigan, Diocese of Leeds; Dr Meg Whittle, Diocese of Liverpool; Fr Dominique Minskip and Dr David Smallwood, Diocese of Middlesbrough; Canon Anthony Dolan and Dr Graham Foster, Diocese of Nottingham; Rev Dr David Lannon, Diocese of Salford; Fr Michael Clifton and Fr Charles Briggs, Diocese of Southwark; Fr Ian Dickie, Fr Nicholas Schofield and Tamara Thornhill, Diocese of Westminster; Dom Philip Jebb OSB, Downside Abbey; Fr Andrew Headon, Iris di Domizio Jones and James McAuley, Venerable English College, Rome; Vera Orschel, Pontifical Irish College, Rome; Fr Peter Harris and Dr Javier Burrieza, Royal English College, Valladolid; Rev Dr Michael Sharratt and Dr Alistair MacGregor (RIP), Ushaw College; Fr Thomas McCoog SJ; Fr Hans Boerakker MHM, St Joseph's Society For Foreign Missions; Fr Tom Kiggins, St Patrick's

Missionary Society; Fr Edmund Hogan, Society of African Missions; and Fr Raymond Barry (RIP), the Spiritans.

Dom Anselm Cramer OSB, Dom Andrew McCaffrey OSB and Mrs Sue Goodwill, Monastic Library, Ampleforth Abbey; Sr Mary Joseph McManamon OSB, Librarian, Venerable English College, Rome; Rev Michael Dolan and Anthony Cornwell, Talbot Library, Preston; librarians at the British Library in London and Boston Spa; staff of the National Archives at Kew; librarians at Rhodes House, Oxford; and librarians at the University of York and the Minster Library, York.

Dr John Davies; Dr Peter Doyle; Mgr John Dunne; Fr Sean Finnegan; Mgr Timothy Galligan; Dr Mark Goldie; Elizabeth Grose; Fr Eamonn Hegarty; Paul Kennedy; Mgr Basil Loftus; Professor Alan McClelland; Francis McCrickard; Fr Peter Mansfield; Canon Cyril Moverley (RIP); Patrick Sice; Fr Brian Taylor; Fr Ken Taylor (RIP); and Louise Ward.

Professor Bill Sheils, my supervisor at the University of York, for his skilful academic guidance and friendship.

Dom Luke Beckett OSB and Fr Nicholas Schofield for kindly reading the manuscript and for their many helpful suggestions and comments.

Colin Mason, Edward Reeves and the staff of Family Publications, Oxford.

My wife Trina for lovingly supporting me during the years of research and writing. This book is for her.

James Hagerty

ABBREVIATIONS

AAW, Bo	Archives of the Archbishop of Westminster, Bourne Papers
AAW, Hi	Archives of the Archbishop of Westminster, Hinsley Papers
ABA	Archdiocese of Birmingham Archives
ACSA	Archives of the College of St Alban, Valladolid
ADHN	Hexham and Newcastle Diocesan Archives
ALA	Archdiocese of Liverpool Archives
AMHM, CAM	Archives of the Mill Hill Missionaries, Campling Papers
AMHM, KEN	Archives of the Mill Hill Missionaries, Kenyan Papers
AMHM, ROM	Archives of the Mill Hill Missionaries, Roman Papers
AMHM, UGA	Archives of the Mill Hill Missionaries, Ugandan Papers
ASA	Archdiocese of Southwark Archives
ASV, Scat., Fasc.	Archivio Segreto Vaticano, Scatola, Fascio
AVEC, Scritt.	Archives of the Venerable English College, Scritture
BDA	Brentwood Diocesan Archives
CO	Colonial Office
DAA	Downside Abbey Archives
IRM	International Review of Missions
LDA	Leeds Diocesan Archives
NAEd.	National Archives, Education
NDA	Nottingham Diocesan Archives
PICA	Pontifical Irish College Archives
SDA	Salford Diocesan Archives
SHDA	Shrewsbury Diocesan Archives
SPMS	St Patrick's Missionary Society
TLP	Talbot Library, Preston

INTRODUCTION

Arthur Hinsley's priestly ministry spanned fifty years. It was a life of service fulfilled diligently, loyally and modestly by a man of unyielding faith and intense patriotism.

The most significant, unforeseen and final stage in Hinsley's career began in 1935 when, at the age of 69, he became Archbishop of Westminster in succession to Cardinal Francis Bourne. Hinsley had no ambition for high office and his appointment to Westminster was not what he had wished for. Having just returned from Africa, where he had recently served as Apostolic Delegate to the British Colonies, he was in desperate need of rest and recuperation and the prospect of going to London filled him with foreboding. In England news of his appointment was greeted with disbelief in some ecclesiastical circles.

On the completion of his African ministry and beset by eczema, Hinsley had gratefully accepted the sinecure of a Canonry of St Peter's Basilica in Rome. To all intents and purposes he was *in sepulchro* but like Lazarus he emerged from the tomb and his appointment to Westminster transformed the last few years of his life. Initially overawed by the prospect before him, but bound by loyalty to the Bishop of Rome, Hinsley soon recovered his characteristic dynamism. He proceeded to undertake his duties at Westminster not burdened with the frailties of age but with a confidence bred of a long-held faith and maturity, vast experience, and in the knowledge that it was his last opportunity to contribute to God's work on earth. If his translation to Westminster was unexpected, his ensuing episcopate was to be even more surprising, for this ageing Yorkshireman brought a personal warmth and exercised a style of open and vigorous leadership hitherto unknown in the upper echelons of the English and Welsh Catholic Church. The first Yorkshire-born cardinal since St John Fisher was a priest whose personal qualities and directness of speech appealed not only to his co-religionists but also to those beyond his own faith community. Hinsley commanded respect if not always popularity and his words and actions helped to overcome the suspicions of those who considered Catholics to be less than loyal to crown and country.

Hinsley had not followed the path normally mapped out for those who achieved clerical eminence. He had studied for the priesthood at

St Cuthbert's College, Ushaw, and at the Venerable English College, Rome. Following ordination in 1893 he returned to Ushaw as a minor professor and then became a curate in Keighley. He subsequently became the founding headmaster of St Bede's Grammar School in Bradford, a missionary rector in the Diocese of Southwark and a part-time lecturer at St John's College, Wonersh. In 1917 he was appointed Rector of the Venerable English College and was created titular Bishop of Sebastopolis in 1926. Two years later he was sent as Apostolic Visitor to the British African colonies to initiate the modernization of Catholic mission schools in accordance with British policy. From 1930 until 1934, as titular Archbishop of Sardes, he remained in Africa as Apostolic Delegate to co-ordinate missionary endeavours. On his return from Africa Hinsley genuinely thought his career was over and looked forward to a time of restful tranquillity. He found the Pope's unexpected decision to send him to London profoundly disturbing and protested vigorously to Cardinal Raffaele Rossi, Prefect of the Sacred Consistorial Congregation, that he be allowed to remain in Rome. His entreaties were ignored and, as ever, Hinsley obeyed the papal will.

Hinsley's career was never entirely free from controversy. As a student in Rome he was challenged to a duel by the editor of a communist newspaper – an unusual event in the annals of the *Venerabile*. As a young priest at Ushaw he confidently entered the Modernist debate which reverberated around the late nineteenth- and early twentieth-century Church. After a strong disagreement with his bishop he was incardinated into another diocese. Against his own wishes and in defiance of the English and Welsh Hierarchy he was appointed Rector of the *Venerabile*. There he successfully prevented the civic authorities and town planners from demolishing part of the college. In Africa he challenged colonial administrators who ignored government ordinances and refused to acknowledge the rights of the Church. And at Westminster, where he arrived so unexpectedly, he aroused the ire of Italian cardinals, right-wing Anglicans, left-wing Catholics, Soviets, Fascists and Nazis. His relations with his brother bishops were never easy but he was not as uncompromising or as secretive as his predecessor. On more than one occasion he expressed his frustration at the inner workings of the Hierarchy and the views and actions of the bishops. His public devotion to King and country was as unacceptable to some bishops of Irish descent as was his ecumenical 'Sword of the Spirit' movement to the more conservative bishops. But all recognised that Hinsley was a man of principle, a doughty fighter for his Church and a lover of British institutions. He was also a pastor of souls and this remained the bedrock of his ministry irrespective of people, place, circumstance or preferment.

Like others, Hinsley expected a younger and fitter man to take on the bed of nails at Westminster, one who would introduce a fresh approach and revitalise the Hierarchy, but his appointment is less surprising in the light of other considerations. First, although Hinsley's age firmly identified him as a stop-gap appointment, he would take to Westminster substantial experience of training priests, English and African education, and a sound working knowledge of the Papal Curia and Vatican Congregations. Secondly, he was well-known in Rome if not in Westminster, Whitehall or the drawing rooms of the English Catholic aristocracy. His orthodoxy, his life-long commitment to the Church, his achievements in Rome and Africa, and his fierce loyalty to both the papacy and British Empire had long been recognised and appreciated by the Pope and the Vatican and British officials with whom he had worked. Thirdly, Hinsley's vision and experience of the universal Church was far wider and greater than any possessed by an introspective English and Welsh Hierarchy weakened by years of idiosyncratic leadership, divisive disputes and the jealous defence of episcopal jurisdictions.

Hinsley was a pragmatic bishop, one who realised that he could only administer his large diocese and lead the national Church with the help, advice and support of others. He did not regard himself as a scholar but willingly considered the opinions of those whom he thought able, articulate and, above all, orthodox. To guide him, he chose advisers irrespective of class, education or age. He wrote prefaces and forewords to the books of others but left no published work of theology. He had the experience to produce a manual on the training of priests but never did so. He left no diaries or memoirs or anything that might appear to suggest a personality cult. His archive contains Pastorals, his *Ad Clerum*, working papers and official correspondence. His letters, written in his distinctive firm sloping hand, are to be found in a variety of archives, religious and secular, private and public. Copies of his speeches and articles can be found in newspapers, pamphlets and journals. Some of his early wartime sermons and broadcasts were collected and published as *The Bond of Peace and other War-Time Addresses* in 1941. The pace at which he worked left him little time for writing but he always found time for his priests and his people.

Hinsley was appointed to Westminster at a turbulent time in British history, for the death of King George V in 1936 was followed in the same year by the abdication of King Edward VIII. The Archbishop's immediate entry into the public domain as a Church leader was not particularly auspicious for he unfortunately mishandled the protocol expected on such state occasions. In more routine domestic issues such as education and social welfare, however, he displayed a more confident touch. The rights and status of Catholics and their institutions were frequently challenged by government and Hinsley and the bishops were continually on their guard to protect and advance those legal and social advantages which their predecessors had fought for and won. In order to mobilise the Catholic community on social issues, Hinsley energetically pursued a policy of Catholic Action consistent with recent papal pronouncements but his enthusiastic approach and overly bureaucratic procedures were not always welcomed or imitated by his episcopal brethren.

In foreign affairs, the stability of Western Europe was disturbed and Catholic loyalties divided by the rise of totalitarian dictatorships, the Italian invasion of Abyssinia, the Spanish Civil War and ultimately the Second World War. Throughout the whole of this difficult period — virtually his entire time at Westminster — Hinsley was required to lead the national Church and his loyalties, stamina, qualities of leadership and diplomatic skills were frequently and thoroughly tested. From all of this he emerged as a staunch and vociferous opponent of those who denied religious conscience or infringed human rights. He was critical of the Italian invasion of Abyssinia and incurred the wrath of those Italian cardinals who supported Mussolini. His description of Pope Pius XI as 'a defenceless old man' in the face of Italian armed might was received with horror in the Vatican and for this he was temporarily denied promotion to the College of Cardinals. He supported the Catholic General Franco against the atheistic Republicans in Spain but the alliances of Catholic Italy with Nazi Germany and of democratic Britain with Soviet Russia pushed his religious loyalty and patriotism to the limit. In Anglo-Vatican and Anglo-Irish relations his interventions were significant but not always successful. His uncompromising stance on Italian fascism, Irish wartime neutrality and Irish republican terrorism made him unpopular in both Rome and Dublin. His distaste for Fascist Italy, Nazi Germany and the USSR was never concealed and his wartime speeches, while welcomed by the Allies, were condemned by Hitler's propagandists.

Hinsley proclaimed the Second World War to be a Christian crusade and to be effective and successful in this venture he invited other Christian denominations to combine through the Sword of the Spirit movement. 'The Sword', headed by Hinsley and led by his chosen Catholics, sought to renew Christian values in the social order and international relations but his ecumenical approach alarmed conservative Catholics and not for the first time highlighted the difficulties he experienced in leading a Hierarchy so long accustomed to either ignoring or disagreeing with Westminster. Nevertheless, he was *de facto* senior spokesman for the English and Welsh Hierarchy and through his wartime radio broadcasts he became a figure of national prominence. Allegedly, Winston Churchill said that he and Cardinal Hinsley were the only two people he trusted to speak on behalf of the nation in time of war. The government turned to him, as President of the Hierarchy, in all matters relating to Catholic engagement in public life and in that role he had to lead and collaborate with his brother bishops to protect the unique status and maintain the morale of his Church, one so often identified with foreign and now enemy regimes. In all these undertakings, not always facilitated by independent-minded bishops, Hinsley maintained scrupulous adherence to the Church's *magisterium* and unwavering loyalty to his country.

Hinsley's patriotism was not jingoistic nor can it be associated simply with the circumstances and demands of war. His love and affection for his country and its empire was life-long: it was evident in his approach to the education of Catholic boys and their preparation for life; it was pronounced as he trekked across British Africa; and it was proclaimed as he spoke for the Allied cause during the Second World War. It matured as he lived in Christian communities in Rome and in Africa and was demonstrated in peace and in war. It was inherent in his concept of a human society that enshrined the virtues of Christianity protected and fostered in the British Empire. The Russian Patriotic War, where people gave their lives for a godless state, did not equate with Hinsley's understanding of patriotism.

To Hinsley true patriotism was essentially a Christian virtue and in his studies of St Thomas Aquinas he would have read that 'after God, it is to parents and fatherland that man is most indebted. Consequently, just as it is the function of religion to pay cult to God, so, in a secondary degree, it is the function of *pietas* to pay cult to parents and fatherland'.

To St Thomas 'Religion will put man into his proper relationship to God. Piety will enable him to honour and serve his parents and his country'. In this context it is easier to understand the motto he chose for the *Venerabile* in 1922 – *Pro Petri Fide et Patria*. In war the obligations of patriotism demand that people give their governments the same kind of respect that is owed to their parents. A country can be seen as God's instrument in creating, directing and contributing to the general well-being of people and so long as a monarch and his or her representatives remain in office they possess authority and therefore demand respect. Jesus had said to his disciples 'render unto Caesar the things that are Caesar's' and according to Pope Leo XIII this pertains even when power resides in 'an unworthy mandatary'.[1]

The second duty of patriotism, according to St Thomas, is preferential love which orders people to show a special love and respect to the country in which they were born, 'so much so that the good citizen does not hesitate to face death for it'. Yet this does not demand that the state becomes the final end and is placed above God, a position totally opposed to Catholic teaching. When condemning totalitarianism, Pius XI warned that transgressing the limit of what is just and right, especially when it develops into an immoderate love of one's nation, becomes the source of wrongs and injustices, and men dispense with charity and forget the universality of God's human family.

The third obligation of the patriot is obedience to legitimate authority but totalitarianism usurps the authority of God and makes the state the be-all and end-all of the citizen. In democratic states power derives from the people but in turn the electorate draws its authority from God so there can never be blind submission to a state. Yet to withdraw legally acquired authority citizens must only use lawful means and if a government remains in office legitimately then citizens must submit to it. The invasion of one's country by a foreign power presents difficulties, for whilst the citizen is not bound to obey the invader he is compelled to acknowledge an existing legitimate authority which tacitly ratifies an invader's regulations as long as they do not prejudice the liberty of Christian conscience nor patriotic dignity.

Thus patriotism can be taken beyond the narrow confines of the place or land of birth. While people are always tied to the country of their birth, they owe a debt of justice and charity to a wider community of which they are also citizens. The same patriotic obligations apply in this situation. Where men live in lands other than their birth country they must loyally co-operate in promoting common welfare. There can be no conflict between the virtues of patriotism and legal justice, for both are essential to build a better world and humankind has a duty to God to exercise both.[2]

Hinsley's patriotism therefore was firmly based on Christian principles and was proclaimed throughout his adult life and especially during his African ministry and the Second World War. During that conflict the Ministry of Information was delighted to acquire his services for propaganda purposes but his pronouncements were not made to order. Hinsley spoke on issues that he saw as being fundamental to the Allied cause and the good of Christianity. His radio broadcasts reached 3 million people during weekday broadcasts and over six million on Sundays, and to some non-Catholics the Cardinal assumed a central but unwelcome place in English national life. Hedley Henson, former Anglican Bishop of Durham, claimed that Hinsley had replaced the Archbishop of Canterbury as the spiritual leader of the nation. Extreme Protestants considered him to be presumptuous in claiming to speak for all Christians but his patriotism made it difficult for them to condemn him outright. J.A. Kensit of the Protestant Truth Society, whose father had been murdered by a Catholic in 1902, exemplified those who welcomed the Cardinal's patriotism but found it hard to accept his religion. 'Your utterances of loyalty to the British cause in the present struggle', he wrote to Hinsley in 1940, 'have been received with no little gratification, and no-one is surprised that your English blood freezes at the thought of a Nazi or Fascist overthrow of British liberty'. The Vatican's past attempts to overthrow Protestantism, Kensit argued, were mirrored by the present Italian-dominated papal curia's support of fascist regimes but bravely Hinsley disagreed with them. 'In Italy', Kensit wrote, 'your Church is enthusiastically pro-Axis, whilst here you courageously take a stand for British interests'. Hinsley's outspoken comments about Ireland's alleged sympathy with Germany also forced Kensit to admit that Hinsley was 'not *persona grata* with the followers of the Roman Catholic Church in Ireland' but if Hinsley were able to convince the Irish, through their bishops, to hand over their southern ports to the British then 'such would constitute a practical step in your patriotic campaign'. Kensit lumped Eamon de Valera, Mussolini, and Hitler together and for good measure threw in Joseph Kennedy, the United States Ambassador to Great Britain, who, he claimed, attempted to whitewash Germany's military conquests. Kensit suggested to Hinsley that he should make representations to the Vatican that 'such notorious sons of the Church should be publicly reproved and excommunicated. Mere platitudes about principles of freedom are futile'. 'Whilst you might be a losing caste with your Italianised headquarters', he concluded, 'you would at least be showing some consistency in the light of your patriotic speeches and writings'.

Kensit recognised that for Hinsley and for many others in the Church, hostility to Hitler, although in the foreground at the present time, was probably not as profound as their dislike of Stalin and Churchill's attempts to forge an Anglo-Soviet alliance which threatened the Prime Minister's support from Catholics and movements like the Sword of the Spirit. Yet Kensit was not to let Catholics occupy the high ground and, quoting Mussolini, Franco and Pétain, argued that their oft-unspoken affinity for fascism might fan the spirit of defeatism should Hitler invade the British Isles. The invaders, he argued, would find many prepared Catholic minds on which to work. The people of this country should not forget that for six-and-a-half years from February 1933 when the Nazis came to power, to September 1939, when the war broke out, the English Catholic press had glossed over the misdeeds of Hitlerism against humanity. Not even the attacks on the Church were treated as news and *The Persecution of the Catholic Church in The Third Reich* was published after war broke out. Catholics in Germany had tried to convince Hitler that working with the Church was in his interests but this had met with little Catholic criticism in England compared with the Church's attacks on the USSR.[3] Kensit's letters and books highlighted the very real dangers in the public perception that Catholics were allied to the nation's enemies. It was for this very reason that Hinsley continued to speak out and carefully protect the Catholic name.

Historians of the English and Welsh Catholic Church in the twentieth century have generally examined Hinsley's career in the context of his time at Westminster and their approach and interpretation have tended to be similar: a superficial survey of his Westminster years followed by the judgement that they were brief but eventful. Specific studies of contemporary British Catholic history have scrutinised Hinsley's role in more detail and have arrived at slightly modified interpretations of his reputation but restricted by space and confined by focus they do not provide a complete picture of the Cardinal's life. Similarly, histories of missionary institutes and the African Church have considered Hinsley's contribution only in the context of Africa and are therefore restricted in analysis and conclusions. However, Fr John Carmel Heenan's *Cardinal Hinsley,* Thomas Moloney's *Westminster, Whitehall and the Vatican: the Role of Cardinal Hinsley (1935-1943)*, and Kester Aspden's *Fortress Church* are studies which include longer and wider perspectives of the Cardinal's life. Heenan's work suffers from an almost hagiographic approach whilst Moloney's and Aspden's works, though valuable, are deliberately limited in range and coverage.

Heenan claimed that *Cardinal Hinsley* was not a biography but 'a memoir' compiled with great reluctance and as a result of much pressure. It appeared only six months after the Cardinal's death and the urgency to transmit words to paper, combined with the fact that many of the major personalities were still alive, restricted Heenan's analysis of many important events and developments. Heenan was devoted to Hinsley and was very close to him. He had been a seminarian at the Venerable English College during Hinsley's rectorship and following the Archbishop's arrival in Westminster he became an adviser and speechwriter. His memoir, described by himself as 'un-ambitious work' may be considered too subjective but, as he pointed out, he intended to present 'while his living personality is still vivid, a sketch of a great and holy man.' In that, Heenan was successful and there emerges a portrait of a very human character – impulsive, dynamic, diligent, indiscreet, pious, and warm. Heenan's work is largely anecdotal but nevertheless it provides a unique contemporary understanding of a priest who so obviously animated the loyalty and affection of others. The narrative concentrates mainly on Hinsley's career as Rector of the English College and as cardinal–archbishop, two areas where Heenan could write with confidence, yet there are many details on Hinsley's earlier life often overlooked by later historians. *Cardinal Hinsley* may suffer from immediacy and an inadequate research base but it is an indispensable source that informs later and more detailed analyses of Hinsley's life and episcopate. Fr Andrew Beck described the book as an 'episodal outline', 'the fruit of a truly Roman *pietas*, moving in its affection, downright, direct and distinguished in its vigorous prose'. He wrote that Heenan's book was 'brilliantly successful' despite its shortcomings and uneven treatment of the Cardinal's life. Beck was as fulsome as Heenan in his appreciation of Hinsley but unlike Heenan he emphasised the lasting importance of Hinsley's African ministry in the development of the Universal Church and the due recognition accorded him by Pope Pius XI, 'the Pope of the Missions'.[4]

Moloney drew upon a wider range of sources than Heenan and his erudite and stimulating study of diplomatic relations between Westminster, the Vatican and Whitehall, demonstrates how Hinsley, an increasingly prominent figure in British life, guided the English and Welsh Catholic community through a series of domestic and foreign crises. In his treatment of Hinsley's early life and career Moloney follows the accepted interpretation but departs from other studies when, like Beck, he emphasises the importance of Hinsley's African ministry. Up to 1927 Hinsley's work had been almost entirely devoted to ecclesiastical education but, Moloney claims, his time in Africa rescued him from the routine of seminary life and enabled him to contribute substantially to the development of the indigenous African Catholic Church. It also gave him the opportunity to preach the benefits of the Catholic faith within the boundaries of a benevolent British Empire. Hinsley had total devotion to the former and great respect for the latter and in his view a combination of the two provided the optimum conditions for the Christian progress of humankind. His time in Africa also allowed him to deviate from the traditional career path of a diocesan bishop and brought him to the notice of a grateful Roman Curia and imperial government. When this part of Hinsley's career is considered, his appointment to Westminster becomes more understandable.

In *Fortress Church* Kester Aspden analyses the English and Welsh Hierarchy's approach and response to social and political issues in the first sixty years of the twentieth century. Aspden deals competently with Hinsley's role in this context but the scope of his work, like that of Moloney, necessarily precludes a fuller analysis of Hinsley's career. In *The Venerable English College, Rome*, Mgr Michael Williams gives a first-rate overview of Hinsley's rectorship of the English College and provides both a useful antidote to Heenan's restricted view and supplements the researches of Moloney and Aspden. The two most recent studies of English cardinals, Bellenger and Fletcher's *Princes of the Church: A History of the English Cardinals* and Schofield and Skinner's *The English Cardinals*, draw upon all of these studies and both contain useful synopses of Hinsley's life and career but neither claims to be a biography.

To many, the history of the Catholic Church in twentieth-century England and Wales is personified in the dominating figures of Cardinals

Bourne, Heenan and Hume who between them ruled Westminster for 67 years out of 100 years. They were indeed very special men who in their own unique ways influenced not only the Catholic community which they served but also the wider society in times of significant social and religious change. Cardinal Griffin and Cardinal Godfrey are not generally seen as prominent churchmen but in the case of Hinsley it can be argued that he too should be ranked alongside those regarded as important leaders of the Catholic Church in this country. His career has long been overlooked in its entirety and consequently his reputation, whilst never denigrated, has not been accorded the full measure it deserves. From a working class background Hinsley became a Prince of the Church; that in itself is an achievement worthy of respect and admiration.

The aim of this book is to add to work already undertaken and provide a much fuller account of Hinsley's life and career. To achieve this I have consulted sources which were neither relevant nor available to other studies and have expanded on aspects of Hinsley's life which have been previously overlooked. In particular, his early life and student days, his work in Bradford and in Southwark, his African ministry, and his experiences as a diocesan bishop are dealt with in some considerable detail. There emerges a picture of a conscientious priest who regarded his vocation as an immense privilege and a huge responsibility and whose commitment to his Church was almost equalled by the love and respect he had for his country.

Chapter One

FROM BOYHOOD TO PRIESTHOOD

1865 – 1900

Carlton: 'My Native Place'

Arthur Hinsley was born on 25 August 1865 at Carlton in Yorkshire, an ancient village on the road between the market and abbey town of Selby and the port of Goole on the River Ouse. At the time of Hinsley's birth, the Anglican parish of Carlton-cum-Snaith had a population of approximately 750.[1] Parish records show that branches of the Hindslay, Hindesley, Hinslay, or Hinsley family had lived in Carlton and the neighbouring village of Snaith, immediately to the south but separated by the River Aire, since at least the seventeenth century with the male members being predominantly artisans and inn keepers.[2]

Arthur was the second of four children born to Thomas Hinsley and his wife Bridget, née Ryan, formerly of Cloonascragh near Tuam in County Galway. They had married in 1858 when Thomas was twenty-three and Bridget probably in her late teens. Their eldest child, Charles Joseph, was born in 1859; Annie Elizabeth was born in 1861 and Alfred Thomas, born in 1869, was the youngest of the four.[3] In his biography of Hinsley, Fr John Carmel Heenan presented an idyllic picture of a hardworking father and a pious mother, typical, he claimed, of the kind of Catholic home which produces priests. Hinsley's mother, wrote Heenan, 'had that profound influence upon his character normally exercised by the mother of a priest. She gave him his first lessons in piety, while his father . . . showed him the nobility of a true craftsman'.[4] It was certainly a close knit family surrounded by many relatives. When Hinsley was confirmed by Bishop Robert Cornthwaite of Beverley on 11 October 1874, he was accompanied by his brother Charles and sister Annie and of the 28 children who were confirmed ten were Hinsleys. By 1871 the family lived at 15 North End (now Convent Lane), a modest redbrick terrace house down a narrow lane adjoining the grounds of St Mary's Catholic church. Thomas, a joiner, employed two men and two boys.

33

Other Hinsleys in the village and district were employed as a blacksmith, a labourer, a carpenter, and a gardener.[5]

At the time of her marriage to Thomas Hinsley, Bridget Ryan worked in the service of the Catholic Stapleton family and lived in Carlton Hall their Jacobean home. The Hall with its integral chapel and adjoining estate was located to the east of the main north-south road which bisected the linear village.[6] The Stapletons had been staunch recusants: from 1664 until 1668 their chaplain was a relative, Fr Thomas Thwing, who was executed at York in 1680 amid the anti-Catholic persecution following the Titus Oates Plot.[7] In 1839 a collateral branch of the family, the Stapletons of Richmond in North Yorkshire, who were decidedly lukewarm in their support of the Catholic faith, succeeded to the Hall and estates. In the following year their ancient title of Beaumont was revived and Miles Thomas Stapleton, who now became the 8th Baron Beaumont, celebrated by remodelling the Hall. This included the conversion of the chapel into state rooms and Beaumont informed Canon George Heptonstall, the chaplain, and Bishop John Briggs, Vicar Apostolic of the Yorkshire District, that they should look for another place of worship. Heptonstall bought land and a legacy from Beaumont's cousin, Catherine, Lady Throckmorton, paid for the erection of a new church and the maintenance of its clergy. In 1842 St Mary's, located at the north end of the village, was opened to serve a Catholic population of about 200.[8] Relations between Beaumont and Canon Heptonstall deteriorated when the priest refused free pews for the Beaumont family in the new and financially independent 'episcopal church'. Beaumont responded by making Catholics pay a toll when they crossed over his bridge from the south of the river to attend Sunday Mass. Like many other English aristocratic Catholics the 8th Baron did not welcome the growing power of their bishops and at the Restoration of the Catholic English and Welsh Hierarchy in 1850 he expressed his displeasure by joining the Church of England.

George Heptonstall, born at Tadcaster, educated at St Cuthbert's College, Ushaw, and the Venerable English College, Rome, was thus the last chaplain to reside at Carlton Hall and became the first post-Reformation Catholic missioner at Carlton.[9] It was Heptonstall, the contemporary and former colleague of Nicholas Wiseman at the *Venerabile*, who baptized the two-day-old Arthur Hinsley and then later educated him at a little school in a cottage adjoining the church.[10]

Without citing his sources, although it could have been the Cardinal or his relatives in later life, Heenan described Hinsley as a determined and energetic little boy who, surrounded by a caring family, studied earnestly, served Mass for Canon Heptonstall and helped his father in the joiner's shop.[11] The inference is unmistakable but we are left to make our own comparisons.

On the death of Canon Heptonstall in 1875 Mgr Edward Goldie became the missioner at Carlton. Goldie, educated at St Cuthbert's College, Ushaw, had been secretary to Bishop Robert Cornthwaite of Beverley from 1865 to 1875 and was subsequently financial secretary to the diocese. It was Goldie who arranged for Hinsley to leave Carlton in 1876 and begin his studies for the priesthood at Ushaw as a student of the Diocese of Beverley. Twenty years later, in September 1896, the recently-ordained Hinsley attended the funeral of Mgr Goldie at St Wilfrid's, York. On his appointment as Archbishop of Westminster in 1935, Hinsley wrote to Mrs Etheldreda Shattock, a great niece of Goldie, saying that it was Goldie, 'his greatest friend and benefactor' who had 'got me to Ushaw and later to Rome'.[12] It is very likely that Goldie arranged for the support of Bishop Cornthwaite but before his death Canon Heptonstall had also ensured that with the substantial income from a fund bestowed by Lady Throckmorton and additional financial help from the Himsworth family who owned land in Carlton, the Hinsleys would be able to send Arthur to train for the priesthood. Such was the generosity of Mr and Mrs Himsworth to ecclesiastical education and the diocesan deaf and dumb institute that Bishop Cornthwaite obtained a papal blessing for them during his visit to Rome in 1878. Thomas Himsworth had stood as Hinsley's confirmation sponsor.

Hinsley's first eleven years, therefore, were spent in a village strongly associated with recusancy and among a small but steadfast Catholic congregation which was dependent, like many others, upon the financial support of a Catholic gentry family. But this background, so typical of many English Catholics of the time, was given another dimension by his descent from Anglo-Irish parentage. 'Arthur's mother was a saintly Irishwoman, his father of hardy Yorkshire stock', wrote Heenan, and Hinsley, he continued, 'seems to have inherited the best qualities of both races'.[13] He had also come under the influence of priests who were part of the revival of early and mid nineteenth-century English Catholicism and whose education, training and outlook were Ultramontane yet whose priestly ministry was rooted in the practicalities of the English mission.

Ushaw

Ushaw was one of four English seminaries for secular priests and served the new dioceses which had formed part of the Northern District before the restoration of the English and Welsh Hierarchy in 1850. The other seminaries were at St Edmund's, Ware, (for the old London District), Prior Park (for the old Western District), and St Mary's College, Oscott (for the old Midland District). In addition, the major religious orders had their own seminaries.

Seminary training and Catholic higher education was in a state of transition at this time. The change in ecclesiastical organisation after the Restoration of the Hierarchy in 1850 had a knock-on effect on the management of seminaries. Instead of serving eight geographically extensive vicariates, the seminaries now served thirteen independent dioceses and their progress was seriously impaired by divisive episcopal disputes over jurisdiction and finance. Some dioceses, such as Liverpool, Birmingham and Leeds, opened their own diocesan seminaries. To meet the enormous costs of running the seminaries, bishops were compelled to admit lay students and, in consequence, a secular tone crept into the curriculum and ethos of what were essentially religious institutions. The academic brilliance of converts such as John Henry Newman, added a new dimension to contemporary Catholic learning but also highlighted its relatively poor quality. The English and Welsh Hierarchy's ban on Catholics attending Oxford, Cambridge, and the older universities was seen by the Catholic laity who could afford it as a serious social limitation and the prohibition was often ignored. To obviate all these problems, and despite the cost, some bishops decided to establish their own diocesan seminaries, and in this they had the support of Cardinal Manning.[14]

Bishops and seminary presidents disagreed over many other crucial details. Faced with the necessity of providing more priests for the rapidly developing urban missions, the majority of bishops favoured shortened theology courses. Some bishops, however, like Alexander Goss of Liverpool, were critical of the poor quality secular courses offered to seminarians and feared that most newly-ordained priests would enter a secular world educated to a lower level than some Catholic laymen. They also questioned the advisability of training seminarians in semi-monastic surroundings when most would be dispatched to one-man urban missions. Other bishops, such as the Ultramontane Robert Cornthwaite of Beverley, a former Rector of the Venerable English College, Rome, adopted a conservative attitude towards the free-thinking tendencies of contemporary academia and, like Manning, strongly supported the continued ban on Catholics attending the universities. Since 1835, a way round this had been for lay Catholics and seminarians to obtain external degrees from London University. Catholic seminaries were affiliated to the university and Ushaw had prepared students for London degrees since 1863. This affiliation introduced a stronger secular influence on the seminary curriculum and, in particular, on the wider reading of literature and philosophy. The more reactionary bishops argued against this contending that the correct nature of seminary studies would be vitiated and that the education and formation of priests would be replaced by cramming, coaching and exposure to unwelcome texts and influences.[15]

In the midst of all this, St Cuthbert's had its own peculiar problems, and its historian has commented that the years 1876-1890, when Hinsley was a student there, were 'the unhappiest that Ushaw was to know'.[16] The college was governed by the Bishops of Hexham and Newcastle, Beverley, Salford, Liverpool, and Shrewsbury, and as Hinsley arrived at the college, Robert Tate, the sixth president, had just died. During the next fourteen years there were to be five presidents – Francis Wilkinson, Bishop James Chadwick of Hexham and Newcastle, William Wrennall, William Dunderdale, and James Lennon. This frequent turnover, wrote Fr Milburn, 'suggests dissension, instability of government, harm to the college in its different branches; and in general such was the picture'.[17] Francis Wilkinson, who had previously been vice-president, was not of the same high calibre as his illustrious predecessors, Tate and Charles Newsham. The heavy responsibility seriously affected his health and by September 1877 he was dead. Bishop Chadwick acted as interim president for a short while before being succeeded by William Wrennall in October 1878. Under Wrennall's presidency, but against his advice, the number of lay students was reduced in accordance with the bishops' stipulation. Ushaw became more of a seminary and less able to compete, not only with Ampleforth, Downside, and Stonyhurst, but also with the newer and rapidly growing Catholic colleges such as Cotton College,

Ratcliffe, and St Bede's College, Manchester, all providing for the sons of an emerging Catholic middle class. Never robust, the financial affairs of the college deteriorated, and Wrennall resigned as the bishops appeared either unable or unwilling to consider long-term solutions to the problems faced by Ushaw. In January 1886 he was replaced by Canon William Dunderdale of Salford Diocese but within a month his health had broken down and he was immediately replaced by James Lennon. Affected by ill-health and with serious doubts over his competency, Lennon struggled on for four years until he too was replaced in October 1890, by Bishop Thomas Wilkinson of Hexham and Newcastle. Under Wilkinson, the college's fabric and finances improved, academic changes were introduced, and the link with London University gave way to one with Durham University when, in 1896, *Propaganda Fide* finally agreed that clerical students could attend state universities.

The Seminarian

Such then, in outline, is the background to Hinsley's studies at Ushaw, not that a teenager living away from home would be aware of anything other than the most obvious changes to his daily routine. However, Hinsley was to be directly connected with Ushaw for eighteen years, and later, during his time as a professor at the college, he was to contribute significantly to the reforms introduced by Bishop Wilkinson. Unfortunately, we have no record of Hinsley's feelings as he left Carlton for Ushaw, and we can only surmise at his impressions as he compared the flat, agricultural surroundings of his native village with the hills and mining communities around the college when he arrived on 16 September 1876.[18] St Cuthbert's had been established at Ushaw in 1808. Its original quadrangular shape was dominated by a plain three-story front and it was described as being very much 'like a factory'. Throughout the 1840s and 1850s there had been almost continual extensions and alterations and during Hinsley's time as a seminarian St Joseph's Chapel, which had been designed by Augustus Welby Pugin in 1845, was replaced in 1884 by St Cuthbert's Chapel designed by Dunn and Hansom.[19]

The contemporary academic structure of the college was as follows:

a) *Seniores*   staff
b) *Professores*   minor professors
c) *Theologi*   Divines (three divisions)
d) *Philosophi*   Philosophers (two divisions)

e) *Litterae Humaniores*
    i rhetoric   age 18 years
    ii poetry   age 17 years
    iii syntax   age 16 years
    iv grammar   age 15 years
f) *Rudimentorum*
    i high figures   age 14 years
    ii low figures   age 13 years
    iii 1 underlow   age 12 years
    iv 2 underlow   age 11 years
    v 3 underlow   age 10 years[20]

Hinsley entered in second underlow and studied English, Arithmetic, Bible and English History, Geography, French and Latin. As he progressed through the college he embarked on additional courses in Greek, Algebra and Geometry, and Classical History. With him from the Diocese of Beverley were Edwin Carr, John Hanlon, and Frederick Mitchell, adding to the other thirty-six Beverley students out of a total college roll of 375. The tall, reserved, and self-contained Hinsley developed slowly and it was not until he reached *Litterae Humaniores* that he really began to make progress. The regular reports received by Bishop Cornthwaite give the impression that Hinsley was of above average ability, diligent, in good health and well behaved.[21] His examination marks were consistently creditable. Certainly, Hinsley did not cause his bishop grief as other diocesan students had done. Mgr Wrennall reported to Cornthwaite in November 1883 that among seminarians from Leeds, created a separate diocese in 1878, 'losses have been great' and seven had left the college. He tried to allay the Bishop's conviction that something was seriously wrong at Ushaw and was at pains to convince him that the spiritual direction the students were receiving was correct.[22] By this time, however, in accordance with Manning's policy, Cornthwaite had his own small but expensive seminary of St Joseph's in Leeds. The diocese was paying out over £20,000 a year for its seminarians at Ushaw, Leeds and Rome.[23]

Hinsley was later described by his contemporary Canon Frederick Mitchell, Administrator of Leeds Cathedral at the time of Hinsley's appointment to Westminster in 1935, as a steady and earnest student of a genial disposition with a habit of close application to his studies. He continued successfully, if not spectacularly, and obtained very good marks and positions in Greek, Latin, English, French and even Mathematics, which was never his strong point.[24] Later, Canon Mitchell and others reminisced about their time at Ushaw, and remembered life outside the classroom – the trips down the valley to the river, eating pies at Mrs Pearson's Hill Top, and the physical demands of college sports which were numerous, varied and strenuous. They remarked that the newly introduced game of tennis was effeminate, unlike the arcane and violent games that the Catholic colleges had copied from the great English public schools. However, they admired the skill and athleticism of the young Rafael Merry del Val y Zulueta who had joined the college in 1883 and who was an expert tennis player.[25]

On 7 October 1883, Hinsley received the tonsure and was admitted to the clerical state. In 1885-1886, whilst in the second division of Philosophy, he became an acolyte, the highest of the four minor orders. Meanwhile, his academic studies continued. In Poetry he had been prepared for matriculation at London University, in Rhetoric he was entered for the university's Intermediate Examination in Arts, and in the first year of Philosophy for the final B.A. exam. His first attempt at the London external degree examination was surprisingly unsuccessful but in September 1887 he became a minor professor and taught syntax and rhetoric for three years. He also prepared some of the older students for the London degree and had the embarrassing experience of taking the exam with them. Fortunately, in October 1889, he was successful, offering mental philosophy as his major subject and emerging as the top of the class.[26]

The Venerable English College

The Venerable English College, Rome, often referred to as the *Venerabile*, is on the Via di Monserrato off the Piazza Farnese and stands on the site of a fourteenth-century English hospice that had originally been under the direction of the English crown.[27] After the Reformation it was taken over by the papacy and became a haven for English pilgrims and exiles. On the advice of Cardinal William Allen, who had already founded a continental seminary at Douai, it was established as a seminary for English and Welsh students by Pope Gregory XIII in May 1579. Early students were compelled to take the 'missionary oath' – a promise to return to England and Wales to minister to the beleaguered and persecuted recusant community. If caught, they faced torture and execution. Over forty of the *Venerabile's* students were martyred for the Faith, and this apostolic spirit permeated the college's ethos during succeeding centuries.

During the Napoleonic Wars and the French occupation of Rome, the college was closed and its students were disbanded. Ironically, though there were still anti-Catholic laws on the statute books, the students returned to England where even French émigré priests were welcomed and new Catholic seminaries were established, including Ushaw. In 1818, the *Venerabile* was reopened with a new constitution. Among the first students were Nicholas Wiseman and George Heptonstall.[28]

Hinsley's academic success identified him as a prospective 'high flier' and in October 1890 he was sent to the *Venerabile* for further studies in Theology and to prepare for ordination. The college Rector was Monsignor William Giles who had occupied the post since 1888. Giles had already spent thirty-six years in Rome, first as a student at the *Collegio Pio*, as *ripetitore* at the *Venerabile*, Vice-Rector of the *Pio* and, after 1865, Vice-Rector at the *Venerabile*. Giles, a fine artist, was an affable man and an easy-going rector; administration, enforcing rules and disciplining students were not his strong points.[29] The college atmosphere was relaxed and debate was encouraged. On one occasion Hinsley took advantage of this. He had read an article in a Milan newspaper advocating communism and took issue with it. His response, which he had translated by an Italian seminarian, was so aggressive that the editor challenged him to a duel. Irrespective of the prospect of imminent death or wounding, the liberty taken by Hinsley was, even by the standards of Monsignor Giles, against the college rules and he received a severe dressing down from the Rector. Giles felt that the breach of the rules was so serious that he considered sending Hinsley home but after some thought decided that he could stay and privately proclaimed that the article was 'uncommonly fine'. It was the first public instance of Hinsley coming to the defence of his Church. Thereafter he conscientiously continued his studies, obtained a Doctorate in Divinity from the Gregorian University, a Doctorate in Philosophy from the Academy of St Thomas, and was ordained for the Diocese of Leeds on 23 December 1893.[30]

An Energetic Professor

In the following year Hinsley returned to Ushaw as a professor of Moral Philosophy, full of the revived interest in Scholastic Philosophy, and aware that other students, like him, would be sent to Rome inadequately trained in philosophy unless the weakness was addressed by the English seminaries as the bishops had requested. *The Ushaw Magazine* recorded that:

> To give effect to the strongly expressed desire of the Pope that Philosophy should be studied more deeply, the course of Moral Philosophy has been considerably increased, the class time almost doubled; and to make this possible, a second professor of Moral Philosophy has been added to the staff in the person of Arthur Hinsley, D.D.[31]

Hinsley quickly established circles for the study of philosophy and a college branch of the Roman Academy for the Study of Aquinas. He frequently visited local book shops, where he often bought books for his students, and his friends called him 'bocca'. He was also given responsibility for the college's Big Library of over 40,000 volumes. 'Dr Hinsley' reported the Ushaw Magazine,

> has been entrusted with the custodianship of the library, and is busily engaged, with an array of helpers, in carrying on a work that has long been needed – weeding out duplicates and worthless editions that occupy valuable space. This work, with that of compiling a new catalogue, is one of great labour, in the successful completion of which we shall greet reason for satisfaction and gratitude to all engaged in it.[32]

In late 1896 and early 1897, Hinsley became publicly involved in the contemporary Modernist debate and embroiled in correspondence with the Catholic biologist St George Mivart. Modernism was the label attached to those Catholic thinkers and writers who attempted to synthesize the basic truths of religion and the methods and assumptions of modern scientific thought, using the latter as the necessary and proper criteria.[33] Modernists judged what was true or right in accordance with recent experience, regardless of whether the process or the outcome ran counter to Church teaching, accepted dogma, or tradition. The movement gathered pace in the 1890s, during the liberalizing pontificate of Leo XIII, while Hinsley was a student at the English College, but whereas some seminarians found it difficult to reconcile what they were being taught with present day scientific thought, Hinsley appears to have had no doubts about the Church's teaching. The leading proponents of the various strands of Catholic Modernism were Alfred Loisy, a French priest, the Jesuit George Tyrrell who had converted from the Church of Ireland, and Baron Friedrich von Hügel, an Anglicised Austrian. Loisy has been described as a critic and historical scholar; Tyrrell as an apologist, and von Hügel as a biblical scholar and theologian. Working inter-dependently, they adopted a critical approach to contemporary Catholic thought and dogma, and, like others, were encouraged by the fresh approach to philosophical studies and social problems stimulated by Leo XIII. However, Rome reacted negatively to Modernists and other liberal Catholics attempting to obtain freedom of scholarship within the Church and the movement was ultimately condemned by Pius X in 1907.

Under the title *Veritas*, Hinsley corresponded with Mivart through the columns of *The Tablet* and defended the Church's position. Mivart's response to Hinsley's first letter in *The Tablet* was: 'Who is this Hinsley who is seeking to obtain some cheap renown regardless of the harm he does'.[34] The very orthodox Hinsley probably saw no harm at all in his stance and his correspondence with Mivart came to the attention of the influential Downside monk Dom Aidan Gasquet, resident in Rome, and his adviser Mgr James Moyes both of whom commented favourably on the strength of Hinsley's arguments against the Modernists.[35] Hinsley's students also knew very well that *Veritas* was Hinsley as he would enter Philosophy lectures and begin a discussion on his latest letter to *The Tablet*.[36]

Looking back on this era at Ushaw over sixty years later, contemporaries of Hinsley had different impressions of him. In 1935, Canon Frederick Mitchell remembered him as a diligent and sincere contemporary.[37] Fr Godfrey Dix, writing about the professors, remarked that Joseph Corbishley, who succeeded Wilkinson as President in 1909, was held in great respect; Rafael Merry del Val, later to become Cardinal Secretary of State, was a gentle and dignified teacher of French; whilst Hinsley was a quiet, unassuming professor, and not a strict disciplinarian.[38] Fr Edwin Bonney, a student of Hinsley's and subsequently choirmaster and lecturer in English at Ushaw, wrote that 'the ardour and zeal' with which Hinsley

> threw himself into his work, and the self-sacrifice with which he devoted himself to the interests of his scholars will not readily be forgotten by them and could not but excite regret for his departure.[39]

Heenan's assessment of the situation, however, was that Hinsley's exit from Ushaw was welcomed by some and was made inevitable as much by his own imperfections as by those of any reactionaries among his fellow professors. To the end, he wrote, Hinsley was an impatient man and his modern, direct approach proved too abrasive for some of his colleagues at Ushaw.[40] Hinsley had said, 'I am bent on coming out of my shell some day, either sooner or later; perhaps later rather than sooner, but out I will come'.[41] When he returned from Rome, he had jettisoned the self-containment and reticence that a working class boy would have hidden behind in the presence of urbane professors and more able and well-to-do contemporaries. Now extremely well-qualified and self-confident, his enthusiasm knew no bounds, but to those not infused with the spirit of Romanità and the *Summa Theologiae*, his interest was not contagious and he soon became disillusioned with those who were not inclined to share his interests and views. Heenan claimed that he was unable to collaborate and that his restless spirit proved too disruptive for Ushaw. On 21 July 1898, after frequent disagreements with his colleagues and those in authority, he left the college, disenchanted mainly by its lack of institutional interest in scholastic philosophy. But there were other reasons. In Fr Heenan's words, Hinsley went away 'a disappointed man . . . who had found too few to share his enthusiasms' but he concluded that because of his impetuous nature 'he must have been a trial to those with whom he worked'.[42]

For the next two years Hinsley worked on the mission as a curate to Canon Edward Watson at St Anne's, Keighley, a textile town with a Catholic population of approximately 4,000. The church, designed by Edward Welby Pugin, had been opened in 1840. The mission elementary school, adjacent to the church, was small, understaffed, and overcrowded, and the children were described as being generally poor and badly clothed and shod. Hinsley became involved in the mission cycling and cricket clubs and with Patrick O'Donnell and other young men would go walking on the hills around the town. He became a familiar figure as he rode around Keighley and until the 1950s there was a framed photograph in the presbytery lounge of him as a curate with his bicycle. But it must have been obvious that although he related well to his friends and parishioners in Keighley greater things were in store for such a talented and educated priest. In 1899, he was approached by leading Catholic laymen in nearby Bradford to become involved in the founding of a Catholic boys' grammar school in the city and in 1900 he left Keighley to embark on another stage in his career.[43]

Chapter Two

THE HEADMASTER

1900-1904

Bradford's Catholic Schools

At the turn of the twentieth century, Bradford was a thriving West Yorkshire city whose economic and occupational life was dominated by the wool textile industry. Its nineteenth-century growth had been phenomenal. The population of the four original townships was 13,000 in 1801, but a century later, as a result of dramatic demographic changes and the annexation of neighbouring townships, the population of the city had risen to 280,000.[1] Energetic and innovative entrepreneurs had mechanised the production of woollen textiles in the early nineteenth-century and this had stimulated local collieries and iron industries. By 1887 Bradford was described as the capital of the worsted industry of England, and many prominent Bradfordians had amassed substantial fortunes.[2] Despite periodic fluctuations in trade, the remarkable progress of the city continued, but its pre-eminence was achieved at a cost. The small town rapidly became a vast, industrial city dominated by mills, factories and a polluted atmosphere. Municipal incorporation in 1847 led to developments in public amenities that slowly improved the quality of life but one of the city's most famous sons, the writer J.B. Priestley, recalled that in the late 1890s, Bradford was still ugly and forbidding.[3]

Irish immigration was a contributory factor in the growth of Bradford's population. In 1851 there were 9,279 Irish-born inhabitants out of a population of 103,778. Bradford had the largest Irish population east of the Pennines, and it was claimed that in the central districts, Bradford was increasingly becoming a 'Catholic town'.[4] The first permanent mission, St Mary's, was established in 1825, but by the 1840s there were over 5,000 Catholics in the town, and a new mission of St Patrick's was opened in 1852. By the end of the century there were another six missions, and the Catholic population had risen to 19,000. Initially, school-chapels had been built, but eventually the Catholic community was able to erect separate churches and elementary schools and, by the end of the nineteenth century, each mission had its own school. Only one of these elementary schools, however, had acquired higher grade status and there were no Catholic secondary schools for boys.[5]

The national Catholic Schools Committee had concentrated their efforts on the provision of urban elementary schools, and there had been a similar emphasis in Bradford and in the Diocese of Beverley and later Leeds. Between the Education Act of 1870 and 1900, seven Catholic elementary schools, as opposed to school-chapels, had been opened in Bradford, despite intense competition from well-resourced Board Schools. The Catholic school population had initially been concentrated in the missions of St Mary's and St Patrick's, but by the end of the century it was located in eight missions and had risen from 2,877 to 4,220. However, there was only one higher grade or middle class school at St Patrick's, and this was for girls. Between 1878 and 1900, the number of Catholics in the diocese increased from approximately 96,000 to over 104,000, and in the same period the number of Catholic schoolchildren on roll rose from 19,000 to 26,000. In 1878, there were 105 diocesan elementary schools, two industrial schools, and seven higher and middle class schools for girls. By 1899 there were 134 elementary schools, eleven higher and middle class schools for girls, and one industrial school. Forty-six schools were run by female religious orders including four girls' boarding schools, and one orphanage, also run by nuns, was described as a Poor Law School.[6] Two attempts had been made by laymen, late in the century, to open boys' secondary schools – one at Ilkley, conducted by Joseph Skelton, and Wharfedale College at Boston Spa – but both were short-lived ventures and neither appeared to have Bishop William Gordon's patronage.[7]

The Bradford Catholic Union

The establishment of diocesan grammar schools was one of Bishop Gordon's principal achievements and in Bradford he received considerable support from the Bradford Catholic Union.[8] In late 1897 the leading Catholic laity of the city proposed that they should imitate their co-religionists in Belfast and Glasgow, and form an organisation to protect and advance the interests of local Catholics. After discussions with Mgr John Motler, the Vicar General and senior priest in Bradford, the proposal was accepted and in May 1898 the Bradford Catholic

Union was established under the presidency of the Bishop of Leeds. Leading clergy and laity were its officers, and each mission, under the direction of 'the senior priest', elected representatives to sit on the central committee and sent delegates to annual general meetings. The Catholic Union's constitution stated that its duty was to 'do all that may be required . . . for the moral, social and educational benefit of the mission. . .' and to achieve these objectives it lobbied political candidates, scrutinised electoral registers, and canvassed voters. The voting power of the substantial Catholic population in the city meant that the Catholic Union was in a relatively strong position to influence political decisions, despite its claim that it was a non-political body.[9]

The development of Catholic secondary education in early-twentieth century Bradford stands as the Catholic Union's greatest success, a manifestation of Catholic middle-class dynamism. In the Diocese of Leeds, which included the vast industrial conurbations of west and south Yorkshire, and a massive rural hinterland to the north, there were no Catholic secondary or higher grade schools for boys and so, in 1899, the Catholic Union, through voluntary contributions, undertook to provide a Catholic boys' grammar school in Bradford. As the *Bradford Daily Telegraph* recorded on 20 January 1900: 'The Bradford Catholics are agitating for a Higher Grade School of their own.' Some members of the Catholic Union had already visited St Cuthbert's School, Newcastle, and obtained the advice of Fr Horace Mann, ex-Ushavian and headmaster of the school. Fr William Brown, the leading educational specialist in the Southwark Diocese, was also consulted. Supported by Canon John Earnshaw of St Patrick's, Bradford, the Catholic Union then called in Hinsley, who had already heard of the proposal.[10]

On 19 February, under the chairmanship of Mgr Motler, the Governors of the new school held their first meeting in the Midland Hotel, Bradford. The minutes record that Houghton House, Drewton Street, a large detached Victorian villa that had served as a cancer hospital, had been rented for one year with an option for a further five year lease. It was also recorded 'that Bishop Gordon be asked to appoint Rev. Dr. Hinsley (who was present at the meeting) headmaster.' The governors agreed to pledge themselves financially to the school for five years, make good any deficit, and solicit subscriptions from the nobility and gentry. Fees were fixed at six guineas per year and boys were to be admitted over the age of nine. The Board of Education sent an inspector to examine the building and plans for the future school, and once approval had been given, work and fund raising began in earnest.[11] In May the *Yorkshire Observer* reported that the Roman Catholics of Bradford had held a bazaar in aid of the new school with the leading Catholics of the city being present in addition to the school's newly-appointed headmaster.[12]

St Bede's Grammar School

Throughout May an Executive Committee of the Governors met regularly in order to finalize plans for the ceremonial opening and the reception of students.[13] On 11 June, Hinsley and two lay teachers enrolled thirty-seven boys, and on the following day Bishop Gordon, President of the Board of Governors, officially opened the new school which was to be named St Bede's Grammar School. The brief ceremony was attended by local clergy and prominent Catholic laity, and also by Fr Louis Casartelli of St Bede's College, Manchester, Fr Norris of The Oratory, Birmingham, and Fr Mann of St Cuthbert's, Newcastle-upon-Tyne, all well-established Catholic boys' grammar schools. The house was blessed by the bishop and a crucifix was placed in a prominent position 'so that no-one entering the school could fail to see under what standard' boys were enrolled. In his speech Bishop Gordon said that in answer to Pope Leo XIII's appeal that Catholics should make a signal offering to the Sacred Heart, nothing would be more suitable than a grammar school which would afford the chance of a good education to Catholic boys of the district and save them from the evil influences of godless schools. The bishop therefore presented the school as the diocesan offering to the Saviour of the World in the Holy Year of Jubilee and dedicated the school to God 'under the patronage of the Venerable Scholar who, in Jarrow's cloister, by prayer and study, became the great Saint and Doctor of Saxon days, and the pioneer of English learning'. Nothing, continued the bishop, gave him so much pleasure as the opening of the school and he praised the courage and generosity of Bradford's Catholic community who had taken up the challenge of 'this grand work'. The school would be 'a home of learning, and, above all, a home of Catholic teaching and Catholic truth'. He was delighted to be able to appoint Fr Arthur Hinsley as headmaster, 'for his high scholastic attainment and his great enthusiasm fitted him especially for the work' and his selection 'secured its success'. St Bede's, the bishop concluded, would be 'the pioneer and model of similar institutions in other towns'. Fr Norris was more specific in his definition of the Catholic secondary school's purpose. Catholic boys' grammar schools, he said, were needed in every diocese to create a Catholic middle class, and enable the Catholic community to prepare itself for the forthcoming legislation on secondary education. The future success of the Catholic community, he contended, depended on such institutions as St Bede's and, after many years of struggling to secure Catholic elementary education, the time had now come to provide for those who were between the clergy and the poor – 'the middle class, the backbone of every religious community'.[14]

At the turn of the century most of the established Catholic boys' schools were either under the control of religious orders or part of a junior seminary. Ampleforth and Downside were located in rural areas and attached to monasteries, whilst seminaries such as St Edmund's, Ware, and St Cuthbert's, Ushaw, educated lay and clerical students. Most of the schools were located in the Midlands and in the south of England and generally only accepted respectable boys from the middle and upper social classes. Most imitated the great public schools and their classical curriculum, although some offered the modern combination of classical and commercial education as provided by the leading London schools. Whatever the underlying philosophy of individual schools, it was becoming increasingly obvious to the laity and clergy in urban areas, that large numbers of poorer but able Catholic boys were being denied a Catholic secondary education to the eventual disadvantage of themselves and the Catholic community.

There had been some developments, however, in the provision of urban grammar schools for middle class Catholic boys. The Jesuits had opened St Francis Xavier's School in Liverpool in 1840, and there followed a series of schools opened by religious orders at Manchester (Xaverian, 1854), Clapham and Southwark (De La Salle Brothers, 1855 and 1860), Preston (Society of Jesus 1860), Manchester (Xaverians, 1862), Croydon (Josephites, 1869), and Kensington (Oblates of St Charles, 1863), all of which entered pupils for university and professional, civil service and military examinations These foundations were followed by Salford Catholic Grammar School (1862), St Bede's College, Manchester (1875), St Cuthbert's, Newcastle (1884), St Bonaventure's, Forest Gate (1884), and St Philip's, Birmingham (1887), and by 1896 with the establishment of St Brendan's College at Bristol, another ten schools or colleges, some conducted by secular priests, were offering Catholic boys in urban areas the opportunity of secondary education. Their work and that of the Catholic public schools was co-ordinated through the Conference of Catholic Colleges established in 1896.[15]

The opening of St Bede's was a major educational development within the Diocese of Leeds and was also a significant departure in the wider provision of secondary education for Catholic boys. In a *Pastoral on Secondary Education* issued in August 1900, Bishop Gordon wrote:

> Of the importance of the work which St Bede's Grammar School is designed to accomplish there can be no doubt. It is meant to supply a want long felt in this diocese. The demand for better education, for an education which shall fit the sons of Catholic parents to compete successfully with their neighbours in the higher paths of life, has forced itself on our attention the last few years with a persistence not to be ignored.

St Bede's, he continued, represented the 'first step' in 'grappling with the difficult question of education' and 'stands alone'. At the head of this venture, the Bishop wrote, 'we have placed the Rev Dr Hinsley, a priest respected by all who know him'. The Bishop solicited support from priests and parents in an attempt to form a Roman Catholic 'middle class'. Such was the importance of the work, he concluded, that there was above all 'a need for permanence'.[16]

The aims which the Catholic Union had set out for the school were:

> 1. To promote God's honour by affording to the sons of the middle and upper classes a thorough training in the knowledge and principles of the Catholic faith combined with a secular education equal in every respect to that which is given in the best public schools in England so that whatever line of life be chosen they may be at no disadvantage through lack of educational opportunities.

> 2. To afford intelligent Catholic boys of a humbler station in life by means of scholarships an opportunity to equip themselves in the higher branches of knowledge which elementary schools do not provide.

> 3. To increase loving devotion to the See of Peter, reverence for Ecclesiastical Superiors, and intelligent interest in public affairs.[17]

It was to be an urban grammar school for boys of all classes, conducted by a secular priest, and dependent upon the financial support of the laity and secular agencies. Mounted on his bicycle, 'the Doctor' undertook frequent trips round the neighbourhood to recruit boys and ensure the school's future.[18]

Hinsley as Headmaster

The Governors and Hinsley attempted to implement the Catholic Union's aims but a severe shortage of money made their task extremely difficult. From 1900 until 1919 the school was housed in Drewton Street and, whilst the reminiscences of the first students were full of fond impressions, the governors had a long and arduous struggle to meet the exacting standards of inspectors and keep the school in existence. Income depended on the number of boys on roll, their success in grant-awarding examinations, modest fees, governor support, and voluntary contributions. Official assistance was limited and inadequate. The Bradford School Board dealt only with elementary education, but the City Council did make grants to the school, as did the Technical Instruction Committee of the West Riding County Council. In 1902 St Bede's was recognised by the Board of Education for the purposes of grant aid but the chronic shortage of funds continued to be the most pressing concern.[19]

The driving personality and role of Hinsley as headmaster were critical factors in the early days of the school. His short time at St Bede's was to be of the utmost importance, for his enthusiasm and intense labours were to lay the foundations for the educational and social development of the school. According to the school's *Annual Reports*, it provided 'an efficient secondary education for boys in a thoroughly Catholic atmosphere'. The curriculum consisted of English, religious knowledge, modern languages taught by 'native professors', classics, history, geography, mathematics, natural science, drawing, shorthand, typing, drill and music. Boys were entered for a range of examinations accredited by the legal and medical professions, Oxford University, London University, the College of Preceptors, the Royal Society of Arts, and northern universities. The school was also a student teacher centre. Early reports on the school's performance were variable. In 1902 the Board of Education reported 'that although the school had made a distinct improvement, the general standard of the work was much lower than that of schools of a similar type in Bradford and surrounding districts'. The governors, anxious to bring the school up to the required standard, were advised by the Board of Education's inspectors to amend the curriculum and offer higher salaries in order to attract better teachers. In 1904 Lord Herries, in his address at the school's Speech Day, emphasised the need for Catholic secondary education, praised the progress being made by the school and encouraged co-operation between Catholics and grant-awarding state and county agencies. In one phrase he summed up what might be seen as one aspect of Hinsley's philosophy for Catholic schools and one which he had outlined at the Conference of Catholic Colleges. 'In their education', said Herries, the schools 'should strive to inculcate a spirit of patriotism, and to teach their young men to take an interest in politics and municipal life'.[20] In the following year, Bradford Education Committee's *Co-ordination Report* congratulated those who founded the school 'on the measure of success it has already attained'.[21]

In 1903 Canon Aloysius Puissant, the Diocesan inspector, had also praised the school's progress but from a religious perspective:

> I examined this year, for the first time, St Bede's Grammar School, Bradford, so far the only higher grade school for boys in the Diocese. The result of the examination has strengthened my conviction of the importance and religious advantage of such schools. While the boys who had attended the school for a considerable time, gave evidence of a sound knowledge of their religion, those who had entered the school only recently, and had before been attending non-Catholic schools, knew very little about their religion and were even in ignorance of some of the most important prayers. From this fact we must necessarily come to the conclusion that, if they remained in those schools to the end of their course, they would have entered the busy world deficient in the most important and the only absolutely necessary science; a science which, if not acquired in early youth or during school years, is very seldom acquired in after years. I consider it, therefore, strongly advisable to establish similar schools in the large centres of population, wherever a sufficient number of boys, belonging to the better classes, can be brought together. Ample provision, in this respect, is already made in the diocese for girls.[22]

Considering his own background, it is unlikely that Hinsley would have agreed entirely with Puissant's reference to the school providing for boys 'belonging to the better classes', and early registers illustrate that he was assiduous in enrolling students from diverse backgrounds where the bond was faith not class. By 1904 the roll had risen to eighty and included boys whose fathers were skilled workers, labourers, professionals, soldiers, merchants, commercial travellers and clerks. They came from Bradford and outlying districts, from local Catholic and non-Catholic schools, and from convent and private schools. At first, all the students were day boys, but eventually Hinsley persuaded the governors to provide accommodation for boarders. A room above St Patrick's Church, rooms in Camden Terrace, and then the huge Victorian mansion of Rosemount Villa in Manningham, one of the better areas of Bradford, both housed the boarders and the headmaster.[23]

Hinsley attended the Conference of Catholic Colleges at Ampleforth in May, 1902, and Bishop William Brown's recollection provides a description of Hinsley at the time. He was, remembered the Bishop, 'a striking figure, tall, erect, trim and active, with a most genial manner and a winning smile'.[24] At the Ampleforth conference, Hinsley outlined his educational philosophy in a wide-ranging address. There had been, he stated, great progress in building up the seminaries and the schools conducted by religious orders but there was now a great need for equality of educational opportunity and the smoothing over of class distinctions in national education. Catholics, he continued, could not 'be insensible to the strength of this growing impulse' as 'our brethren in faith call as urgently for educational uplifting as any portion of the community'. Rapid developments in trade and politics made it imperative that the national education system be remodelled, and that Catholics should be adequately educated to play a full and active role in all aspects of society, and at all levels. Catholic students, he argued, should not by accident of birth and education, be 'kept in a station below that to which they legitimately aspire'. The answer was to provide more Catholic secondary schools, especially in urban areas, to raise standards in elementary schools and facilitate 'organic unity' between them. The curricula of both types of school should complement each other and should be age-related but he recognised that the tendency of Catholic parents to put their children to work was a serious weakness in preventing the full completion of a course at either elementary or secondary level. 'We have, too often', he continued, 'the utmost difficulty in inducing even prosperous parents to leave their children at school until the age of fourteen'. The low value placed by some Catholics on any form of education was a continuing problem but Hinsley did not confine his comments to this and saw this as disappearing with time. Praising the 'sacrifice' of the Bradford Catholic Union and acknowledging the funds provided by local and national agencies, he stressed the need for continued lay support but stated that 'we need it still more from the clergy'. The arduous task of extending secondary education could not be achieved without a wider, coherent approach:

> The cause is not to be confined within the narrow limits of parish interests

or the circle of a single diocese. It stretches out as broadly and as widely as the British Empire, nay is only bounded by the limits of the Church's mission. The work already done in England has been such that only God's special guidance and aid can account for such results amidst such difficulties. More grammar schools are now needed to complete and perfect what has been accomplished, and when that need is recognised, strenuous efforts must be made to knit the component elements of our system into one organic whole of which all the parts shall be living in helpful sympathy.

The ensuing discussion supported Hinsley's views. The extension of secondary education, the creation of a Catholic middle class, episcopal support, Catholic participation in politics, and competition from non-denominational schools, were all points raised by delegates, but Fr Casartelli stressed that 'The greatest difficulty was parochialism. The clergy as a body do not realise the importance of the question'. It was the function of such conferences to 'form Catholic opinion among laity and clergy'. Hinsley's mood was one of urgency and action and his final comments were couched in the contemporary context of the South African War: 'Let us talk over the difficulties afterwards; it is a race for the *kopje*'. And then, as if to re-emphasise the point he had started with and reflecting his own experiences:

> Objections have been made on the score of the class of boys introduced into middle schools by scholarships. Were not the grammar schools meant to lift up, even from the lowest, if necessary, those who could profit by education? The mixing of the classes had educational value for all: the higher would not usually be dragged down, but the lower lifted up, and we had thus to *create* a middle class.[25]

Hinsley played an active part in the proceedings of the conferences. In 1903, at St Edward's, Liverpool, he spoke of the practical difficulties that he and his governors had experienced in Bradford. In the following year, at the Oratory School, Birmingham, he advocated changes in the science curriculum and, in particular, the grant-aid system which distinguished between pupils in different schools. It was obviously an arrangement that disadvantaged Catholic schools and, at Hinsley's instigation, a petition of protest was drawn up and forwarded to South Kensington.[26]

In Bradford, Hinsley had attempted to do this by word and deed. He was enthusiastic and determined, but his manner and methods were abrasive. Despite the support of some parish priests, he inevitably came into conflict with others, who were fighting not only for funds but also for high quality students and numbers in their own parish elementary schools. He had already confronted Canon Simpson when the latter threatened St Bede's by proposing to open a secondary school in his parish of St Mary's. He also had disagreements with his governors and, in January 1902, actually tendered his resignation over the issue of taking boarders but, on that occasion, the governors had given in to his demands. His continued work as headmaster, as a teacher, as an administrator, as a recruiter of boys, and as a fundraiser, began to take its toll on his health, however, and the conflicts with governors over funds and future developments became more frequent.[27]

Hinsley had no doubts about the value of Catholic grammar schools but by 1904 his frustration at the continual struggle to keep St Bede's going was beginning to show. He was concerned that the sacrifices made by the Catholic community since the Education Act of 1870 would count for nothing unless the present generation of bishops, school managers and headteachers overcame the financial and legal problems they faced. He was especially concerned at the lack of coordination and critical of the episcopal bench's approach to secondary education. Unwisely he went into print to vent his feelings.

In a letter to *The Tablet*, Hinsley complained that the whole movement for Catholic secondary education lacked direction and structure and argued for the proper organisation of Catholic educational interests especially at secondary level. 'Their Lordships the Bishops give blessings to isolated attempts at founding grammar schools', he wrote, but 'there generally the matter ends in scattered and chance generosity'. 'Some central body there must be', he continued,

> to point out the ways and means, to regulate the action of local committees, and to take charge of Catholic interests in case of conflicts with inspectors or with local education authorities. The only central body which has so far been active in this matter is the Conference of Catholic Headmasters. But this is entirely composed of priests; laymen who are chiefly concerned in the problem are not represented.[28]

However accurate, these were not comments that bishops and especially William Gordon would have been pleased to read. Hinsley struck chords that may have pleased the laity but they were disconcerting to clerical ears.

Breakdown

In his attempt to keep the school going Hinsley wore himself out and, in June 1904, he attended his last governors' meeting. On 19 July the governors received a letter from Hinsley's brother 'to the effect that owing to the serious illness of the Doctor it was unlikely that he could continue to act as the Headmaster of the school'. Regretfully, the governors accepted Hinsley's resignation, and asked Bishop Gordon to appoint a successor. They also recorded their appreciation of Hinsley's work:

> A vote of thanks was agreed upon. Members of the Board testifying most heartily to the great work done by Dr Hinsley in starting the school and to his devoted energy during the years he has been Headmaster. The Board expressed the view that he would soon be restored to health and vigour.[29]

One of Hinsley's former students later recalled Hinsley's impact on the school. 'With a confidence resulting from mature reflection' and perhaps after having read something about Hinsley in his later years, V.J. Clarkson put down his memories of the formative years of St Bede's. The *esprit de corps* engendered during the pioneering days and 'very non-academic conditions' at St Bede's was due entirely to Hinsley, 'a saint to those who knew his way of life' and who was 'certainly the zealous and humble priest who well and truly laid the foundations of St Bede's'. Clarkson remembered Hinsley cycling around the diocese to recruit students, his simplicity of life and quiet 'unheralded austerity'. He recalled serving Mass for Hinsley when 'the Doctor's' whole being 'was transformed with a devotion that seemed . . . a beautiful passion. . . . ' Out of Hinsley's daily encounters with the boys and the walks with him between the cramped school in Drewton Street and the boarders' house at Rosemount Villa in Manningham there arose 'a loyalty to him that was unique among unsentimental schoolboys'. On the downside, however, he wrote that although Hinsley's 'mental attainments were great' his duties as headmaster 'were many and onerous' but 'the assistance he had on the spiritual life of the school . . . was nil'. Added to this, the governors were unhappy about the direction in which Hinsley was taking the school and he endured much criticism. Yet, according to Clarkson, 'even in his tragic leave taking' when he was ill, Hinsley 'displayed a patience and tolerance towards his critics that was worthy of a priest of God'. 'With sad hearts . . . and none too dry eyes' the senior boys 'took leave of him as, wrapped in blankets', he was driven away.

This tearful scene was played out amid acrimony, however, for later in the letter Clarkson highlights the bitterness surrounding Hinsley's departure. Hinsley was 'almost a nervous wreck' and when his brother collected him he 'became "all blood and thunder" with the bishop, the governors and everybody else in and around Bradford'. Seeing Hinsley's poor state of health, his brother 'took drastic action and removed him to some southern nursing home'. So bad was the headmaster's physical and mental condition that Bishop Gordon felt compelled to withdraw his faculties. The Bishop also took exception to Hinsley leaving the diocese without permission and was less than impressed by Hinsley's brother's forthright denunciation of a situation where he felt that the headmaster had been humiliated.[30]

Hinsley was ambitious for St Bede's but worked at a speed and with an intensity not always to the liking of his governors and, in particular, to Bishop Gordon whose earlier plea for 'permanence' seemed to be seriously threatened by Hinsley's actions. Such was the Bishop's fear of the school's bankruptcy and his disgust with Hinsley that, reputedly, he later said to the Bishop of Clifton, who was considering Hinsley for the headship of Prior Park: 'If you were my worst enemy I might advise you to take him. . . .'[31] Hinsley's enthusiastic but confrontational approach remained a strong personal characteristic and he had a tendency to take action before informing others. Although some of Heenan's account of Hinsley's time at St Bede's is inaccurate, he was correct when he wrote that:

> The governors and Bishop Gordon of Leeds feared that the Doctor would lead them into bankruptcy. They were probably right. They felt that this young enthusiast knew nothing of the art of cautious consolidation. In developing the work of Catholic secondary education in Bradford, he considered only one aspect – the urgency of immediate expansion. The authorities thought him to be a megalomaniac. They were not, therefore, unduly depressed when he resigned, or, rather, suddenly departed.[32]

Heenan claimed that Hinsley had received 'niggardly support'[33] from the governors but this assertion is not borne out by the evidence and, in his later years, Hinsley praised those who had given so much to the school.[34] Both he and his governors were inexperienced in managing a school and it was inevitable that mistakes would be made. With a governing body of twenty-five people, it is unsurprising that occasionally Hinsley acted unilaterally in order to expedite matters. His forthright views and direct action may have caused friction with the governors, many of whom were experienced and successful businessmen, but they continued to maintain the school and by 1912 had subscribed over £4,000 towards its on-going costs. Bishop Joseph Robert Cowgill who had succeeded Bishop Gordon wrote:

> I feel that you deserve the sympathy and encouragement of clergy and laity alike in your struggle to carry on your magnificent work. I cannot sufficiently emphasise the great importance of such schools as St Bede's . . . if our Catholic men are to take their place in the social, commercial and professional life of this country. You may well be proud of your undertaking.[35]

Despite the shadows surrounding his exit from Drewton Street, Hinsley's talents and forceful managerial style had contributed in no small measure to the successful beginnings of St Bede's. Others were to comment later that he left the school with work unfinished but this applies to all headteachers. Hinsley had helped lay very solid foundations and established traditions on which his successors would consolidate.

St Bede's remained at Drewton Street until 1919 when, under the leadership of another dynamic headteacher, Fr Charles Tindall, it moved to Heaton Hall on the outskirts of Bradford. Mgr Hinsley, now Rector of the *Venerabile*, visited the school with Cardinal Bourne in 1925 and was to have opened the new school in September 1939. Sadly, the outbreak of the Second World War prevented him from doing so.[36]

Chapter Three

ON THE MISSION

1904-1917

Sutton Park and Sydenham

After a period of sick leave when he served as a chaplain on board a troopship sailing to India and back,[1] Hinsley finally broke his links with the Diocese of Leeds and was incardinated into the Diocese of Southwark in late 1904.[2] This move, which was not unusual but frowned upon by bishops unless they were arranging it, was probably due to Hinsley's friendship with Mgr William Brown whom he had met at the conferences of Catholic Colleges. Fr Brian Taylor, however, states that Bishop Gordon actually arranged Hinsley's transfer from Leeds to Southwark but there is no evidence to support this theory.[3] In May 1904, Hinsley invited Mgr Brown to be guest of honour and distribute the school prizes at St Bede's in July but, as Brown recalled, Hinsley was not present at the event for 'private reasons', probably due to continuing ill-health and his resignation as headmaster. In the same year, Brown was appointed Vicar General to Peter Amigo who had been created Bishop of Southwark in February 1903.[4] Amigo was subsequently to play a significant role in Hinsley's career.

In Southwark, Hinsley gained valuable and substantial experience of the pastoral ministry. On his incardination, he was appointed first to the mission at Amberley in Sussex and from there acted as chaplain to the Sisters of Charity of Nevers, at Withdean in Brighton.[5] Under Hinsley, Canon John Byrne wrote in 1943, Amberley awoke and during his fourteen months there 'great activity was visible'. It was only a question of time, however, before Bishop Amigo moved Hinsley where his talents and energy could be better used and near the end of 1905 he was transferred to St Edward the Confessor at Sutton Park near Guildford, a one-man mission with a population of approximately 100.[6]

Sutton Place, the focal point of Sutton Park and former home of the Weston family, had a very strong recusant tradition and its domestic chapel was a place of worship for Catholics of the neighbourhood. From St Edward's, built in 1876, Hinsley served a geographically extensive mission but ministered to no more than two dozen families.[7] His presbytery was Vine Cottage, which had housed the stewards of the estate and dated from the sixteenth century.[8] It was a long way from Bradford and a very different environment from the grime of the industrial north. The pace of life was also slower but Hinsley had regained his enthusiasm and vigour.

The Witham family, who owned Sutton Place, leased it to Lord Northcliffe, the press baron and owner of the *Daily Mail*, and he arranged that the chapel should be closed but maintained in good order. Northcliffe and Hinsley became friends and Hinsley often conducted tours of the big house. Northcliffe also allowed Hinsley and his parishioners to hold the annual Corpus Christi procession in the grounds of the mansion, an event that attracted Catholics from Guildford, Godalming, Woking and Wonersh.[9]

Hinsley and Northcliffe collaborated in a scheme to enable the local Anglican voluntary school, which had Catholics and Nonconformists on roll, to arrange for separate religious instruction within the school timetable. In theory, the plan was laudable; in practice it collapsed because of some Protestant agitation and the reliance on volunteers to teach the daily religious classes. Hinsley was one of the volunteers but his mission duties and his thrice-weekly eight-mile cycling trips to teach Church History and then Sacred Scripture at the nearby diocesan seminary of St John's College, Wonersh, meant that his appearances to teach the infants were interrupted regularly. In any case, Bishop Brown wrote that 'teaching the infants was beyond Hinsley's capacity'.[10] Hinsley's period at Wonersh coincided with the publication in 1907 of *Pascendi,* Pope Pius X's encyclical against the errors of the Modernists, and just as he had done at Ushaw, Hinsley waded in against those who doubted or questioned the Church's teaching. To many priests and intellectual Catholics Modernism was a grave crisis and Hinsley's orthodox and unflinching public stand against it enhanced his reputation. In the lecture room he was a pious and an enthusiastic teacher who taught with vigour and authority.

The opening of a Catholic school became a priority for Hinsley and in late August 1908 he called a parish meeting to discuss his plans. With typical forthrightness he informed his parishioners that he had already taken a large house called 'The Firs' near Warplesdon railway station and had arranged for the Sisters of St Clotilde to run the school. He had arranged for the transportation of the children and he had received Bishop Amigo's consent. The autumn term got off to a bright start but the French-speaking nuns soon ran into communication problems with the English children. In January 1909 the school re-opened but with new teachers.[11]

Despite this setback, born out of misplaced enthusiasm, Hinsley's first substantial missionary experience was successful. Known as 'Dr Hinsley' to his parishioners, Canon Kieran-Hyland described him as 'tall, spectacled and benevolent. He was living fire, earnest, scholarly, jovial and sincere. Your interests were at once his.' He also recalled that Hinsley's bookshelves in the old timbered presbytery were stocked with scripture and history material sent for review.[12] Hinsley's historical interests also led him to undertake research into the relics, including those of St Cuthbert Mayne, held at St Edward's. Encouraged and advised by the Downside historians Abbot Aidan Gasquet and Dom Bede Camm, Hinsley began to authenticate the relics and proceeded to have reliquaries made in order to protect them.[13]

In 1911 Hinsley became the rector of Our Lady and St Philip Neri, Addington Grove, Sydenham, a suburban mission opened in 1870.[14] St Philip's had a church but no presbytery and Hinsley was compelled to rent living accommodation. One of his first moves in the parish was to establish a Confraternity of the Blessed Sacrament whose aim was to foster love for Christ through devotion to the Blessed Sacrament. This traditional form of lay association had been given a significant boost by the Eucharistic Congress held in London in 1908 and at St Philip's the confraternity developed rapidly following Hinsley's arrival. The first meeting was held in February 1912 and membership rose quickly to 130, but in accordance with the contemporary dominant position of the rector in mission affairs, it was agreed that no resolution could be passed, no appointment would be made, nor any action taken without Hinsley's permission. He immediately assumed the duty of sacristan and proceeded to consult the confraternity on issues affecting the running of the mission but was soon frustrated by tedious discussions over whether the church should have chairs or benches and by financial restrictions that prevented him opening a boys' club or establishing a scout troop or a boys' brigade. After discussions with Hinsley, the confraternity informed Bishop Amigo that the mission could not support a curate and also decided to postpone the proposed extension to the main body of the church, which had been started in 1882 but was incomplete. Instead, it agreed to repair the existing church and to build a Lady Chapel and a presbytery. It is likely that Hinsley disapproved of this and had Amigo's support, for when the bishop visited the mission in March 1912 he favoured an extension. The confraternity were overruled and on 12 May Mgr Brown, the Vicar General, laid the foundation stone for the church extension.[15]

As he had done at Sutton Park, Hinsley took a great interest in the mission school and was a frequent visitor but once again he encountered problems. The school on Watlington Grove had been erected forty years earlier and the building was totally inadequate for the number of children on roll. As there was no room for the school to expand, Hinsley decided to buy adjacent properties on Sydenham Road which, when the houses were demolished, would form the site of a new school. With the support of Amigo, Brown and his parishioners, Hinsley purchased the two properties at slightly above their market value but the development of the school was postponed because of the outbreak of the Great War in August 1914. After the war, the site was deemed unsuitable for the school and was sold at a loss. There were, however, some successful educational developments in the mission. Both Hinsley and Amigo had requested the Ladies of Mary to establish themselves in Sydenham and at Easter 1915 they opened a girls' school at Newlands Park. The sisters, who travelled daily from Coloma in Croydon, eventually opened St Winefride's convent at Oakwood and in January 1918 a new preparatory and senior girls' school was opened.[16]

The houses bought by Hinsley as the site for the new mission school were used during the First World War as accommodation for Belgian refugees. The women's society, the Society of St Elizabeth, undertook a great deal of work on behalf of the refugee families and the Belgian and British governments provided financial resources and materials. Additional funds were raised by a committee controlled by Hinsley.[17] In another facet of the war, Hinsley was caught up in the aftermath of the massive Silvertown explosion when the munitions factory of Brunner and Mond blew up in January 1917 killing 73 people and damaging over 60,000 houses. The factory was in an industrial area facing on to the River Thames to the north of Sydenham and Hinsley joined the rescue and emergency services tending the wounded and helping to accommodate those made homeless by the blast.

Meanwhile, in the midst of a busy life on the mission Hinsley tried to continue with his classes in Holy Scripture at Wonersh but Fr Joseph Leahy recalled that he was not a great success and tended to lose himself in detail.[18] Inevitably, the pressures and demands of mission duties affected the time for preparation and consequently the quality of his teaching. His absorption in mission life and the difficulties of travelling the long distances to and from Sydenham meant that his timetable was eventually reduced and his later infrequent visits were in the capacity of a canonical examiner. It was at Wonersh that Hinsley came into contact with Mgr Arthur Doubleday, the Rector, and later the second Bishop of Brentwood.

Bishop Amigo's Roman Agent

An outstanding feature of personal relations within the English and Welsh Hierarchy at this time was the animosity between Archbishop Bourne of Westminster and Bishop Amigo. Ironically, on his translation from Southwark to Westminster in 1903 Bourne had actually fought against the advice of the Southwark Chapter in order to have Amigo's name placed on the terna and was convinced that all the good he had done for the diocese would be lost if Amigo did not succeed him. However, Bourne's subsequent refusal to relinquish the trusteeship of his former diocese and his attempts to enlarge the Archdiocese of Westminster led to a breakdown in the relationship between the two men. As a trustee Bourne was technically able to interfere in its administration and this he did frequently, much to the annoyance and indignation of Amigo and his senior priests. Numerous letters passed between Westminster and Southwark but Bourne always refused to sign a new trust deed.

Amigo and the Southwark Chapter agreed to refer the matter to Rome and sought the advice of Cardinal Rafael Merry del Val, the papal Secretary of State. The Cardinal advised Amigo to place the facts before Cardinal Gaetano de Lai, Secretary of the Consistorial Congregation, which had been responsible for the dioceses of England and Wales since 1908, but warned him that the Congregation would wish to consider all aspects of the argument. In September 1910, Hinsley was sent to Rome by Amigo to present a memorandum to Consistorial.[19] In October, having considered both cases, Cardinal de Lai wrote to Bourne ordering him to leave Amigo free to administer his own diocese but Bourne still refused to sign off the trust deeds and instead suggested to Consistorial that Amigo be moved to Plymouth Diocese. Oddly enough, this suggestion was taken up by de Lai but was predictably rejected by Amigo. Fr Francis Sheehan joined Hinsley in Rome and, in March 1911, they presented another memorandum to Consistorial which contained detailed responses to Bourne's objections. In December 1912, Consistorial again decided in Amigo's favour but by then the two bishops were engaged in other disputes over finance and the re-drawing of diocesan boundaries.

In March 1911, Hinsley wrote to Mgr Doubleday at Wonersh, to inform him that Bourne had been in contact with Consistorial about the restructuring of the English dioceses. The central thrust of Bourne's plan was the creation of a diocese that would encompass the whole of London and include a large part of the Southwark Diocese. Naturally, Amigo objected. Rome took no action on Bourne's plan but it did reorganise the metropolitan structure of England and in 1911, by the decree *Si Qua Est*, Consistorial divided the English dioceses into three metropolitan provinces based on Westminster, Birmingham and Liverpool. There were no alterations to diocesan boundaries and Southwark remained within the Province of Westminster. But the matter did not end there. In 1912 an espiscopal and lay commission was established by the Hierarchy to consider the creation of new dioceses. It was another dispute that was to drag on and further weaken the reputation of the English and Welsh Hierarchy in Rome. The increasing antipathy between Bourne and Amigo overshadowed all. Rome was perplexed and unimpressed. Pope Pius X had said that the dispute would end only when one bishop buried the other. Gasquet informed Amigo that 'the Westminster–Southwark business was a public scandal and doing a great deal of harm to religion'.[20] For Hinsley, however, this was a brief but important phase in his career. He was trusted by Amigo but incurred the coolness and eventual hostility of Bourne. He became known to the Roman curia, enhanced his reputation with Merry del Val and Gasquet, and operated for the first time at the centre of diocesan and Vatican affairs.

The English Colleges in Rome

The most significant development in Hinsley's career during his ministry in Southwark began in 1916 and involved the two English seminaries in Rome. During that year, the Benedictine Cardinal Aidan Gasquet, who had succeeded Cardinal Vicenzo Vannutelli as Cardinal Protector of the college in September 1915, initiated proceedings to replace the rector of the *Venerabile* and introduce radical reforms to restore the college to its former status. Of necessity his plan involved the other English college in Rome, the *Beda,* which shared the *Venerabile's* premises.[21]

The *Beda's* origins were recent. In 1852 Pope Pius IX had established a house for English converts who wished to train for the priesthood. Called the *Collegio Pio*, it moved into the *Venerabile* buildings in 1854. It was re-founded by Pope Leo XIII at the suggestion of Cardinal Herbert Vaughan of Westminster and Mgr Merry del Val, and in 1899, when St Bede was created a Doctor of the Church, the college took him as its patron. The transfer of the *Beda* to Via de Monserrato created a complicated administrative situation that Bishop William Giles, Rector of the *Venerabile* and superior of the house, was unable to manage. Giles, who had been Rector of the *Venerabile* since 1888, was charming, affectionate and artistically talented but he was not an administrator. Under his stewardship, the college's internal organisation, fabric and financial management deteriorated considerably. Bishops were unwilling to send their seminarians to a college that had lost its traditional rigour, discipline and vitality. They lacked confidence in the college and its ageing rector. Bishop Giles resigned in 1913, and was replaced in December of the same year by John McIntyre, the 61-year-old Auxiliary Bishop of Birmingham.[22] His appointment was opposed by Archbishop Edward Ilsley of Birmingham who feared that his large archdiocese would suffer in consequence of McIntyre's removal. McIntyre had been Ilsley's secretary for 24 years and his Auxiliary for the last two and the ailing 75-year-old Archbishop did not wish to lose his most trusted adviser. He therefore asked other bishops to oppose the decision, requested Cardinal Vannutelli to remove McIntyre's name from the terna, and protested to Cardinal de Lai against McIntyre's appointment. It was claimed that Bourne wished McIntyre to go to Rome to clear the ground for Amigo to succeed Archbishop Ilsley at Birmingham. This would then open the way for Bourne's nominee to replace Amigo in Southwark.[23]

Bishop Amigo maintained that McIntyre was reluctant to go to Rome[24] but writing in 1944 Fr Thomas Bird of Birmingham, who was a student at the *Venerabile* when McIntyre arrived, claimed that the Bishop was full of joy and expectation at being appointed rector of his *alma mater.*[25] Disappointment quickly set in, however, for the new rector was appalled at the college's decline and he soon lost interest and enthusiasm. The task facing him was daunting and, after consulting with Cardinal Vannutelli, he referred the college's financial and administrative irregularities to the Cardinal Secretary of the Consistorial Congregation. An apostolic visitation of the college under the leadership of Cardinal de Lai was ordered by Pope Pius X in July 1914 and four serious problems were identified – the relationship between the *Venerabile* and the *Beda*; the absence of effective internal organisation and supervision of students; and the dreadful state of administrative and domestic arrangements. The state of affairs was so bad that in 1915 no new students entered the college and the roll was reduced to twenty. Wartime conditions may have been one cause of this but the Belgian, Irish, American and Scots Colleges all had numerous students. Writing from the college to his friend in England, one student wrote: "I wonder where the hitch lies!"[26]

Vannutelli, in poor health, resigned, and was replaced as Protector by Cardinal Gasquet on 10 September 1915.[27] In May 1916, Gasquet visited the college and met Bishop McIntyre who recorded that his Eminence was 'amazed at the amount of restoration necessary to make it worthy of its history, of its purpose, and of the great country which it represents at the centre of Christendom. . . . ' On his appointment as Rector, McIntyre had been urged by Pope Pius to make it more attractive and dignified. It seemed that nothing had changed for, as McIntyre wrote, there were no funds for restoration, prices were high, and rents from college properties were low.[28] Gasquet wrote to the Roman Association, the college's alumni, to inform them of the situation and to plead for financial assistance. Canon Joseph O'Toole, Secretary of the Association, replied to Gasquet:

> We heard with the utmost concern of the state of the College. Your Eminence's interest in the College was a source of joy to us. We are convinced that through your influence present difficulties will be overcome and that great permanent advantages are likely to accrue to our alma mater.

But, he added, the Association's Trust was confined only to the granting of student bursaries; it could not be used for the restoration of the college's fabric.[29]

Gasquet presented four suggestions to the English and Welsh Hierarchy: that the colleges be separated; that bishops alone should authorize the ordination of their seminarians; that the Archbishops of Westminster, Cardiff, Birmingham and Liverpool, should form a board of control; and, finally, the position of rector was not to be for life but in the gift of the pope on the hierarchy's recommendation.[30] When the apostolic visitation ended, in July 1916, the college was placed under the direct control of the Holy See which, as noted above, reserved the right to appoint a rector. McIntyre himself had been appointed by the Consistorial Congregation but of course he was already a bishop at this time. In January 1917 the Congregation of Seminaries nominated Mgr Algernon Stanley and Mgr Serafini as Gasquet's deputies for discipline, and the Benedictine Dom Philip Langdon, Gasquet's secretary, and the Carmelite Fr Raffaele Carlo Rossi as deputies for economy. On 7 February 1917, Cardinal Gaetano Bisletti, Prefect of the Congregation of Seminaries, convened a 'congregation' with Gasquet, the four deputies, and McIntyre, to discuss the visitors' report. In June, Fr Raffaele was appointed Apostolic Administrator.[31]

A New Rector for the Venerabile

The visitors considered that McIntyre was too old to be entrusted with the arduous task of restoring the college's fortunes and that, at twenty-six, Fr John Foley was too young and inexperienced to be vice-rector.[32] During the visitation, therefore, the search had already begun for their replacements but Gasquet's attempts to appoint senior men to the *Venerabile* was affected by the simultaneous need to fill similar positions at the *Beda*. In April 1917 Bourne informed him that the Hierarchy had agreed to the separation of the colleges, and had also decided that Mgr Thomas George, the superior of the *Beda*, should be confirmed as its rector with Fr James Redmond as vice-rector. It was a decision uncalled for and subsequently ignored by Gasquet, for he was hard at work in Rome trying to reach an outcome that was acceptable to him and the Holy See rather than to the English and Welsh Hierarchy.[33] He had already begun to help McIntyre sort out the confusion at the college but had made it clear that he was in charge and that the deputies had executive responsibilities. It was not an easy situation for McIntyre. Looking at the situation from the Diocese of Leeds, Fr John O'Connor, an alumnus of the *Venerabile*, claimed that McIntyre was a hopeless cipher and that the affairs of the college were not in his hands.[34]

In England, meanwhile, Bishop Amigo was preparing the ground for an outcome that would be acceptable to Gasquet and to him. Having already been instrumental in McIntyre's appointment in 1913, he now attempted to engineer a situation that would enable McIntyre, who he claimed 'had no mind for details', to leave the *Venerabile*. In June 1917 he had spoken to Archbishop Ilsley and a practical compromise emerged – that McIntyre should return to Birmingham as coadjutor.[35] Developments in Rome brought the matter to a conclusion. On 8 July, Cardinal de Lai informed Gasquet that McIntyre was to be named not as coadjutor with right of succession, but as auxiliary bishop in Birmingham. To assuage his feelings and avoid a loss of personal prestige, McIntyre was offered a titular archbishopric *ad personam* which he willingly accepted.[36] According to Gasquet, McIntyre rejoiced and was glad to be rid of the English College.[37] Amigo later expressed the view that Consistorial was fearful that it might be confronted with the same problems in Birmingham as had beset the *Venerabile* under McIntyre's control.[38] It was an unfair comment on McIntyre who, although not a natural administrator, had experienced a very difficult situation in Rome. According to some, he had been sent there with Bourne's blessing so that the Cardinal could have a free hand when it came to replacing Archbishop Ilsley. McIntyre's return to Birmingham, therefore, would appear to have been a reverse for Bourne's attempts to influence the succession.

With McIntyre out of the way, the Hierarchy moved to draw up ternas for both the *Venerabile* and the *Beda*. On 6 September, Bourne informed the Hierarchy that he had received official notification of the vacancy at the *Venerabile* and convened a meeting for 25 September[39] He suggested that at the same meeting, a terna for the *Beda* also be drawn up. Before the meeting, Amigo wrote to Archbishop Thomas Whiteside of Liverpool and asked him to propose Hinsley for the *Venerabile*, but, although Whiteside considered Hinsley to be an able man, he thought he would be overwhelmed by the difficulty of the task. As an alternative, he suggested Hinsley's name for the *Beda*.[40] Whiteside later informed Bishop Hugh Singleton of Shrewsbury that he preferred Fr Bernard Kavanagh of St Edward's College, Liverpool, although the Archbishop did 'not want his name to appear in this matter lest he be seen as wire-pulling'.[41]

When the bishops met on 25 September, Hinsley's name was included only on the terna for the *Beda,* but Amigo insisted that he should also be considered as a candidate for the *Venerabile*. Bourne opposed the inclusion of Hinsley's name for both ternas, but was defeated by the other bishops.[42] On the following day Bourne submitted the ternas to Gasquet and informed him that, regarding the terna for the Beda, he had a high opinion of Fr Horace Mann, the first on the list, that he would not trust his students with the second – Arthur Hinsley – and that he did not know the third – James Redmond.[43] The three names on the terna for the *Venerabile* were Fr Bernard Kavanagh, Fr Francis O'Farrell of Portsmouth Diocese, and Fr Ambrose Moriarty of Shrewsbury Diocese. Dr Kavanagh was on the staff of the *Beda* and, therefore, already resident at the *Venerabile*; Fr O'Farrell was serving as senior military chaplain at Aldershot; whilst Dr Ambrose Moriarty was Shrewsbury's Canon Theologian and Bishop Singleton's secretary. All three had been educated at the *Venerabile*.[44]

Gasquet obtained references from the three bishops whose men had been named for the *Venerabile*. Archbishop Whiteside thought that the 'firm' Fr Kavanagh, who was a 'good administrator' and of 'unblemished character', would make 'a good rector'. Bishop William Cotter of Portsmouth regarded Fr O'Farrell as 'an excellent priest', of 'sound ability and a good administrator'. Bishop Singleton, however, informed Gasquet that Dr Moriarty was not eager to return to Rome and that 'only a command' would get him there.[45]

On 18 October, Gasquet informed Amigo that he had presented both ternas to the Congregation of Seminaries and added, 'I don't think the lists of names were well considered'. His own view was that Kavanagh, who had previously rejected the offer of the vice-rectorship, would have no sympathy for the radical changes being considered for the *Venerabile*, and was also strongly pro-Irish; that O'Farrell was a non-graduate and therefore stood no chance; and that Moriarty was not in good health. His money was on Hinsley for the *Venerabile* and Mann for the *Beda*. As if he already knew the outcome, he concluded, 'I do not think Dr Hinsley's appointment will be very popular in every quarter – especially at Westminster.[46] On 28 October 1917, Hinsley was named as Rector of the *Venerabile*. On 8 November, Hinsley wrote to Gasquet to accept the post.[47] Clearly, Hinsley was the preferred choice of Gasquet and Amigo: the former being a long admirer of Hinsley's orthodoxy and vigour, the latter being anxious to have one of his most able diocesan priests in a position of stature in Rome where he could act on behalf of the bishops and perhaps offset the influence of Cardinal Bourne.

Episcopal Reaction to Hinsley's Appointment

On 30 October Cardinal Gasquet informed Archbishop Whiteside that

Hinsley had been appointed 'after a much longer delay than expected. . . .' He wrote: 'I trust that Dr Hinsley will do well. He used to be very interested in studies and Cardinal Billot has always remembered him as a student here'. The French Jesuit Louis Billot, raised to the Sacred College in 1911, had taught Dogmatic Theology at the Gregorian University between 1885 and 1910. As Gasquet predicted, the news about Hinsley's appointment was not welcomed by all the bishops. Hinsley's academic qualifications, his knowledge of Rome and the *Venerabile*, and his educational and pastoral experience may have been impressive but some bishops alleged that his career had been marked by a succession of unfinished ventures and that he was not the right man for the *Venerabile*. He had left Ushaw after disagreements with the authorities and his colleagues; his work at St Bede's could be regarded as incomplete, although much had been achieved in a short time; and he had left his original diocese. Moreover, his opponents considered that he 'lacked the requirements of courage and determination necessary for such a post'.[48] For some bishops, he was also uncomfortably close to Amigo. Bishop Singleton of Shrewsbury was indignant at Rome's decision, and wrote to Archbishop Whiteside: 'I have been informed that the Congregation of Studies has rejected our recommendation to appoint Dr Kavanagh to the Rectorship of the Venerable English College, Rome, and put in Dr Hinsley whom we deliberately left out of the terna we were asked to send up'. He suspected that Dom Philip Langdon, Gasquet's secretary, was implicated in the whole affair. The *alumni* of the *Venerabile* he had spoken to believed that Kavanagh's rejection was due to a declaration, made in answers to an informal proposal by Fr Langdon, that he would not accept the vice rectorship. 'If this was the only chief reason for rejecting the Bishops' strongly recommended nominee', Singleton continued:

> . . .then it looks as though it is useless trying to deal with the problem in Rome. Can anything be done to obtain a reversal of this decision? It was stated at our meeting that Dr Hinsley is not the man for the place and very strongly that Dr Kavanagh is; and can any protest be made against this rejection of our terna which we were asked formally to make, without reference to us? What is the use of calling bishops together for their consideration of and advice upon important matters if this is rejected on such grounds? Who are the advisers whose opinion is worth more than the united hierarchy of England?[49]

The answer to Singleton's final question was that the opinion of the senior English cardinals in Rome, Gasquet and Merry del Val, was valued in the Holy See whereas Bourne's reputation was at a low ebb and his leadership of the English and Welsh Hierarchy was considered ineffective and divisive. At the time that the bishops were trying to replace McIntyre, Bourne was simultaneously manouevering to have his auxiliary, Bishop Manuel Bidwell, appointed as the first *Episcopus Castrensis* of the British Army and assume ecclesiastical control of all military chaplains.[50] In effect, they would be controlled by Bourne. As a member of the Consistorial Congregation, Bourne was in a strong position to influence decisions on diocesan issues and the appointment of bishops but senior Vatican officials disliked him and his methods and were unimpressed by the workings of the English and Welsh Hierarchy. The Hierarchy was nowhere near as united as Singleton claimed and letters from the bishops to Gasquet illustrate their mounting and very intense frustration with Bourne's leadership style. Bishop Casartelli of Salford complained that Hierarchy meetings had become a farce, with discussion limited, standing committees not allowed, and Bourne overruling others. 'We are living under an autocracy', he wrote.[51] Archbishop Whiteside lamented that Hierarchy meetings were not opportunities for frank discussions but simply occasions to rubber-stamp Bourne's decisions. Archbishop Ilsley wrote to Cardinal de Lai and outlined the continuing disagreements between the bishops and Bourne.[52]

Hinsley's Feelings

Hinsley was aware at a relatively early stage about his possible appointment to the *Venerabile* for on 19 June 1916, he called to see Fr Francis Sheehan at Blackheath, to discuss it.[53] He told Sheehan that he had serious misgivings about his candidacy, and that his reasons were part personal, part practical. Primarily, he was genuinely convinced that he could not succeed and he did not wish to see his beloved *Venerabile* connected with his failure. He was also concerned that his appointment would incur Cardinal Bourne's displeasure and as a result the college would subsequently suffer. His position at the college, he continued, would also involve acting with considerable independence and include making hard decisions that might endanger his friendships in Rome. Additionally, part of the mission debt had been paid off at Sydenham, a school was needed, and he wished to complete his work there. Finally, at 51, he thought himself too old and lacking the necessary qualities to take up such a position, although he admitted that his ecclesiastical superiors would be the best judges of that. On the following day, Sheehan wrote to Cardinal Gasquet and expressed the opinion that sending Hinsley to Rome was an experiment worth trying but on the other hand he feared disappointment if Hinsley did take up the post. He felt that bringing pressure on Hinsley to change his mind would be unfair.

A year later, on 21 June 1917, when Amigo wrote to Gasquet trying to force the issue of the rectorship, he informed the Cardinal that both he and Fr Sheehan had again urged Hinsley to go to Rome if the rectorship fell vacant and was offered to him. Hinsley, however, was still diffident about himself and was very depressed for he had received the devastating news that his younger brother Alfred had died at the age of 47 in May 1917 whilst serving as a Quartermaster Sergeant with the Royal Defence Corps. Hinsley was naturally concerned for the welfare of his family. Alfred and Hinsley's nephew Wilfred, who died in Salonika in 1918, were later commemorated in St George's Chapel in Westminster Cathedral. To add to his woes Hinsley had been subpoenaed to appear in court in connection with a disputed will by which Cardinal Bourne stood to benefit considerably.[54] By October 1917, when he had been notified of his Roman appointment, Hinsley's spirits were even lower. Fr Thomas Cambourne, a student priest at the time, later recalled that Hinsley sent him a telegram and called him to Sydenham where he found Hinsley in considerable distress. Hinsley showed him the letter of appointment to the *Venerabile* and lamented that he had been clearing up messes all his life. He was happy at Sydenham and was against going to Rome.[55]

By early November, however, his spirits had recovered and he had changed his mind about his Roman appointment. He wrote to Cardinal Gasquet to express his gratitude for the Cardinal's confidence that 'makes me daring enough to accept the burden of responsibility'. He informed Gasquet that he was arranging with the Foreign Office for the necessary clearance and that he had replied to Cardinal Bisleti 'with all my heart's gratitude and loyalty.'[56] He was to return to the *Venerabile* after an absence of twenty-four years. On 26 November Amigo saw Hinsley leave Waterloo Station for Rome. 'He was', wrote the bishop to Cardinal Gasquet, 'in fine spirits, determined to do his utmost for the *Venerabile*'.[57] He had much to do and was aware that although he had powerful friends in Rome he still had to win supporters in England.[58]

Others who perhaps knew him better rejoiced in his promotion. Eleven of his former colleagues from his student days at the *Venerabile* were delighted that one of their own had been appointed to such a prestigious post and wrote to him before he left for Rome.

> Dear Arthur,
>
> We, the companions of the 'good Old School' unite in offering you our warmest congratulations and affectionate felicitations on the honour that has been conferred on you by our Holy Father in the promotion to the Rectorship of the English College, Rome. We have always been proud of you because of the lustre you have cast on the 'School' by your scholarly attainments and priestly zeal, as well as by the great educational work you have accomplished during your missionary career. We are doubly proud now that your worth and abilities have been so signally recognised by the Head of the Church and by the Episcopacy of this country. In your new sphere you will find ample scope for your energy and abilities. We rejoice in your promotion, and feel sure that your return to the old associations and the congenial atmosphere of Rome will stimulate you to still more fruitful service of the Church. We shall follow your career as Rector of the English College with deep interest, and will pray God to bless and strengthen you in the discharge of the duties of your responsible position. We beg you to accept the enclosed cheque as a brotherly 'consideration' towards the expense you will be put to in changing your quarters.[59]

It was a commendation that Bourne and some other bishops would have disagreed with.

At Ushaw, the difficulties caused by Hinsley's earlier enthusiasm were forgotten and its professors and students sent their heartiest congratulations to him on his appointment at 'this critical time' in the history of the *Venerabile*. It had been many years since an Ushavian 'had ruled over' the Venerable English College.[60] Meanwhile, Hinsley's parishioners in Sydenham presented him with a cheque, a set of robes, and a cross. Hinsley expressed his appreciation but regretted that he had been unable to build an elementary school for the mission.[61]

Hinsley's curate Fr Patrick Roughneen, wrote to Mgr Michael O'Riordan, Rector of the Pontifical Irish College in Rome:

> I promised my late Rector Dr Hinsley – now rector of the English College – to write to you as he is very anxious to meet you. He is leaving London tomorrow Friday and will arrive some day next week, if the Germans do not interfere with the Northern railways.

The new Rector is a very fine priest, a very hard worker on the mission, and notwithstanding his temporal cares, always finds time for a half-hours mediation before 7.15 Mass. You will find him to be straightforward and honest and entirely above the ordinary type of English priest that one meets here in London.

He has been exceedingly kind to me and I think you will find him very anxious to model the English College on the disciplinary system now in vogue at 14 Via Mazzarino [the Irish College's residence 1836-1926] . . . the Bishop told me to take charge of the parish till he finds a Rector to replace Dr Hinsley, a task of no small difficulty. . . .[62]

Chapter Four

THE RECTOR

1917-1930

Arrival

Hinsley was appointed a Domestic Prelate on 14 November 1917 by Pope Benedict XV and arrived at the *Venerabile* later in the month.[1] Robert Meagher, a seminarian from Liverpool and one of the fifteen students in the college, recalled that the arrival of the new rector, 'tall, strongly built, strong jawed . . . fresh featured, and smiling', was like a breath of fresh air. In the following months, recalled Fr Meagher, Hinsley was 'to alter all and make the dead bones of the College live again'.[2] Cardinal Gasquet recorded that when Hinsley visited him he was 'in good spirits and dispositions'. In the evening the Cardinal officially introduced the new Rector to his students who gave a concert in his honour.[3] Later, Gasquet wrote to Bishop Amigo to tell him that Hinsley had arrived and was 'determined to work for the *Venerabile*'. Gasquet also informed Amigo that Hinsley had

> . . .told me all about the very malicious lies and misrepresentations that have been set about in England as to what I have tried to do for the College to pull it out of the miserable state into which it had fallen through years of neglect.

'Nothing short of drastic measures' he concluded, 'will revive it'.[4] On Christmas Eve Gasquet informed Amigo that he thought Hinsley was going to be 'a great success'. Hinsley was aware that English opinions of him (Gasquet) were 'a pack of lies' but he 'must judge for himself'. He also told Amigo that he had warned Hinsley about the Roman Association, the former students of the college, 'who did not manage the College' despite their influence with the Hierarchy.[5]

Less than harmonious relations between the Hierarchy, the Roman Association, and the Cardinal Protector placed Hinsley in a very awkward position. He was very conscious of the fact that not all the bishops favoured the English College for the training and formation of their seminarians nor did they all welcome his appointment. He was also aware of the Association's fondness for the Roman tradition and Bishop Giles' stewardship, their mistrust of Gasquet and the regulars who were now running the college, and their dislike of an interfering Papal Curia. But he was enough of a realist to know that only Gasquet's drive and determination, backed by papal authority, would pull the college out its present deplorable state. Hinsley faced a formidable task, not only of restoring the college's fortunes but also of having to wade through the sometimes turbulent waters of ecclesiastical politics in his attempt to do so. But at least he had powerful support. At the centenary of the college's restoration, Pope Benedict XV wrote to Hinsley to express his high hope for its future. His hope was stronger because of the character, faith and ability of the Cardinal Protector and the traditions of the college which was 'under the eyes of the Supreme Pontiff'. He urged the new rector to recognise the immense possibilities facing young men of the brightest promise who, when ordained and before leaving for the homeland, will have 'filled their souls at the very wellspring with the spirit of the Roman faith'.[6] But the reality was more prosaic and pressing. According to Mgr Richard Smith, Hinsley found 'a down-at-heels college with a great past, an unworthy present, and a problematical future.'[7] During the next ten years, with considerable assistance from Gasquet and Merry del Val, he was to transform the *Venerabile* and not only restore its reputation but enhance it considerably. He acted speedily on the recommendations of the Visitors and seized every opportunity to further the college's prospects. As a result his career prospered.

Transition Period

Hinsley did not assume official responsibility for college affairs until the work of the Apostolic Administrator was completed in February 1918. Even then, the 'congregation' of Cardinal Protector and deputies that had been set up to administer the college continued to meet and it was only after July 1919 that Hinsley attended their meetings.

The Roman Association and others may have been suspicious of Gasquet, Rossi and Langdon but they succeeded, where McIntyre had failed, to rectify the financial mismanagement of the college and clear up the administrative debris left by Giles. The Association was not impressed by this take-over nor the methods employed and in 'Notes for Mgr Hinsley' the Association stated that

> The entire control of the finances of the *Venerabile* appear to have been taken over by San Calisto in February 1917 ... the Reverend Philip Langdon took full control of the College accounts. He took entire possession of the *computisteria*. The key of this office was in his keeping and he kept all accounts with the assistance of one, Domenico. The college staff had no access to this office. Even the salaries of the Rector and Mgr George (of the Beda) were paid by Rev P Langdon.[8]

From Hinsley's point of view, however, it was better that the separation from the Beda was complete, that the college's complicated accounts were effectively re-organised and stabilised, and that the college was restored on the basis of a sound constitution which reflected the nature of the modern college and the work for which its students were being prepared. Such developments took time.

As Rector, Hinsley was in the front line of this stand-off between Gasquet and his detractors in the Hierarchy and in the Association, and having been briefed by Amigo he was 'interviewed' by the officers of the Roman Association in December 1917. In an attempt to allay the Association's fears over the likelihood of a new constitution for the college, Amigo advised Hinsley 'that he should tell them that he was too thoroughly English to allow constitutions to be imposed (by Italians) that did not suit the English character'. Amigo reported to Gasquet that

> Hinsley seemed satisfied after his talk with them. His plain, straightforward manner must have disarmed them. I hope the misunderstandings are now finished and that the *Venerabile* will flourish under its new Rector ... he is determined to do well.[9]

The misunderstandings were far from over, however, and subsequent developments were to reveal Hinsley's misinterpretation of the Roman Association's constitution and the interfering hand of Cardinal Bourne.

Gasquet and McIntyre had written to the Roman Association in 1916 asking for financial assistance towards the restoration of the college property. The Association, whilst sympathetic to the plight of the college, could not address these pleas as constitutionally it was restricted to the provision of student bursaries derived from interest on capital. In the following year, and before Hinsley was appointed, Gasquet persuaded the English and Welsh Hierarchy to issue a joint pastoral letter appealing for funds for the restoration of the college. This was read out in all churches on the last Sunday of October 1917 and eventually raised the considerable sum £5,181.10s.6d.[10] The prominent role of the Roman

Association in both the collection and distribution of the money came as a complete surprise to some of the Hierarchy. Bernard Ward, the recently consecrated Bishop of the new Diocese of Brentwood, had actually written the pastoral but, as he told Gasquet, he had not even mentioned the Association in the appeal nor was he aware of its involvement. Only at the Low Week meeting of the bishops in 1918 did he hear that the Association 'should hold the money and supervise its expenditure'. Cardinal Bourne informed the bishops that this had always been the intention but Ward, and probably others, was unconvinced.

Archbishop Whiteside of Liverpool and Bishop Singleton of Shrewsbury, the former an *alumnus* of the college, were most certainly aware of the Association's role in the matter. In September 1917, before the appeal was launched, Singleton received a letter from Canon O'Toole of St Joseph's, Birkenhead, and Treasurer of the Association, informing him that the rectorship and the appeal had been discussed with Whiteside. O'Toole asked for Singleton to use his influence with the episcopate and wrote that all the Association was asking for in 'proceeding in the matter of the appeal' was a 'workable scheme between us and the bishops'.[11]

Acutely aware of his junior position on the episcopal bench, Ward told Gasquet that 'I did not contradict' Bourne but added 'it seems a very unusual method of procedure'. He concluded, 'I hope we shall not have trouble about it'.[12] But trouble there was, for the Roman Association which had supervised the collection would not send the money to Rome given the unfavourable rate of exchange and without knowing how it was to be used. The majority of bishops were against this rather intransigent attitude but nevertheless Ward told Gasquet that the money collected would 'be expended by the Association'.[13] Not surprisingly, Gasquet found this unacceptable and only through the support of Amigo, who advised 'prudence', and the intervention of Cardinal Bisleti were the funds eventually released and secured for the Protector and the college authorities.[14]

In December 1918, during a visit to the college, Bourne told Hinsley that he knew nothing of the Roman Association and its difficulties with the college authorities. It was a strange admission for in a separate discussion with Mgr Mann of the *Beda*, he said 'that the Roman Association was quite right to take a stand'. He further told Mann that the English and Welsh bishops could not approve the new constitutions for the college and that the future management of the college should be vested in the four Archbishops of England and Wales. Gasquet placed the facts, as he understood them from the reports of these conversations, presumably from Hinsley and Mann, before Cardinal Bisleti who replied that he would ask the Pope to immediately settle the dispute between the college and the Roman Association. On hearing of this, Bourne backtracked, denied that he had anything to do with encouraging the Association to take an active part in the administration of the college, and promised Gasquet that he would 'set the situation right' at the next Low Week meeting.[15]

In his first annual report, for 1918-1919, Hinsley informed the Hierarchy of very positive developments. The *Venerabile* and *Beda* had been formally separated in 1 January 1918 and all outstanding financial issues had been settled. He told the bishops that 'the utmost cordiality exists between the colleges, and the *Venerabile* is deeply interested in the success of the *Beda*'. A start had been made on repairing the college's fabric 'made necessary by the condition of disorder and decay into which the premises had fallen' but important documents had been lost amid the confusion left by the previous administration and there was evidence that the previous system of management had left the college in a parlous state. There were accommodation and hygiene problems and many health and safety issues to contend with. 'Much remains to be done', he reminded the bishops, 'if the college is to be decent and continue to be an honour to the name it bears'. The Pope, Hinsley reported, was injecting funds into the college and his generosity was 'in stark relief to the monies held back by the Association of the English College' which he claimed, in typically forthright style, 'was injuring the college morally and materially'. The assertions of the Association that 'the Regulars' were interfering 'was not in accordance with the facts', he emphasised, and he finished with a forceful statement of his own position:

> The Rector does not intend to be a puppet, as he has been accused of being, but he does place himself entirely and unreservedly in the hands of his lawful superiors the Bishops of England, represented here by the Cardinal Protector, and our Holy Father the Pope.[16]

By late 1919 the differences between the college and the Roman Association had been resolved. The Association handed over £4,900 to the college, presented the Pope with £1,000 and provided bourses for students. Both Cardinal Gasparri and Cardinal Gasquet thanked Canon Moriarty, President of the Association, for its help and support. Hinsley had successfully cleared one obstacle.

The Boss

The Rector and the 'congregation' were faced with four major tasks: to re-organise the college's domestic arrangements; to restore and modernize the college building; to increase the number of seminarians; and to re-introduce rigour into academic studies. To solve the first problem, Hinsley persuaded a refugee community of Elizabettine nuns from Northern Italy who had been occupying the college's summer residence of Monte Porzio to look after the college's dining, laundry and cleaning routines. By November 1918, they were in the college and immediately effected positive changes.[17] Sister Diomara de Zotti wrote later that it was impossible to describe the disorder and filthy condition of the whole building through lack of cleaning.[18]

The second problem was more expensive to solve and Hinsley's frequent correspondence with Gasquet refers to the huge problems caused by the poor state of the college's buildings. With Padre Rafaele, Hinsley successfully arranged for the amicable separation of the *Venerabile* and *Beda* and the attendant accounts were eventually settled. Arrangements were also made to lease some of the college's property in order to generate income.[19] But improvement work on the college and at Monte Porzio was dreadfully slow and serious domestic issues began to demand more of Hinsley's time. In August 1918 he reported that the nuns at Monte Porzio had been struck by typhus but the necessary changes at the college to accommodate the nuns were incomplete.[20] In September he informed Gasquet that he had managed to get a supply of wood to heat the college during the winter months.[21] It was not until November 1918, a year after his arrival, that Hinsley was able to tell the Cardinal that work at the college was complete and that the Rector did not have to go to the Gregorian University for his meals.[22]

During the next few years money was obtained to make significant improvements to the college and physical conditions improved dramatically. Remedial work was undertaken to rectify serious structural problems, central heating was installed, bedrooms, washing facilities, corridors and study rooms were modernized, a *salone* was provided, the student common room was enlarged, a new organ was installed in the chapel, and a swimming pool was built in the garden.[23] The increasing number of students caused Hinsley to think of providing more facilities for relaxation and he gleefully informed Bishop Ward that he had been able to acquire a billiard table from the British Red Cross for £50 rather than its value of £150. 'By degrees', he informed the Bishop, 'I think everything is getting into order'.[24] Such was his determination to make improvements that at first the Sisters thought he was a workman because he used to carry building materials around the college. A new swimming pool was built and college tradition has it that the Rector 'baptized it' by being the first to dive in.

In 1925, the internal problems were compounded, and the college's future seriously threatened, by the plans of Benito Mussolini, the fascist Prime Minister of Italy, for the improvement of Rome. The scheme, which involved the demolition of the crowded and dirty Via dei Cappellari and the creation of a covered market, included the proposed demolition of a substantial part of the college and the loss of the small garden. The college authorities had fifteen days in which to lodge an appeal and Hinsley set to work at lightning speed. In December 1925, he mounted a press campaign in England. At first, only *The Universe* covered the college's plight, reporting that 'the energetic Rector has not been caught napping' but in the New Year it was taken up by *The Times* of London which carried a sympathetic leader and a special article entitled 'A Threatened Foundation'. In another edition *The Times* included photographs of those parts of the college affected by Mussolini's plans – the third library, the *guardaroba* and the Martyrs' Chapel. Provincial newspapers in England and Wales also carried the story whilst in Italy it was followed up by *Tribuna* and *Il Giornale d'Italia*.[25]

Hinsley kept the Hierarchy informed of developments. In 1926 he confidently informed Bishop Doubleday, the new Bishop of Brentwood, that he thought the college was safe from 'expropriation altogether, garden and everything'[26] but he later told Archbishop McIntyre that he was going to appeal to the Governor of Rome.[27] In a further letter to McIntyre he told the Archbishop that he was employing 'delaying tactics' against the Roman authorities but he was concerned that the considerable expense incurred may restrict student entry.[28] Eventually, thanks to the intervention of Senator Cremonesi, the Governor of Rome, the plans were modified but it was not until 1929, after the signing of the Lateran Pact between Italy and the Vatican, and when Hinsley was Apostolic Visitor in British Colonial Africa, that the *Venerabile* was finally saved from loss of land and damaging alterations. As Mgr Williams concluded, the mobilisation of the successful opposition to the *Piano Regulatore* was a combination of Hinsley's prompt action and private negotiations. *The*

Universe reported that 'the Rector's untiring labour, persistent courage and diplomatic ability succeeded in averting the threatened destruction of the splendid fabric entrusted to his charge'.[29]

Since his appointment and often with the assistance of Cardinal Merry del Val, Hinsley was actively engaged in selling and purchasing property. Especially important to him was the acquisition of an adequate summer residence to replace Monte Porzio which was considered to be too small for the growing number of students. In April 1917 papal permission had been given to sell Monte Porzio, by November 1918 it was up for sale, and so advanced were the arrangements that the *villeggiatura* was held at the former friary of Montopoli where Hinsley celebrated the Armistice and sang the *Te Deum* in the presence of the students.[30] By March 1920 Hinsley had purchased a replacement, Palazzola, in the Alban Hills.[31] So enthusiastic was he about Palazzola and such was his determination to have it that Hinsley made a special journey to Genoa to complete the deal before the owner had chance to sell the property to another prospective buyer. Aspects of this purchase soon passed into college folklore. The cutlery at Palazzola bore the initials 'CA' representing the previous owner Carlo Amaldi. Students noted that the initials were interchangeable with 'Collegio Anglorum'.[32]

The dreadful condition of the college's buildings and properties were obviously a cause of great concern to the college authorities but so too was the low number of students. At the outbreak of the First World War, there were thirty-three students but during the war years the number had fallen dramatically. In April 1918 Hinsley reported to Gasquet that there were only seventeen students in the college. All attended the Jesuit-run Gregorian University but they complained to Hinsley about the content of the studies and the quality of the teaching.[33] Despite this, in 1919 Hinsley was able to report to Gasquet that the college had produced six doctorates in the last year. He informed Gasquet that during a recent visit to England he persuaded the Archbishops and Bishops of Southwark, Liverpool, Middlesbrough, Leeds, Salford, Menevia, Brentwood, Nottingham, Plymouth, Shrewsbury, Hexham and Newcastle, and Malta to send a total of twenty new students. As an aside he told Gasquet that despite being overlooked for the rectorship Moriarty gave him 'a warm welcome' in Shrewsbury but, he continued, 'the feeling of soreness is still there and will last some time'.[34]

Such was the rate of progress that at the beginning of the academic year 1919-1920 there were forty-four students on roll – eleven from the previous year and thirty-three new men representing nearly every diocese and seminary in England and Wales. In addition, there were sixteen applicants for the following year. Hinsley had certainly made an immediate impact and the numbers were to rise continuously over the next few years.[35] At the start of the 1922-1923 college year there were sixty-five students on roll and by 1927-1928 there were sixty-eight.[36] The college was now faced with the problem of inadequate accommodation.

The immediate impact that Hinsley had upon the college did not go unnoticed by the Hierarchy. At their annual Low Week meeting in April 1919 it was recorded that

> Having heard the report of His Eminence the Cardinal and the Bishop of Brentwood, who had recently been in Rome, and the accounts received by other Bishops from their students, the Bishops decided to congratulate the Rector, Mgr Hinsley, on the excellent state of the College.

They also thanked the Roman Association and hoped that they would 'continue to have friendly relations with the college authorities'.[37] Accordingly, Bourne wrote to Hinsley to say that 'their Lordships desired me to congratulate you very sincerely on the present excellent state of the college'.[38] The successful transformation of the *Venerabile* was due of course to the combined efforts of Gasquet, Rossi, Philip Langdon and Hinsley but it was the Rector who drew the plaudits from a grateful Hierarchy. In 1924 Cardinal Bourne wrote to Hinsley to congratulate him 'on the success of your constant efforts for the improvement' of the college and again in 1927 thanked him for his 'continued successful government of the college'.[39]

In 1926 the Rector reported that 'the spirit of our men is excellent. There is a healthy public opinion and a tradition of earnestness, loyalty and regularity'. Hinsley expected hard work but he also encouraged an active social life within the college. A magazine was introduced, visiting speakers were invited to address the students, there were plays and Gilbert and Sullivan operettas, there were sports teams, and there was a debating and other societies. It was, wrote Mgr Williams, not unlike an officers' mess: an isolated and 'a very English sort of existence' boosted by occasional high points such as the visit of King George V and Queen Mary to Rome in 1923. This limited social existence was forced upon the college by its Constitution and rules which forced the students into each other's company and restricted social contact with any other than ecclesiastical personnel.[40] Hinsley also introduced a more systematic academic regime and his reports to the bishops reveal that few details of a student's personal qualities, application and performance escaped his attention. He was conscious of his responsibility to the bishops but above all he was aware of his important role in preparing young men for the priesthood. According to Mgr Smith, there developed between Hinsley and his students 'a human bond, sublimated by the grace of vocation'.[41] But ensuring the balance between a student's academic education at the Gregorian, a thorough preparation for his priestly life in England and Wales, and his existence in an expatriate college was not easy. He managed to engage English Spiritual Directors, Frs Moss and Cotter, but the presence in the college of Dr William Heard of Southwark was not of any great value, as he was unsociable, 'silent, stern, and cynical', and displayed 'a superiority' that Hinsley found unsettling.[42] Such was the difficulty of obtaining an appropriate Spiritual Director that Hinsley actually offered to take up the position himself and resign as Rector.[43] He had tried hard on more than one occasion to acquire the services of English priests to act as tutors, or *repititores*, within the college but he was not always successful. Despite opinions to the contrary, for the college was not seen as a post-graduate institution, Hinsley managed to preserve the college's library in its entirety and, as at Ushaw, had it catalogued.[44]

The relative value of post-graduate theological studies in Rome and elsewhere on the continent was discussed openly after 1923 when Cardinal Bourne announced his wish to set up a Catholic Faculty of Theology and Philosophy at either Oxford or Cambridge. Typically, Bourne had not consulted the Hierarchy and many of them shied away from the practical ramifications of the proposal – its costs, the potential insularity of such an institution and the consequences on the English College. Bishop Casartelli immediately wrote to Gasquet to say that the scheme had to be opposed otherwise it would damage the college.[45] The proposal was dropped.

Roman Agent

Like his predecessors, Hinsley acted as the Roman agent for some of the English and Welsh bishops but it was huge distraction from the rectorship and took up considerable time and effort. Most of his work for the Ordinaries seemed to be occupied with unusual and difficult matrimonial cases which had been referred to Rome for a solution. It was tedious and bureaucratic for he had to ensure that he had the correct documentation, attend appropriate Vatican departments and wait upon Vatican officials for decisions. However, it earned money for the college and Hinsley devised a system to record the work he undertook for each prelate. By April 1918 he was representing Archbishop Whiteside of Liverpool and wrote to the Archbishop that 'I will gladly take up the work and do all in my power to serve the diocese and Your Grace in any possible way'.[46] When he left for Africa ten years later he had processed 179 petitions from Liverpool.[47]

Unfortunately, when acting on behalf of Bishop Ward of Brentwood during 1919, Hinsley again confronted Cardinal Bourne. Bishop Ward of Brentwood did not wish his seminarians at St Edmund's College, Ware, to be members of the college's Combined Cadet Force. However, Cardinal Bourne, the President of St Edmund's, was very much in favour of such manly and patriotic pursuits, even for seminarians, and insisted that they participated. Neither prelate would back down. To resolve the situation Ward asked Hinsley to raise the matter with Cardinal Bisleti at the Sacred Congregation of Seminaries.[48] Bourne told Cardinal Bisleti that the C.C.F. was an accepted feature of all English public schools, both Catholic and non-Catholic, and that parents and public opinion expected it. It was good, he argued, for clerics to be exposed to discipline and obedience. Bisleti initially advised the bishops to sort out the matter themselves[49] but no resolution was reached and Ward proposed to withdraw his students and send them to St John's College, Wonersh, in the diocese of Southwark.[50] At first Bisleti opposed this but eventually wrote to Ward and told him that in order 'to avoid continual friction' he was pursuing the correct course. He further told Ward that 'this is the only way to keep peace with Westminster'.[51] In his correspondence with Ward, Hinsley was less than discreet and spoke of the dispute with Bourne as if it was a military conflict. In Rome Hinsley was assisted by Bishop Amigo and the two of them took Ward's side unreservedly.[52] 'The Bishop of Southwark', Hinsley told Ward, 'is fighting your battles like a warrior'. Aware of Bourne's temperament and strength of character, Hinsley advised Ward that he was in for a 'tough bit of fighting'. Eventually, Ward was successful and his students did not face the rigours of the C.C.F. In June 1919 Hinsley congratulated him on his triumph and accepted the bishop's invitation to visit Brentwood. But

Bourne was not pleased with the outcome and wrote a 'terrible letter' to Bisleti who immediately summoned Hinsley and told him that the Roman Curia, from the Pope downwards, was indignant with Bourne's stance for he had told the Cardinal that his decision to support Ward would be followed by diplomatic and political consequences. Bourne's correspondence, Hinsley told Ward, was met with horror and disgust by Vatican authorities and Bisleti charged Hinsley with ascertaining the reaction in England. Amigo's offer to take Ward's students would not have endeared him to Bourne nor would Hinsley's energy on Ward's behalf have increased his popularity in Westminster. In his role as agent Hinsley came into contact with other Sacred Congregations. A dispute with the Franciscans over control of missions in the diocese of Brentwood, forced Bishop Ward again to call upon Hinsley to represent him before Cardinal de Lai at the Sacred Consistorial Congregation.[53] On another occasion he had to discuss the whole issue of the English bishops' faculties relating to marriage cases with Cardinal Merry del Val.[54]

The college was an important centre of English Catholic life in Rome and Hinsley frequently hosted visitors and presided over commemorative events. In January 1918, in Gasquet's absence, he welcomed guests to celebrations commemorating the centenary of the re-opening of the college under Nicholas Wiseman. When Archbishops Frederick Keating of Liverpool and Thomas Williams of Birmingham received the pallium they were entertained at the college in June 1921. On 14 February 1922 Hinsley's powers of diplomacy and tact were severely tested when he hosted a dinner at the college to celebrate the coronation of Pope Pius XI. The major guests were Cardinals Gasquet, Bourne, and Logue of Armagh. Relations between Bourne and Logue had been extremely strained during the Great War and subsequent Irish troubles and the Vatican observed Anglo-Irish friction with sadness and displeasure. The prospect of Bourne and Logue at a dinner was fraught and was a potentially explosive situation but it passed off harmoniously. Hinsley wrote to Amigo to tell him that Gasquet proposed the Pope, Bourne judiciously spoke of Logue as a great protagonist for Church and country, Logue proposed peace and union among Catholics, and Hinsley proposed a toast to Mgr Donald Mackintosh, Rector of the Scots College who had been recently appointed Archbishop of Glasgow. It was a masterstroke in bringing the British Hierarchies together and Count John de Salis praised Hinsley for successfully presiding over this minor 'Peace Congress'. In May 1923, in a mark of improving relations between Great Britain and the Holy See, King George V and Queen Mary made a state visit to Rome when they had a private audience with Pope Pius XI. Cary Elwes, a student of the college, presented the Queen with a bouquet of roses tied with red, white and blue ribbons.[55] At very different level, Hinsley had the pleasure of presenting a group of pilgrims from St Bede's Grammar School to the Pope in 1925 during the school's silver jubilee year.[56]

Relations between the *Venerabile* and the Pontifical Irish College in Rome were strained throughout the first few years of Hinsley's rectorship. The outbreak of the Great War gave Asquith's Liberal government an opportunity to defer its decision on Irish Home Rule but the Easter Rising of 1916, continuous Republican activity and savage English reprisals meant that during and after the war Ireland was a hotbed of violence, rumour and intrigue. The establishment of Howard's Mission in 1914 gave the British government direct access to the Pope and the opportunity to use the Vatican as a moderating influence on the Irish Hierarchy which was inevitably involved in Irish politics. With no corresponding Irish Mission, the Irish College was the principal channel of communication through which the Irish bishops tried to counteract British influence in the Vatican and the attitude of the Rector of the Irish College, Mgr Michael O'Riordan, and his successor Mgr John Hagan, generally reflected their Hierarchy's policies. The two Rectors were fierce nationalists and their correspondence includes letters from prominent Irish churchmen and politicians about the Irish situation. In 1916 O'Riordan had been investigated by the police for allegedly publishing and circulating a pamphlet on the Easter Rising and in 1918 had prepared the defence for seditious Irish priests opposed to conscription in Ireland. Both men disliked Gasquet, whom they regarded as an enemy of Home Rule, and the arrival of a British Mission to the Vatican in 1914 added to their suspicions of British influence.[57] Count John de Salis, who succeeded Howard as British Minister to the Holy See in 1916, reported to the Foreign Office that intelligence described the Irish College as a nest of intrigue against England and the Allies but he knew nothing of actual conspiracies. He reported that his relations with the college were delicate rather than difficult but he did not doubt its sympathy with Irish nationalism.[58]

An article on the Irish situation, allegedly emanating from *Venerabile*, and published in *L'Osservatore Romano* in December 1918, so incensed Hagan, now the Rector, that he refused to attend the *Venerabile's* celebrations to commemorate the centenary of the *Venerabile's* re-opening. Hagan told Hinsley that the article was 'gratuitously offensive to a land I hold dear'.[59] The Irish College referred to the English College as 'the colony' and never missed an opportunity to make disparaging comments about the *Venerabile* or Hinsley. O'Riordan and Hagan, of course, were in the difficult position of trying to appraise Vatican officials of the Irish situation and their bishops' actions without appearing to be openly hostile to Great Britain. They both considered that the British government's attitude to small nations at the post-war peace conferences contrasted starkly with its attitude to emerging Irish nationhood and consequently they distanced themselves from English activities in the Eternal City. In December 1920 Hagan declined Hinsley's invitation to the *Venerabile's* patronal feast-day celebrations. During the war, he wrote, such festivities were not held 'while might trampled on right' and he felt ill-disposed to visit the college given the present situation in Ireland where the same principle was being applied by Great Britain. He told Hinsley that he had no wish he to be 'in the company of individuals . . . who to say the least have given no public sign that they dissociate themselves from the deeds perpetrated by their government'.[60] In the same year de Salis reported that there was very active propaganda being carried on in Rome in favour of a republican outcome to the deliberations over Ireland's future. As if to emphasise the Vatican's extreme caution, the Pope personally reprimanded both Mgr Hagan and Mgr Salotti, a senior Vatican official, over demonstrations held at the Irish College during the Terence McSwiney affair. Ireland, it may be said, derived little solace from the Vatican.[61]

After the signing of the treaty creating the Irish Free State and the Province of Ulster, High Mass was sung in the college chapel on 15 January 1922 and was attended by Count John de Salis and the British Ambassador to the Quirinal. Three days later Irish peace was celebrated in the college 'by a concert during which all present rose and drank the undying friendship of England and Ireland and sang the chorus "God Save Ireland" '.[62] No-one from the Irish College was present but Anglo-Irish relations in Rome steadily improved. In 1923 de Salis reported that the agitation formerly carried on in Irish Circles in Rome against England was 'practically dead' and by 1926 inter-college relations had also thawed.[63] Hagan attended Hinsley's episcopal consecration and Fr M J Browne at St Patrick's Maynooth took this as a sign that Hagan 'had yielded to the spirit of the times'[64] but when Henry Chilton replaced Sir Odo Russell at the British Legation in 1929, Hagan did not pay his respects to the new minister as did the Rectors of the Scots, *Beda*, and Canadian Colleges and the Vice-Rector of the *Venerabile*.

Hinsley's Legacy

When Hinsley arrived at the *Venerabile* the omens for him were not good. Edward Ellis, later Bishop of Nottingham, recalled that the students saw little of McIntyre but Hinsley 'was a new broom and many people were against him'. There were, he wrote, 'outbursts' against the new Rector and his reforms. Some even objected to him removing fleas from bedding on the grounds that the martyrs had fleas in their beds.[65] Mgr Richard Smith, a former student at the *Venerabile*, wrote that when Hinsley was appointed Rector, his 'cronies gave him six months at his new post' for his early years as a priest had been a series of 'false starts' and he had arrived at the *Venerabile* with 'the reputation of not being able to stay on one course'. Such unfavourable sentiments lingered but twelve successful years on the mission in Southwark had enabled Hinsley to put his early failings behind him. And indeed, despite his alleged failings at both Ushaw and Bradford, his achievements in both places had been considerable. Against all the odds, he remained as full-time Rector of the English College for ten years and then *in absentia* for three years.[66]

The energy and restless spirit that had worked against Hinsley at Ushaw and Bradford were to his advantage in Rome. In spite of the reservations of others, he rescued his beloved *alma mater* from the financial chaos, physical deterioration, academic underachievement and communal torpor into which it had sadly sunk.

The restoration of the college's fabric and the purchase of Palazzola were of the greatest importance in the improvement of the material conditions in which students lived, studied and relaxed and these achievements were among Hinsley's greatest legacies to the *Venerabile*. But more importantly he proceeded to re-establish the *Venerabile* as a major seminary and its traditions and its reputation was handsomely restored. After a little less than a year in the post he said to Bishop Ward that 'the *Venerabile* is very much alive'[67] and with the help of others he ensured that the college resumed the fullness of life and regained its former status and the respect it had lost. Even the Roman Association was won over to his side and such was their approval of his efforts that he was made President of the Association in 1921. When their representatives met in Rome in 1922 Hinsley welcomed them wholeheartedly. They were impressed that the Rector who was supposed to lack courage and determination had made such good use of the Restoration Fund. One wrote that Hinsley had brought the college and Association into 'a wholly new and intimate relationship which it is to be hoped may be permanent'.[68]

To the seminarians Hinsley was a frightening but an inspirational figure. He never forgot the importance of his role or the obligations of his students. They were not allowed to underestimate the awesome responsibilities facing him nor his high expectations of them. His application to prayer and study were exemplary. His preparation of men for the priesthood was rigorous and his discipline was fierce, but he was temperamental. John Carmel Heenan recalled that 'A man of moods, he was liable to become unduly depressed by occasional transgressors' yet he was elated by student success. Hinsley was 'a man of powerful character', 'a Rectorial Mr Chips'. Under him, Heenan recalled, 'the *Venerabile* was a contented house'.[69] Moloney perceptively noted that the students responded promptly to the firm leadership of 'the Boss', related to his humour and understanding, and developed a healthy respect for his ferocity on matters of principle but they 'only imperfectly comprehended his deep and quiet unconscious craving for companionship'.[70]

It was not difficult, wrote Mgr Smith, to measure Hinsley's achievements at the *Venerabile* simply 'in terms of material progress' but there were other important facets to Hinsley's rectorship. The physical improvements he introduced, necessary and important though they were, were overshadowed by his enormous personal influence on the students. Hinsley was quick to recognise the academic talents of others and developed them accordingly. Among the students he was enthusiastic and vibrant and could be 'young at heart' but he was also the Rector and he 'never lost his grip or lacked for authority'. 'Those who thought he did not rule', wrote Mgr Smith, 'were judging from superficial observation'. He may have 'lacked many of the qualities which are considered indispensable in a superior' and the students may have been able to read his moods 'like a barometer' but they did not question his authority or doubt his sincerity of purpose. The *Venerabile* had to be given mind, heart and lungs and Hinsley provided all. By sheer strength of effort and personality he restored college life and forced the *Venerabile* to shed its intellectual and corporate malaise. His approach was always courteous and charitable and he created a bond between him and his students that was 'sublimated by the grace of vocation'. It was Hinsley's 'crowning glory', wrote Smith, that he breathed 'a noble spirit' into the college based on *pietas* – 'the mutual obligations of ruler and ruled, obligations of affection and reverence and responsibility'. Hinsley's rectorship, concluded Smith:

> was historic not only for the material prosperity it brought or for the rise in our repute; but most of all, for that new spirit which he breathed into a body that was old and tired, renewing its strength for fresh effort in all the joy and generosity of youth.[71]

On Hinsley's death former students recalled the former Rector as 'a legend of a golden age'. Mgr John MacMillan, a student under Hinsley and Rector of the college during the Second World War wrote of 'the dear old Boss' with sincere affection. Hinsley, he reflected, was a 'lovable and inspiring character' whose friendship was 'warm and unfailing'. The Rector had inspired him as 'no other man'.[72]

Mindful of the enormous responsibility of producing priests, Hinsley's primary concern was that seminarians should leave his care 'moulded in solid virtue.'[73] Williams described 'the Hinsley spirit' in the *Venerabile* as disciplined, earnest and loyal to Rome – qualities that he successfully instilled into his students.[74] Addressing the Catholic Union of Great Britain in 1926 Hinsley emphasised the importance of thorough preparation for the priesthood 'to enable a weak man to become an Ambassador of Christ, His Minister and the dispenser of the mysteries of God'. And Rome, in his view, was the best place where a man could be trained for there he would receive

> formation of heart and mind and character which fit him to be an instrument of Christ, a vessel of election to impart the Gospel to God's people; and there is no place in the world where he has such and so many opportunities of filling heart and mind, soul and sense, with the spirit of the Church, "the mind of Christ".[75]

Rome was the living heart of the universal Church where students were inextricably linked with the communion of saints, the apostles and the martyrs. For him the *Venerabile* was the most ancient and historic monument of English life and English faith in Rome. He pleaded therefore that it should remain 'the crown and apex of our English system of clerical education' and appealed for the Union's financial support.

Hinsley's theology was strictly orthodox, as earlier demonstrated by his stance in the debate on Modernism, his support of Thomistic studies at Ushaw and his vigilance against doctrinal errors while at Wonersh. The *Venerabile* experienced a memorable period of competent leadership, growth and development. There is some evidence, however, to suggest that Hinsley himself was not entirely happy with progress made by his students and the reputation of the college. He was meticulous in his reports on students and was not disposed to favour those who did not match his expectations. If possible he would arrange for students unsuited to the physical or academic rigours of Rome to be transferred. In 1927, when he was about to leave the college for Africa, he wrote to Bishop Doubleday that 'Our position in Rome at the (Gregorian) University has been as low as that of any college – or lower; and I do want to secure men who will help me lift us up.'[76] His choice of men and the education and training they received under him was ultimately to allay his fears.

Mgr Williams noted that Hinsley's stewardship had more than a domestic influence 'since under him were formed spiritually, theologically and culturally the churchmen who were to mould English Catholic thought right into the 1970s'.[77] From among his students, eleven were raised to the episcopate. John Carmel Heenan and Bernard Griffin became Cardinal Archbishops of Westminster and Joseph Masterton, Francis Grimshaw and George Patrick Dwyer became Archbishops of Birmingham. Other bishops included Edward Ellis (Nottingham), Joseph Halshall (Auxiliary in Liverpool), Thomas Pearson (Lancaster), Cyril Restieaux (Plymouth), Joseph Rudderham (Clifton) and Gerard Tickle (Bishop of the Forces).[78] As Williams commented: '. . .it is doubtful if the extent of the influence of the English College on the hierarchy can be equalled in such a limited number of years'.[79] Their commitment to serve the English and Welsh Church was instilled in them by Hinsley. In 1922 he had introduced a new coat of arms for the college. Its motto was 'For the Faith of Peter and the Fatherland' and its features included references to the supremacy of Peter, the martyrs, St Thomas of Canterbury, St Edmund of East Anglia, the papal colours, the heavenly kingdom and the traditional hospitality of the college. On his episcopal consecration he took as his motto 'They return rejoicing' and in a reference to the seminary his coat of arms showed seed being scattered.[80]

In his regular contacts with senior members of the Roman Curia,

Hinsley came to the favourable notice of the Vatican. Meanwhile, Cardinal Gasquet, always anxious to consolidate the position of the English Catholic community in post-war Rome and foster the continued improvement of the *Venerabile*, proposed that Hinsley be raised to the episcopate as a mark of gratitude for his work and respect for the college. He recorded in his diary:

> April 30, 1926. Audience with Holy Father. Discussed many things. Strongly recommended Fr Philip (Langdon) to Holy Father for a post in the future. Also asked him to honour Mgr Hinsley, Rector of the English College, by making him a Bishop.[81]

Pope Pius XI acceded to Gasquet's request and Hinsley was consecrated as titular Bishop of Sebastopolis by his friend Cardinal Merry del Val in the college chapel on 30 November 1926, the 33rd anniversary of his ordination as a deacon.[82] He became the ninth Rector to be consecrated since the college's restoration. He received a pectoral cross from the Pope and gifts from the students, Merry del Val, Gasquet and Langdon.[83] Hinsley was now in the happy position of being able to ordain his own students but he feared that he might be sent back to England as a diocesan bishop. *The Tablet* reported that those who knew of Hinsley's achievements would not be surprised by his promotion. It signified great satisfaction on the part of the Holy Father and all ecclesiastical circles with whom the Rector came into contact and for the rector of a national college to be raised to the episcopate while still in post was an unusual but welcome mark of distinction. Hinsley thanked *The Tablet* and its readers for their congratulations and their earlier support in saving the *Venerabile*.[84]

Mgr Richard Smith recorded in the college magazine that Hinsley had been consecrated 'whilst he was still vibrant' and that his mitre had been a reward for 'what in another would be his life's work'. The last nine years in Rome, he claimed, were only a fraction of what Hinsley had done. 'Much', he continued, 'remains to be done and the Holy Father leaves him in the college to do it, with this new honour upon him as an unmistakable mark of official approval of the past and of official encouragement for the future. . . .'[85] Outside the college, however, inter-related political developments were taking place that would affect Hinsley's future and they did not involve the *Venerabile*.

In 1927 Hinsley was appointed Apostolic Visitor to the British colonies in Africa with the task of inspecting Catholic schools conducted by missionary institutes and judging how they could be integrated into the planned educational reforms of the British imperial government.[86] He was to remain as Rector of the college while in Africa between 1928 and 1929 but when he was sent back to Africa as Apostolic Delegate in 1930 he was compelled to resign the rectorship. The editor of *The Venerabile* wrote in fulsome praise of Hinsley. He was 'its greatest rector' since the college's restoration, a strong leader and a fine example to those in his care:

> Of that energy of spiritual life which made itself felt throughout the whole community, that infectious, unswerving loyalty to the Holy See, that stimulating example of unassuming, deep learning, that spirit of *pietas* which characterized the relations between rector and men, that veneration of, and loyalty to our great traditions – in a word, all the vital force he has infused into the Venerable English College, estimation is not possible here.[87]

At his farewell celebration Hinsley's moving address to his former students 'breathed the very essence of his Rectorship, to cultivate that spirit of Catholicity and *Romanità* which was the distinguishing mark of this college, and, he was convinced, the true remedy of the difficulties the Church has to encounter'.[88] One former student defined *Romanità* as:

> the enemy of a one-track mind; it canonises the social virtues; it has learnt to penetrate appearances knowing that the outside of the Minerva gives no clue to the profusion of decoration within; it has understood that there are more ways of doing things than one, simply because it has been brought up against methods different from the English; it has acquired a great respect for logic while learning that it is not incompatible with compromise. . . . In a word, *Romanità* is Catholicism with a small 'c'; it is a universality of outlook that will give the devil a monopoly of nothing save sin. It reverences erudition, it appreciates the place of art, it enjoys humour, it is intensely curious and largely tolerant.[89]

Heenan wrote that the Roman spirit was almost impossible to define. To him the essence of *Romanità* was personal loyalty to the Holy Father and a devotion to the Church that was neither national nor parochial. Students at the *Venerabile* were educated and trained at the very heart of the universal Church, close to the pope and the tombs of the apostles, in the shadow and tradition of the English and Welsh martyrs, and in a college that encouraged study, devotion, prayer and honest debate. These were vital elements of their formation that would influence and guide them in their priestly ministry. Hinsley, Heenan wrote, had both imbibed this spirit as a student and inculcated it in others as Rector: 'For many he was its incarnation'.[90]

Hinsley sang High Mass in the college on the Feast of the Epiphany 1930. On 2 February 1930 he left the *Venerabile* for the last time as Rector and 'after a mournful leave taking' departed once again for Africa.[91]

Chapter Five

CATHOLIC MISSIONS
AND COLONIAL POLICY

Anglo-Vatican Relations 1914-1927

In 1927 Hinsley was entrusted with a task of crucial importance for both the Church and the British government when he was appointed Apostolic Visitor charged with inspecting and reporting on Catholic educational provision in British colonial Africa. The imperial government's insistence on harmonizing educational provision in its African colonies compelled missionary institutes to comply with British policy and the Church required someone in the field who possessed experience of the British educational system and on whom it could rely to protect its interests. A man of Hinsley's patent loyalty to the Holy See and his support for the concept of a benevolent British empire was ideal for the post. His appointment also coincided with the Church's post-war missionary policy and through his efforts in Africa the Vatican was brought into closer contact with British imperial politicians and administrators.

Relations between Great Britain and the Holy See improved steadily after December 1914 when Sir Henry Howard established a British diplomatic mission in Rome and became Envoy Extraordinary and Minister Plenipotentiary to the Papal Court. This was the first overt official contact between Britain and the Holy See for 350 years and was a deliberate British attempt to offset strong Austro-German influence within the supposedly neutral Vatican. The Austro-Hungarian Empire was a faithful supporter of the Papacy whilst German Catholicism was vibrant; the papal curia could hardly be indifferent to their governments. In November 1914 Cardinal Gasquet had complained to Foreign Secretary Lord Grey that 'with all the Catholic interests in the Empire it seems absurd that there should be no official means of communication between the British Government and the Pope. The matter has been very evident in this great crisis. . . . '[1]

Howard, a member of a prominent English Catholic family and a veteran diplomat, quickly established an official British presence in Rome. His objectives were to obtain information for the Foreign Office and advance British interests. Cardinal Gasquet's residence at San Calisto became the informal base of the British Mission[2] and soon after his arrival in Rome in 1917 Hinsley was involved in diplomatic exchanges between the Holy See and Whitehall.[3] The private visit of King George V and Queen Mary to the Vatican in 1923 further strengthened the ties between Britain and the Holy See and in 1926 an agreement was reached for the opening of a permanent Legation. Sir Odo Russell, who had succeeded Count John de Salis, reported that Anglo-Vatican relations were, 'as in the preceding year, of marked cordiality.'[4]

In his report to the Foreign Office in 1926, Russell described the nature, organisation and extent of Catholic missionary activity, approximately 30% of which occurred in British colonial territory, and the recently-elected Pope Pius XI's view on Great Britain and the British Empire. According to Russell, Curial opinion of Great Britain had changed:

> His Holiness seldom fails to give expression to his affection and regard for Great Britain and his confidence in the good sense and stability of the British character. This esteem, I find, has communicated itself to a greater part of the Pope's entourage, and has produced a much keener appreciation than existed a few years ago of the importance of the British Empire as a whole as a factor in world peace and, indirectly, in the progress of many of the ideals for which the Roman Catholic Church stands.[5]

Finding the Right Man

It had been one of the 'chief tasks' of the Legation during the year to 'nourish this sentiment and ensure that it was translated into practical effect by the nomination of British subjects to important ecclesiastical positions in the British colonies and mandated territories'. But the Holy See was experiencing difficulties owing to the lack of sufficiently qualified British candidates in missionary institutes and Russell advised the British government that attempts to interfere directly by nominating candidates would be unwelcome to the Vatican. The Holy See had acknowledged the principle of limited British involvement in appointments and Russell was confident that it would not act in a manner likely to make the administration of British colonies more difficult. For the Vatican it was a question of finding the right men.

Russell highlighted the differences between Pius XI and some of his predecessors. The new pope's approach was one of drawing the Church away from political and national affiliation and concentrating its attention throughout the world on its role 'in the religious and missionary sphere'.[6] Russell felt compelled to alert the Foreign Office to such developments and remind it of the Catholic Church's 'tenacity of purpose and length of vision'. The Foreign Office, however, was more concerned with the 'factious defiance of government and disloyalty' among contemporary Catholic prelates and had been trying since November 1926 to obtain prior notification of senior ecclesiastical appointments in the Empire in an attempt to exert greater influence over the Holy See's nominations. Russell's view was that the current position of being informed in advance about the nomination of Apostolic Delegates with a right to discuss other appointments was sufficient in the circumstances and advised the Foreign Office accordingly.[7] Nevertheless, he was instructed to approach Cardinal Pietro Gasparri, the Papal Secretary of State, to suggest that not only should high ecclesiastical appointments in the British Empire be filled, so far as possible, with suitable British candidates, 'but that His Majesty's Government should be allowed some measure of supervision over candidates selected by the Pope. . . . [8]

When Russell met Gasparri and his officials, the Vatican diplomats 'showed a friendly disposition' but were 'opposed to any participation in the Pope's unfettered choice, a point of view maintained in all post-war concordats, and even seemed disinclined to agree to any prior notification of appointments'. They argued that Britain's 'reluctance to interfere with the work of the Church was well-known and appreciated' and that although submitting to Britain's request to participate in appointment procedures may appear innocuous to Britain it would encourage countries such as France and Italy that were not so modest in their demands of the Vatican.

Russell continued lobbying to attain the British government's primary objective – 'namely some measure of control over the Vatican's selections of Vicars Apostolic and Prefects Apostolic in backward regions in the Colonies and Mandated Territories.' Here there were no concordats or formal agreements to guide policy and direct action. In some ways this was advantageous for, as Russell pointed out, 'experience has shown that . . . relations with the Vatican are best regulated by verbal understandings and personal contact'. The strategy soon proved fruitful, for an informal agreement was eventually made regarding the appointment of British prelates to posts within the Empire. Whilst the Vatican did not, nor was it ever likely to, cede the initiative, it acknowledged the mutual benefits accruing from a closer Anglo-Vatican relationship. For its part, the British government felt that a point had been made and the Vatican would be more circumspect in future appointments. Russell wrote that:

> the agreement seemed likely to serve as a signpost to the Vatican that his Majesty's Government was not completely disinterested in its appointments, but expected these to be made in accordance with British interests and in recognition of the goodwill shown to Catholic missions in the British Empire generally.[9]

Gasparri accepted that the British government had a 'normal right to discuss' ecclesiastical appointments but Russell's continued requests for further British involvement 'evinced distinct petulance' from the Cardinal.[10]

The next annual report from the Legation illustrated the benefits of harmonious diplomatic relations between Britain and the Holy See. There was confirmation of the opening of the Legation, there was informal agreement on the notification of ecclesiastical appointments in the British Empire, and the Vatican 'whilst binding themselves to no agreement on the matter shows every desire to fill vacancies in the Dominions and Colonies with delegates of British nationality.' One consequence of this final arrangement was that 'Bishop Hinsley, Rector of the English College in Rome, was appointed Visitor Apostolic in Africa for the purpose of inspecting all the chief Catholic missions in British territory and reporting on their efficiency', particularly with regard to education.[11] The diplomat Alec Randall later claimed that Hinsley's appointment, made without canvassing by British diplomats, was particularly welcome to their government.[12]

The Sacred Congregation for the Propagation of the Faith, the Vatican department responsible for the Church in missionary lands, had an ulterior motive in establishing closer links with the British government. Propaganda's attempt to co-ordinate the activities of its dependent missions in relation to mutually advantageous policies of colonial powers was in pursuance of Pope Pius XI's policy of *politique du présence*. The Pope and Cardinal Willem van Rossum, the Redemptorist Cardinal Prefect of Propaganda, wished to install their own men on the missions to direct and control missions and missionaries in accordance with a centrally formulated policy. The appointment of Hinsley to the special post of Apostolic Visitor to the Catholic Missions in the British Colonies in Africa was therefore a significant move in this direction. His specific instructions were to urge the missionaries to concentrate on the schools, to ensure the provision of Catholic education for the Africans, and to offset the influences of government and other denominations.[13]

African Schools

Education in British colonial Africa had been largely provided by missionary institutes and was seen by the government as a means of fulfilling its moral obligation to civilize and develop indigenous races. In the post-war period, however, the concept and provision of African education was subjected to more radical analysis and secular influences, and became more closely related to concepts of eventual self-government and economic development. Leftist and liberal writers criticized educational practices in the colonies and 'suggested a growing commitment to the idea of a synthesis of European and African culture, the need for a clear distinction between Christianity and English social habits, and the need for a more equal partnership between Europeans and Africans.'[14] Missionaries would no longer be expected, or required, to produce African Christians with European social habits.

Progressive colonial officials saw the chief responsibility of government as 'assisting native races in their progress towards the attainment of conditions of modern civilization which are best suited to the country and the chief element in this progress is education.'[15] To implement this philosophical change, the political will was needed to provide a relevant, coherent, and adequately funded system of education. The British government took up the challenge of modernizing native education, and throughout the late 1920s and 1930s proceeded to invest in colonial education and its administration. In the process, it placed heavy philosophical and practical demands upon missionaries and required them to reconsider their purpose, a purpose it had originally supported. The 1920s and 1930s were decades of change and re-appraisal. Such changes were the result of two critical reports on African education.

In 1920 the Foreign Missions Conference of North America, which was linked to the World Conference of Missions made up of the Anglican, Methodist and Free Churches, approached the trustees of the American Phelps-Stokes Fund to finance a study of native education in Africa. The trustees of the fund agreed to the request and established a commission whose terms of reference were to investigate the educational needs of the people, to see if those needs were being met, and to formulate plans to bring about suggested changes. Four commissioners examined educational provision in East and West Africa and published their reports in 1922 and 1924.[16] The reports added considerable weight to the arguments of those who countenanced change in Africa and they advocated a modernized system of colonial education. They emphasised that the educational policies of both colonial governments and missionaries were inadequate, inefficient and unrealistic as far as the majority of Africans were concerned. Evangelization was the primary aim of missionaries; education was not always considered a priority. Where missionaries did provide education it was not properly administered. Although missionaries were praised for their zeal and devotion, the commissioners reported that many failed to appreciate the full significance of education in the development of African people. Not surprisingly, secular and missionary educators replicated the ideals and organisational patterns established in their home countries but in the African context this led to inappropriate and confusing ideas of education. To some Europeans in Africa, education was a means of imparting knowledge or vocational skills. To some it was concerned with mental development but only in a secular sense. To others it was about bible study and Christian practice together with basic instruction in the rudiments of reading, writing, and arithmetic.

These views were inadequate in the singular and confusing in their entirety, and the situation was compounded by the outmoded pedagogical methods of colonial educators. The commissioners reported that there was insufficient supervision of African educators and that the education provided was leading to indifference and apathy among those it was supposed to benefit. Essentially, it was the organisation and administration of colonial education that was at fault: 'Governments and missions have not applied the sound principles of administration which are increasingly recognised in other undertakings of importance'. There was a lack of supervision and inspection, and little co-ordination between governments, missions, and commercial interests. There was also a need to reconcile the superficial form of education for the majority of people with the more advanced education provided for those who were destined for political and other forms of leadership.[17]

The commissioners, however, did not detach the spiritual dimension from the provision of a more systematic, relevant and self-sustaining form of colonial education based ultimately on native leadership. In their first report they stated that: 'The Christian religion . . . cannot be limited to the Sunday services or the devotional exercises at the opening of school or even to the teaching of the Bible.' Rather, 'every school act and every act in life should have a religious significance.'[18] The second report stated that Christianity and missionaries had a critical role: the 'right type of education is very closely akin to the right type of Christian nurture, and there seems to be no part of the world where teachers and missionaries, living in the spirit of Christ and proclaiming His simple Gospel by word, life and deed, can render a larger service for the spread of the Kingdom of God than in Africa'.[19]

The Catholic Church in Africa

There were 111 Catholic mission territories in Africa on Hinsley's appointment in 1927 and of these 51 were under the British flag. Nineteen of these were subject to the Apostolic Delegate for South Africa. Mauritius and the Seychelles, also under British rule, were the only two sees ruled by Ordinaries. In British East Africa there were twenty major missionary territories and ten in British West Africa. Generally speaking, West Africa came under the French sphere of influence; the Congo was under Belgian control, whilst East Africa was predominantly British. These three states together with Italy, Portugal and Spain, controlled 95% of the continent; the remaining 5% was made up of Abyssinia, Liberia, and Egypt.[20]

Ecclesiastical structures and boundaries were extremely flexible as Propaganda responded to local developments and missionary expansion. At the highest level of ecclesiastical jurisdiction, missionary territories were sub-divided by Propaganda into vicariates and prefectures. There were eight in Tanganyika, two in Uganda, three in Kenya, one in Northern Rhodesia, two in Nyasaland, four in the Anglo-Egyptian Sudan, six in Nigeria, three in the Gold Coast, and one in Sierra Leone. Other, and smaller, ecclesiastical divisions were based on independent missions within vicariates or prefectures. In Northern Rhodesia, for example, there was a vicariate, a separate prefecture, and an independent mission. Propaganda was responsible for the appointment of vicars apostolic, prefects apostolic, and superiors. In all of British African possessions secular priests ran only two dioceses, both in South Africa.[21]

The superior of an independent mission possessed limited ecclesiastical jurisdiction over a defined area. If evangelization succeeded to a point where the growth of a mission called for an extension of jurisdiction, the area would be raised to a prefecture. The Prefect Apostolic had some of the powers and dignity of a bishop but was not consecrated. A vicariate was a much larger missionary area and had a Vicar Apostolic as its head with the jurisdiction, dignity, and the title of a consecrated bishop. Within prefectures and vicariates there may have been missions under the charge of different religious orders. Prefects Apostolic and Vicars Apostolic were appointed by the Pope and acted in his name with delegated apostolic powers to teach, minister, and rule. Thus the Pope reserved to himself the general care of missions in territories that had not yet been raised to dioceses. Superiors, Prefects Apostolic and Vicars Apostolic sent annual reports to Propaganda.[22] At the summit of ecclesiastical arrangements in Africa in 1927 were two Apostolic Delegates. Archbishop Bernardus Gijlswijk was Apostolic Delegate to South Africa, and Archbishop Andrew Cassulo was Apostolic Delegate to Egypt and Arabia.[23] There were huge areas of sub-Saharan Africa with no visible ecclesiastical head, and many vicars apostolic but not one with overall authority. When Hinsley went to Africa his episcopal status was no higher than that of the Vicars Apostolic but his unique authority lay in the letter of appointment given to him by the Pope. Hinsley's secretary read out this letter at the first meetings between Hinsley and the missionary leaders.

British Catholic missionary commitment in British colonial Africa was insignificant compared with that of other European countries. The British Mill Hill Missionaries (the majority of whom were Dutch) had two missions in Uganda, one in Kenya and one in Cameroon. The English Province of the Society of Jesus had missions in Northern and Southern Rhodesia. The remaining missions were in the care of fourteen European institutes. Some, such as the French Holy Ghost Fathers (the Spiritans) and the French Society of African Missions, had Irish seminaries and large Irish contingents within their ranks. But British Catholic missionaries were in a minority and this was reflected particularly in the ranks of the Vicars Apostolic and Prefects Apostolic. In 1927 there were four Irish Vicars Apostolic, one Scottish Vicar Apostolic, one Irish Prefect Apostolic, and one English Prefect Apostolic. Of these, only two represented British institutes – the Jesuits and the Mill Hill Missionaries.[24]

Notwithstanding national identities, differences in internal organisation, and variations in strategies, missionary institutes had to collaborate and acknowledge the authority of the sees, vicariates and prefectures established by Propaganda. Occasionally, institutes attempted to arrive informally at a division of labour and responsibility but more often it was imposed by Propaganda.[25] The granting of jurisdiction and special faculties to a representative of one institute was for Propaganda an exercise in balancing the practical needs of the Church against wider diplomatic interests, and illustrated the very reason for Pius XI's policy of de-nationalizing missionary activity. The delegation of authority to a particular priest usually reflected the numerical superiority of his institute but as van Rossum reminded missionary superiors in 1929, Propaganda would always ensure that the Roman position dominated rather than a national or an institutional one. The Prefect's authority had been greatly strengthened by the Code of Canon Law, promulgated in 1917 by Pope Benedict XV, which gave the Church a universal legal Code. Power was well and truly vested in Rome and in Vatican departments.[26]

The British government could not ignore missionary activity within the empire. Depending upon circumstances, the presence of a missionary Church could be a civilizing influence, a cohesive and stabilizing factor, or a focus for dissent and opposition. The British government generally recognised the value of Catholic missionary endeavour in the empire and in return the Church benefited from British protection. The Catholic Church became a major source of support and development not only in colonial Africa but also across the British Empire.[27] The Church was able to consolidate on the evangelizing and educational progress it had made in Africa during the late nineteenth and early twentieth centuries and begin to implement the missionary encyclicals of Pope Benedict XV, *Maximum Illud* (1919), and Pope Pius XI, *Rerum Ecclesiae gestarum* (1926).[28] These seminal documents called for increased but centrally co-ordinated missionary endeavour, the formation of an indigenous priesthood, the creation of new ecclesiastical structures, and an end to institutional rivalry. This process was not entirely without difficulties and tensions as state, Church and missionary institutes attempted to further or defend their interests.

African Catholics

The growth of the Catholic community in Africa was hampered by the outbreak of the Great War. After 1918, however, the pace of conversions and baptisms quickened and there was a dramatic rise in the Catholic population. Contemporary statistics, which include South Africa, are not entirely reliable but indicate general trends. Garnered from official and missionary sources at varying dates, they were collated, often repeated, and then presented as annual returns.[29]

In 1914 there were approximately 540,000 Catholics in British Africa. Of the islands, Mauritius had the greatest Catholic population with 122,424, whilst on the mainland, Uganda had the largest number of Catholics with 230,568. The overall figures for 1919 support the claim that progress was interrupted by hostilities, that missionaries had difficulty in maintaining their levels of commitment, and that consequently growth was slow. By 1919 the total had risen only by around 20,000.[30] In 1922, however, the year of Pius XI's election, the number of African Catholics had risen to 699,083 – an increase of over 139,000 since 1919. This total probably includes a combination of re-adjusted wartime figures and the post-war increase. Additionally, Catholics of the former German territories of Tanganyika (16,756 in 1922) and Togo (about 25,000 in 1922) must also be factored in to the total. Undoubtedly, there were substantial increases between 1914 and 1927, when the figures for the latter date included returns from all vicariates and prefectures. In the Gold Coast, for example, the total went from 11,827 in 1914 to 41,955 in 1927; Southern Rhodesia from 4,618 in 1914 to 18,285 in 1927; and in Nigeria from 15,839 in 1914 to 56,568 in 1927, indicating significant increases in the Catholic populations. Similarly, there had been a substantial increase in Catholics in the Republic of South Africa from approximately 90,000 in 1914 to 165,630 in 1927.[31]

By the time of Hinsley's arrival, the total number of Catholics in British African possessions had reached 988,732. The increase of nearly 299,000 since 1922 represented the fruits of an enormous impetus from the centre, financial support from non-missionary lands, and a huge effort on the part of missionaries.[32] The Catholic missions had made enormous progress in Africa during the latter part of the nineteenth and the first two decades of the twentieth century. The number of missionaries had increased, ecclesiastical organisation and structure had developed, the Catholic population had grown substantially, missionary involvement in education continued to expand, and there were signs of an emerging African priesthood.

Convergence of Interests

A number of factors and forces converged to make the 1920s a creative period in Catholic missionary outreach to the African continent.[33] Driven on by the philosophy of the papal encyclicals and especially by the determination of Pope Pius XI and the practical application of Cardinal van Rossum, missionary institutes not only consolidated their earlier efforts but also increased them. The deleterious impact of the Great War was overcome relatively quickly and, indeed, stimulated the expansion of non-German institutes. The centralizing tendencies of Propaganda, strengthened by the 1917 Code of Canon Law which gave greater power to Rome, paid dividends. Missionary personnel increased and financial investment through the Association for the Propagation of the Faith also grew. The Church continued to grow numerically, a fact regularly and triumphantly proclaimed by *Fides*, Propaganda's broadsheet, but it had a remarkable tendency to simplify the most complex situations and elaborate perceived success. Nevertheless, a resurgence of interest in the African missions, the advent of new, energetic male and female missionary institutes, and the continued growth of the Catholic population added a sense of urgency to the need to create more permanent ecclesiastical jurisdictions and an indigenous clergy. All these developments, however, affected and, in most cases impaired, relations with non-Catholic missionaries.

The Church continued to play an active role in the development of African education but the nature and quality of missionary schools and the extent of missionary co-operation with the British government and Protestant institutes were variable. Missionary responses to educational initiatives manifested an uneven Catholic position that was unacceptable to Propaganda. It had to demonstrate to its missionaries that co-operation and collaboration with the government, tempered with a Catholic bias, would ultimately lead to efficient schools, a better-educated population, an African Catholic middle class, indigenous priests, and a permanent local Church. Propaganda's motive in compelling missionary institutes to adapt to British colonial educational policy was that the Catholic Church could not afford to lose its dominant position in education, otherwise its future in Africa was in jeopardy. Cardinal van Rossum was aware that Great Britain's new education ordinances introduced across its colonies constituted a serious threat to Catholic schools and therefore to the influence of the Catholic Church. From Propaganda's perspective these newly-introduced education ordinances were of the greatest importance. Hinsley's appointment as Apostolic Visitor emphasised their significance and their potential consequences. He was sent to deliberate with colonial administrators and place the Church's position before them and impose a uniformity of approach among missionary institutes. He was also required to shore up the confidence of some prelates who were badly shaken at the prospect of interference from both Rome and London and facing the prospect of radical change.

Cardinals Gasquet and Merry del Val may have influenced Hinsley's preferment but his personal qualities and practical experience served to make him a strong candidate for a particularly complex and difficult African assignment. After a faltering start in Ushaw and Bradford, he had forged an impressive reputation for himself as the rector of a major seminary in Rome. His knowledge of English Catholic secondary and seminary education was substantial. Throughout his time in Rome he had become familiar with the personnel and workings of the papal curia. The development of positive diplomatic relations between Great Britain and the Holy See, and informal agreement on papal appointments, were also to Hinsley's advantage. His obvious loyalty to both Pope and King meant that his selection for Africa met with approval in the Vatican and aroused no objection in Whitehall.

Hinsley was entrusted with a task of crucial importance for both Church and state. He was sent to inspect and report on Catholic educational provision in British colonial Africa where missionary institutes of all denominations were compelled to comply with changing British policy. A man of religious orthodoxy who was loyal to the Holy See and who possessed experience of the British educational system was ideal for the post of Apostolic Visitor.

Chapter Six

APOSTOLIC VISITOR

1928-1930

Preparations

Although Hinsley was a very active man, he was accustomed to the relative comfort of the English College. Travelling was confined mainly to ecclesiastical departments within Rome and visits to Palazzola. Trips to England were infrequent. His visitation to Africa, however, involved a formidable amount of travelling and considerable discomfort for a man in his early sixties. In January 1928 he embarked on a two-year journey that took him over 35,000 miles from South Africa to Central and East Africa, the Belgian Congo, and West Africa. When he returned to Rome in November 1929 he had visited all the Catholic ecclesiastical divisions in British colonial Africa with the exception of the Anglo-Egyptian Sudan. He had witnessed a growing and vibrant section of the universal Church.

On December 17, 1927, *The Tablet* commented on the importance of Hinsley's visitation. Education was an essential part of the missionary effort 'but at the present time the question of the schools has an especial urgency in view of the anxiety evinced by the British government to bring native education up to the standard of maximum efficiency'.[1] By the time of this report Hinsley was well advanced into arrangements to leave Rome for England and then Africa. On 2 December he had received a note from Cardinal van Rossum stressing the importance of the mission schools and the need for the Holy See to 'have a man on the spot'. On the following day he received a copy of the British government's *African Education Ordinance* of 1927 from Archbishop Francesco Marchetti, the Secretary of Propaganda, and immediately set about familiarizing himself with its contents. On 7 December he had an audience with Pius XI and two days later he met with Randall of the British Legation, van Rossum and Marchetti to finalize agreement on his responsibilities and authority. Again, van Rossum 'spoke of the schools.' During his last days in Rome he also met with the Jesuit Fr Henri Dubois, an experienced writer on missionary affairs, an expert on the use of vernacular languages and an adviser to van Rossum. Another visitor was the Abbot Primate of the Benedictines who spoke of the Benedictine mission at Lindi in East Africa. By 18 December Hinsley had received his brief and faculties from the Vatican, and in the evening of the same day he dined with the staff and students at the *Venerabile*. The next day he left for London.[2]

His preparations continued in London. Of particular urgency and importance was the need to make contact with officials of the Foreign Office and Colonial Office. To facilitate this he received the assistance of the Catholic peers Lord Fitzalan-Howard and Lord Lovat. Fitzalan-Howard gave him a letter of introduction to see Sir H. W. Ormsby-Gore, Parliamentary Under-Secretary for the Colonies, and Sir William Tyrell at the Foreign Office.[3] Lovat took him to meet permanent officials at the Colonial Office.[4] On Christmas Eve, Hinsley met with Fr Engelbert Giersbach, a Benedictine monk of St Ottilien Abbey in Bavaria. Recently ordained, Fr Giersbach had been studying in London and was on his way to the mission at Lindi. Hinsley decided that Giersbach would be useful as his secretary and on the following day he wrote to the Archabbot of St Ottilien to ask permission to take Fr Giersbach with him to Africa. His petition was successful.[5]

Hinsley spent the next month reading about Africa at the Colonial Office library and, in line with requirements for all colonial officials going to Africa, attended a Swahili language course at the London School of Oriental Studies.[6] He was also anxious to meet with missionaries either on leave or studying in England. Among these was Fr Caysac Joseph of the Spiritans' seminary at Castlehead in Lancashire, with whom he discussed the institute's recent ordinations and general missionary issues. Castlehead had been established in 1916 by the Spiritans in an attempt to enlist English seminarians into a predominantly Franco-Irish institute. The Jesuit Fr William Bodkin, Rector of Heythrop College, also called to see Hinsley and reported on his recent visitation to the Society's mission in Southern Rhodesia. On 26 January he received a visit from the German Benedictine missionary Bishop Thomas Spreiter, former Vicar Apostolic of Dar-es-Salaam and since 1923 Vicar Apostolic of Eshowe in Zululand. Their discussion concentrated very much on the relationship between missionary education and the development of an indigenous priesthood.[7]

On 3 February 1928 Hinsley and Fr Giersbach set sail from Southampton for Cape Town on the *SS Walmer Castle*.[8]

Hinsley's South African Itinerary

On 20 February, Hinsley arrived in Cape Town and was welcomed by Bishop Bernard O'Riley, Vicar Apostolic of the Cape of Good Hope (Western District). The South African authorities ensured a smooth passage through customs and the Governor General placed a car at Hinsley's disposal. During the next few days the Imperial Secretary (the Catholic Sir Bede Clifford), the Governor General, and the prelates, clergy and laity of the Cape Province formally received and entertained him.[9] It was a pattern to be repeated wherever he went during the next two years.

Hinsley's first speech gave a strong indication of his views and the urgency that he attached to his visit. In his usual, uncompromising way, and displaying the prejudices of the time, he said that 'Never before in the history of the world has such formidable danger arisen as exists in Africa today – a welter of savage native tribes clashing with civilization. Unless within twenty-five years the native population is converted to Christianity there will be disaster on a grand scale. . . .'[10] The 'disaster' for Hinsley, of course, would be the Church's inability to evangelize successfully in Africa and see Africans succumb to a mixture of western materialism and, potentially even worse, conversion to Islam.

Hinsley immediately set about familiarizing himself with the realities of the African mission. In late February and throughout March he made unofficial visits to Catholic schools, convents and missions in Cape Province, the Orange Free State and the Transvaal. He also had discussions and attended conferences on education and general missionary issues with the Vicars Apostolic, mission superiors, and the Apostolic Delegate, Archbishop Gijlswijk.[11] His impressions of Catholic missionary progress and education in South Africa were publicly articulated although, strictly speaking, they were not part of his brief. He was, *Fides* reported, impressed with the material progress of South Africa but noted with concern the unsettling social effects of encroaching materialism on Africans. He praised the work of the missions, Catholic organisations, and in particular the apostolate among the miners of the Rand, but, at a Catholic education conference at Johannesburg on 17 April, he castigated the governments of the Transvaal and Cape Province for their lack of state aid to Catholic schools. He was eager to point out the beneficial effects of state aid 'and elucidated very thoroughly the system of grants employed in England.'[12]

On 8 March Hinsley left South Africa for Basutoland where he was met at Roma by the veteran missionary Bishop Jules Cenez, a French Oblate of Mary Immaculate (OMI), who had been Vicar Apostolic since 1909. The nineteenth century origins of the Oblate mission had been fraught with difficulties but during the twentieth century there had been spectacular progress. In 1900 the Oblates had 30 schools; in 1927 they had 120 and one seminary at Roma, and it was this facet of their ministry that particularly interested Hinsley. As he was to do throughout all his visitations, he concentrated on obtaining a comprehensive picture of the work being done by missionaries, 'for the better education of the natives', on moral training, the use of the vernacular, vocational training, teacher training, and on their general contribution to African life. He also expressed two important but rather contradictory principles. First, having stated that Africa was composed of a 'welter of savage tribes', he now exhorted Basutos, 'who were respectful to all authority', to continue to show obedience to their chiefs, thus indicating a relatively sophisticated political system with which he was only superficially familiar. Secondly, he stated that higher education, for those carefully selected, should take place, where possible, within the boundaries of the African's own country. Did this imply, therefore, that Africans were to be denied the benefits of a superior western education? Did this principle apply, for example, to those seminarians who were to be educated in Rome or in other European cities? Such statements, issued with Hinsley's usual forthrightness, illustrate his unfamiliarity with the African cultural situation and the international missionary Church. Emphasizing the value of traditional authority, for example, may have been acceptable to an African audience but the authoritative nature of the Catholic Church, like the introduction of European political and administrative structures, was bound to conflict with tribal customs as experienced missionaries and colonial administrators would amply testify. And, although educating African élites within the local context would obviate the need for them to be taken out of their cultural milieu, it would impose upon missionary institutes the huge burden of providing higher and seminary education. Additionally, Hinsley's apparent intention of preventing

Africans from being educated in the European seminaries of missionary institutes would also discourage those European missionaries already suspicious of British political domination.[13] From the outset, Hinsley's almost uncritical acceptance of the benefits of British imperialism and his unwavering Catholic faith and service to the Church led him to make straightforward pronouncements on complex issues.

From Basutoland Hinsley travelled to Durban where he stayed with Bishop Henry De Lalle OMI and again toured schools and missions. From there he visited the 'young vicariate' of Eshowe and it was there that he wrote up his report on Basutoland for Propaganda. He also inspected the missions of the Trappist Mariannhill Fathers in Natal[14] before visiting Swaziland and then returning to Johannesburg. From there he undertook an extensive but unofficial survey of missionary provision in Johannesburg, Mafeking and Pretoria before setting out for a two-day inspection of missions in Bechuanaland on 24 April.[15]

Hinsley's Itinerary in East, Central and West Africa

Hinsley travelled over 1,200 miles in the two Rhodesias under the guidance of Mgr Robert Brown, the Jesuit Prefect Apostolic of Zambesi. Jesuits of the English Province had been the original missioners in Rhodesia but now Polish Jesuits, Mariannhill Fathers, White Fathers, and Irish Capuchins supported them.[16] Throughout June Hinsley was in the Vicariate of Shiré with Bishop Aneau and the Vicariate of Nyasaland with Bishop Guillémé where he observed the medical ministry of Benedictine sisters[17] and for the first time encountered Protestant opposition. The veteran Anglican missionary Archdeacon Charles Johnston, who had been in Africa for over 50 years, complained vehemently to Hinsley at Lituli mission about the zealous and energetic Catholic missionaries who, he claimed, had invaded Protestant 'spheres of influence'.[18] The Protestants were very active along the coast and Hinsley recorded in his diary that 'our Fathers' were 'very excited about the opposition' but anxious about government intervention to delineate missionary territory.[19] He did not record his own course of action.

In Tanganyika Hinsley was able to see the damage inflicted on German missionary settlements during the Great War and the efforts taken to restore provision. During July and August he undertook visits to the many missions and convened a bishops' conference to discuss educational issues.[20] From Tanganyika he sailed, in late September, for a short but intensive visit to the Muslim-dominated island of Zanzibar. On the island there were nearly 16,000 Catholics served by 21 priests supported by lay brothers, nuns, and catechists.[21] He then returned to Tanganyika and the Kilima-Njaro mission for eighteen days before progressing, on 3 November, to Nairobi in Kenya. Within two days he had convened a conference of the local ordinaries to consider the latest developments in African education.[22] By the end of December 1928, Hinsley had travelled over 15,000 miles by rail, car, boat, and on safari. He was, by his own admission, very tired. At the end of the month he completed his reports on his visitation for van Rossum.[23]

In January 1929 Hinsley moved to the Mill Hill Fathers' Kenyan missions in Kavirondo Prefecture where Mgr Gorgorius Brandsma received him. Later in the month he visited the White Fathers' missions in the Uganda Vicariate and at Rubaga celebrated with them the golden jubilee of their arrival in the protectorate. With the very experienced missionary, Bishop Henry Streicher,[24] he toured the impressive mission station at Villa Maria, the headquarters of the White Fathers, with its convent, training college, hospitals, schools, shops and printing presses. It was one of a network of stations established by the French missionaries in the British protectorate.[25]

Hinsley's next visitation was to Bishop John Campling and the Mill Hill Fathers at Nsambya, near Kampala, to where they had been sent by Propaganda in 1895 'to prove that the Catholic Church was not exclusively French.'[26] There, Hinsley inspected missions, schools and hospitals and before leaving Uganda and East Africa he visited Makarere College, a secular university with a growing reputation for advanced education in medicine and agriculture.[27] The final destination in the first part of Hinsley's journey was to have been the Anglo-Egyptian Sudan where the Italian Verona Fathers ministered to a small Catholic population but this did not take place. The Sudan was acknowledged to be difficult missionary territory because of Muslim fanaticism and divisive disputes between Christian missionaries and Hinsley had insufficient time to devote to it.[28]

In June 1929, after travelling over 20,000 miles since landing at Cape Town, Hinsley undertook another 3,000-mile journey across the Belgian Congo towards the missions of West Africa. On his way, he again paid unofficial visits: to the White Fathers at Albertville and Kabalo; to the Spiritans at Kongolo, and Kindu; to the Sacred Heart Fathers at

Ponthierville and Stanleyville; to the Scheut Fathers at Leopoldville; to the Redemptorists at Matadi; and to the Jesuits at Kisantu. As he had done in South Africa, he was prepared to comment publicly on aspects of missionary endeavour strictly outside his remit. The Belgian Congo had a population of 15 million and of these Catholics accounted for approximately 600,000. Nevertheless, Hinsley felt that excellent progress was being made and his observations 'on conditions both spiritual and material were enthusiastic'. In particular, he praised the wide range of missionary activity – in evangelization, industry, transportation, education, medicine and hygiene. He was especially interested in the scholastic organisation within schools, and the surgical and medical teaching foundation established in the Congo by the University of Louvain.[29]

He began his visitation of West Africa in British Cameroon where he met Mgr Peter Rogan of the Mill Hill Fathers and Prefect Apostolic of Buea.[30] The total Catholic population in West Africa was 332,989. There were three ecclesiastical divisions in the Gold Coast, five in Nigeria, and one in Gambia-Sierra Leone. 133 priests and 65 nuns ministered across the region and in addition to their other missionary duties taught, presumably with native help, 60,000 children in 1,180 schools.[31]

Following yet another conference with bishops and mission superiors in Lagos,[32] Hinsley left Nigeria on 1 October for Accra in the Gold Coast and conducted visitations of the three ecclesiastical territories there. His final brief visitations were to the Gambia and Sierra Leone, under the care of Bishop John O'Gorman and the Spiritans.[33]

Missionary Expectations of Hinsley's Visitation

In May 1928 *Fides,* Propaganda's missionary news service, proclaimed that Hinsley was undertaking a momentous journey of investigation in the name of the Holy See.[34] Not unnaturally, the experienced Vicars Apostolic, Prefects Apostolic, and mission superiors regarded the official visitation with a mixture of approval, expectation and apprehension. Anyone familiar with *Rerum Ecclesiae* and Propaganda's agenda would be aware that Hinsley would not simply report on schools but also convey his impressions of overall missionary effectiveness. No-one doubted the importance of the Visitor's mission.

In January 1928, Mgr Brandsma of the Kavirondo Prefecture, Kenya, wrote to Dr Schut, the Mill Hill Missionaries' agent in Rome, that 'It is interesting to read that Dr Hinsley . . . is coming out to see our school work. We shall receive His Lordship well'. Hinsley's visit, he wrote, 'should prove a great help and we shall make use of it'.[35] By May Brandsma was particularly anxious for Hinsley to arrive, for he was aware that at the end of the month there was to be an education conference and 'the Government wished Bishop Hinsley to be present'. Hinsley's impending visit, he wrote, had resulted in Protestant authorities 'taking note of us'.[36] From his own point of view he had another motive for Hinsley's early arrival. He felt that the Apostolic Visitor might be able to extricate him from the financial difficulties he faced in his new prefecture, difficulties compounded by additional expenditure on schools and the parlous state of the American economy. 'I do hope', he wrote, 'that Mgr Hinsley will be able to assist considerably, otherwise it means ruin financially. Heavy expenses on education and buildings and America closing down. We cannot keep our head above water in this way and before long resignation will be the only thing left'.[37]

Mgr Brandsma's Mill Hill confrère, Mgr Peter Rogan in Cameroon, had recently returned from an educational fact-finding tour of Europe, and was 'anxiously waiting for Bishop Hinsley'. Rogan found the new educational ordinances 'almost impossible to understand',[38] and felt very isolated. He was desperate to visit the Spiritan Bishop Shanahan in Nigeria in order to negotiate for his seminarians to be transferred to Nigeria and to obtain advice and ideas on education.[39]

The *Missionary Annals* of the Spiritans reported in April that Hinsley's appointment was important in the context of the British government's attempt to re-organise the African school system. It concluded that Hinsley would have to 'watch out' for the interests of the Catholic missions in the new system 'for the reins are now in the hands of the government.' Hinsley's appointment was welcomed because it was considered that hitherto the Protestant missionary societies 'had been able to keep more in contact with the government in the development of details than have Catholics.'[40]

Like the Mill Hill Missionaries, the Jesuits in Southern Rhodesia viewed both the proposed system of African education and Hinsley's arrival in a positive light. The editor of *The Zambesi Mission Record* was of the opinion that the imperial and colonial governments were now acting upon the principle of co-operation rather than control. It was also 'a sign of hope and good augury for the future of the missions' that Hinsley had been delegated to help the missions co-operate with the governments in the various British colonies.[41] Mgr Robert Brown later confirmed this positive reaction to Hinsley's appointment when he wrote that during such a period of crisis for African education, the Pope 'chose for the important task of guiding the movement as far as possible into paths which would lead to true enlightenment, one who had already shown unmistakable talent for leadership and who was otherwise well equipped for the task.'[42]

Hinsley's visitation, however, was not welcomed by all missionaries. An imposition by Propaganda could not be avoided but this one was obviously linked to a far-reaching British policy with serious implications. Fr Thomas Gavan Duffy who was visiting Catholic communities in Africa at the time, provided a slightly cynical but nonetheless objective forecast of Hinsley's mission, the success of which depended not solely upon the Visitor:

> Let us hope that Bishop Hinsley, who, at least, talks the language of the Administration, and who presumably carries in his head, or in his bag, the many splendid statements published in the course of the long struggle for the Catholic schools in England, will have the good fortune to secure on the part of the colonial authorities a reasonable attention to our reasonable Catholic claims. Rome dearly loves a problem that can be solved by settlement with powerful people; and the British national sport is compromise; so the principals at headquarters should have a thoroughly good time during the years that it will take to come to an agreement. But meanwhile, unless the men on the spot keep up the local agitation, they will find themselves sans grant, sans schoolmasters, sans schools, sans everything.[43]

Chapter Seven

IMPOSING VATICAN POLICY

Imposing Uniformity

Hinsley's major task was to harmonize Vatican and British educational policies in colonial Africa. To fulfil this he had to inspect and evaluate the nature and quality of missionary education, assess the impact of the government's educational initiatives on Catholic provision, state Vatican policy very clearly, and formulate common strategies that were in Vatican and British interests.

It was very clear that there was no monolithic Catholic approach to missionary education in Africa and attitudes and methods varied tremendously. Some institutes were pioneering and energetic; others were hesitant and cautious. The fulfilment of missionary charisms was greatly influenced by leadership, geography, and local circumstances. The huge distances separating missions and the diversity of cultures combined with differing missionary ideologies to produce a mixture of approaches, further complicated by the fact that very few of the prelates and missionaries with whom Hinsley dealt were British. Many, if not all, were averse to British ideas and policy.[1] The Apostolic Visitor, therefore, had to convince missionaries of the benefits of reformed colonial education, impose Vatican policy as far as African education was concerned, and persuade colonial administrators of the value of mission schools. This was achieved through a series of conferences attended by Vicars Apostolic, Prefects Apostolic and mission superiors, and at meetings with local officials. Hinsley listened and advised but left no one in any doubts about his views of the British Empire, British intentions, and, as far as the missionaries were concerned, the will of the Vatican.

Discussions with the Ordinaries, superiors and civil authorities largely determined his judgements and actions. They were the leaders and decision makers and had to be convinced of the mutual benefits of Church-State co-operation. The Vatican had signalled its will to modernize mission schools and through its 1927 Ordinance the British government had specified the intended nature of African education and defined its future development. The interpretation and implementation of these twin policies by missionaries and administrators, however, was not uniform and Hinsley was confronted with a range of peculiar historic and current circumstances which determined relationships between missionaries and colonial civil servants.

Hinsley in East Africa

In June 1928 Hinsley visited the Vicariate of Nyasaland, where he made it very clear that Rome wanted to make a contribution to the education of the people of Nyasaland and assured the Governor of the co-operation of the Catholic Church. On 5 July he wrote to Bishop Mathurin Guillémé, the White Father Vicar Apostolic, outlining the fundamental policy to be adopted and measures by which it might be achieved. There was no doubt about the source of authority, and no room for interpretation:

> Schools are a means to reach the masses, and it is my mission to insist that missionaries concentrate their efforts on schools. Schools are more important than churches. The school is the vestibule into the church. The sacraments are given in the church, but it is in the school that you prepare the subjects of the sacraments. Therefore at the Sacred Congregation of the Propagation of the Faith I have been told to state clearly that where a choice is to be made between building a church and building a school, it is the school that is to be chosen.

Hinsley gave reasons to support the statement. The school was important because the people themselves wanted education. The Church could not afford to be accused of keeping Africans in a state of ignorance. Catholic schools were also able to counteract the influence of other denominations and paganism. The government offered precious financial help. And finally, in order to develop an African clergy, good schools from which suitable candidates come forward had to be provided. Hinsley then suggested to Guillémé and the other missionary prelates how the position might be improved. Each mission should have good buildings and must be well-equipped; Africans must be trained as teachers and experienced ones should be re-trained; there should be a teachers' training centre; missions should obtain a printing press and publish their own text books; and education secretaries should be appointed to supervise the system. Experienced missionaries were probably unimpressed by such practical but fairly obvious suggestions; after all, they had been striving to achieve most of these since their arrival in Africa. Guillémé had been on the

African mission since 1884.[2]

From 6-9 August 1928 Hinsley convened a four-day conference at Dar-es-Salaam, in Tanganyika, to discuss the latest developments in colonial education and the serious difficulties thrown up by the new education ordinance of the colony. He had already met with Rivers-Smith, the Director of Education. Present at the conference were Vicars Apostolic Bishops Henry Gogarty of Kilima-Njaro, Gabriel Zegler of Dar-es-Salaam, Joseph Sweens of Nyanza, and Bartholomew Wilson of Bagamoyo. Monsignori Cagliero, Prefect Apostolic of Iringa and Edward Michaud, Apostolic Administrator of Tabora were also present, as was Bishop Gallus Bernhard Steiger OSB, Abbot Nullius and Superior of Lindi. Their combined jurisdiction covered 373,000 square miles and contained over 105,000 Catholics and they represented five missionary institutes.[3] Even before Hinsley's arrival, the missions and the authorities had collaborated in the development of a school system based on recognition, supervision and grants. The Governor had met with representatives of all the missions in September 1925 to consider the way forward and since that meeting there had been steady, if cautious, co-operation. Illustrating a fundamental concern over the new funding arrangements, there were some institutes and mission superiors who did not wish to be tied to the government by a 'golden chain' of grants and subsidies,[4] but Hinsley wished to consolidate this arrangement and his most important objective was to engage the Ordinaries and superiors in dialogue about education and then issue an unambiguous declaration of position and intent. The outcome was to his satisfaction: the missionary prelates of Tanganyika Territory formally accepted the principle of co-operation with the government but refused to sacrifice any of their rights as Missionaries or the religious character of their school system.[5]

Keldany noted that 'here as elsewhere a policy of co-operation with the education authorities was duly reached.'[6] According to *Fides*, the meeting 'bore fruit' for on his return to Nyanza, Bishop Sweens immediately appointed Fr Rivard as Secretary of Education for Catholic Schools, to organise mission schools 'according to the regulations of the government.' Fr Rivard had already attended a conference called by the civil authorities at Bukoba where, in line with government directives, a central school was to be opened for the Catholics of the district.[7] Not all institutes needed Hinsley's encouragement, however. The Spiritan Fr Michael Witte had started a catechist training school at Kabaa in 1925 and

Mgr Wilson had opened a teacher training school at Morogoro in 1926 staffed by well-qualified Irish Spiritans. There were sound educational developments taking place before Hinsley's visitation.[8] Similarly, Hinsley was able to witness the advances made in the provision of an indigenous priesthood when, on the feast of the Assumption at Tabora, he ordained three African priests who had been trained by the White Fathers.[9] On the following day, as if to emphasise the point and in accordance with the recent encyclical, a discussion with Bishops La Rue and Guillémé took place on the advantages of regional and inter-vicariate seminaries.[10]

In November Hinsley visited the seminaries and all the major educational institutions in Kenya and chaired a Catholic Educational Conference at Nairobi. It was in this colony that the mission schools were perhaps under the greatest threat. Kenya was made up of four ecclesiastical divisions – the Vicariate of Nyeri and the Prefecture of Meru in the care of the Consolata Fathers, the Prefecture of Kavirondo in the care of the Mill Hill Missionaries, and a part of the Vicariate of Zanzibar served by the Spiritans and the White Fathers. There were nearly 43,000 Catholics in the colony. As he had done in South Africa, Hinsley spoke forcefully and publicly about Catholic education. It was, he claimed, unfortunate that the previous Ordinance of 1924 disregarded the work done by the missions but more damaging now was the fact that the Catholic missions had no direct representation on Kenya's educational advisory committees. And, really forcing home the point that Catholic education was undervalued and under-resourced, the bishop concluded: 'It seems very strange to me that up to last year our schools received no grants-in-aid'. This issue and those of future co-operation with local governments and the education of women and girls were among many discussed by the bishops and superiors. They also considered the methods of the less than co-operative Director of Education, H. S. Scott, whose objective was to rid Kenya completely of all mission schools or at least leave them as second best to those run by the government.[11]

In January 1929 Hinsley visited the Uganda Protectorate where he saw evidence of more harmonious Church-government relations. When Hinsley met the Ordinaries on 22 and 23 January, he was told that education in the Protectorate was working smoothly. There had been internal inquiries into African education in 1902, 1914, and 1919 and the report of the third inquiry proposed that government should take a more active role in education. In 1923 the Governor of Uganda,

Sir Geoffrey Archer, invited Eric Hussey, Director of Education in the Sudan, to investigate and report on schools in the protectorate. Hussey found the mission schools to be inefficient and ineffective and Archer proposed a network of government schools in which the teaching of religion would not be excluded. In response, Bishops Streicher and Biermans submitted a memorandum suggesting the appointment of a director of education for the colony, common secular syllabuses, trained African teachers, regular school inspection and government grants but they would not surrender control of their schools.

The British government appointed a consultative commission to study the situation in Uganda. Its report coincided with the Phelps-Stokes Report on East Africa and both arrived at the same conclusion: the need for efficient education in Uganda was so great that there could be no development without government intervention and assistance. It also agreed that there should not be a government monopoly of schools and that no progress could be made without the full co-operation of the missionary institutes. An Advisory Council was formed that included representatives from all the major denominations and Hussey was appointed Director of Education. In spite of his earlier criticisms of mission schools, the missionaries found Hussey to be 'conciliatory'.[12]

Bishop John Forbes, coadjutor Bishop of Nyanza had been responsible for Catholic mission schools in the Ugandan Vicariates until 1925, when Bishops Streicher and Beirmans replaced him with Fr Edward Michaud of the White Fathers and Fr James Minderop of the Mill Hill Missionaries. They supervised and inspected schools, acted as education secretaries, and liaised with the government of the protectorate. Later a Secretary-General was appointed for all Catholic education. Following Bishop John Campling's arrival in 1925, there was a determined effort to co-operate with government educational policy which involved Catholics, Anglicans and Muslims. This had a positive side-effect for, as Fr Tourigny commented, 'the work of the Educational Secretaries of the various religious bodies proved a happy basis for improving Catholic-Protestant relations in the following years.'[13]

Streicher and Campling had to be vigilant, however, for there were occasions when misunderstandings and disagreements arose. Then the bishops closed ranks. The sharing of grants in the two vicariates in Buganda, for example, caused difficulties as Hussey gave the two groups of Catholic schools the same amount as he had done for one group of Protestant schools. Campling complained whereupon Hussey simply asked Streicher to forward his share to Campling. Streicher wrote that this was the second time that Hussey had appeared to drive a wedge between the bishops. He added: 'my fraternal relations with Bishop Campling are more precious to me than any government grant.'[14]

Campling was under no illusions about Hinsley's visit. He was especially concerned to present a united front to Hinsley and avoid any expression of anti-government bias. He was very much aware of Hinsley's agenda and that of Propaganda and in October 1928, in a letter to the Bukedi mission superiors, who had asked for a separate meeting with Hinsley, he wrote:

> I would be absolutely averse to any meeting for the purpose of discussing educational matters with Bishop Hinsley which is not fully representative of the whole Vicariate. We are all at one, with the same educational policy and syllabus. The Apostolic Visitor has not come out for the purpose of discussing educational affairs, nor have we been requested to draw up any programme for him: he has laid down his own and he informs me that he will hold a conference with the Ordinaries either in Rubaga or Nsambya. He takes it for granted that the Ordinaries know and can explain their whole educational system and policy. He will visit each mission station, inspect your schools and carry away his report. If you have any important matter to put before him, you will have the opportunity to do so, but I expect to accompany him. I would add a word of warning and advise you not to display any anti-government sentiment which will assuredly damage the name of our Society in Rome.[15]

Hinsley moved back to Tanganyika and the recently erected Vicariate of Bukoba where 29,000 Catholics were under the care of the White Fathers. Once again he inspected schools, visited missions and met with local prelates and superiors. From there he made a return visit to Kenya where at Mumias in April, in the presence of government officials and Ugandan and Kenyan Church leaders, he described the educational scene as he observed it and delivered yet another forthright statement of policy. First of all, he commented on British officialdom's fairness, a remark which diverged slightly from that made at Nairobi in October. Secondly, he praised missionary pioneers and their success 'in the uplift of the native.' Finally, he concluded with an unambiguous statement of the policy that he had brought with him and one that had been confirmed during his visitation:

We welcome the co-operation of the Government for we have now reached the stage when we cannot do without Government, but on the other hand Government cannot do without us, and the Government knows it. We want to join with all those who have the same great cause at heart that we have and with those who will not interfere with our essential principles. We believe that the Colonial Office has put its seal of approval on our principles. We are prepared to co-operate with all in anything in which we can conscientiously co-operate and we are convinced that there never will be an attempt on the part of the British Government to interfere with our essential principles and religion. The principle of our English system is to give us perfect liberty in all that regards our religion but to insist on efficiency on the material side.[16]

On Hinsley's return to Kenya Colony in March, the earlier concerns about Scott's negative view of denominational schools were confirmed and Hinsley discussed the implications with Mgr Brandsma and Fr Doyle. The Protestants were already succumbing to Scott's policy and were 'surrendering as expected'. The Anglican Archdeacon Owen stated that some Protestant missionaries, especially the Scotch Mission, were ready to lose their schools rather than give any advantage to the Catholics and that 'anti-Romanism seemed to be the only uniting dogma of the various Protestant denominations'. Such a situation was to Scott's advantage, but in April Brandsma submitted a memo to the Director on behalf of the Ordinaries protesting against the grading of schools, the inequality of the grants-in-aid system, and the constraints placed on the teaching of religion to those in government boarding schools. Scott backed down; the denominational character of grade A and B schools was retained and Roman Catholic grade C schools were to receive a greater share of the grant-in-aid. In his diary Hinsley wrote: 'This we gained by sticking to our principles'.[17]

After fifteen months, in which he had travelled 20,000 miles, Hinsley issued a prepared statement that described the Church's position in East Africa and contained five major observations. First, he was aware that material progress was detaching Africans from their traditional culture and drawing them into a detribalized situation where they needed and demanded education to prepare them for contact with Europeans. Secondly, the government had awakened to the necessity of education. Missionaries were to play a part in directing this 'crushing tide of progress', a development that had both beneficial and deleterious effects, but must be prepared to deliver practical as well as intellectual and religious education. Thirdly, Hinsley referred to the education of African womanhood. Only the Catholic Church, he stated, could 'wield the heroic might of our vowed and consecrated sisterhood' and evidenced this by the work of Catholic nuns in the apostolic work of the Church in Africa. Fourthly, he called upon the Vicars and Prefects Apostolic to realise that new methods were required in the new conditions. It was not enough simply 'to occupy the field'; poorly educated teachers in ill-equipped schools were not good enough 'to give the people the deep intelligent faith needed as civilization advances with giant steps'. Schools and teachers had to be brought to a standard of excellence that satisfied both native aspirations and government regulations. Finally, he called for centralized teacher training institutes which would enable missionaries to adhere to the principle of 'Catholic schools with Catholic teachers and a Catholic atmosphere for Catholic children'.[18]

Hinsley in West Africa

Hinsley then moved on to West Africa where, following the Nigerian Education Code of 1926, which unlike others failed to mention the concept of co-operation, hundreds of inefficient bush schools were closed down. On 31 August 1929, Hinsley and the Ordinaries of Nigeria and British Cameroon met to discuss the repercussions of this development and to devise a strategy that would avert a further crisis. Present were Bishop Thomas Broderick, Vicar Apostolic of Western Nigeria; Bishop Joseph Shanahan and his coadjutor, Bishop Charles Heerey of Southern Nigeria; Mgr Rogan; Fr L. Freyburger, Pro-Vicar of the Bight of Benin; and Fr A. Schal, Pro-Prefect of Eastern Nigeria. The Visitor presided over a frank and sometimes fearful discussion as the prelates and superiors expressed their deep concerns about government restrictions and government encroachment into what had previously been their exclusive preserve. There were also internal dissensions. Prelates such as Broderick, adhering faithfully to de Brésillac's theory of adapting Christianity to local conditions, wished for education to be based on arts and crafts and all that the African required on a daily basis. Schools, he reported to Rome, were needed in order to attach the Africans 'more certainly to their country and to avoid turning them into déracinés'. It was not a theory that Rome, Hinsley or indeed many Africans subscribed to. Hinsley wrote in his diary that Broderick was 'anxious to keep the natives in natural simplicity and did not push education' nor did he wish to train African teachers. But Hinsley persuaded the doubters to follow his line; there could be no delaying the inevitable. Too many mission schools were inadequate and sub-standard and Hinsley recognised this. In his subsequent discussions with the colonial government he declared his optimism at Catholic progress on the coastal strip but it was, however, tempered by Muslim expansion in the interior which, to him, 'cast a dark shadow'.[19]

In a statement on behalf of the bishops, Hinsley said that the Catholic Church was prepared to co-operate with the various governments but that it would resist undue interference. The Ordinaries, of course, saw the value of government financial support but could not contemplate Catholic schools managed or dictated to by a non-Catholic organisation. From this position emerged a common Catholic education policy that recognised the value of government educational reforms, despite their initial unpopularity, pledged collaboration, and placed the school at the centre of Catholic action.[20] The final policy declaration of the Ordinaries had Hinsley's imprint all over it: a new situation faced the missionaries and they had to adapt in accordance with both colonial developments and papal pronouncements. In view of the rapidly changing conditions of Africa and in ready obedience to the Holy See, the prelates pledged that while the essential ministerial work of the missionary could never be neglected, the school was to be regarded as the heart of each missionary organisation in each Vicariate and Prefecture.[21] The consequences of such a clear statement of intent were enormous for the institutes. To provide the improved and more efficient schools demanded by government ordinances, missionary schools had to have better teachers, effective management and new syllabuses. In addition, further financial investment and an increase in personnel would be required by missionary institutes, and Irish missionaries especially took up the challenge in Nigeria.[22]

In the *Lagos Daily Times*, Hinsley summarized his views after meeting with the bishops and missionary leaders. He repeated his agreement in principle with the educational schemes proposed by the government and the Church's desire to co-operate. But he was uncertain about the willingness or ability of local authorities and officials to implement the schemes for the majority of the people and felt that imperial policy had not always animated colonial officials. He noted that it was only recently that local authorities had actually become involved in the delivery of education whereas the missionaries had been providing education for nearly fifty years. In a final statement he again reiterated Catholic policy:

> As far as Catholic missions were concerned, they were prepared to co-operate with he governments of the various British territories in Africa in the education and general improvement of the native African, although that was not to be taken to mean that they would agree with them in every scheme that might be put forward. For instance, there was a noticeable tendency of educating the African as part merely of machinery for the production of wealth for the benefit of others. The Catholic missions will support no such policy. Education, they believe, should aim at the uplifting of the whole of mankind, and the development of the individual man for the sake of his temporal as well as his eternal happiness.'[23]

From 5 to 7 October 1929 he convened and chaired an education conference at Accra in the Gold Coast and once again 'ascertained the views of the leading missions.'[24] Present were Bishop Augustus Hermann, Vicar Apostolic of Lower Volta; Bishop Ernest Hauger, Vicar Apostolic of the Gold Coast; and Mgr Morin, Prefect Apostolic of Navrongo in the Northern Territories. Bishops Hermann and Hauger were Dutch priests of the Society of African Missions; Mgr Morin was a White Father.[25] Bishop Hermann declared that the government reforms were 'a devastating blow to Christianity and civilization' and, like others, he was extremely fearful of the consequences.[26]

But there had already been positive developments. The Church in the Gold Coast had gone some way to organizing its combined educational efforts. Hinsley was relatively optimistic about the situation and was delighted that the government did not interfere with missionary educational enterprises as long as they met prescribed quality standards. This was in accord with the 1925 British Memorandum on African Education, a code which also specified that education must be based on character training 'and that without character training on Christian and moral lines there can be no true education.'[27] In an address at Cape Coast he praised the British government's approach and support:

> The British Government gives full liberty to Catholic schools. I can speak without prejudice because I have seen what is being done all over Africa. I am an Englishman but I am also a Catholic and a Roman, I am proud to say. Wherever I have seen the British Government at work I have met with the most ardent desire never to offend the religious feelings of any Christians.[28]

Hinsley's Advocacy of Mission Schools

Throughout his visitation Hinsley placed an uncompromising emphasis on one aspect of Propaganda's overall policy – the vital importance of schools in the development of Catholicism in Africa. In August 1928, at the Ordinaries' conference at Dar-es-Salaam, he strenuously urged the bishops to co-operate with government educational developments and develop schools as quickly as possible.[29] It was a message that shocked some Ordinaries and missionaries but one that was to be repeated at all the conferences.

Local education ordinances enacted in the various colonies during the mid-1920s compelled missionaries to provide more efficient schools. Most institutes accepted that the primary method of evangelization was through the schools, but there was an uneven provision across the vicariates, prefectures and missions. This was due as much to variations in missionary ideology and zeal as it was to official intervention and financial support. Missionaries recognised that to lose schools because they were sub-standard would render their essential task much more difficult. Efficient schools offered the prospect of financial support, the continuation of an apostolate, an embedding of Christianity within the community, and the maintenance of Catholic influence. The schools, therefore, were critical to Propaganda, Hinsley and to most missionaries, but not to all. For mission purists 'the only proper aim was evangelism and although educational and medical services earned secular praise, they diluted energy and funds for evangelization and made missions vulnerable to government control.'[30] Many missionaries argued that they were priests and not teachers.

In eastern Tanganyika the conservative and cautious French Spiritans adhered firmly to the Lieberman tradition of establishing bush-schools as primary centres for evangelization rather than education. Since the 1850s the Spiritan motto had been 'holiness rather than scholarship.' They were slow to adopt Hinsley's message and left him frustrated.[31] In western and northern Tanganyika, however, the Irish Spiritans and the White Fathers, who were not noted educationalists, realised the importance of schools and acted upon Hinsley's advice.[32] The White Fathers were recognised for their cultural sensitivity and with the Fipa people of Southern Tanganyika, their flexible approach allowed a religiously receptive people the opportunity to adapt Catholicism to their local culture.[33] But even the White Fathers were taken aback by

Hinsley's powerful emphasis on schools. 'L'école, toujours l'école et plus que jamais l'école', complained one of the Fathers after Hinsley's visit to Lubwe in May 1928.[34] In Nyasaland some White Fathers complained to Bishop Guillémé that Hinsley's schools policy was 'profane' and a *magni passus extra viam* – not their business, and a waste of time and scarce manpower.[35] But Lavigerie's earlier theory of Christianising native communities without disturbing their culture changed after Hinsley's visitation and he 'gave the White Fathers sufficient incentive to double their efforts in school matters.' Under Fr Jan van Sambeek, the White Fathers in Central Africa increased their schools, improved opportunities for conversion, and successfully deflected Protestant encroachment and influence. Fr van Sambeek was Hinsley's kindred spirit and alive to the threat of other forces. 'If the Catholic Church does not organise the school system together with the government', he wrote, 'the Protestants and the African Bolshevists will take it over'.[36] Mgr La Rue interpreted van Sambeek's and Hinsley's motives, and therefore the Vatican's, rather more cynically, but probably with a degree of truth, when he stated to Cardinal Marchetti, Secretary of Propaganda, that the main reason for Hinsley, and his supporters, choosing to build schools rather than churches 'was, of course, not the concern for the education of the Africans. Schools were seen as an excellent way of barring the Protestants from entering the Vicariate, and it would also assure the growing sympathy of the English administration.'[37]

Bishop John Campling had firmly stated his educational policy on his arrival at the Mill Hill Upper Nile mission in 1925. Each mission school should be an elementary vernacular school; catechumenate schools should be realistically graded; catechists should be properly trained; and intermediate, technical and normal schools should be opened. Campling's ideas caused friction among his priests. His view, like Hinsley's, was that 'education is to be put first'. Some missionaries disagreed: for Fr George Speirings, missionary work came first and he declared that he would rather leave the country than acquiesce to the bishop's policy. Fr Henry Rottgering held a different view, however. He felt that it 'was better to make one good Catholic than a hundred baptized heathens', that the standard of catechetical knowledge was appalling, and that 'school is one of the means' to remedy the situation.[38]

In southern Nigeria the influence of the Spiritan tradition and the driving, if loosely organised, enthusiasm of Bishop Shanahan meant that there was a strong emphasis on the place of schools within mission structures.[39] According to Shanahan, the school, the centre of the mission, would have failed in its principal object if it failed to Christianise, to bring the life of God to the children and to train them to grow in it. That was its primary function 'and no school would be completely successful as long as a single pagan child remained outside its portals and its influence.'[40] This approach, deliberately developed and consolidated by the training of African catechists, directly involved local people in the apostolate and rooted the mission in its local culture. But the school had both educational and liturgical facets, for the school was the church and the church was the school. Students were educated into basic literacy and also into the proper liturgical practices of the Church, and African catechists became indispensable collaborators with the Spiritans in developing the Lower Niger Mission. Bishop Shanahan used schools to preach the gospel message through a system of biblical and liturgical catechesis which captivated the people's interest.[41] In Southern Nigeria a range of schools, including two aided secondary schools, and from 1928 St Charles's Teacher Training College at Onitsha, built on the efforts of earlier attempts to provide African teachers and catechists. When compared with Protestant provision at secondary level, however, the Catholics were seriously outnumbered.[42]

Hinsley had preached expansion and he was impressed with Shanahan's schools extension programme if not the actual organisation of the vicariate. But elsewhere in Nigeria the situation was uneven. Religious rivalry was a spur for Shanahan and he proved a worthy adversary. In Nigeria there was at times 'an atmosphere of war' – a rather unedifying contest between denominations to erect schools and impose influence. Ever since the late nineteenth century a proliferation of schools, even in close proximity, had been a manifestation of this competition. In Southern Nigeria there were 2,243 denominational schools in 1921 with 3,683 teachers catering for 137,235 pupils. In this situation the Catholics held their own, but in Western Nigeria the situation was different, for the White Fathers were almost exclusively French and taught through the medium of their own language. For Nigerians, English was the language for advancement, and Protestant schools were regarded as being superior to Catholic schools run by European institutes where English was not the medium of instruction. The White Fathers' philosophy was based more on the direct apostolate and the building up of Christian communities rather than evangelization through schools. In the north, as will be shown, the government restricted all Christian missionary activity in a Muslim dominated region.[43]

Hinsley's 'schools first' policy was not new to the Jesuits. In 1896 the Society's Superiors in Rome had instructed all missionary rectors that 'no Residence should be without a school, and if a school is impossible then a Residence should also be considered impossible.' It was a policy that had prospered on Jesuit African missions and especially in Southern Rhodesia where they had made good progress. Fr Alfred Burbridge[44] was closely involved in the Southern Rhodesian Missionary Conference which in 1922 had proposed a government department to deal specifically with African education. In 1928 he became the Roman Catholic representative on the Advisory Board for Native Education. The Jesuits and education officials were on amicable terms,[45] and the educational system uniquely placed responsibility on the missionaries to act as superintendents and inspectors of their own schools. They were therefore closely integrated with government policy and their inspection reports determined the amount of subsidy. Whilst some other denominations opposed this close relationship, the Jesuits were content to accept generous government grants.[46]

In the colony there were three grades of schools – boarding schools under the direction of Europeans; day schools also under the direction of Europeans; and day schools in out-stations offering basic literacy and English. The Catholics had more first grade and second grade schools than any other denomination and the Jesuits had an unparalleled reputation as educationalists. Their commitment to the education at a higher level of all whites and, with the Marianhill Fathers and Dominican Sisters, to the provision of basic and vocational education for all, earned the respect, financial support, and co-operation of government officials. Both Harold Jowitt, Director of Education for the colony, and Hinsley were extremely impressed by what they observed and inspected. Jowitt regarded the mission school at Drifontein as a model to be imitated by other mission schools. Hinsley referred to the school, under the care of the Sisters of the Most Precious Blood, as 'one of the most alive missions in the country.'[47]

Hinsley was further heartened when in May 1928 he visited Gwelo in Southern Rhodesia with Mgr Brown and laid the foundation stone of a new school-chapel being erected by the Jesuits. Hinsley declared that schools were at the centre of missionary work and, possibly reflecting on his own nineteenth-century English experience where rectors of urban missions built school-chapels, said that where necessary the school and the church might have to be the same building. As Brown reported, 'It was curious ... that one of the points insisted on by Bishop Hinsley during his tour was that, in the present circumstances, it was even of greater importance to build and equip schools rather than churches, and the ideal was school-chapels.' Hinsley was simply affirming the obvious Jesuit missionary commitment and their convergence with British and Vatican policy. The sight of a beautiful new native church prompted local white Catholics to begin collecting funds to erect one for themselves.[48]

There were missionary prelates elsewhere who, whilst agreeing with Hinsley, were not in a position to introduce many changes. In southern Ghana, Bishop Ernest Hauger had opened hundreds of small schools since his appointment as Vicar Apostolic of the Gold Coast in 1925, but in central Ghana the Society of African Missions struggled to become established, and the White Fathers were not allowed in to northern Ghana until 1929.[49]

Relations with Colonial Officials

Relations between missionaries and colonial officials were influenced by nationality, different interpretations of government educational policy, and regional variations in implementation. Different philosophical and religious views, inflexible opinions, misunderstandings and the disputed application of policy inevitably led to friction. The resolution of such difficulties required patience and sensitivity. In west and South Africa there was a record of some colonial governments assuming direct responsibility for the establishment and maintenance of schools through modest financial assistance. In east, or tropical Africa, however, there was some opposition to the mass education of Africans, and also to education with a religious dimension.[50] During his visitation Hinsley had ample opportunity to observe the differences in interpretation of policy and the administration of education in the colonies. He also became very much aware of the government's determination to implement its policy.

Although the government White Paper of 1925, and colonial educational ordinances prior or subsequent to its issue, had emphasised a partnership between state and voluntary educational agencies, the government reserved the right to supervise all educational institutions and enforce prescribed standards and regulations. Not unnaturally, this caused some concern among missionaries. Progress depended very largely on personalities and the relationships between missionaries and local officials. Fearful missionaries, who in many cases were not English, regarded government reforms with suspicion. A critical and negative official attitude towards missionary religious aims and educational methods accentuated the problem. C.B. Smith, the Director of Education in Southern Provinces of Nigeria, reported that missionaries and officials found it hard to see eye-to-eye in the matter of schools and education. The divide between the religious and the secular approach tempered relations between Catholics and state officials from 1926 to 1929.[51]

Catholic missionaries faced serious problems on all fronts. They lagged behind the Protestants in the provision of schools and they could not afford to upgrade their elementary schools or provide secondary schools. In western Kenya, for example, Mgr Bransdma's Prefecture was very heavily in debt. Two catechist training schools had to be closed and other schools were threatened. Brandsma considered resigning, despite the promise of financial assistance from van Rossum and Hinsley. Only an American begging tour wiped off the debt. Additionally, the Kenyan administration placed its own unwelcome interpretation on government policy. From a Catholic point of view, reported Hinsley, it was a land of trouble and menace. In 1929 the Director of Education, H.S. Scott, issued *A Memorandum in Regard to the Education of the African in Western Kenya*. Its contents caused great anxiety among missionaries of all denominations for the *Memorandum* outlined a grading system whereby the basic bush school staffed by missionaries or African catechists would receive no grant. The proposed 'Grade B' elementary schools would be run by the missions but paid for by the government. 'Grade C' schools were to be managed by local native councils and financed by the government. Above standard five they were to be non-confessional and have boarding facilities with denominational hostels. Denominations would have to finance any extra staffing. Despite the outcry from missionaries, Scott remained firm in his resolve to have some form of non-confessional education and prepared to impose Grade C schools, and he went even further when, following discussions with the Kavirondo Native Council, he openly stated 'the native has indicated in no uncertain terms that he no longer wishes to be educated in institutions which are controlled by missionaries.'[52]

Already disturbed by Scott's non-confessional proposals, the Ordinaries were incensed by the Director's assertions about African anti-missionary opinion. Hinsley was alerted and immediately sent a letter of protest to the Colonial Office Advisory Board in London and contacted Propaganda. Whilst Hinsley acknowledged the goodwill of the British authorities he was distressed by the anti-missionary stance of some local officials.[53] The British Minister to the Holy See was obviously informed as his annual report for 1930 included details of the dispute. Some apprehension was expressed in Propaganda about Scott's comments which, the Minister reported, 'were warmly repudiated by the natives.'[54] Letters of protest also appeared in local Kenyan newspapers. Scott was temporarily silenced and backed down but he continued to advocate non-denominational secondary schools run by local native councils His 1929 report 'insinuated that the Catholic Church knew very little about education, and that the Catholic missionary would be a dubious educator for the African native.'[55] In its annual review of colonial educational developments, the *International Review of Missions* reported in 1929 that 'there were difficulties in tropical Africa.'[56]

A conference, held at Dar-es-Salaam in March 1929, highlighted the growing divergence between officials and missionaries. It was attended by directors of education from South Africa, Southern Rhodesia, Basutoland, Bechuanaland, Kenya, Nyasaland, Tanganyika, Uganda, and Zanzibar, and therefore represented a wide range of systems. Missionary institutes, however, were not represented. The conference recognised the missionary contribution to African education but was not satisfied that Roman Catholic missions, in particular, were aware either of the speed of educational development or that natives required education not evangelization. Missionaries, the delegates accepted, had to accept the importance of 'efficiency'. The employment of qualified and registered English teachers to teach English in the Kenyan schools was also discussed. With a large number of French, Italian and Dutch missionaries this was an obvious problem for the Catholics. A joint denominational approach led to discussions with Scott and facilitated the continued and extended use of Swahili. But it was only an interim measure and the Churches had to pay for books and teachers. After the conference the Governor of Kenya informed the Colonial Office that 'the Director of Education has discussed the position with the leaders of the Protestant and Roman Catholic Churches and that little difficulty in ensuring the adoption of the principles is anticipated.'[57] However, Hinsley's comments on the conference and his subsequent actions in Kenya, indicated his anxiety. 'Everything', he wrote, 'seems to point in the direction of neutral schools and government schools for higher education'. Catholics had to reject strenuously any developments that separated education from religion.[58]

In July 1929 Rivers-Smith, Director of Tanganyika, wrote to the Colonial Office that the subject of grants-in-aid to mission schools 'presented considerable difficulties and requires delicate treatment.'[59] The government, however, was not going to be lenient and the memorandum on principles to be observed in making grants in aid to missionary and denomination schools was to be as rigorously applied as it was in England. 'Aided institutions', the memorandum stated, 'cannot be inferior substitutes for government schools.'[60]

The obvious difficulties of finding extra money, training and employing approved teachers, and meeting externally imposed standards did not always prevent development in missionary education. *Fides* reported that in East Africa many missionaries viewed educational reforms with satisfaction. In Tanganyika Bishops Michaud and Birraux obtained government approval for central schools at Tabora and Ujiji. They were costly undertakings but gave 'a healthy spurt to mission education activities in many parts of East Africa.' Admittedly, continued the *Fides* correspondent, there were possibilities that such reforms might work against Catholic interests but in those cases 'the Catholic missionary would have to express disagreement.' Such had been the case in western Kenya.[61]

Yet in some colonies neither the Catholics nor other denominations could justifiably complain about government financial support for schools. Educational expenditure in Uganda increased from £8,231 in 1922 to over £56,000 in 1929; in Tanganyika it increased from £8,058 in 1921 to over £127,000 in 1931; and in the Southern Province of Nigeria it rose from £72,900 in 1922 to nearly £215,000 in 1929. But in Nyasaland educational expenditure only rose from £3685 in 1926 to £12,184 three years later.[62]

Hinsley's relations with colonial officials in West Africa were also influenced by circumstances leading to different interpretations of the educational codes. To Sir Graeme Thomson, Governor of Nigeria, Hinsley expressed 'a legitimate pride in British administration' and assured him that the bishops and missionary superiors realised that he was 'striving to follow a policy of all-round fair play'. They were, he wrote, grateful for the protection and kindly disposition of the colonial administration and that any criticism should not be interpreted as disloyalty. Yet, Hinsley continued, he feared that some officials tended to discriminate against Catholics and were not abiding by their own ordinances. Some had doctrinaire attitudes towards Catholic schools whilst others delayed developments in Catholic schools and did not advocate the education of African women. He could not, he threatened Thomson, 'tell Rome that in Nigeria the spirit of the Colonial Office is not being observed'.[63] While Thomson recognised difficulties in the implementation of policy, his position was seriously tempered by the strength of Islam, especially in Northern Nigeria where British rule was 'still tentative' and where local factors had to be taken into account.[64] Hinsley's response was that if there are laws and ordinances then they should be obeyed and implemented irrespective of religious groups or local conditions and complained that Koranic and Christian schools were treated differently.[65]

Catholics had received considerable assistance from the government in the Gold Coast but Hinsley told the Governor, Sir Alexander Ransford Slater, that he disagreed with the political decision to restrict the expansion of Christianity in the colony. Hinsley considered that the mission schools in the Gold Coast to be among 'the best in Africa' but the Government was wrong, he argued, in preventing Catholics from opening schools. It was further at fault by suspecting the loyalties of French-Canadian White Fathers in the Northern Territories and not allowing Catholic students to exercise the Conscience Clause when attending non-Catholic schools. He told Slater that: 'I am bound to state that we cannot consent to a system which encourages the idea that one religion is as good as another'.[66]

The Impact of Hinsley's Visitation

When he left Africa on 30 October 1929, Hinsley summed up the experiences of his visitation. His first accolade was for the British government for allowing freedom of worship and liberty to Catholic schools. He was leaving, he said, with a deep love of Africa and its enthusiastic people and with full confidence in their future. He expressed his deepest admiration for the missionaries but was anxious that the Church seized the opportunity to consolidate on their efforts before the invasion of other 'wretched isms'. The government had awakened to the necessity of providing appropriate education for the Africans, and the missionaries 'were trying to direct the onrushing tide.' The principal aim of missionaries was the eternal salvation of the African but, he added, 'they must also be prepared by careful training to minister to the intellectual and corporate needs' of the people, and he again referred to the opportunity to advance African womanhood through the Church's female institutes and through other apostolic ventures such as teaching and nursing. His final comment, emphasizing the need to erect an indigenous Church, was that while the missionaries had begun the work 'there must be native priests, native sisters and native brothers to supplement their efforts.'[67]

British diplomats had worked hard for the appointment of a British subject to an important ecclesiastical post in the British Empire, and Hinsley's appointment as the only British Apostolic Visitor was of great significance. But it was a long way from embassy niceties and carefully crafted communiqués to the practicalities of the mission and colonial service. The two-year visitation was a physically tiring and mentally draining experience for Hinsley and on occasions the bishops commented on his fatigue. And whether they agreed with his message and methods or not, it is apparent that Hinsley made a tremendous impression on prelates and missionaries. They were also aware that certainly Rome, and perhaps Hinsley, had under-estimated the magnitude of his task but admired him for his conscientiousness and determination. In September 1928 Bishop John Campling of the Upper Nile, anxiously waiting for Hinsley's visit, wrote to the Mill Hill agent in Rome to say that he thought Hinsley had found that his visitation was 'a far bigger job than expected'. Later, in July 1929, he wrote, 'I greatly admire him for he is a very courageous man.'[68] Campling's colleague, Mgr Bransdma, wrote to Dr Schut to say that throughout the visitation and discussions, he and Hinsley had become good friends. Hinsley, he wrote, is 'a very fine man, his visitation will do a lot of good for the African mission.'[69] Reporting on Hinsley's methods he wrote: 'He is extremely tactful and prudent, yet he can be very firm when needed.' He was, for example, annoyed at the 'stagnation' among the French Holy Ghost Fathers in East Africa;[70] yet in Nigeria the success of their confrères had impressed Hinsley. Despite differences in their approach to schools, priests of the Society of African Missions were similarly impressed by the Apostolic Visitor. His appointment was a wise choice, their missionary magazine reported, and his physical stamina and intellectual qualities were outstanding. His visitation, the report concluded, was 'a feat physical and mental of which any ecclesiastic may be proud.'[71]

Some bishops felt that Hinsley's visitation strengthened resolve, restored confidence, and gave a fresh impetus to missionary activities. Mgr Brandsma, who lacked not only self-confidence but also that of some of his missionaries, wrote that from his point of view 'It is almost providential that Bishop Hinsley came here . . . for now we have his valuable help and advice.' Hinsley, he claimed, pushed matters more strongly and had resolved the impossible educational position they had found themselves in before his visit.[72] In Rhodesia the Jesuits were 'spurred on to a decade of major effort on the educational front' by Hinsley's visit.[73] But they were in no doubt about the immensity of the task facing them and the need to raise standards either through the employment of better educated and more expensive salaried white teachers or through the slower process of educating, with government financial assistance, native teachers. The task was 'no light one for Bishop Hinsley' either, but 'no one could ask', they recorded, 'for a more competent delegate.'[74] And in Rhodesia Hinsley also stimulated the White Fathers, mainly through the efforts of Fr van Sambeek, to increase their educational commitment. As Mgr Brown recorded:

> Up to the present time the main work of the (White) Fathers has been directed to the evangelization of the natives in the vicariate and comparatively little attention has been given to education as such, but in the present circumstances and particularly after the words of Bishop Hinsley to the assembled community, the White Fathers with their wonderful energy and thoroughness have embarked on a scheme of systematic instruction and education of the natives, and the start made at Rosa with the Normal School under the enlightened direction of Fr van Sambeek is a sure sign that in this, as in all the other projects they undertake, it will be carried through to success.[75]

The influence of Hinsley's visitation on missionary schools was considerable. Protestant educational provision, especially at secondary level, was far superior to that of the Catholics prior to the Phelps-Stokes report, but following Hinsley's mission the Catholics were compelled by his direction both to begin to raise elementary standards and extend secondary provision. Efficient primary schools and a greater number of secondary schools, Propaganda and Hinsley realised, were excellent means of evangelization, consolidating claims to missionary territory, and influencing the future development of the Church, colony or protectorate.

In two pioneering generations the Catholic missions had built up a system of African native schools for the most part without government assistance and had earned the respect and support of their converts. Government educational reforms of the mid-1920s threatened this system and geographically disparate missions were confronted by a philosophical and administrative onslaught. But there was no united Catholic point of view and missionary prelates offered no coherent plan of action to cope with the inevitable transformation of schools. The Church could not afford to stand by and leave others to formulate and dictate educational policy. During his two years in Africa Hinsley made it very clear that this was not an acceptable course of action.[76] His forceful intervention and his dynamic leadership of missionary conferences strengthened missionary resolve and galvanized the actions of hitherto isolated and vulnerable prelates. He had a major influence on the subsequent nature of missionary education and Church-government relations and, most importantly, he was able to express Vatican strategy in relation to British policy and transmit it undiluted across the British colonies. From this emerged the beginnings of a uniformity of ecclesiastical purpose and approach. In its review of 1930 the *International Review of Missions* reported cryptically that Hinsley's visitation had 'led to a re-organizing of educational personnel and a reconsideration of policy.'[77] *The Times* was more fulsome in its tribute to Hinsley's first African mission and recalled his dominant and forceful personality in ensuring the mutual benefits accruing to the Church and state, but particularly to the Church, through the imposition of Vatican policy:

> From the first, his candid, vigorous personality commended him to the colonial officials – never backward in recognizing the beneficial influence of Roman Catholic missionaries on native character. He was always ready to tell them home truths and to warn them of the dangerous effects of a superficially western education on the minds and morals of Africans. At the same time he fully refused to allow any Roman Catholic missionaries to adopt an attitude of non-cooperation; exerting his whole power and influence on the side of such parts of the government schemes as seemed to him practically expedient.[78]

Hinsley's own appraisal of his work was simple and straightforward. The

British government realised that it could not do without missionary schools if education was to spread among the masses of Africans in its territories. Missionary schools had been a great civilizing influence and government recognised their value. The government's desire for educational efficiency was shared by the Holy See, and it was the Pope's anxiety to know how Catholic schools fared in Africa and his desire to see them brought up to externally recognised standards of excellence that was the main reason for Hinsley's visitation. 'Yet', he concluded, 'it was not only to make reports to Rome, but the hope of stimulating and encouraging all the workers in our schools with the Pope's own enthusiasm for higher standards in education that inspired me.'[79]

Throughout his visitation Hinsley presented a common Catholic educational position to missionaries and colonial officials. His emphasis was on Church strategy and planning rather than missionary improvisation, and his leadership of regional discussions and the creation of a more coherent missionary opinion enabled the Catholics to obtain concessions from administrators. It also hastened the Colonial Office's implementation of an African educational policy based on collaboration and partnership with missionary and voluntary agencies. In addition, Hinsley's stated educational aims, based on the foundations of Christianity, and their achievement in Africa, secured through a partnership between the universal Church and the British Empire, were difficult for colonial officials to gainsay. After Hinsley's visit it was no longer possible for colonial officials to ignore Catholic opinion or the contribution of Catholic mission schools. Heenan wrote that Hinsley's success was attributable to his practical acumen:

> By humility in dealing with pious missionaries fearful of change and by his intransigence in his relations with such officials as he found too ignorant to appreciate the importance of religious education, Mgr Hinsley encouraged wise compromise and was able to suggest solutions for most of the outstanding problems dividing the two parties.'[80]

As it was not the central objective of Hinsley's remit as Apostolic Visitor, his impact on the development of Catholic seminaries in British colonial Africa during his visitation was less immediate and obvious than his effect upon schools. Nevertheless, his meetings and discussions with missionary leaders highlighted the problems facing the African Church in the development of an indigenous priesthood. Seminaries were expensive institutions to maintain and there was no government assistance; seminarians had to be educated at least to a good standard of secondary education yet there were few Catholic secondary schools; the logistics of providing central seminaries to serve a number of institutes were complex and expensive and not always to the liking of the missionaries, or their mother houses in Europe, who feared a loss of identity; and staffing the seminaries often meant denuding the ranks of European seminaries.

Reports to Rome

Hinsley's reports to Propaganda reflected his methodical and uncompromising approach to his Visitation. Throughout the course of his travels he sent regular reports back to Rome and on the conclusion of the Visitation he submitted a 31 page summary of his findings and recommendations.[81] It contained many positive comments about the Church's progress on the continent – the zealous labours of the missionaries, the rapid growth and development of Catholic communities, and the generous predisposition of the British government towards the Catholic Church. But it also contained some uncomfortable reading about the missionaries' capabilities to exploit their opportunities, their disunity and the worrying problem of colonial officials preventing Catholic expansion either out of personal secularism or from fear of conflict with other religious denominations. Such was Hinsley's forthright and open approach, it is likely that the reports contained nothing that he would not have said directly to the missionaries.

The Africans, Hinsley reported, were drawn to the Church in ever-increasing numbers and there remained 'the opportunity for a harvest of millions of souls'. The crude and primitive religions long practised by the Africans were at last 'giving way to light as the dawn breaks upon them'. He had been received warmly and reverentially 'as the representative of the Great Father and Chief of the Catholic Church' and whatever setbacks and failures there may have been 'our missions give ample motive for consolation and hope. . . . ' The erection of missions, churches and schools for 'the thronging multitudes' gave an immediate opportunity to the Church to extend the Kingdom of God in Africa.[82] The statistics he sent back to Propaganda were eagerly seized upon by *Fides* which reported in 1930 that it was 'becoming ever more clear that Africa is moving rapidly and that the barque of ancient fetishism is floundering . . . the progress of catholicity is enormous . . . the whole country is on the march toward the Church'. The African phenomenon was, however, but one feature of the expansion of missionary activities for ' . . .the multiplication of mission territories', *Fides* reported, 'has continued at the same pace, the most rapid which the history of the Church has ever registered'. From 1922 until 1929, 78 new missions had been created across the world, with 23 being established in 1929. Such developments, as Hinsley's reports attested, were accompanied by the erection of the Church's administrative structures and the growth of the indigenous priesthood.[83]

In his final report Hinsley referred to 'the practical fitness of our European Mission workers'. The Church was growing remarkably, he wrote, and not only were missionaries required in substantial numbers it was necessary for them to have a wider range of scientific and pastoral skills than those possessed by the traditional missionaries. Africa was changing at 'lightning speed' and colonial governments were beginning to provide educational and medical facilities but in their schemes, he lamented, 'the true end of life is little in view'. Missionary institutes, therefore, should be alive to this danger and should 'seek to direct the crushing tide of progress'. In particular, he emphasised the opportunities for the 'consecrated sisterhood', who were 'essential to apostolic work in Africa', and the need to educate African women. Prelates in Africa and Missionary Superiors were aware of these developments but the time had come for them to make further progress:

> The Vicars and Prefects Apostolic . . . realise that new methods are urgent in the new conditions. It is not enough now to occupy the field. A vast number of poorly built and poorly taught out-schools, controlled by occasional visit from a distant central station by one priest, are not enough to give the people the deep intelligent faith needed as civilization advances with great steps to seize on the minds and bodies of the African. . . .

In response to these circumstances, Hinsley advocated co-operation with government, better schools and more medical missionaries. But, he wrote 'European missionaries cannot hope to perfect the work they have begun. Native priests, native sisters, and Native Brothers there must be in plenty to supplement their efforts'. There had been some progress in the training of African seminarians but as he recognised 'the work of forming a native priesthood is a slow process and many failures cause disappointment'. But there were signs of great promise and to fulfil this the need to establish and develop good schools became 'the most urgent need' if the African Church was to develop under African leadership. It was, he realised, an exorbitantly expensive course but there was no alternative as the Church could never consent to a government monopoly in education. The training and employment of African catechists – 'heroic men' – was one way of circumventing the problem at a base level but their education and training was rudimentary and they could not hope to replace well educated Europeans.

The most serious obstacle to missionary progress was what Hinsley referred to as 'want of united action'. The missionaries may have recognised one Lord, one Faith and one Baptism, he recorded, but it had to be admitted that 'our missionary work is conducted by a great number of orders or congregations or institutes and that there are sometimes petty jealousies among different organisations'. Missionaries worked in isolation and seldom met to consider the 'great issues of their work'. There were many different nationalities, even within the same Institute, and consequently nationalism sometimes tended to overshadow other considerations. The remedy, suggested by many of the Vicars and Prefects Apostolic, was the appointment of an Apostolic Delegate who would be able prevent friction, remove doubts and difficulties, and settle questions that may arise with the government on school questions, on marriage laws and property. Hinsley added, 'Our Holy Father alone can tell whether this desires of the Ordinaries . . . will be wise and feasible'. In this way, he added, a senior prelate could supervise the implementation of a coherent policy and ensure united action. Such an approach was also needed, he wrote, 'to offset the work of the Protestant sects whose principles of faith are so vague and fluid that they can accept any compromise, all the more readily if it keeps out Catholics'. His view on Islam was rather different for he reported that one of the saddest considerations of his Visitation had been the recognition that Catholic missionaries had made little headway against the Moslems. He suggested a more scientific approach to the training of missionaries in the precepts and teachings of Islam and in Arabic.

The missionaries, he emphasised, had to accept government involvement in education but they had to be vigilant, for increased government funding very often meant greater secular supervision and control and increased competition from non-denominational schools. Aware of government criticism of the missionaries he wrote:

It is said by Directors of Education that missionaries seek to get all they can from the government but give corresponding services grudgingly in return. Our generosity and self-sacrifice for the schools should not only remove their reproach but set an example to the officials themselves who are not always perfection in the same direction.

There was need to co-operate, therefore, both for the good of the Africans and for the Church.[84]

Internal dissension and poor leadership and management were debilitating factors. In his report on the Vicariate of Shiré Hinsley stated that there was 'want of harmony between the Fathers and the Ordinary', a disagreement arising out of conflicting views over education. Some missionaries asked for secret interviews with Hinsley who ascertained that whilst some missionaries wished to consolidate and take advantage of government funding the French-Canadian Bishop, Mgr Auneau, disagreed. More than this, Hinsley wrote, Auneau was swayed by anti-British sentiments and was not entirely straightforward in his dealings with colonial administrators, the missionaries and even the Apostolic Visitor. Hinsley wrote:'He does not understand English well; he certainly has no sympathy with English ways and English mentality'. Auneau was, he concluded, 'a good man but not alive'. He was against the higher education of Africans and the quality of the schools in the Vicariate was generally of a low standard.[85]

The Prefect Apostolic of the Upper Nile, Bishop Vignato of the Verona Fathers, incurred Hinsley's displeasure for his attitude towards the government and control of the Prefecture. The colonial administrators were not disposed to watch Catholic missionaries monopolize education and prevented them from training their own teachers. Vignato was unwilling to challenge this nor would he censure priests or antagonize other missionary institutes. Hinsley told him that he had to. According to Hinsley, the Bishop was cultured but disorderly, he had no breadth of outlook, he was suspicious of others, he had favourites and most importantly would not fight for the schools. Hinsley considered that Vignato was incapable of ruling the Prefecture and wrote a three page memorandum suggesting improvements.[86]

In the Vicariate of Zanzibar Hinsley differed strongly with Bishop Neville, the Holy Ghost Father and Vicar Apostolic, over the quality of missionary schools. He found Neville 'alive' to some developments but not to education and considered that he was 'ill informed' even about his own vicariate. There was much more that could be done, reported

Hinsley, but Neville was not the man to do it. He was, Hinsley wrote, 'timid' and 'lives in the last half of the last century'. He had no initiative and relied almost completely on his Vicar General who lived in Nairobi. The upshot, wrote Hinsley, was that 'he cannot make up his own mind on any practical subject himself, but is suave and elusive until his judgment is decided for him by his Vicar General. . . . ' Neither of them were attracted to any progressive initiatives and did 'not really wish to educate the natives'. Neville was 'like wax' in the hands of government officials, had done nothing to develop an indigenous priesthood and was basically ignoring the instructions of the Holy See. Hinsley saw 'no hope for improvement under such a regime' and called Neville 'a dead letter'. He asked for Fr Bernhard, Neville's Vicar General, to be removed as he was obstructive and anti-British.[87]

His criticism were not confined to missionary leaders in East Africa. In his report on the situation in West Africa he wrote that 'the predominant impression after visiting the mission stations and the schools in Nigeria, the Gold Coast and Sierra Leone is one of disappointment and anxiety'. His disappointment arose because of the lack of unity among the missionaries and his anxiety stemmed from his fear over the future development of the Church in West Africa. The interests of the institutes, he complained, were put before the needs of the Africans or the instructions of the Holy See. Nationalism among the institutes was a debilitating factor leading to both indifference to British government reforms and dissension between missionaries. A major reason for this state of affairs was that the Mother Houses of most missionary institutes were in mainland Europe. They were neither British nor Roman. He concluded:

> Sorrowfully but candidly I feel bound to express my conviction that some better organizing power and some more efficient driving power is urgently wanted in West Africa than is displayed by the various Mother Houses if the Church is to make or maintain any real progress.

His solution was the introduction of a higher ecclesiastical power: 'In West Africa the direct presence and control of Rome through a Permanent Representative on the spot seems to me as necessary and in certain respects even more necessary than in East Africa'.[88]

Hinsley returned to the *Venerabile* on 15 November 1929.[89] At the end of 1928 the Vatican had expressed its pleasure with Hinsley's achievements during the first year of his visitation[90] and by December

1929 the Holy See's satisfaction had increased. Cardinal Gasparri wrote to the British Minister to the Holy See to express his gratitude for the cordial welcome and co-operation afforded to Hinsley during his visitation of the British African colonies. Bishop Hinsley, he wrote, had made a most successful journey.[91]

Chapter Eight

LARGER FIELDS AND WIDER HORIZONS

1930-1934

The Role of the Apostolic Delegate

On 9 January 1930 Hinsley was named as Apostolic Delegate to the British Colonies in Africa with the title of Archbishop of Sardes. His jurisdiction included the whole of Africa under the control of Propaganda apart from those territories under the supervision of the Apostolic Delegates of South Africa, Egypt and the Congo.[1] Notwithstanding these huge exceptions, there were sixty ecclesiastical divisions under his jurisdiction, covering nine million square miles and with a total population of 80 million. His authority extended over eighty percent of the African continent. For the next four years Hinsley was the visible presence of the Holy See in British colonial Africa.[2]

An Apostolic Delegate is responsible for overseeing the condition and status of the Church within a defined territory and informing the pontiff of related developments. As the pope cannot exercise personal vigilance over the universal Church, legates or delegates are appointed to fulfil this function. These purely ecclesiastical offices stem from the constituted government of the Church and the pope's power to send a representative to any part of the world. Historically, the exercising of delegated authority has been related to the preaching of the Gospel in new missionary areas. An Apostolic Delegate's authority does not extend to interference with the normal jurisdiction of an Ordinary but he takes precedence over all Ordinaries in his territory who are not cardinals.[3] The purpose of an Apostolic Delegate is to strengthen the Church throughout his territory and to confirm, unify, and facilitate the labours of the Ordinaries.[4]

As no formal diplomatic relations existed between the Vatican and Great Britain in 1930, there was no official requirement for prior discussions with the British government over Hinsley's appointment and this also is the reason why Hinsley was appointed Apostolic Delegate rather than a Papal Nuncio.[5] However, as illustrated by Hinsley's choice as Apostolic Visitor in 1927, there was an informal agreement that there would be some consideration of British concerns before senior ecclesiastical appointments were made in the British Empire. There were already Apostolic Delegates serving in the Empire but Hinsley became the only English-born prelate in the foreign service of the Holy See.[6]

As Hinsley's second African appointment was breaking new ground as far as the Vatican and the British colonies were concerned, his terms of reference appear to have been deliberately left imprecise by Propaganda. His main duty was to ensure that the wishes of the Pope and the policies of Propaganda were adhered to, and this had to be accomplished without undermining the authority of the Ordinaries or the activities of the missionaries. A second task was to establish ecclesiastical structures that guaranteed the authority of Rome, provided a framework that effectively directed missionary energies, and ended the insularity and nationalistic dimensions of missions. As a result of his earlier visitation and recommendations, a third task was to continue to re-orientate and co-ordinate missionary educational systems in response to British reforms.[7] Like all delegates, Hinsley was charged with exercising direct surveillance of religious activities within his territories. He was also responsible for furnishing Propaganda with information and advice and ensuring open channels of communication between Rome and the missions. The range of his duties as Apostolic Delegate were essentially defined by the Vatican but greatly influenced by his own previous Visitation reports.[8] Hinsley later suggested that his remit was too vague and comprehensive and that others in Africa regarded his arrival with some distaste. The French, he claimed, resented his appointment; the Italians, the Portuguese, the Spanish did not accept it easily; and the Delegates of the Belgian Congo, South Africa and Egypt considered that the new Apostolic Delegate's powers invaded their jurisdiction. But Propaganda had confirmed that his activities were confined to British African colonies and that other non-British areas were not to be visited.[9]

Archbishop of Sardes

That the Vatican had been considering Hinsley's second African appointment for some time is apparent from the sequence of events that led up to Propaganda's announcement on 9 January. On 5 December

1929, the Papal Secretary of State, Cardinal Gasparri, wrote to the British Minister to the Holy See:

> The Holy See has learnt with great satisfaction that the Right Reverend Monsignor Arthur Hinsley, Titular Bishop of Sebastopolis, Apostolic Visitor, has received during his visit to the Catholic Missionary Schools situated in British territory in Africa, the greatest courtesy and all possible facilities on the part of His Majesty's Government in those regions. . . . Monsignor Hinsley, in fact, made a most successful journey. . . . The Holy See hastens to express its most cordial thanks for the courtesies accorded to the Visitor Apostolic by the Governors, residents, Commissioners and all British officials. . . . Moreover, the Holy See has also learnt with pleasure from the report of the Visitor, of the benefits of liberty and justice enjoyed by the Catholic missions in His Britannic Majesty's Colonies.
>
> I therefore beg Your Excellency to be so good as to convey to the British Government an expression of the Holy Father's lively gratitude. . . .[10]

Prefaced by the comment that 'British relations with the Holy See were tranquil', the British Minister reported to the Foreign Office that Hinsley had returned at the end of 1929 after a two-year tour of practically the whole of British territory in Africa, where he had inspected Catholic mission schools 'with a view to seeing how they could best co-operate with the different colonial administrations in carrying out a programme of native education'. Hinsley 'expressed his warmest appreciation of the sympathy and assistance he had received from the various British authorities and the Holy See officially expressed their gratitude to His Majesty's Government on the same account.' Without referring to Hinsley's promotion, the Minister concluded 'that at the end of the year the Vatican informed His Majesty's legation that Mgr Hinsley had been appointed to visit the Sudan, the only important part of Africa he had left untouched, and the request for similar facilities was acceded by His Majesty's Government.'[11]

On 29 December Cardinal van Rossum informed Hinsley that he was to return to Africa with increased responsibility. On the following day he had a long talk with Cardinal van Rossum and Archbishop Marchetti about the African missions and British policy. Van Rossum instructed him to proceed to London, once all the necessary documentation was complete, and meet with colonial officials. Hinsley was now compelled to resign as Rector of the *Venerabile* and on the Feast of the Epiphany he sang his last Pontifical High Mass at the college.[12] On 8 January he met with Bishop Shanahan of Southern Nigeria and together they discussed missionary affairs with Marchetti, who also instructed Hinsley about his duties and responsibilities regarding Vicars and Prefects Apostolic.[13] On 9 January Hinsley received written notification of his appointment and on the following day learned of his appointment as titular Archbishop of Nazareth. This title was subsequently changed and he became Archbishop of Sardes in succession to Archbishop Eugenio Pacelli who had been elevated to the Sacred College of Cardinals.[14]

Hinsley wrote of his sadness at leaving the *Venerabile* but expressed great confidence in the Church's future in Africa. Of his own forthcoming contribution to the development of the African Church, and possibly conscious that this was likely to be his final appointment, he wrote: 'If the forces which remain to me in my advancing years can be of any good to the Faith in Africa, I give them most gladly'. And then he made a telling comment about those with whom he was returning to work and the missionary rivalries that Popes Benedict XV and Pius XI had urged be consigned to the past. It was obvious that he had encountered such rivalries on his previous visit.

> It is interesting to note that in my territory I have priests of fourteen institutes: White Fathers, Holy Ghost Fathers, Missionaries of Lyons, Benedictines, Mill Hill Fathers, Missionaries of Verona and Consolata, Franciscans, Capuchins, Jesuits, La Salette Fathers, Picpus Fathers, Sons of Mary Immaculate, and the Company of Mary, and in their ranks are found members from almost every nation in Europe. I look forward with joy to representing the Holy See among them, out on the field of the apostolate where for the most part differences of institute and nation are buried and men strive to meet on the common ground of consecration to the advance of the interests of Jesus Christ.[15]

The editor of the Society of African Missionaries' journal greeted Hinsley's appointment with pleasure. His successful visitation had placed him in close contact with the problems associated with establishing the missionary Church in Africa and had prepared the way for him to undertake a wider and more extensive mission. He was confident that Hinsley's preferment 'will give a wonderful impetus to the young but growing African Church' and that as 'a direct representative of Rome living in close touch with the actual conditions of the apostolate, his guiding presence will tend to unify missionary effort and . . . advance the general interests of the Catholic religion. . . .'[16] A non-Catholic official held a similar view. Before departing for Africa, Hinsley addressed the Advisory Committee on African Education in London. At the end of his speech the Committee's secretary remarked, 'I have a feeling that from now on the Catholic missionaries in British Africa will find their task easier and better appreciated by the authorities; this causes me great pleasure.'[17]

Visitation to the Anglo-Egyptian Sudan

Hinsley and Fr Giersbach sailed from Naples on 7 February for a visitation of the Anglo-Egyptian Sudan.[18] Hinsley had planned to visit the Sudan in 1928 but, according to Bishop Campling, was directed instead to South Africa 'to undertake a difficult task for Cardinal Gasparri'.[19] In January 1930 the British Minister to the Holy See informed the Under Secretary of State for the Colonies of Hinsley's forthcoming visit to the Sudan to inspect the Catholic schools and missions as he had done in other British African colonies. He added: 'Mgr Hinsley is a most loyal and patriotic Englishman and will be much missed at the English College in Rome. . . .'[20] However, Ogilvie-Forbes, the British Minister to the Holy See was under no illusions about the difficulties facing Hinsley in the Sudan:

> This is considered a difficult mission field. Moslem fanaticism, the wild Shilluk tribes on the one hand, and competition from other Christian bodies, Protestant, Greek Orthodox, and Coptic, on the other, are stated to hamper the activities of the Roman Catholic missions. In the Southern Sudan especially, the system of zones, where Catholic and Protestant missionaries are, by law, excluded from working in the same area, has been a subject of grievance to the Vatican. . . . [21]

On 2 February Fr Giersbach had written to J. G. Mathew, the Secretary for Education in Khartoum to inform him of Hinsley's visit and his episcopal promotion. Hinsley arrived at Khartoum on 17 February[22] and Major-General H.J. Huddleston, who reported his arrival to the Foreign Office, stated that he had every reason to believe that Hinsley's appointment 'will prove of great benefit to the Sudan government in furthering educational work in the areas of the Sudan in which the Roman Catholic missions work'.[23]

The difficulties outlined by the British Minister to the Holy See did not hinder Hinsley's energetic visitation and he astounded Sudan veterans by travelling over 5,000 miles in fifty days, visiting eight missionary areas before returning to Cairo. Sudanese Catholics numbered less than 15,000 out of a population of 3.5 million and were under the care of Italian Verona Fathers who had ministered in the Sudan since the 1870s together with a small number of Austrian missionaries.[24] As on previous visitations, Hinsley convened an educational conference with Vicars Apostolic Silvestri of Khartoum and Stoppani of Bahr el Ghazal, and Prefect Apostolic Zambornardi of Bahr el Gebel. He also held meetings with the government's Secretary of Education.[25]

Hinsley did not have a major impact on the Sudan during his period as Apostolic Delegate and could do no more than help the missionaries consolidate their position. During 1931, the Vatican and the British Chargé d'Affaires in the Sudan, presumably with Hinsley's knowledge, submitted informal requests to the Sudanese government to allow missionary expansion but restrictions were not lifted.[26] Hinsley's only direct and successful intervention came during late 1930 when, after consultation with Bishop Silvestri of Khartoum, the Italian missionaries, and British officials, he was able to regularize missionary landholdings consequent upon the effects of the Great War and simultaneously de-nationalise missionary terminology. Instead of referring to the 'Italian Catholic Mission' and the 'Austrian Catholic Mission', Hinsley insisted that they were in future to be known as 'the Roman Catholic Mission'.[27]

Hinsley's report to Rome on his Visitation to the Sudan was as direct as his previous submissions from East and West Africa. The very size of the territory led to a complicated administrative situation further componded by the strong Moslem presence and Britain's uncertain policy for the region. Nevertheless, Hinsley felt compelled to alert Propaganda to weaknesses in Catholic provision. He was especially harsh on Bishop Silvestri who 'by want of prudence and tact, . . .seems to have alienated the government and estranged the clergy and the people'. It was true that he and the Verona Fathers had made good progress but the Bishop's interference in the detailed affairs of other missionary institutes and his intemperate and unmeasured language inflamed an already complex situation. In the Vicariate of Bahr el Ghazal he felt that the Italian language was 'too much in evidence' and that there should be 'but only Catholic' transmitted through the vernacular. He found the efforts of Bishop Zambornadi to be characterised by 'tactful zeal' but the Bishop and his missionaries were hampered by 'unacceptable administrative zoning' imposed by the Foreign Office and designed to prevent inter-religious rivalry.[28]

On 29 July 1930 Hinsley arrived at Mombasa in Kenya where he established his residence. Groves claimed that this was because 'East Africa was his more particular concern. . . .'[29] It was certainly the region with the greatest Catholic population and the most numerous missionary personnel.

The Church and Colonial Administrators in East Africa

Education continued to pre-occupy the missionaries and remained a major issue in all the British colonies. After his visitation of 1928 and 1929, Hinsley was well placed to influence and monitor educational developments during his time as Apostolic Delegate but the world economic crisis of the early 1930s restricted the ability of colonial governments and missionary institutes to implement educational reforms. The global financial depression adversely affected the income of the Association for the Propagation of the Faith (A.P.F.) and funds available to Catholic worldwide missions dropped from over 66m lire in 1929 to 38m lire in 1933.[30] Cardinal Salotti, Secretary of Propaganda, estimated that the central missionary funds of the Church declined by 50% between 1931 and 1936.[31] Similarly, the income generated by direct fund raising on behalf of missionary institutes declined and the ability of the Church to continue its expansionist missionary programme was severely hampered.

The financial picture across the British African colonies was mixed. The imperial government's insistence on a policy of colonial economic self-sufficiency led to variations in income and educational expenditure. In poorer colonies, declining income from the A.P.F., grants-in-aid, and the institutes' own sources restricted educational developments.[32] In some colonies, economic retrenchment re-opened discussions about the nature of African education and responsibility for its provision. However, other colonial governments made limited progress within the terms of their educational ordinances and some institutes even managed to extend and improve provision. But overall, funds were inadequate and the situation was exacerbated by those local administrators who maintained a secular philosophy of African education and who continued to display antipathy towards missionaries and disregard the historical, actual and potential contribution of mission schools.[33]

Despite economic stringency and some official opposition, there was progress. Throughout 1931 and 1932 Hinsley reported very positively on aspects of missionary educational development in East Africa. In Tanganyika Territory the Holy Ghost Fathers had developed their teacher training school and central school in the Bagamoyo Vicariate whilst in the Kilima-Njaro Vicariate their minor seminary, training centre and central school were flourishing. The White Fathers had opened new schools in the Tanganyika Vicariate and were planning new schools in Mwanza and Bukoba Vicariates. The Consolata Fathers had a central school in Iringa Prefecture and the Benedictines had opened two educational centres at Lindi.[34] In 1932 the Benedictines also opened a central school at Perahimo. In Nyasaland there had been a change of official attitude and the Education Ordinance safeguarded religious teaching. Seminaries were opened in Shiré and Nyasa Vicariates and a new teacher training school had been established in Nyasa. Under the direction of the zealous Fr Jan van Zambeek, the White Fathers had a flourishing seminary and teacher training school in Northern Rhodesia. The Polish Jesuits in Broken Hill faced difficulties but other Jesuits were developing education in Barotseland and had established a seminary at Mariathal in 1931.[35] A Catholic high school and central school had been opened in the Zanzibar Vicariate. The Mill Hill Missionaries had opened a new school at Yala in the Kavirondo Prefecture under the direction of Canadian Christian Brothers. And the Consolata Fathers' seminary in Nyeri produced two African priests who were ordained by Hinsley. In Kenya, despite the opposition of the Director of Education, the Holy Ghost Fathers, supported by Hinsley in 1928, had eventually opened an 'inter-vicarial' high school at Kabaa in 1930 under Fr Witte. The government was obliged to make grants-in-aid.[36]

Hinsley regarded Uganda Vicariate, under the inspirational leadership of the White Father Bishop Streicher at Katigondo, as the most outstanding mission field. Here there were flourishing schools, African priests and African-run missions. In the Vicariate of the Upper Nile, the Mill Hill Fathers were developing schools and seminaries at lake Victoria and Nyenga. In Buganda the Verona Fathers remodelled their school at Gulu in 1928. Teaching Brothers of the Sacred Heart were invited to take over the school in 1932 and teacher training schools were established for boys and girls.[37] Hinsley could feel well satisfied that his earlier visitation was paying such handsome dividends. The Christian but not Catholic

International Review of Missions acknowledged his influence when it reported in 1932 that 'In Tanganyika territory, in Kenya and Uganda, the Roman Catholic Church is building up a fine system of education for boys and girls under the direction of Archbishop Hinsley'.[38]

However, the situation was not entirely favourable and Hinsley informed readers of *Fides* that 'If the above be thought too roseate a story of East African missionary success, we hasten to admit that there is another side. . . . '[39] Catholic schools had been closed in Swaziland during 1930 due to financial problems and in Tanganyika, as the financial crisis took hold, the financial Retrenchment Commission restricted educational progress. It proposed that education should be handed back to the missions but with the government reserving the right to inspect and to fund where possible. Secularists claimed that this scheme would simply revert to pre-ordinance days and return power and influence to the churches. Hinsley forcefully rejected such loud and persistent assertions and claimed that only the Catholic missionary 'has the certain knowledge of the nature and content of education'.[40]

Hinsley repeatedly acknowledged that the Colonial Office recognised the importance of religious instruction and, in principle, enabled Catholic missionaries to deliver it, but he demonstrated that local officials did not always implement this policy. Collaboration was laudable and necessary but the practice was not always two-sided.[41] He was concerned particularly by the secularism manifested by some local officials and noted the ambiguous stance of others who ' . . .though not wholeheartedly trusting the Catholic missionary, recognise that he is an indispensable ally of order and discipline. . . . '[42] More dangerous were those officials who ignored regulations and actively encouraged African antipathy towards missionaries. The Local Native Schools of Kenya, run by tribal elders, were cited as an example. At Nairobi in October 1928 Hinsley and the Ordinaries had emphasised their opposition to Local Native Schools, claimed that they contravened previously agreed Church-government arrangements, and argued that the opening of secular schools would introduce unfair competition. They also pointed out that to tax all Africans to pay for Local Native Schools would be unfair, as the taxes collected would only be used to satisfy the wishes of those who opposed mission schools. But their most important criticism was that Local Native Schools encouraged pagan elders to perpetuate their pagan customs contrary to the religious education element of the

Colonial Office's Educational Policy of March 1925.[43] Hinsley suspected that the development of Local Native Schools and a growing anti-Catholic attitude, particularly among the Kikuyu, was fostered by white officials, who regarded Catholic schools as inferior and was also a result of Catholic opposition to female initiation rites rather than African dissatisfaction with mission schools.[44] But the problem of native schools was not confined to Kenya. Tanganyika Territory had Native Authority Schools and Nigeria had Native Administration Schools.

In the former German territory of Tanganyika, the development of indirect rule by Sir Donald Cameron also included the opening of Native Authority Schools. After his arrival in 1925, Cameron pushed ahead with them as part of the build-up to a modern system of government based upon indigenous authority and traditions. Initially, there was co-operation between missionaries and officials but the situation deteriorated during the early 1930s, partly due to the growing doubts among missionaries about government intentions and also because of the economic depression. The Advisory Committee on Native Education, which included missionary representatives, was convened only three times between December 1930 and March 1933. The meetings of colonial Directors of Education, from which missionaries were excluded, seemed to be taking precedence.[45] The marginalization of the mission schools and the reduction of income led to friction between officials and missionaries who saw their work and influence threatened. Missionaries were angered by apparent government ingratitude for their previous efforts and sacrifice. After re-establishing education in post-war Tanganyika in the absence of a formal colonial structure, the churches were now relegated to be junior partners in education, a situation exacerbated by Native Authority Schools being better funded than voluntary schools.

The economic depression severely affected the missions, their status and further progress. Expenditure on education in the Protectorate slumped from £122,666 in 1932 to £86,704 in 1934 and five government schools were closed. Government schools suffered a 40% staff reduction between 1930 and 1934. Mission schools had their income reduced by 45%[46] and the White Fathers were compelled to dismiss sixty-eight inadequately trained catechists.[47] Such decisions sowed seeds of doubt in African minds about the sincerity of the missionaries, who were perceived to be in collusion with the European administrators. Despite this, the annual Report to the Mandates Commission of the League of Nations in 1934 stated that in Tanganyika an outstanding feature of missionary work had been the marked increase in the activities of the Roman Catholic missions who applied to register over two hundred new schools in the Kigoma District, and over one hundred in the Iringa province, apart from several hundred applications spread over other provinces.[48]

The Church and Colonial Administrators in West Africa

Educational developments in Nigeria during the early 1930s were the cause of much tension between the missionaries of all Christian denominations and local officials. E.R.J. Hussey, Director of Education of the combined Northern and Southern Provinces from 1929 to 1936, attempted to re-structure educational provision and set about establishing a system that would ultimately preclude and in the meantime minimize the missionary contribution. New education ordinances were introduced in 1926 and expenditure, particularly on government schools, increased up to 1930. In times of economic stringency, Hussey was forced into a policy of retrenchment but he continued with the re-organisation of the education system that he had introduced on his arrival. Economic constraints also compelled him to accept the continued involvement of the missions.[49] The Catholic Ordinaries had to confront Hussey in order to maintain and develop their schools. Hussey's restrictions were unacceptable to the Catholics as were his proposals to introduce higher studies for a small number of students.[50]

As well as being anti-denominational, Hussey's reforms also had wider political and social implications and in his report to Propaganda on the conclusion of his visitation, Hinsley had warned against the education of a *déclassée* elite in Nigeria leading to dangerous voids between educated and uneducated Africans and between colonial administrators and a detached but vociferous African intellectual minority.[51] The majority of white opinion in Nigeria reflected Lugard's view that an educated African élite could easily engage in political subversion. Sir Hugh Clifford, the Catholic Governor-General of Nigeria from 1919 to 1926, may have been critical of the school system, but he also accused British expatriates of being afraid of African advancement. Hussey's reforms seemed to vindicate this allegation. Primary education was extremely basic and skills training was restricted to agriculture and handicrafts; West African certification replaced prestigious English examinations at the Middle School level; and third level awards were officially defined as inferior to those from British institutions. Such developments were regarded by most missionaries as serious constraints on the advancement of Nigerians, and considerable opposition was engendered among Christian groups.[52] Catholic missionaries, like others, feared that after much good work their efforts would be negated, that there would be a reversion to illiteracy and paganism, and that political discontent would be fomented among Nigerians.[53] Missionary endeavours had concentrated on schools and success, in terms of converts and the development of a Catholic community, was based on them. Government restrictions not only threatened the *status quo* but also prevented the continued expansion of the missionary field, especially in the north.

The genuine difference in philosophy and method between missionary and administrator in Nigeria was manifested in deliberate local official interference in missionary activities[54] and to a large extent this was the result of Colonial Office opposition to uncontrolled missionary expansion, particularly in the north. There was extreme sensitivity about arousing the wrath of the emirs and missionary incursion into the north was severely curtailed. There were, in other words, areas where the missionaries were not wanted. In December 1930 J.H. Oldham, Secretary of the World Missionary Conference, wrote to Sir Graeme Thomson, the retiring Governor-General, complaining that the policy contravened earlier government pronouncements about religious freedom and toleration and that local officials were obstructive and 'irritating'. Thomson, who had informed the Colonial Office that his administrators had to handle 'some very rebellious missionaries', advised Oldham that the policy remained unchanged. Limited expansion had been permitted by Thomson after 1927[55] but he wrote to Oldham, 'I wish to impress upon you again the supreme importance of the selection for posts in the Northern Provinces of broadminded men of tact and good education. . . .'[56] Of course, missionaries had one view of civilizing the African; the administrator had another. Administrators claimed that the missionaries produced relatively well educated but rootless and potentially subversive individuals. Colonial officials preferred a more deferential African based within subservient communities. More importantly, the Colonial Office did not wish the missionaries to enter the northern territories and destabilize Muslim educational and social arrangements.[57]

In developing the policy of indirect rule, colonial officials had introduced the concept of African administered schools into Nigeria before the Great War. They were encouraged in the inter-war period, especially in those areas in the Northern Province inadequately served by mission schools. In the Southern and Eastern Provinces missionaries and the more discerning Africans viewed these secular schools, often administered by illiterate African chiefs and tribal leaders, as poor alternatives to the education provided by the missionaries. The Nigerian nationalist press also demonstrated that educated Nigerians, anxious to assume control themselves, were extremely sceptical about the value and effectiveness of Native Administration schools and the motives of the colonial power in promoting them. There were others who suggested that missionaries were afraid that they would be compelled to alter their methods, face competition, and lose their influence.[58] The reduction in Nigerian educational expenditure in the early 1930s compounded the situation. The salaries of teachers in mission schools were cut by 15%.[59]

Hinsley maintained the stance he had taken in Kenya. At Lagos in 1929, he and the Ordinaries and Mission Superiors had resolved to adopt the resolutions of the Kenyan Ordinaries' conference of October 1928. They would co-operate but would not cede their rights and their preferred option was to deal with central administration rather than local African councils. In this way they could at least guarantee some income and avoid the hostility of those who were not only anti-Catholic but also uneducated. Earlier British efforts to influence Native Administration Schools in British Cameroon by forcing them to introduce a minimum of moral training had failed. Catholic missionaries considered that the secularism of such schools threatened all their achievements and the continued existence of Catholic schools. Speaking on behalf of the Ordinaries of Nigeria and the British Cameroon in 1934, Bishop Francis O'Rourke, Vicar Apostolic of Benin Coast, said that all Catholic missionary authorities opposed Native Administration Schools which they regarded as secular, superfluous and a waste of money. The *Nigerian Daily Times* expressed its agreement with this opinion and discouraged the policy of dividing educational administration and funding between central and local authorities. Nevertheless, Hinsley and the Ordinaries were unable to resolve the situation, which continued into the 1940s.[60]

A contentious issue among missionaries was that of reconciling the primary spiritual purpose of the missionary with the work of teaching. Hinsley addressed this dilemma in July 1932. 'To reconcile the demands of the sacred ministry,' he wrote, 'with the technical and routine duties of school direction would seem under the circumstances superhuman.' It was a situation familiar to him. He had been a priest and headteacher in Bradford; he had been a missioner and lecturer in Sydenham; and he had been a priest and college rector in Rome. He was conscious that there were not enough missionaries and was also aware of the bureaucratic demands for higher educational standards and the need for specialist educationalists. Such demands necessarily impacted upon missionary resources. The difficulties were real and would continue as long as African education was in its early stages of development. It was a problem not easily solved but Hinsley was optimistic that the steady recruitment of properly trained missionary sisters and brothers would bring some relief 'to the harassed apostolic pastors'. Above all, he pointed to the solution and the alternatives should that not be realised:

> More priests for Africa's conversion must be forthcoming at the earliest possible moment: now is the opportunity given us for immense gain of souls: the opportunity neglected, the gain will go to the many-headed monster of error, secularism, materialism, at best to sectarianism.[61]

Training missionaries in the latest educational methods had to be implemented, however, and in 1931 and 1932 Hinsley negotiated with the Colonial Office and principals of Catholic teacher training colleges in England for the provision of one-year training courses in modern teaching techniques, the use of English, and an understanding of the English educational system. They were to be provided at St Mary's College, Strawberry Hill, and St Charles's, Kensington.[62] The Colonial Office wished the Catholics to work together in the scheme and Hinsley successfully enlisted the Jesuit Archbishop Alban Goodier,[63] formerly Archbishop of Bombay and Roman Catholic representative on the Advisory Committee on Education in the Colonies, to liaise with the Colonial Office, the training colleges, and London County Council. In exchange for government funding, the teachers were to return to the mission and work in schools receiving grants-in-aid. In April 1931 the Joint Board of Catholic Missions accepted the courses and in Africa the Ordinaries and Superiors were encouraged to make use of them. On 2 December 1932 R. V. Vernon at the Colonial Office informed Fr Basil Gudgeon of the Joint Board that both the courses at St Mary's and St Charles's had been approved.[64] The impact of such developments, however, would only be felt after Hinsley's departure from Africa.

Hinsley himself appeared to be not entirely satisfied with his role as Apostolic Delegate. The Church had made progress in numerical terms and in the development of ecclesiastical structures but the Apostolic Delegate found that he could not impose the Vatican will through a remit that was as wide as that of the Visitation had been specific. Vigilance of missionary activities was difficult. Based at Mombasa, he could not easily travel to all areas within his jurisdiction. Travelling was time-consuming and costly and his expenses did not cover his requirements. His car had been provided by the Catholic Union of Great Britain, Fr Giersbach was unpaid, and he employed three servants. He summed his difficulties in a letter to Cardinal Pietro Fumasoni-Biondi who had succeeded Cardinal van Rossum as Prefect of Propaganda in 1933:

> The difficulty of establishing new Delegations, especially in these critical times, is readily understood. Yet I consider it my duty to inform the Sacred Congregation of the needs above indicated and the somewhat strange position of the Mombasa Delegation due to the vagueness of its designation and the vast extent, at least nominally, of its territory.[65]

Carlton Hall, home of the Stapleton family, where Hinsley's mother worked in service.

LEFT: *Hinsley's red brick family home at 15 North End, Carlton.*

BELOW: *St Mary's Church, Carlton, which was opened in 1842 and where Hinsley was baptised.*

*Arthur Hinsley as a student at the Venerable English College, Rome. He stands in the
centre of the back row; in the centre at the front is Bishop Giles.*

ABOVE: *Fr Hinsley as a curate at St Anne's, Keighley.*

OPPOSITE: *St Cuthbert's College, Ushaw, where Hinsley was a student and later a professor.*

ABOVE: *Fr Hinsley with the first teachers and students of St Bede's outside the school in Drewton Street, Bradford.*

LEFT: *Fr Hinsley as the first headmaster of St Bede's Grammar School, Bradford.*

OPPOSITE TOP: *The Church of St Edward the Confessor, Sutton Park.*

OPPOSITE BOTTOM: *Our Lady and St Philip Neri, Sydenham, where Hinsley served as Rector from 1911 until 1917. The church was demolished following severe bomb damage in World War II.*

ABOVE: *Cardinal Francis Aidan Gasquet OSB, Cardinal Protector of the Venerable English College and Hinsley's patron in Rome.*

OPPOSITE TOP: *St John's College, Wonersh.*

OPPOSITE BOTTOM: *St John's College Wonersh. The chapel.*

ABOVE: *Mgr Hinsley when appointed Rector of the Venerable English College, Rome.*

RIGHT: *Outside the Venerable English College, Rome, in the 1920s.*

OPPOSITE: *Pope Benedict XV, who supported the restoration of the Venerable English College, Rome.*

ABOVE: *Bishop Hinsley's coat of arms as Rector of the Venerabile. The seed being sown refers to seminarians and the harvest of souls. The motto is 'They return rejoicing'. Like their predecessors from the English College, priests are going to work on the home mission.*

OPPOSITE: *The celebratory dinner in the Venerabile following Hinsley's episcopal consecration in 1926. Included are (left to right): Bishop Amigo, Bishop Hinsley, Cardinal Gasquet and Cardinal Merry del Val.*

ATLANTIC

OCEAN

EUROPE

MEDITERRANEAN SEA

ASIA

MOROCCO

MOROCCO

ALGERIA

TUNISIA

LIBYA

EGYPT

Cairo

ARABIA

RED SEA

Nile R.

RIO DE ORO

FRENCH WEST AFRICA

GAMBIA

SENEGAL

PORTUGUESE GUINEA

FRENCH GUINEA

Freetown

SIERRA LEONE

LIBERIA

IVORY COAST

GOLD COAST

DAHOMEY

Niger R.

NIGERIA

CAMEROON

RIO MUNI

FRENCH EQUATORIAL AFRICA

Congo R.

BELGIAN CONGO

CABINDA

ANGLO-EGYPTIAN SUDAN

ETHIOPIA

ERITREA

FRENCH SOMALILAND

BRITISH SOMALILAND

ITALIAN SOMALILAND

UGANDA

KENYA

URUNDI

Kilimanjaro

TANGANYIKA

Zanzibar

ATLANTIC

OCEAN

ANGOLA (PORTUGUESE WEST AFRICA)

KATANGA

RHODESIA

MOZAMBIQUE (PORT. EAST AFRICA)

MADAGASCAR

SOUTHWEST AFRICA

BECHUANA-LAND

TRANS-VAAL

Johannesburg

UNION OF

ORANGE FREE STATE

NATAL

BASUTOLAND

SOUTH AFRICA

Cape Town

CAPE PROVINCE

INDIAN

OCEAN

ABOVE: *Africa 1919-39 showing the colonies visited by Hinsley during his time as Apostolic Visitor and Apostolic Delegate.*

OPPOSITE: *Pope Pius XI, the Pope of the Missions.*

LEFT: *Cardinal Willem Marinus van Rossum CSSR, Prefect of Propaganda Fide (Congregation for the Propagation of the Faith).*

BELOW: *Bishop Hinsley with an African chief during his period as Apostolic Visitor.*

Chapter Nine

BUILDING THE AFRICAN CHURCH

The Growth of the African Catholic Community

The parts of Hinsley's reports to Propaganda that could be made public and which placed the Church's advance in a favourable light were given due prominence in *Fides*. In particular, the growth of the Catholic community was celebrated by the frequent publication of statistics. Accepting that 'the cynic describes statistics as the superlative degree of inexactitude', Hinsley nevertheless bombarded Propaganda with as many as he could lay hands on. They were for him, Propaganda and the Pope, evidence of startling missionary progress in Africa. They also served to enhance Hinsley's reputation in Rome although he would never consider them in such a way.[1] Sometimes using the name *Pistis* ('Faith'), but more often under his own title, Hinsley reported in great detail on the Church's progress. In 1935, under the headline, 'Africa in the Van of Missionary Progress', *Fides* published figures for the final year of Hinsley's delegacy. 'The progress of the Catholic Missions in Africa', it stated, 'does not seem always and everywhere to be realised.' Readers were referred to the recently published *Guida delle Missioni Cattoliche* and figures were presented to illustrate 'the brilliant progress of the Church in British Africa, East and West.'[2]

In 1931 there were 1,136,770 Catholics, including catechumens, in East Africa, representing an increase of 76,392 since 1930. The majority (412,733) were in Uganda. In October 1930 over 70 missionary priests, brothers and sisters passed through Dar-es-Salaam into East Africa thereby, to some extent at least, meeting Hinsley's aspirations for more missionary personnel. By 1931 633 European and African priests, 224 lay brothers, 844 European and African sisters, and 8,680 catechists served the Catholic community. There were over 174,000 pupils in mission schools.[3]

Hinsley was aware that quantity did not always equate with quality and in Africa the variety of geographical, social and political conditions rendered almost every mission unique. A summary of missionary progress

161

in East Africa during 1932 and 1933 illustrated the numerical variations and also the relationships between the various facets of Catholic missionary activity. Hinsley readily explained some of the differences. There were, for example, few Catholics in the Sudan because of the destruction of missions by Muslims who prevented evangelization by 'a vast track of fanatic hatred', and 'the unpromising character of the tribes.' To the south in sparsely populated Tanganyika, the Great War and its aftermath had retarded progress but, according to Hinsley, missionaries were 'making consoling headway'.[4] By 1934 the number of Catholics in East Africa had risen by 88,569 since 1933. 913 priests including 96 African priests, 421 European and 39 African lay brothers, and 997 and 623 African sisters served Catholics within the same areas. By any standards, this was a striking advance. In addition, there were over 10,000 African catechists. 330,000 catechumens were preparing for baptism, and over 240,000 children were being educated in 5,891 elementary schools.[5]

Progress in West Africa did not equal that of East and Central Africa. Hinsley reported that missionaries in these regions faced many problems – climate, terrain, history, and the character of the population – and emphasised the difficulty of staffing the missions. Nevertheless, there had been an increase of just under 30,000 Catholics between 1933 and 1934.[6] In Northern Nigeria the small Catholic population had been augmented by the migration of Catholic Nigerians from the Southern Province after the opening of railway routes to the north. And although colonial regulations attempted to restrict Catholic and Protestant missionaries in the north to rural areas, Catholic incomers migrated to towns such as Kano, and Kaduna. Here and along the railway routes, missionary stations, churches and schools were established and priests ministered to Catholics in camps established by the government for migrant workers.[7] In the Northern Province in 1930 there were 3,950 Catholics, six missions, fourteen schools, and 867 pupils. By 1934 these figures were correspondingly 5,396, six, 27 and 1,790 but the Church was migrant rather than indigenous.[8] In 1934 the figures, West Africa were: Nigeria and British Cameroon 227,356; Gold Coast and British Togoland, 111,682; Sierra Leone, 7,198; and Gambia, 2,900, giving a total of 349,136. Twenty-four European brothers, 138 European and six African sisters, and 2,896 African catechists assisted 249 European and six African priests. Approximately 183,000 were being prepared for baptism and there were over 73,000 pupils in 1,069 elementary schools.[9]

Hinsley was forever optimistic. Even in 1931, at the height of the economic crisis, he wrote of an 'undaunted perseverance' that drove him and others on. Nor was he deflected by the complaints of other denominations who claimed missionary rights or the persistent attempts by administrators to restrict missionary activity to geographical zones. In October 1932, in a report on the Benedictines in East Africa, he bluntly expressed his opinion of those who would stand in the way of Catholic progress:

> This amazing recovery and progress of the Benedictine Mission in Tanganyika is not viewed with equanimity by non-Catholic missionaries. Some there are who would restrict this onward march by artificial boundaries. Each 'denomination', they consider, should be assigned to it a special and exclusive district. We have heard of the system before – *cujus regio, ejus religio*; but the failure of such a scheme was, and is, as certain as its conception is preposterous. The liberty of the Black man is as sacred as that of the White man. In the name of consistency we urge that that those who go about scattering bibles and crying up private judgement should not imprison freedom of conscience within lines drawn upon a map. The Catholic Church has the Divine Commission to preach the Gospel to 'every creature'. Her apostles cannot permit that the tribes who call for their teaching and ministrations, should be forced to wait till this or that other body of missionaries without a clear mission find it convenient to intervene.[10]

The expansion of Benedictine missions and those of other institutes across Africa naturally aroused hostility and impaired relations with Protestant denominations. The contemporary commentator J.W.C. McDougall wrote that 'differences between the missions are so immense that co-operation at any time is a signal triumph of grace.'[11]

In Nigeria all missionary expansion faced the determined and combined opposition of Muslims and colonial officers. Before 1927 the government severely restricted all Christian missionary expansion but a relaxation of the rules by Governors-General Thomson and Cameron allowed missionaries to expand into prescribed and carefully delineated 'pagan' areas. Expansion was dependent upon the acquisition of a 'certificate of occupancy' and this in turn was linked to the missionaries agreeing to teach Classes of Religious Instruction in secular schools. Lukewarm about delivering 'C.R.I.' but eager to have certificates, Protestant and Catholic missionaries resisted either official or other denominational attempts to be confined to zones. In the Kabba region, Holy Ghost Fathers and Protestant missionaries disputed each other's territory so much between 1932 and 1934 that colonial administrators were compelled to adjudicate.[12] Confronted with such altercations, local officials simply found new reasons for withholding certificates of occupancy. Public and acrimonious disagreements among missionaries made it easier for them to discourage expansion. In his critique of British administration in Nigeria, the former colonial officer, W.C. Crocker, wrote that the central issue for administrators was Christianity versus Islam and not inter-Christian rivalry or Christianity versus African deism or any other form of worship. Christianity, he argued, was generally ill-suited to Nigerians, that few really understood its tenets, that it was not as structured as Islam, and that it was being introduced into Africa as it declined in Europe. The vague notions of Christianity with its inner morality and self-discipline were likely to create anarchy for the African. However, he wrote, 'Just as Islam appears to be a better religion for the African than Christianity, so Roman Catholicism appears to be better than Protestantism. It makes more allowance for his human nature, and, there being no right of private judgement, it lays down exact rules'. The Catholic parish, he continued, also replaced tribal groups.[13]

When, in 1932, Propaganda sent the Capuchins to Barotseland and the Conventuals to the Northern Rhodesian Copperbelt, 'Catholic missions were opened everywhere, often on the doorstep of a Protestant mission.'[14] In 1934, Dr Diana Brown, a Protestant medical missionary in Northern Rhodesia, wrote that

> The Romanists have arrived. We do not propose giving way to Rome but shall, with God's help, go on. It is a tremendous pity, however, that in so huge a continent so much of which is still unoccupied by a Christian body, there should be any invasions such as this, or rivalry as is scarcely avoidable following such an invasion.[15]

Such sentiments had little effect upon Hinsley, and his unsympathetic view of ecumenical collaboration was stated very clearly in a reply to Fr Jan van Sambeek in May 1934 on the issue of Catholic children attending non-Catholic schools. The White Father had forbidden Catholic children to attend non-Catholic schools but he could neither provide Catholic schools nor Catholic teachers. By this time Hinsley had left Africa and was in Rome but the retired Delegate's response was predictable and categorical:

Establish yourself firmly in those parts not worked by Protestants . . . then with the help of your teachers extend yourself to Protestant areas . . . and establish your own schools. We can never surrender the principle: Catholic schools for Catholic children in Catholic atmosphere and with Catholic teachers. . . .[16]

Faced with this uncompromising instruction, van Sambeek wrote to Propaganda and was advised that in such difficult circumstances he could not prevent Catholic children from attending non-Catholic schools. Contrary to Propaganda's perceived policy and earlier directions, Hinsley's advice was ignored. Fr Oger wrote that Hinsley's reply to van Sambeek 'showed a complete ignorance of the situation: there were no 'parts not worked by Protestants'; and there were no teachers.'[17]

Ecclesiastical Structures

The creation of new ecclesiastical structures in missionary lands was an integral part of Pius XI's plan to develop young Churches. In Africa, Propaganda responded to the continued growth in Catholic numbers, increased missionary activity, and changes in education by constantly developing organisational arrangements for an effective ministry. These devolved upon missions, prefectures and vicariates. Hinsley had observed the deployment of missionary personnel, the effectiveness of missionary structures, and the exercising of ecclesiastical authority during his time as Apostolic Visitor. As Apostolic Delegate he was unable to interfere in the affairs of the Ordinaries but he wielded great influence. He advised Propaganda on the status of the African Church under his jurisdiction and, where necessary, suggested refinements to the organs of Church government, the introduction of new missionary institutes, and the reallocation of missionary jurisdiction.

In two separate developments Hinsley was involved with the Holy Ghost Fathers. The combination of events showed him to be quite ruthless if not entirely successful. In early March 1933, summarising the Holy Ghost Fathers' pioneering exploits and successes in East Africa, Hinsley wrote that further organisational developments were contemplated. Nairobi was to be a new vicariate dismembered from the Vicariate of Zanzibar which embraced Zanzibar, Pemba, and a large portion of Kenya. The islands of Zanzibar and Pemba, forming a distinct British Protectorate, were 'to be speeded up in the race for excellence' by being erected into a separate vicariate. Thus, he concluded, 'Zanzibar in its 70th year is renewing its youth and giving birth to a most important new Vicariate of Nairobi. For such courage and supernatural enterprise, gratitude to God and unstinting admiration are due from all who have at heart the cause of the African missions.'[18]

On 24 March 1933 Sir Richard Rankine, the British Resident in Zanzibar, informed the Colonial Office that Hinsley had expressed dissatisfaction with the lack of progress in the Holy Ghost missions on Zanzibar and Pemba and put forward a proposal to re-allocate missionary responsibilities in the vicariate. The scheme necessitated the removal of the Holy Ghost Fathers from the islands and their replacement by German missionaries, the Benedictines of St Ottilien. The Germans would be given their own vicariate based on Zanzibar. The Holy Ghost Fathers would extend their activities from Bagamoyo and Kilima-Njaro and form the nucleus of the new mainland vicariate of Nairobi. The Spiritan Bishop John Heffernan, who had only been appointed Vicar Apostolic of Zanzibar in 1932, naturally objected. Whilst he knew that Hinsley could not replace him, Heffernan saw the redeployment of his institute's personnel as a serious threat to his influence and that of the Spriritans and sought the informal advice of Rankine. The Resident 'guardedly expressed his objections' to Hinsley's plan.[19]

Rankine, who considered Hinsley to be 'loyal and above suspicion', sought further advice from London on 25 April 1933. Senior civil servants in the Colonial Office had no prior knowledge of the scheme and were unsure whether Hinsley was acting alone or whether his plan was 'part of some general RC movement'. It was suggested that Cardinal Bourne might be consulted, as he had been previously, but the idea was dropped due to Bourne's illness and the realisation that one archbishop could not interfere in the affairs of another. The employment of German missionaries raised a more important political issue. German Protestant missionaries were already working on the mainland and therefore German Catholic missionaries could not be denied access. But the revival of an organised German missionary effort through German institutes was a potential problem. Officials were of the opinion though that if German 'political propaganda' did appear it would be more likely to come from German Protestants rather than German Catholic missionaries who were 'much more amenable to control' by the British. Another prejudice forced its way to the surface when one official wrote that he 'would far rather have a German than a native of the Irish Free State – which appears to be the alternative. . . .'

The Colonial Office was not in favour of Hinsley's suggestion and advised Rankine that Heffernan and Hinsley should settle the issue themselves. Rankine was told that he could not interfere with Archbishop Hinsley's 'dispositions' but that he should nevertheless try to discourage him. Care was needed in handling the two prelates for 'the Roman Catholic Church usually controls its missionaries a good deal more effectively than do the authorities of other denominations'. He was counselled to 'walk warily'.[20]

Hinsley's reason for attempting to reorganise the Zanzibar vicariate probably lay in his comparison of the Holy Ghost Fathers' methods and results with those of other institutes. During the 1920s the Catholic population of the Zanzibar Vicariate had grown slowly, and educational progress was unspectacular compared with other areas of Africa. By 1931 there were approximately 66,000 Catholics in the vicariate and in the following year there were 70,000.[21] Superficially, this represented progress but the statistics concealed regional variations, especially between the mainland interior, the islands and mainland coastal areas. Islam dominated some regions of the vicariate and Catholic missionaries faced an uncompromising battle to win souls. Hinsley admitted as much in his report on missionary progress in British East Africa for 1932 when he stated that

> One other observation is necessary to explain the comparatively fruitless efforts in the coastal regions of East Africa. It is just in such parts that Mohammedan influence is greatest, and it is well know that the chief block to progress is Islam. So it is not surprising to find that in Bangeuolo of Northern Rhodesia with its 35 Fathers, 12 Brothers and 37 Sisters there are more visible gains than in Kenya and Zanzibar where there are 90 Fathers, 30 Brothers and 193 Sisters. Along the coast of Kenya and in the islands of Zanzibar and Pemba the religion of Mohammed is strong, while in the highlands and more particularly in Kavirondo (Kisumu) Catholicity is more free to advance.[22]

Despite these almost insurmountable obstacles facing the Spiritans and other institutes, Hinsley displayed frustration that the Spiritans in particular had not done more and was irritated by their lack of progress. Yet he had earlier spoken with admiration for their achievements in the Vicariates of Kilima-Njaro and Zanzibar. The Catholic population was growing and there were flourishing schools and seminaries. He reserved special praise for the Catholic High School of Kabaa near Nairobi, 'perhaps the finest scholastic establishment of East Africa'.[23]

The resignation in 1930 of Bishop Neville, the Spiritan Vicar Apostolic of Zanzibar, and the death of the Spiritan Bishop Grogarty, Vicar Apostolic of Kilima-Njaro, may also have influenced Hinsley into thinking that the time was ripe for change and the introduction of a more vibrant approach.[24] Hinsley described Neville as a man of 'gentle zeal'. Maybe his zeal was too gentle for a man of Hinsley's determination and enthusiasm. In 1932 he had reported with satisfaction that the mission of Kilimbero Valley had been ceded by the Consolata Fathers to the Capuchins of Dar-es-Salaam 'thus promising a greater and faster development'. Hinsley wanted the same for the Vicariate of Zanzibar but on this occasion his plan did not materialise.[25] Both Neville and Grogarty were replaced by Spiritans – Heffernan and Joseph Byrne. The only change in the ecclesiastical structure of Kenya was the creation in 1932 of the Vicariate of Kisumu from the Prefecture of Kavirondo. The new vicariate was placed under the direction of the Mill Hill Missionaries.[26]

Hinsley may have been thwarted but his position reflected the view of Rankine's predecessor, Sir Alan Pim, who, approaching the educational problem from a different perspective, reported that in those areas under the control of the Arab aristocracy there was a 'lack of dynamism'. Since 1924 the British had introduced political changes on Zanzibar with the intention of moving it towards colonial status but the dominance of the Arab aristocracy, complicated by the presence of Asian and African cultures, prevented a smooth transition to indirect rule. A report to the Colonial Office in 1932 stated that in education 'racial, class and caste distinctions have crystallised into stagnation' and there were no effective policies to counter this and provide an effective government education service. Although Koranic schools on Zanzibar had increased their enrolments in the 1920s, there had been very little progress in any other form of education. Muslim opposition to other schools was also exacerbated by Zanzibar's economic decline. The government had little money to invest in education and grants-in-aid to mission schools were reduced by 45% between 1930 and 1934. On the mainland, in those coastal areas facing the island, missionaries confronted the same major problem: 'the strength of Islam prevented any noteworthy success'. On Zanzibar Christian progress was largely confined to immigrant Africans from the mainland. So, although Hinsley was critical of missionary progress, he was being less than fair to those who faced such fierce and uncompromising opposition. The Spiritans had ministered in the vast Vicariate of Zanzibar and its predecessor, the prefecture of Zanguebar, since 1863 and had experienced bewildering political changes. In addition, the withdrawal of German missionaries from the vicariate during the Great War had seriously weakened Catholic missionary endeavour on both islands and in Kenya. A renewed missionary campaign, therefore, had to start almost from scratch after 1918. Little wonder that the Spiritans were overwhelmed and progress was so slow.[27]

In Southern Nigeria the Holy Ghost Fathers were more aggressive in their approach than their confrères in East Africa but were hampered in the fulfilment of their apostolate by a serious personnel shortage. Following a report to Rome, Bishop Joseph Shanahan was charged by Propaganda, *sub gravi*, to increase the number of missionaries in his vicariate. In 1920 only nineteen European priests and 928 Nigerian catechists ministered to over 25,000 Catholics and 71,000 catechumens. By 1929 there were over 81,000 Catholics and over 88,000 catechumens.[28] It was a difficult situation for Shanahan who was not only concerned by his confrères being so heavily outnumbered by Nigerian catechists but was also anxious about the quality of doctrinal instruction imparted by his local assistants. So, without the knowledge or permission of the Council of the Holy Ghost Fathers in Paris, Shanahan went to Ireland and persuaded Cardinal Logue and the Irish Hierarchy to provide temporary secular missionaries for Nigeria. They agreed that for five years he could recruit from among recently ordained Maynooth priests who were awaiting appointments in Ireland.[29]

Although the Irish bishops agreed to Shanahan's proposal, it was not entirely popular. Young priests found that the United States of America was a more amenable environment in which to wait for an Irish appointment. Between 1920 and 1926 twenty recently ordained priests went annually to the U.S.A. compared with only two per year to Southern Nigeria. Spiritan missionaries in Nigeria did not view the proposal favourably either. Some Spiritans objected to Shanahan's unilateral initiative and asserted that 'he would rather see the whole Congregation go to the devil than humble himself.'[30] French Spiritans, already uneasy at the emphasis on schools and isolated because of English language restrictions imposed by education ordinances, were anxious about being marginalized and outnumbered by Irish seculars and Irish

Spiritans. Using the example of the Maynooth Mission to China, others suspected that there was a deliberate intention among some seculars, both in Ireland and among those who volunteered for Nigeria, to establish a secular vicariate based on Spiritan African territory. It was also noted with some dismay that there was indifference to Spiritan fund raising in Ireland where they had rich and exclusive secondary schools. Irish seculars did not experience the same problem and would be able to raise sufficient funds for a separate vicariate.

Shanahan's handling of the situation and his style of management led to defeat for the Irish Spiritans. Eventually drawn in, the Spiritan Council in Paris proposed that Spiritans from the wealthy U.S.A. Province be drafted in to Nigeria and that the vicariate be divided between the Irish and Americans, but the Irish Province resisted this. The Council also suggested that the seculars, whom they could ill afford to lose, be placed under the guidance of their own men. The Spiritans in Nigeria accepted this but Shanahan failed to provide adequate induction and left the young seculars without direction. But more importantly, neither the Council nor Shanahan reckoned with the personalities and determination of the seculars, Fr Patrick Whitney, ordained in 1920 for the Diocese of Ardagh, and Fr Thomas Ronayne, ordained in 1913 for the Archdiocese of Dublin.

Whitney had been recruited by Shanahan on his visit to Maynooth and on account of perceived public antipathy against the Spiritans had actively engaged in fund raising and propaganda for them.[31] He had also volunteered for Nigeria where he quickly came to the conclusion that the Spiritans not only lacked organisation but failed to provide adequate training and direction for the seculars. He was also concerned to hear of the proposed division between the American and Irish Spiritans. Accordingly, Whitney felt unable to continue extolling the virtues of his erstwhile mentors. The Spiritan Council considered the possibility of incardinating the seculars, but Whitney and his colleagues refused this alternative and instead, confirming the earlier fears of some Spiritans, decided to establish their own missionary institute staffed by Irish secular priests and unfettered by history and reputation. In 1925 Ronayne visited Rome to discuss and promote the formation of an Irish secular missionary institute with its own vicariate in Nigeria. Whilst there he met with Hinsley at the *Venerabile*.

Hinsley was the catalyst in the formation of the secular institute and in deciding the fate of both Shanahan and the Vicariate of Southern Nigeria. When he undertook his visitation of East Africa in 1928 he was not impressed by some Holy Ghost Fathers whose achievements, attitudes and moral standards, he claimed, left much to be desired. Some Spiritans felt that Hinsley was opposed to their interests, and Shanahan may have had prior warning of Hinsley's zealous and critical approach. Probably fearing the worst, he became restless as the time approached for the Apostolic Visitor's arrival. Fox claims that in July 1929 Shanahan met Hinsley at Calabar and explained that he was departing immediately for Ireland leaving Bishop Charles Heerey, his coadjutor since 1927, in charge of the vicariate. With Heerey, Hinsley discussed the shortage of priests and convinced him of the beneficial impact that an influx of English speaking seculars would have.[32]

Hinsley was subsequently unimpressed by the situation in Southern Nigeria. So appalled was he by what he later observed of Shanahan's leadership and organisational skills that he considered his character and administration to be unworthy of a person of his experience and position – a serious and damning judgement on Shanahan's stewardship and on a fellow bishop. In Hinsley's opinion, the ailing Shanahan now lacked the necessary qualities of a spiritual leader and administrator and consequently the Spiritans were not completely fulfilling their missionary obligations.

From Sierra Leone Hinsley wrote to Whitney saying that he favoured the formation of 'a society under the direct orders of the Holy See' – an ambitious plan but one which, if it materialized, would immediately aid the Nigerians – and invited him to Rome to expedite matters.[33] Soon after his return to Rome in November 1929 and following his reports to Propaganda and the Spiritan Council on Shanahan's vicariate, Hinsley invited Whitney to formally propose the formation of a new institute and arranged for him to meet with van Rossum. On 14 December van Rossum verbally approved St Patrick's Missionary Society and directed it to work in Southern Nigeria subject to the approval of the Irish Hierarchy. In January 1930 the Hierarchy formally approved the formation of the secular institute.[34] On being informed of the development, Bishop Heerey observed that 'the Irish Province is dead as far as missionary work goes.'[35] Hinsley, meanwhile, had invited Shanahan to Rome on the understanding that both he and Heerey were in favour of the introduction of the Irish seculars. If Shanahan failed to arrive, wrote Hinsley to Whitney, 'things will be settled with or without him . . . starving souls cannot wait on personal convenience.' If Shanahan was afraid of Spriritan wrath then he (Hinsley) would bear it. Shanahan duly arrived and on 8 January 1930 met with Cardinal Marchetti and Hinsley to be informed of the fate of his vicariate.[36]

Shanahan's vicariate was dismembered. As the result of negotiations during 1930 involving the Irish Hierarchy and the Spiritans, Whitney's secular priests were given the Calabar and Ogoja areas for a trial period and in October 1930 seven seculars left Ireland for Nigeria.[37] German Spiritans were assigned to the Benne area and the missions of Muri and Munchi; whilst the Irish Spiritans retained jurisdiction over Igboland and the Rivers and Delta areas east of the River Niger.[38] St Patrick's Missionary Society, the name adopted by Whitney for his new institute, was formally established in March 1932[39] and in 1934 the Vicariate of Southern Nigeria was replaced by the Vicariate of Onitsha-Owerri under the leadership of Bishop Heerey. Spiritans in Nigeria felt bitterly disappointed that the Mother House in Paris had not been more robust in 'the struggle with Hinsley' and were hurt by Propaganda's ungrateful division of the territory where they had laboured so long and at great human cost. They had lost some of their most established and wealthiest missions.

Hinsley insisted with Propaganda that Shanahan, now ill and partially sighted, should resign and enable his young coadjutor to take control over Southern Nigeria and tighten up its administration. On 9 February 1931 van Rossum instructed the Spiritan Council to request Shanahan's resignation and warned them that Shanahan should not know that either Rome or the Apostolic Delegate had been involved in the decision. In March, Shanahan was asked by Superior General Fr Le Hunsec to tender his resignation to Rome, which he duly did. Van Rossum replied that 'after mature consideration and the sanction of the Holy Father, his resignation was accepted.'[40] Shanahan had expected to be the first superior of St Patrick's Missionary Society, which he had encouraged from the outset, but no offer came. Instead, he retired in 1931 after having ordained the first Nigerian priest and returned to Ireland. It was rather an unfortunate end to a missionary life of high endeavour and substantial achievement, but neither Hinsley nor van Rossum would allow sentiment to deflect them from their purpose. To his credit, Shanahan did not bear a grudge against the seculars or harbour antipathy against those who had made unkind comments about him but was pleased that his hard pressed Spiritans had been given support in the form of a fully-fledged missionary institute. Hinsley wrote that Shanahan 'was delighted' with the new arrangements.[41] For his part, Hinsley had concluded a successful outcome to a serious problem and had played an important part in the founding of a new missionary institute which would go on to work alongside the Spiritans and be instrumental in the further development of the African Church.

Hinsley's attempts to impose a new order in East Africa involved the Mill Hill Missionaries but were less controversial than his relations with the Spiritans. In 1918 Bishop John Biermans, Vicar Apostolic of the Upper Nile, convened a meeting of Mill Hill missionaries to discuss their ministry in East Africa. It was decided to sub-divide the vicariate into four districts – Buganda, Busoga, Bukedi and Kavirondo. The missionaries in each district were to hold six-monthly meetings and report to Biermans on the outcomes. Two representatives from each district were to meet with Biermans annually. By mid-1923 the missionaries at Erigi in the Kavirondo district were convinced that 'the part of the vicariate situated in Kenya should form an entirely separate mission' and Biermans and advisers were of the same opinion.

Eight missions had been established in western Kenya from the Upper Nile Vicariate and in 1925 Propaganda approved the erection of the Prefecture Apostolic of Kavirondo under the direction of Fr Gorgonius Brandsma, a Mill Hill Missionary then working in the Belgian Congo. The new prefecture, which contained flourishing missions, was to receive £1,800 and a share in the school and factory at Buluba. Over the next few years the prefecture made very good progress in purely statistical terms. In 1927 the Catholic population was 19,014; by 1930 it was 28,599; and by 1932 it was 34,930. During the same period the number of pupils in Catholic schools rose from 8,725 to 17,055 and the number of missions grew from eight to fourteen, yet the number of priests and catechists had not increased significantly.[42] By 1932 there were only 25 priests and 949 catechists. The Mill Hill Fathers regarded Hinsley's first visit in 1928 as an opportunity to suggest the erection of a new vicariate centred on Kavirondo and under their leadership. It would be a fitting accolade to their efforts and would raise the profile of the institute.[43]

In July 1928 Brandsma wrote to Dr Schut in Rome to say that the Fathers in the Kavirondo Prefecture wanted to suggest to Hinsley that

Kavirondo be erected into a vicariate. Such a change, he argued, would be of ecclesiastical and civil benefit.[44] When Hinsley did arrive he was impressed, and thought it strange that Kavirondo was not a vicariate and Brandsma not a bishop.[45] In December 1928 Brandsma informed Schut that 'Bp Hinsley's secretary mentioned to me that he expected that we would soon be raised to a Vicariate as Bp Hinsley saw the advantages everywhere and would advocate for it everywhere.' Yet at this stage Hinsley was only Apostolic Visitor. Nevertheless, in April 1929 Brandsma confirmed that Hinsley had requested Propaganda to give consideration to the suggestion.[46] As Apostolic Delegate, and armed with more influence, Hinsley continued the lobbying. In July 1931 he informed Biermans that he had recommended to Propaganda that Kavirondo be erected to vicariate status. Excellent progress had been made, Kavirondo was a growing centre, and the residence was appropriate for a bishop. However, a cathedral would have to be built.[47] Fortified by this support, Biermans wrote to van Rossum in October 1931 and reminded him that the institute had made the same request in 1926. Van Rossum replied that he should 'await developments.'[48]

Hinsley and Brandsma, however, faced opposition to their proposal from some of the institute's personnel and dissension appeared within the ranks of the Mill Hill Fathers. Fr Herbert Doyle, mission superior at Kavirondo, informed Hinsley that some missionaries had little confidence in Brandsma and that if a new vicariate were created they would find it difficult to see his name on the terna let alone vote for him. There was some unease, he claimed, among missionaries about the Prefect's organisational ability and especially about his financial acumen. Brandsma had almost bankrupted the prefecture in an effort to expand missionary activities. Only the closure of two catechist centres and a begging tour in the U.S.A. had reduced the overdraft. The new vicariate, it had to be recognised, would begin its existence heavily in debt. Hinsley acknowledged this but the dominant and most persuasive factor for him was that Kavirondo, despite its financial instability, contained a greater number of Catholics than the other two Kenyan vicariates combined and was making impressive and substantial progress.[49] In February 1932, disturbed by developments, Doyle told Brandsma that he 'washed his hands' of financial arrangements in the prefecture but facing an overwhelming tide in favour of the new vicariate, he informed van Rossum that the institute's own visitators agreed with Hinsley and that all the Fathers now accepted the Delegate's proposal.[50]

Schut was reluctant to emphasise Doyle's serious reservations but could not conceal from Biermans the degree of clerical opposition to Brandsma.[51] Van Rossum agreed with Biermans that raising Kavirondo to vicariate status 'would contribute very largely to the progress and prestige of the Church in Kenya'[52] but the problem lay in finding a suitable Vicar Apostolic. Schut informed Biermans that van Rossum, having been fully appraised of the problem in Kenya, was worried that Brandsma's name might not even be on the terna.[53] Such an outcome would be embarrassing for the Church and for Mill Hill. To raise the prefecture to a vicariate but not simultaneously promote the Prefect would raise, or confirm, doubts about the wisdom of Brandsma's original preferment. Bransdma himself was very concerned at the subsequent slow rate of progress and in January 1933 wrote pessimistically to Schut saying that he expected 'to be removed' and that Mill Hill was 'ominously silent' on the matter.[54] Hinsley, however, was not and in June 1933 Schut informed Biermans that the Apostolic Delegate preferred Brandsma whose name eventually topped the terna. Brandsma was consecrated in the same month.[55]

In the four years of his delegacy seven new vicariates were erected – Salisbury, Bukoba, Kisumu, Kumasi, Equatorial Nile, Ruwenzori, and Onitsha-Owerri. Four new prefectures – Umtata, Bulawayo, Kaduna, and Jos, and one *abbey nullius* (Perahimo) – were erected. Some changes, for example those in Nigeria, arose out of Hinsley's dissatisfaction with Shanahan's stewardship and his practical attempt to provide a more structured approach to the needs of a rapidly expanding community. Others, for example those in East Africa, were created to facilitate the better organisation of a rapidly expanding Catholic community. In Kenya the Prefecture of Kavirondo was erected into the Vicariate of Kisumu whilst Uganda received a new mission territory in the Vicariate of Ruwenzori. The Prefecture of the Equatorial Nile was detached from northern and eastern Uganda and raised to the status of Vicariate whilst Tanganyika's ecclesiastical divisions were increased by the new divisions of Bukoba and Mwanza (formerly of the Vicariate of Nyanza), the *Abbies Nullius* of Perahimo and Ndanda (previously of the Prefecture of Lindi), and by the erection of Tukuyu. The Passionist Fathers were allocated the districts of Dodoma and Kondoa-Irangi. In Northern Rhodesia the Italian Conventuals were given charge of Ndola in the

Copper Belt region and the Irish Capuchins took over Livingstone. In 1933 the Vicariates of Bangweolo and Nyasa were divided and a new independent mission of Lwanga was established in between them. But Lwanga's appearance on the ecclesiastical map did not meet with the approval of some White Fathers. Its vastness, difficult terrain, and lack of population militated against the infusion of valuable missionary personnel and the development of a successful mission.[56] As Fr Ogez wrote, 'This inappropriate division of territory was soon apparent and was remedied four years later.' In 1937 Lwanga was reduced in size and the territorial divisions of Nyasa and Fort Jameson were readjusted. It is possible that Hinsley considered that the energetic and inspirational van Sambeek was the man to develop Lwanga for he became the first Administrator of the new mission in October 1933. His appointment as Vicar Apostolic of Tanganyika in 1936, three years of limited missionary success, and Hinsley's absence may have convinced Propaganda of the need to revise its earlier decision.[57] In the Anglo-Egyptian Sudan Kodok was erected as a new mission and in the Gold Coast Kumasi was erected as a new vicariate. As a result of the dismemberment of Southern Nigeria, the new prefectures of Benue, Jos and Calabar were established and Gambia was erected as an independent mission.[58]

Hinsley was successful in developing Church structures and creating others in response to the growth and development of the Catholic community under his supervision. When he returned to Rome in 1934 he could claim with some justification that he had redrawn the map of the Church in large parts of Africa.

An Indigenous Priesthood and Missionary Personnel

The imperative need to provide African priests for the future development of an indigenous Church was another issue to be addressed by Hinsley and his regular reports kept Propaganda abreast of progress. Developments were extremely slow, very uneven, and highlighted significant differences between East and West Africa.

In May 1931 Hinsley visited the vicariates of Nyasa and Shiré and saw the recently-opened seminaries.[59] Following his visits to Uganda, Kenya and Equatorial Nile later in the same year, he reported that although progress was slow there were positive advances. In the Equatorial Nile Prefecture the Verona Fathers at Gulu had opened a central seminary. In the Upper Nile Vicariate, the Mill Hill Fathers were building a senior seminary at Lake Victoria whilst they also had a minor seminary at Nyenga. In Uganda, under the White Fathers, there were forty-six African priests and ten missions were already in the care of indigenous priests. The major seminary at Katigondo and the minor seminary at Bukalasa were paying handsome dividends and progress was substantial. The Consolata Fathers had established a seminary at Nyeri and Hinsley had already ordained two African priests there in 1931.[60]

On 8 December 1931 Hinsley again visited the White Fathers to consecrate the new church at their seminary at Katigondo 'where the ceremonies and the plain chant were of as high an order of excellence as could be expected in any seminary in Europe.' He had every reason to be satisfied with the efforts of the White Fathers, for five African priests had been ordained at Katigondo during the year, bringing the total to 46 since 1913.[61] Two weeks later he blessed the building of the White Fathers' minor seminary and central school at Ujiji in Tanganyika. The complex had been transformed from derelict buildings abandoned by German missionaries during the war into an extensive and promising missionary centre.[62] In April 1933 Hinsley reported confidently that by looking at the number of African aspirants to the priesthood, the 'future is bright.' There had been 1,200 seminarians in 1932 but the figure had risen to 1,439 in 1933 with 1,115 in the minor and 324 in the major seminaries. Tanganyika was 'still marching ahead' with 471 minor seminarians but Uganda was 'leading the avant-garde' with 112 students at the two major seminaries of the White Fathers and Mill Hill Missionaries.[63] In the following year he reported that there were 1,339 seminarians of whom 234 were in the major seminaries.[64] Yet the development of an indigenous priesthood continued to be desperately slow. In 1932 there were only three African priests in Kenya, forty-six in Uganda, nineteen in Tanganyika, and nine in Mauritius.[65] In 1933 there was a total of seventy-eight African priests and ninety-six in the following year. The majority of these were in the Uganda Vicariate where in 1934 there were fifty-two African priests and twelve major missions were entrusted to them. The numerical progress of the Church in East Africa continued to outstrip its ability to provide missionaries and, particularly, African priests. Seminaries demanded priest-scholars; they were labour intensive and expensive. The missionaries became victims of their own success. Newcomers substantially augmented their ranks, but they were never sufficient. In 1931 663 priests ministered to just over one million Catholics.[66] In 1932 there were 845 missionary priests; and by 1932 there were 847 missionaries and 78 African priests. By 1934 1.2 million Catholics were served by 913 European missionaries and 96 African priests.[67]

In the same year there were 249 European but only 6 African priests in West Africa. Hinsley reported that caring for nearly 350,000 Catholics, preparing 183,000 catechumens and maintaining over 1,000 schools 'must task the energies of this personnel to the utmost.' The formation of an indigenous clergy, however, no matter what the cost, was taken seriously. There were 129 students in minor seminaries and twenty students in major seminaries. Quoting a Vicar Apostolic, Hinsley said that the triumph of the missions would be complete 'when the Church in Africa is manned by Africans.'[68]

The training and ordination of African priests, as already noted, was an issue that divided European missionaries. The Jesuits were particularly sensitive to accusations that they were reluctant to prepare Africans for the priesthood. In Southern Rhodesia there were over sixty Jesuits from the English Province serving parishes in and around Salisbury. Mgr Robert Brown, the Jesuit Prefect Apostolic, decided, after consulting his priests, that Africans were to be trained primarily as catechists. Although not entirely defiant, such a decision was not exactly in the spirit of recent encyclicals, which encouraged the formation of an indigenous clergy. However, Bishop Aston Chichester SJ, who succeeded Brown in 1931 and became the first Vicar Apostolic of Salisbury, held a different opinion and began to educate African boys in preparation for seminary training. After touring Uganda to witness the progress being made there under the White Fathers, he opened a seminary at Chishawasho Farm in 1933. He actions did not receive overwhelming support from the Jesuits nor did his decision to employ Dominican Sisters win approval in Rome. And Fr Philip Beisly who had been Rector of St George's College, Salisbury, and who had been appointed Superior of the Jesuit Mission in 1931, refused to provide the staff that Chichester wanted for his new seminary. Chichester struggled on: 'I must do what Rome wants but there are some of our people who do not want me to have African priests,' he wrote.[69] Meanwhile, other Jesuits parried complaints about their approach. Their critics cited developments elsewhere in Africa where indigenous clergy had taken on roles as seminary professors, mission rectors, teachers and administrators. The Society's own Visitor, Fr

William Bodkin, had reminded his Rhodesian confrères in 1925 of the Pope's intention to raise the African priesthood and hoped 'that it will not be so long delayed in its realisation.' In 1930 the Jesuits replied to Canon Joly by asserting that they did not oppose an African priesthood and 'could not afford to let it fall out of sight.' But they maintained the right to prepare seminarians in a thorough and proper fashion and opposed the presentation of immature candidates. The ordination of the first Rhodesian priest took place in 1947.[70] Although Hinsley's reports contained evidence of progress, the formation of an indigenous clergy developed very slowly in Africa compared with other missionary territories. In 1933-1934 only 9% of Africa's priests were indigenous compared with 22% in China, 42% in Japan, 57% in India, and 75% in Indo-China.[71]

Hinsley did not allow the work of the lay brothers and sisters to go unnoticed, for he realised their importance in the fulfilment of the apostolate. No one, he wrote, could rightly appreciate the work of the lay brothers until they had seen the fruits of their incomparable practical and artistic skills and he cited the cathedrals, churches, hospitals, seminaries and schools that they had built. Their skill was matched by a life of labour, poverty, and obscurity and they deserved 'reverent admiration.' He noted that in East Africa substantial numbers were from Germany, Belgium, Holland, Switzerland and France, where they received their training, but there were relatively few from England, Scotland and Wales.[72] At Perahimo, under the care of the St Ottilien Benedictines, he reported that in addition to the construction of mission buildings, lay brothers had surveyed and built roads and drained marshes. Seventeen missions were served by thirty-five monks assisted by forty-six brothers and fifty sisters from Tutzing in Bavaria. The sisters worked in the schools, hospitals and leper camps. Their work, he wrote deserved 'unbounded admiration'.[73] As the basic training of most brothers and sisters was less intellectually demanding than that of seminarians, the number of Africans in the lay apostolate grew rapidly. In 1933 there were 365 lay brothers in East Africa; by 1934 this had risen to 421. Within their ranks there were thirty-nine Africans. Among the sisters there were 623 Africans out of a total of 1,620 in 1934.[74] The situation was very different in West Africa where Hinsley reported that in 1934 the missionary territory was not so 'completely staffed as on the East Coast.' The shortcoming was particularly felt in relation to 'the body of auxiliary forces.' There were only 24 lay brothers and 138 European sisters, and 6 African sisters.[75]

The increase in the number of female missionary institutes was a significant factor in the development of the Catholic Church in Africa during the inter-war period. By 1939 there were 176 institutes of men, 247 institutes of women, and 61 institutes of brothers working on the missions.[76] However, because of the constraints of Canon Law female institutes were restricted in their activities, especially in medical work. Heenan relates, in anecdotal form, an important intervention of Hinsley that led eventually to a change in the rules governing the medical ministry of sisters. A Mother Superior requesting permission for her nuns to be trained as midwives approached the Apostolic Delegate to help improve the conditions under which African women were giving birth. Hitherto it was considered unseemly for a nun to attend a confinement. However, Hinsley saw the problem faced by both mothers and nuns and sensibly advised the Mother Superior that, whilst attendance would be a strict contravention of the Rule, the virtue of charity could not be ignored.[77] Hinsley subsequently took up the issue with Rome. The prohibition was eventually lifted in 1936 and female missionaries began to play a more central role in the wider aspects of specialist missionary provision.[78]

Hinsley's Influence

Arriving in Africa from a non-missionary background, Hinsley was, as Propaganda doubtless wished, completely objective but also completely Roman and untainted by the nationalist and institutional jealousies of the various missionary orders. He took with him to Africa an inflexible approach to the priestly ministry, a dynamic view of the contemporary missionary apostolate, and unbounded optimism in the future of the African Church.

Heenan's assessment of Hinsley's approach to the development of African Catholicism was that it was essentially pragmatic and that the Archbishop's greatest contribution was the co-ordination of missionary activity through the sheer force of his personal qualities and decisive action. According to Heenan, Hinsley was unwilling to accept that the discussion of policy should be restricted to the members of a particular religious institute or directed in a defined area exclusively by priests of similar nationality. He abhorred parochialism and nationalism and less by persuasion and exhortation than by strenuous action he welded missionary effort into a more completely unified programme. There is evidence partially to support this contention and it is likely that Heenan confirmed his own conclusions after discussing the Archbishop's African experiences with Hinsley in Westminster. It is evident that Hinsley convened meetings where his agenda and that of Propaganda compelled local leaders of different institutes and nationalities to discuss and agree common policies. They would then be expected to adhere to and implement those policies. Undoubtedly, Hinsley was a strong character and Heenan was correct in his appraisal: the Ordinaries and superiors knew that the Delegate came armed with papal authority and they respected his determination to exercise it. But Hinsley also conducted meetings with professionalism and tact. Mgr Birraux, wrote that Hinsley presided over conferences with distinction and competence. 'He was always the dauntless chief of us all, and in spite of the length of these meetings, delicate manoeuvring and his own weariness which grew as time went on, he never wavered from his purpose or lost his patience.'[79] There were, of course, those who expected him, being English and not being a missionary, to be too ready to compromise with British authorities whilst imposing Propaganda's will. His African record demonstrates this assertion to some degree. Yet notwithstanding his respect for the Empire, Hinsley's Romanism always directed his opinions and actions. It can be claimed that his ambitions for both Empire and Church coincided, but the latter always took precedence.

There were some, such as Fr Oger, who did not agree with Hinsley's approach while he was in Africa. There were others who unwittingly passed critical judgment on the extent and durability of Hinsley's achievements after he had left Africa. In 1937 Fr McCarthy, Secretary General for Education to the Catholic Missions in Tanganyika, lamented that

> ...in Tanganyika there are nine vicariates and three prefectures directed and controlled by six different missionary societies, each with its own ideas, codes of rules and regulations, its own system of education and finances and manner of life, all of which are guarded, pursued and adhered to with grim missionary determination as being the one and only. . .[80]

If this savage verdict was applied to all the colonies included in Hinsley's delegacy, then his impact was indeed only partial for the regimental independence of missionary institutes appeared to have survived Hinsley's previous onslaught. Without further evidence it is difficult to prove if this development was widespread but it is clear that during his second period in Africa Hinsley, with a different remit and restricted by distance and age, was communicating by letter and occasional visits rather than by a programme of personal visitation. His impact therefore was less immediate. He had, of course, few options for he could not replace those missionaries who failed to respond to Propaganda's bidding or colonial policies.

Yet as Apostolic Delegate Hinsley could point to a substantial increase in the Catholic population and the erection of twelve new ecclesiastical structures. Here the successful missionary efforts of others influenced his decisions for he, like some Ordinaries, saw that the administration of vast areas with newly-evangelized peoples had to be better organised and responsive to the needs of the local Church. It was a development demanded by Propaganda and one that was handled firmly by Hinsley, as the Nigerian example demonstrates. The erection of new ecclesiastical divisions cut across colonial boundaries and missionary territories, reduced the influence of institutes, and imposed a structure instantly recognizable and understood by all engaged in missionary activity, if not by Africans or colonial civil servants. But the chain of command and the essence of Church authority were established and being developed in Africa and these, despite some initial and inevitable missionary opposition, would, in the future, eventually pass to an indigenous priesthood supported by their own lay brothers and sisters. On leaving Africa in 1929, Hinsley had emphasised Pius XI's missionary encyclical, when he said that European missionaries could not hope to perfect the work they had begun: there had to be African priests, sisters, and brothers to supplement their efforts.[81]

In the development of education, overall progress was perhaps less substantial than Hinsley must have expected during his delegacy, considering the groundwork he had undertaken during his visitation. There were, however, mitigating circumstances caused by the financial difficulties faced by the colonies and Christian missionary institutes of all denominations. Catholic education continued to develop but not at the pace and with the uniformity which Hinsley had hoped for. Understandably, the situation was beyond his control and he and the missionaries had to respond as best they could to financial restrictions. Financial retrenchment had a knock-on effect regarding the provision of seminaries but they were not the only cause for slow progress in the formation of an indigenous clergy. Hinsley was able to indicate pockets of progress, as with the White Fathers, but the idea of an African clergy was not one that appealed to all missionaries and limited secondary provision meant that the required standards of entry deterred many potential African seminarians.

The fulfilment of Propaganda's and Hinsley's objectives involved difficult decisions but he proved equal to the demands and strains of leadership. In education, the creation of new ecclesiastical structures and the provision of seminaries, he was occasionally compelled to stand against administrators, Ordinaries and missionary institutes. His steadfastness and determination were illustrated in Kenya and in Nigeria where he proved to be as unyielding to his own missionaries as he was to colonial administrators. And yet, where merited, he dispensed praise and tributes with immense gratitude and respect. He admired all missionaries, whatever their shortcomings, and their attempts to enhance the Church in Africa. The huge differences between East and West Africa were readily acknowledged but he would not allow institutional or geographical and socio-political considerations to be excuses for a lack of missionary progress.

The effectiveness of Hinsley as Apostolic Delegate has to be assessed in a slightly different way from his visitation. His duty to impose central authority on the missions through his presence was, given the nature of his remit and the extent of his territorial responsibility, much broader and less clearly defined than that of an Apostolic Visitor. But he had established a reputation and formed relationships during his first visit that enabled him to continue not only towards the fulfilment of what he considered the final stage of his career but, more importantly, to the establishment of a strong and loyal African Church. Whilst he never belittled the efforts of the pioneering missionaries and their successors, he consistently pointed the way towards the fulfilment of Pius XI's vision and encouraged the formation of a fully African Church as part of the universal Church. When he retired as Apostolic Delegate in 1934, and thanks to the endeavours of the missionaries he sought to direct, the African Church was nearer to achieving that goal. The African Church had grown during his time in Africa and had moved some way towards the recruitment and involvement of educated African Catholics in developments which took their Church further along the path to maturity.

The contemporary assessment of Hinsley's work in Africa was

favourable. When Hinsley retired to Rome in 1934, Sir Charles Wingfield, newly-appointed British Minister to the Holy See wrote that

> ...during the whole six years of his time of office, he showed immense energy, travelling far and wide, reorganising schools and setting up new missionary districts. In an article of the most cordial nature, the *Osservatore Romano* stated that the memory of the first Delegate to Africa, his zeal and faithfulness, would never be forgotten in the continent where he had deserved so well of the Church and of Christendom.[82]

The Vatican was indeed full of praise for Hinsley's African achievements and on 25 May 1934 *L'Osservatore Romano* published the official appreciation of his African ministry, stressing his loyalty to the Pope and Holy See:

> Very recently, the usually robust Mgr Hinsley was struck down by a long illness contracted while in the midst of his apostolic activity and made all the serious because of his advanced age. It would have been difficult for him to carry on with his work which has met with universal satisfaction in the vast and difficult fields of his labours during the last four years or so. . . . The marvellous activity of the Apostolic Visitor enriched by pleasing results was crowned by the erection of the Apostolic Delegation for British Africa on 11 January 1930. No-one could have been more suitable than Mgr Hinsley to fulfil the office of Apostolic Delegate. He was, therefore, chosen for this by Pope Pius XI. . . .

> The new apostolate, motivated by a love for the Catholic missions and entrusted to him, showed Mgr Hinsley to be a an excellent administrator. . . . The departure of Mgr Hinsley from the missionary field will be the cause of real sorrow amongst the indigenous faithful and particularly amongst the Ordinaries and missionaries whom he has guided through his assiduous co-ordination and organisation. In these distant missions his indelible memory will live on because of the great work of this first Apostolic Delegate to British Africa . . . a most active and zealous promoter of the missionary cause, a faithful interpreter of the directives of the Pope of the Missions and the Scared Congregation for the Propagation of the Faith. . . .[83]

Sixteen years later, Douglas Newton offered a similar appreciation when he wrote that

> Hinsley's work in Africa was regarded both in Rome and in British colonial circles as an achievement of the highest order. His belief in personal contact, his sympathy and tact, no less than his administrative ability, won a happy co-operation among the various nationalities making up the missionary body, as well as with colonial officials, and proved of inestimable value both

to native education and to Roman Catholic missions generally.[84]

In 1934 Wingfield wrote that some observers in Rome considered Hinsley's African achievements merited and deserved promotion to the College of Cardinals and that his presence in Rome would be a useful asset to the British government and to British Catholics for since the death of Cardinal Merry del Val in 1930 there had been no English cardinal in the Vatican. It was not to be, however. A thirty-seven year old papal diplomat, Mgr Antonio Riberi, born in Monte Carlo and on duty in Ireland, replaced Hinsley in Africa. Pius XI, who had called Hinsley 'Africanus', created him a Canon of St Peter's Basilica, the first Englishman to be appointed to the Canonry since the aristocratic Bishop Algernon Stanley in 1919. The erstwhile Apostolic Delegate, exhausted by his labours and affected by stress-related eczema, looked forward to a relatively luxurious, sedate and uneventful retirement.

Chapter Ten

'HABEMUS DUCEM'
ARCHBISHOP OF WESTMINSTER

1935

The Death of Cardinal Bourne

Cardinal Francis Bourne died on the first day of January 1935. He had been Archbishop of Westminster since 1903 and a cardinal since 1911. On hearing of the Cardinal's death, Hinsley wrote to Bishop Amigo who for so long had been Bourne's adversary and who had used Hinsley in his efforts to thwart him: 'May we all meet in heaven where there will be no question of divisions but unending peace and unbroken friendship'.[1]

When Hugh Montgomery, Secretary of the British Legation to the Holy See, reported the Cardinal's death to Foreign Secretary Anthony Eden, he informed him that Bourne had never completely recovered from the serious illness which had struck him down during his last visit to Rome in December 1932. The Cardinal's death, he wrote, had been greatly felt among British Catholics although his influence had lessened during the last two years of his life because of his enfeebled state of health. Montgomery told Eden that although Bourne was only *primus inter pares* among the bishops of England and Wales, he 'was regarded by his Catholic compatriots as their undisputed leader, while his many statesmanlike qualities, his tact and patriotism, and unfailing commonsense had won him the respect of his Protestant fellow countrymen'. He reported that there was great uncertainty both in England and in Rome as to the succession to the Archbishopric of Westminster, 'as there seemed no obvious candidate for this very important post' and he informed Eden of the general view in Rome that an English diocesan bishop, such as Archbishop Thomas Williams of Birmingham, would be the likely successor to the late Cardinal.[2]

After the Cardinal's Requiem Mass, his interment in the Galilee Chapel at St Edmund's College, Ware, and the customary period of mourning, the Cathedral Chapter, having officially been informed that the see was vacant, elected a Vicar Capitular to administer it. The Chapter then had the responsibility of drawing up a terna of names and submitting it to Rome. Inevitably speculation began over who would follow Bourne. Recent tradition suggested that it would be one of the English and Welsh Hierarchy. On 14 January, Bishop Amigo, the senior suffragan of the Archdiocese, presided over a meeting of the Chapter and later informed Cardinal Raffaello Rossi, Secretary of the Sacred Consistorial Congregation, that the arrangements for compiling a terna were complete. He was insistent that in addition to the terna submitted by the Chapter, all the bishops 'should have a voice in this appointment'.[3]

The English and Welsh Hierarchy in 1935

In 1935 there were seventeen diocesan bishops in the English and Welsh hierarchy. At their Low Week meetings, under the presidency of the Archbishop of Westminster, the bishops would, in theory, discuss and arrive at decisions on matters of mutual concern and interest but none felt it his duty to interfere in the running of another's diocese. There was an acute awareness of protocol and among some bishops an even stronger sense of independence. Under Bourne's presidency, personal relationships were severely strained and there was only superficial unity. His fellow bishops disliked Bourne's autocratic methods and Rome was well aware of the unhappy situation.[4]

Many on the episcopal bench had lengthy diocesan experience. Bishop Amigo, consecrated in 1904, was the senior bishop; Joseph Robert Cowgill of Leeds was consecrated as coadjutor there in 1905; while William Cotter of Portsmouth was consecrated as Auxiliary Bishop there in 1905. Thomas Henshaw of Salford, Archbishop Richard Downey of Liverpool, Archbishop Thomas Williams of Birmingham, Joseph Thorman of Hexham and Newcastle, John Barrett of Plymouth (a former Auxiliary in Birmingham), Archbishop Francis Mostyn of Cardiff (formerly Vicar Apostolic for Wales and subsequently Bishop of Menevia), Thomas Shine of Middlesbrough, Wulstan Pearson of Lancaster, and Arthur Doubleday of Brentwood had all been appointed to their sees during the 1920s. Lawrence Youllens of Northampton, John McNulty of Nottingham, Michael McGrath of Newport and Menevia, Ambrose Moriarty of Shrewsbury (consecrated as coadjutor in 1932), William Lee of Clifton, were recent appointments, having been consecrated in the 1930s. Cowgill and Moriarty had been educated at the *Venerabile* while the majority of the others had been educated at the major seminaries in England or on the continent. The Benedictine Pearson of Lancaster had been educated at Douai and Belmont while Youllens had been trained for the African missions. Some bishops had coadjutors or auxiliaries and these too were eligible for the vacant see.[5]

Speculation: Archbishop Downey and Others

The bishop whose name was most frequently canvassed as the next incumbent of Westminster was Richard Downey who had been Archbishop of Liverpool since 1928. Born in Kilkenny, Downey was aged fifty-four. Educated at St Edward's College Liverpool, London University, Upholland College, and the Gregorian University in Rome, he was ordained in 1907. The Archbishop had a fine intellect, was an excellent public speaker and a formidable controversialist. He was a prolific author, a co-founder of *The Catholic Gazette*, and a member of the editorial board of *The Clergy Review*. He was a member of the British Psychological Society, the Aristotelian Society, and an Honorary Fellow of the Philosophical Society of England. He was also an external examiner in Philosophy at the National University of Ireland, from where he received an honorary degree. Most of his career had been spent as a lecturer or professor at seminaries for the Carmelites and Oratorians in London but, in addition, he had also worked for the Catholic Missionary Society and gave Catholic Evidence Lectures from 1911 to 1926. He returned to Upholland as Vice-Rector and Dean of Theology and Philosophy in 1926. His accomplishments and achievements were particularly appreciated in Ireland and he had received the freedom of Kilkenny in 1930, Sligo in 1931, Limerick and Waterford in 1932, and Clonmel in 1934. For many, the diminutive Downey was head and shoulders above the rest of the bishops. 'In Downey', Moloney commented, 'there was not only promise but achievement'.[6]

When Cardinal Bourne died, Downey was in Australia attending the International Eucharistic Congress in Melbourne. After the Congress, he had begun a busy lecture schedule in order to raise money to fulfil his ambitious plans for a new Liverpool cathedral. The Australian press was full of admiration for the Archbishop and once news of Bourne's death had been received, was convinced of his forthcoming preferment to Westminster. The Perth *Daily News* stated that Downey had been mentioned as a possible successor to Bourne.[7] Melbourne's *Star* was more forthright, stating that 'Dr Downey was considered the likely successor to the late Cardinal Bourne'. When asked for his comments, Dr Duhig, Archbishop of Brisbane, replied, 'I cannot speak on that. No one can say who will be appointed'. But, he added, 'Archbishop Downey is an outstanding man'.[8] The *Northern Star* published a photograph of Downey whom it 'expected to succeed Cardinal Bourne as Archbishop of Westminster'.[9] Downey's decision to cut short his visit fuelled the speculation. On 11 January the *Melbourne Herald* published the news that Downey had decided to leave Australia. The Archbishop told the paper that 'his hurried departure had no connection with the necessity for the filling of the vacancy caused by the death of Cardinal Bourne'.[10] Two days later the Brisbane *Mail* proclaimed that Dr Downey had been 'called back to England' and he had accordingly informed his host, Dr Duhig.[11]

On his way home Downey stayed in Ceylon and India. There too, the press published stories about his likely promotion. The *Illustrated Weekly of India* considered him to be the 'most likely successor to the late Cardinal Bourne as Archbishop of Westminster'.[12] The *Ceylon Daily News*, however, was more circumspect about the man and his future:

> There will be one question this time which will beat as great an expounder of problems and solver of propositions as Dr Downey. The question is: Who will be the next Archbishop of Westminster? Who will be the leader of Catholicism in England?

Under the heading 'The Next Cardinal' the article continued,

> Do we see a cardinal in Dr Downey? Shall we here and now visualize His Grace's episcopal purple intensifying and strengthening into the cardinalatial scarlet? Shall we say "Your Eminence to be?" Not an unreasonable question, as anyone almost is a cardinal-in-*posse*, or used to be, according to the older tradition of that sacred office.[13]

To the *Times of Ceylon* Downey himself offered a more prosaic comment: 'The appointment is entirely a matter for the Pope, and no one can say in advance on whom the choice will fall'.[14]

In late February, Downey arrived in England with nearly £2,000 for his new cathedral. He immediately added to the speculation about the vacant see by staying at Clergy House, Westminster, and then celebrating Mass in the cathedral on the following day. The Australian press, still anxious for news of their recent visitor, picked up on this. *The News* of Adelaide reported that his stay at Clergy House now strengthened previous suggestions about Downey going to Westminster.[15] A crowd of 20,000 Catholics greeted him warmly on his return to Liverpool and the *Birmingham Daily Mail* reported that 'the fact that many entertain the hope that Dr Downey may succeed to the vacant Cardinal-Archbishopric of Westminster adds to the interest which his return has aroused'.[16]

Newspapers in the British Isles were also interested in Bourne's successor. On 22 March, the London *Evening Standard* speculated that, as required by the terna, Downey's name was but one to be proposed by the Cathedral Chapter of Westminster. The other two, it claimed, were those of Bishop Edward Myers and Bishop John McNulty. Myers, aged sixty, was born in York and educated in Belgium, at St Edmund's Ware, Christ's College Cambridge, and Oscott. In 1918 he was appointed President of St Edmund's and had been Auxiliary Bishop of Westminster since 1932. McNulty, aged fifty-six, was born in Manchester of Irish parentage. He had been educated at Douai, Ushaw, Oscott, St Edmund's Cambridge, and Friburg, and had been Bishop of Nottingham for three years. Two of the three names, claimed the *Evening Standard*, had been on 'the original list' sent to the Pope.[17] In the following days, the *Daily Express* and the *Sunday Dispatch* published the same names.[18] The *Daily Express* added that the Pope would announce Downey's appointment and create him a cardinal on May 19, the date set for the canonisation of Blessed John Fisher and Blessed Thomas More. In Ireland, the *Cork Examiner* also took up this link between the appointment of Bourne's successor and the canonisation ceremony but added that either Downey or Amigo would receive the cardinal's hat.[19]

'Lazarus Come Forth'

On the day of Bourne's death Hinsley had complained to Bishop Amigo that he had very little to do 'in the way of work'. He had recovered from the paratyphoid that drove him out of Africa and the eczema that had severely afflicted him during the summer of 1934 and was ready for something to do 'which will make me forget myself'.[20] Being a Canon of St Peter's may have been a dignified sinecure where he lived in state in St Peter's and attended conventual Mass, Vespers and various papal functions but for a man of Hinsley's restless energy it was a frustrating end to a very active life.

This inactivity was to cease dramatically when Cardinal Rossi, Secretary of the Consistorial Congregation, called the Archbishop to visit him in early March 1935. The men had known each other since 1917 when together with Cardinal Gasquet and Dom Philip Langdon they had begun the successful restoration of the English College. Hinsley hoped that his friend would offer him a post in one of the Vatican Congregations and rescue him from the monotony and obscurity of the Canonry for as Mgr Elwes wrote later, 'To an essentially active and large minded man, life in the *Canonica* of St Peter's was deadly. With little or no outlet for his abilities and energy of character he had begun to fret and even decline'.[21] To all intents and purposes he was *in sepulchro*. Instead of offering Hinsley a job, however, Rossi explained that he had been asked by Pope Pius XI to solicit Hinsley's views on Bourne's successor. Somewhat surprised, Hinsley replied that he was unable to advise the Pope as he did not belong to the Westminster diocese and had no knowledge of its priests. Rossi suggested that as a former Rector of the *Venerabile*, Hinsley must have met several ecclesiastics and prelates who had visited the College and therefore might be able to 'name several, half-a-dozen, maybe, without discriminating between them'. Again, Hinsley's answer was negative. Rossi then informed Hinsley that the Pope considered him to be the obvious choice. Hinsley was physically shaken by the suggestion and told Rossi that he could think of many reasons why he should not go to Westminster. Rossi advised him to write them out and he would present them to the Pope. At their next meeting Hinsley gave his reasons but after reading them Rossi put them to one side and said what Hinsley must have expected: 'The Holy Father asks for obedience. Is it obedience?' There could only be one answer.[22]

Hinsley must have informed Bishop Amigo almost immediately for before his appointment was announced publicly Amigo wrote: 'It must have come upon you as a terrible shock'. But if Hinsley's promotion was a shock to him it was as much a surprise to British diplomats in Rome and close observers of the ecclesiastical scene. Montgomery wrote to Anthony Eden that in discussions about Bourne's successor 'The name of Mgr Arthur Hinsley, Canon of St Peter's and former Apostolic Delegate for Missions in Africa, was scarcely mentioned' and reported that two other prelates resident in Rome, both much younger men, were considered to have better prospects than him. According to Montgomery, they were Monsignor Charles Duchemin and Monsignor William Heard.[23] Charles Duchemin was Rector of the *Beda*. Aged fifty-nine, English but of French descent, Duchemin was educated at the Benedictine school at Downside, and Trinity College Cambridge. He was a solicitor for eight years before studying at the *Beda* where he was ordained in 1918. From 1921 until 1928 he was a curate in England, first at Peterborough and then at Wandsworth. Duchemin had undertaken some important roles whilst still a curate. He had accompanied a delegation of English bishops to the United States in 1918, represented Cardinal Bourne at international conferences and acted as chaplain to the British Delegation at the Chicago International Eucharistic Conference of 1926. As a trained solicitor, he was also able to advise on legal matters and in 1927 he was appointed the first registrar of the Society of Our Lady of Good Counsel, an organisation dedicated to providing legal aid for the poor. In 1928 he returned to Rome as Rector of the *Beda* and was appointed a Domestic Prelate in the same year.[24] Monsignor William Heard was aged sixty-one and a Scotsman. Educated at Fettes College Edinburgh, and Balliol College Oxford, he also was a trained solicitor. He was received into the Church in 1910 and had been a student at the *Venerabile*. Ordained in 1918, he was a curate in Bermondsey from 1921 to 1926 before being appointed an Auditor of the Sacred Roman Rota in 1927.[25] To the more seasoned Vatican watchers, these two must have been rank outsiders in the succession stakes. It was very unlikely that the Holy See would impose either of these relatively inexperienced priests on a Hierarchy so notoriously insular and lacking in unity and for Montgomery to take the candidacy of these two priests seriously indicates a lack of understanding of the ecclesiastical situation in England and Wales.

On 25 March, Hinsley officially informed Sir Charles Wingfield, British Minister to the Holy See, that he had been chosen to succeed Bourne. 'It appears', reported Wingfield, 'that Archbishop Hinsley, who is not an ambitious man and feels the weight of his years, made a strenuous attempt to decline preferment'. However, the Pope, 'in his masterful fashion', appeared 'to have practically commanded acceptance'. Wingfield proceeded to elaborate on the Pope's reasons, and hinted that the appointment might be to the British government's advantage in its bid to develop diplomatic relations with the Holy See:

Mgr Hinsley's name would not appear to have been proposed by the English bishops or to have been on the list, which in accordance to custom, was sent in by the Chapter of Westminster; it may thus be assumed that his appointment was due to the personal initiative of the Holy Father, who is said to have wanted someone who was at the same time as English and as Roman as possible. The new Archbishop appeared to fulfil both these qualifications for he is of pure English birth and upbringing, and has spent a considerable part of his life in Rome, including thirteen years as rector of the English College. Archbishop Hinsley has a special devotion to the Papacy and to the present Pope, with whose centralizing tendencies, in matters purely spiritual, he is in sympathy, and there is reason to suppose that he would welcome the appointment of an Apostolic Delegate to England.[26]

Hinsley must obviously have been aware of the speculation surrounding Downey for on the same day he wrote to him, aware that he too would be surprised and, no doubt, disappointed.

> Our Holy Father has demanded of me the sacrifice of obedience. In fear and trembling I have submitted. He has appointed me Archbishop of Westminster.
>
> In the strength of obedience to the Vicar of Christ, relying on the intercessions of the Patrons of the diocese of Westminster – the Immaculate Mother of God, St Joseph and St Peter – as well as the powerful help of our glorious Martyrs and especially Blessed John Fisher and Blessed Thomas More, so soon to be canonised, I take courage to come to you.
>
> My few remaining years and all my energy I give unstintingly to work with you for the Church in England.
>
> One thing I desire most earnestly. On every important matter I want to give you my complete confidence. I seek your confidence in return, your advice, your frank criticism and your co-operation. *Quam bonum et quam jucundum habitare fratres in unum:* the grace that flows from our unity will stream down to the least object of our pastoral activity. Our Catholic Action, on the Education Question, on all our Catholic interests we must be *cor unum et anima una* so that the Catholic Hierarchy in Great Britain may be seen to be a single front in the bitter campaign being waged against God and against His Christ.
>
> Your Grace, I beg you to pray for me, a poor frail instrument of God, and I implore your support in the heavy task laid upon me.[27]

He asked Downey if he would regard the letter as confidential until the official announcement was made in *L'Osservatore Romano*. Downey replied, promising prayers and assistance. Hinsley was delighted and told Downey that he had been cheered up and 'given a tonic of courage' by his reply. The help that Downey pledged would prevent him from succumbing to the weight of responsibility he was to face. He was, he concluded, 'overwhelmed just at present'.[28] Hinsley wrote an exactly similar letter to Bishop McNulty of Nottingham on the same day, thus indicating that perhaps McNulty's name was also on the terna. McNulty replied by telegram and assured Hinsley of his deep respect and loyal co-operation.[29]

On 26 March, the day after the official notification of his appointment, Hinsley stood with Pope Pius XI in the Vatican and admired reproductions of Holbein's portraits of the two *beati*, John Fisher and Thomas More. '*Tales ambio defensores*' uttered the Pope to Hinsley – 'Such are the protectors I invoke' – the words of St Ambrose on seeing the bodies of the martyrs Gervasius and Protasius. The Pope told Hinsley that he had decided to place Fisher and More on either side of himself on the Papal Medal of the year and advised Hinsley to take them as his special patrons in Westminster – John Fisher, the model of pastors, and Thomas More, the ideal layman – and also the motto he himself had applied to them. Hinsley willingly agreed and when his Metropolitan coat of arms was devised he included the symbol of a dolphin from the shield of John Fisher and the symbol of a cockerel from that of Thomas More.[30]

On 2 April, in an unusual mark of respect and approval, the Pope personally conferred on Hinsley the pallium, the pure woollen band worn on the shoulders, representing the fullness and authority of the metropolitan archiepiscopal office. Those present included Monsignor Heard, Monsignor Duchemin, Dom Philip Langdon, Procurator of the English Benedictines, and Monsignor William Godfrey, Hinsley's successor as Rector of the *Venerabile*. On the next day Hinsley attended the last solemn public consistory for the canonisation of John Fisher and Thomas More and later in the month left for London 'the capital of the empire, and of the Protestant world and, in a place where all were strangers to him, to take up the thread of the complicated administration, and somehow to continue a great ecclesiastical tradition'.[31]

Reaction to Hinsley's Appointment

Staff and students at the *Venerabile* could not hide their delight at Hinsley's appointment. 'The enthusiasm with which the great news was received by *Venerabilini* here and in England defies expression', wrote the editor of the College's magazine.[32] The reaction elsewhere, however, was mixed.

As Rector of the *Venerabile*, Hinsley had been host to the English and Welsh bishops on their *ad limina* and other visits to Rome. He had also acted as the Roman agent for some of the bishops and knew the outstanding personalities among the Catholic laity. In fact, he knew more about England than he had intimated to Cardinal Rossi and was enough of a realist to understand that his appointment would not be entirely popular. Circumstances militated against him. It was argued by some that following Bourne's long episcopate, the English and Welsh Church required a younger and more vigorous leader. Hinsley would have agreed. He considered that he was old, sick, and out of touch. In London he knew almost nobody. His knowledge of government departments and personnel was confined mainly to the Colonial Office. Among the priests in the Westminster diocese he counted very few friends and acquaintances.[33]

When reporting the death of Cardinal Bourne, whom it described as 'A Great English Cardinal', *The Times* commented that when he was chosen for the metropolitan see of Westminster in 1903, the appointment was received by his own communion with surprise and grave doubts.[34] The same could be said about Hinsley's appointment but whereas Bourne was the youngest of the English bishops with a bright future, Hinsley was an old man with a distinguished career behind him. Fr William Gordon Wheeler wrote that in England, and especially in Westminster, Hinsley's appointment 'caused no little surprise as the new Metropolitan was in his seventieth year and relatively unknown in his own country'.[35] Hinsley's former colleague, Bishop William Brown, Auxiliary in Southwark, recalled that 'many doubted his ability to fill the great post with success'.[36] Heenan wrote that 'the appointment to the Archdiocese of Westminster of Monsignor Hinsley, a retired and ailing missionary, was not received by all English Catholics as a sign of great wisdom in the Holy See. . . . Some pious priests were doubtless content to praise the Holy Ghost for the Hinsley appointment. Many others, equally pious, were inclined to blame what they took to be an ill-informed Consistorial Congregation'.[37] To some senior ecclesiastics Hinsley's appointment was an imposition by the Vatican – an ultramontane by training and experience planted in the midst of a cisalpine and traditionally introspective Hierarchy.

Writing from the Foreign Office, Stephen Gaselee commented that because of his age and health, Hinsley's appointment, 'was an interesting and unexpected choice'. He continued: 'His selection shows that the Vatican still pays attention to the influence and sentiments of the old *English* Roman Catholics by passing over, in favour of Mgr Hinsley, the more distinguished Archbishop of Liverpool, Dr Downey, who represents the Irish RC immigrants now forming so important an element of RC life in the British Isles'.[38] Unlike Bourne and Hinsley, who were both of Irish descent but had proved themselves to be staunchly patriotic – Bourne during the Great War and Hinsley in Africa – Downey was Irish by birth and it is likely that his Irish roots and nationalist leanings counted against him in the eyes of both the English Catholic aristocracy and the British government. Above all, Downey's link with the Cork-born controversial Archbishop Daniel Mannix of Melbourne seriously weakened whatever chance he may have had of succeeding Bourne. Mannix had spoken out against Australian involvement in the Great War and such was the British government's fear of his effect on Irish nationalists that as he attempted to visit Ireland in 1920 the Royal Navy had escorted his ship to Penzance. Thereafter Mannix was prohibited by the British government from speaking in areas with large Irish populations. When he was in Ireland in 1925, the English and pro-Treaty Irish press had refused to print the details of his tour. On his tour of Australia in 1934 Downey had met Mannix at the Eucharistic Congress at Melbourne and in *The Universe*, on 1 March 1935, Downey subsequently wrote of his brother archbishop 'almost in terms of reverence'; a man he claimed, 'of such stature that he has no parallels in these days, but belongs to an age of giants'.[39] Such sentiments were unlikely to impress the British government or the Vatican which was so anxious to foster good relations with Great Britain. The *Bulletin* of Sydney reminded its readers that when Downey was in Australia many may have prophesied that he would become Archbishop of Westminster but commented that Westminster was an appointment reserved traditionally by the Vatican for Englishmen.[40]

The Universe and *The Catholic Herald* welcomed Hinsley. Fr Bernard Grimley, editor of *The Catholic Times*, observed that he was 'sympathetic with anything that makes for progress and a man of extra-ordinary ability'. The *Yorkshire Post* quoted Bishop Amigo, who had known Hinsley for over thirty years, as saying that he had always admired Hinsley 'as a man of downright sincerity and outstanding character. If he has any action to take he will always go about it in the most direct fashion, and he has no time for half-measures'. The prospects for improved relations between Westminster and Southwark, therefore, looked promising. Canon Frederick Mitchell, a contemporary of Hinsley at Ushaw and Administrator of St Anne's Cathedral, Leeds, wrote that Hinsley's 'appointment as Archbishop will undoubtedly be a popular one. He has the admiration and confidence of the English government and everyone else'.[41] The English Jesuits, some of whom had met Hinsley in Africa, immediately offered their support. In their journal, *The Month*, in a side swipe at the disastrous feuds between Bourne and Amigo, the editor wrote: 'We can give our new Archbishop, as we have given his predecessors, our unstinted allegiance with the full assurance that none but spiritual motives were concerned in his appointment, and that he comes to us fresh from the intimate counsels of the Holy Father'.[42]

The Tablet, still owned by the Archbishop of Westminster and under the editorship of Ernest Oldmeadow, reported that Hinsley had left the 'dignified quiet proper to a canonry in the Vatican Basilica' and had been 'called upon to shoulder the heaviest of life's burdens as successor to that great and venerated chief, Francis Cardinal Bourne'. Under the heading *Habemus Ducem,* Hinsley's career was described, in rather gushing terms, from his time at the *Venerabile* and through his visitation and delegacy in Africa. It was noted diplomatically that 'our new leader', unlike Nicholas Wiseman, did not have erudite books to his name but had 'active sympathy with sacred learning'. The Church in England, it continued, was favoured with fine intellects in Archbishops Downey and Williams, both of whom had also spent much time in seminaries but had demonstrated how abstract academic learning could be transferred to 'gracious pastoral wisdom'. It was, however, the emphasis on the relationship between Westminster and the other sees that appeared to be the thrust of the editorial. The 'monarchical episcopate' enabled the Ordinary to run his own diocese; a Metropolitan was not a 'High King'. Nevertheless, it continued, Catholics in England would have noticed that under Bourne immense authority and importance was ascribed to the Metropolitan of Westminster. Similarly, Westminster Cathedral was much more than the largest and most important of the English Catholic churches. It possessed a national and imperial pre-eminence which came to the fore on state and other notable occasions. Thus, it concluded, though not in a theological sense, 'the occupant of the see of Westminster holds a unique position'.[43] It was a proposition that was soon to be tested by Downey.

The non-Catholic press proffered its own views on Hinsley's appointment. The *Church Times* announced that Hinsley's selection 'has caused considerable surprise outside the Roman Communion' but assured him of the good wishes of those Christians not of the Roman allegiance. Like other newspapers, the *Church Times* had expected Downey to be appointed but reminded its readers of the dark intrigue that had surrounded Archbishop Manning's selection in 1865.[44] Cosmo Lang, Archbishop of Canterbury, welcomed Hinsley on behalf of the Anglican Communion and hoped that the cordial personal relations that had existed with Cardinal Bourne would continue and that 'in spite of all our differences we may have chances of co-operation for the common good'.[45] *The Times* reported that Hinsley's appointment was well received and that he was admired as a man of great energy and enthusiasm.[46] *The Sunday Times* commented that many names had been mentioned as successors of Bourne but 'among these was not that of Mgr Hinsley'. It went on to state that Hinsley's appointment would be welcome as his successful African experience gave him an outlook that extended beyond Europe. On a rather surprising note, however, and following the lead of the *Cork Examiner*,[47] it concluded that although he had been named as Archbishop of Westminster, Hinsley should not expect to receive the cardinal's red hat: 'For that, Archbishop Downey of Liverpool may be considered to have the first claim'.[48] It was a story that was to run, rather insensitively from Hinsley's point of view, in the months following his arrival in Westminster.

In April, the *Manchester Evening News* and *Daily Express* were also of the firm opinion that, despite being at Westminster, Hinsley would not receive the cardinal's hat. Correctly, it was pointed out that there was only precedent to link the College of Cardinals with the post at Westminster. Downey or Amigo, therefore, was likely to be the next English cardinal.[49] Even the *South Wales Echo and Evening Press* offered an opinion, stating that Downey's claims would prevail over those of Hinsley.[50] In August, the *Manchester Evening Chronicle* claimed that both Hinsley and Downey would be created cardinals whilst other newspapers also included Archbishop Williams of Birmingham.[51] In Australia, the Sydney *Bulletin* took a different and perhaps more realistic view. Hinsley was *persona grata* in Rome, and 'he will of course become a cardinal'. Of England's thirty-eight cardinals, it concluded, and allowing its readers to draw their own conclusions, only four had been Irish.[52]

Induction

Hinsley left Rome for England on 24 April and was welcomed at

Victoria Station on the following day by Bishop Amigo, Bishop Butt, Viscount Fitzalan, his nephew Stephen Hinsley and a substantial crowd anxious to get a glimpse of the new Archbishop. On 26 April, Hinsley presented himself to the Provost and Chapter of Westminster Cathedral and took formal possession of his see. Three days later, on the deferred feast of St George and during Pontifical High Mass, he was installed as fifth Archbishop of Westminster according to traditional rites of veneration and enthronement. The Senior Canon, Monsignor Martin Howlett, carried the pallium up the nave towards the altar. 'Behind him, under a canopy, came the archbishop, a tall and upright figure in purple, with his long silken train behind him. As he walked his hand hovered in benediction to right and left over the kneeling congregation, most of whom, seeing him for the first time, observed that he looked much younger than his 71 years'. At the *Gloria* 'his voice was heard for the first time sounding clear and resonant across the great spaces of the Cathedral'. His sermon began with praise for Bourne, for 'his gifts and attainments which fitted him to be Archbishop of Westminster'. He asked for prayerful support for the Pope and those statesmen endeavouring to maintain peace based on Christian principles. Not surprisingly after his years in Africa, he called for support of the missions. The sermon also indicated that Hinsley had quickly become familiar with English matters or had been well-briefed. He referred to the on-going schools problem, the importance of the media, loyalty to religion and country, and the forthcoming canonisation of John Fisher and Thomas More. His words took on a more powerful dimension when he launched into a call for the development of the apostolate of the laity – Catholic Action – the Pope's favoured method of apolitical involvement in social and political affairs. Catholic Action took to itself 'the shield of faith and the whole armour of the spirit. Only one ambition fires the movement – to gain the acceptance and observance of the Catholic principles of morality, of justice, of charity, in all the relations of life, domestic and civic, national and international'. In retrospect, his inaugural sermon may be seen as a blueprint for his episcopate – active and outward looking. His words were to enthuse some but concern others.[53]

In the following days Hinsley held receptions for his diocesan priests and for the laity who wished to offer him a welcome. Several thousand people 'from many strata of life' paid him their respects in the Throne Rome at Cathedral House. It was, noted *The Tablet*, 'an event in which convention was swept aside in an enthusiastic mixing of classes'.[54] In May, along with many thousands of English pilgrims, Hinsley returned to Rome for the canonisation of Blessed John Fisher and Blessed Thomas More.[55]

In April 1935, *The English Churchman*, obviously aware of the dynamic personalities of Hinsley and Downey, had warned its readers that there could be 'some sparks' between them. In Bourne's time, it continued, there were strained relations between north and south, and despite Hinsley being of a more genial disposition than Bourne, his attempt to be a unifying factor in the hierarchy might prove difficult.[56] And, in June 1935, it was Archbishop Downey who cast the first but very brief and unnecessary shadow over Hinsley's arrival. He accused Hinsley of ignoring Metropolitan protocol by granting an indulgence to Catholics in the Diocese of Hexham and Newcastle which was within the metropolitan see of Liverpool. Downey sent a memorandum to the canon lawyers in Hexham and Newcastle for them to consider the relative claims of each Metropolitan. They came out in favour of Downey who informed Hinsley that he could not grant the indulgence.[57] Hinsley's response indicated that he cared little for such trivialities but by doing so publicly he left no-one in any doubt as to his position among the Hierarchy. He carefully pointed out to Downey and to everyone else that by authority of Letters Apostolic *Si qua est* of October 1911, quoted by the canonists, he had constitutional precedence over other Metropolitans in England and Wales, certain privileges and distinctions of pre-eminence. He was *Praeses Perpetuus Angliae et Cambriae*, or permanent president of the English and Welsh Hierarchy, and could wear the pallium anywhere in those countries. By virtue of these privileges, he was able to grant such an indulgence. As far as he was concerned, that was the end of the matter.[58] *The Tablet*, meanwhile, ever anxious to promote the seniority of Westminster, had not helped by referring earlier to Hinsley as 'the primate' although admitting that this was not strictly accurate. Oldmeadow attempted sensitively to calm the situation by writing that:

> . . .It should go without saying that Archbishop Hinsley will know – as his beloved predecessor in the same illustrious see always knew – how to use his privileges and rights with delicate regard for the prestige and dignity of others.

Fr Andrew Beck recalled that the general opinion about Hinsley, 'in so far as such things are measurable' was one of a very friendly welcome to a very lovable pastor. . . .' He continued that 'such criticism of the Cardinal as there was came to birth after his appointment and not because of it'.[59] The Catholic aristocracy welcomed Hinsley. The Duke of Norfolk and his three cousins – Lord Howard, Baron Rankeillour, and Viscount Fitzalan – all experienced and influential in British public life, offered support, advice and the benefits of their contacts in Parliament and in government. Their likely part in Hinsley's appointment and his reception cannot be underestimated for Hinsley was born on a Howard estate and maintained contact through Lord Herries while at St Bede's.[60] Hinsley's appointment of the Old Roman, Fr Val Elwes, as his private secretary, not only provided him with a link to the *Venerabile* but also another contact with establishment Catholics for Elwes was related to the aristocratic Clifford and Petre families.[61]

Why was Hinsley appointed?

Charles Wingfield maintained that Hinsley was sent to Westminster on the initiative of the Holy Father who 'wanted someone who was at the same time as English and as "Roman" as possible'; in other words, someone who would bring the English and Welsh Hierarchy closer to Rome whilst simultaneously cementing improving relations between the Vatican and the British government. Westminster was, after all, the premier see in the Empire and, as Wingfield wrote, Hinsley had proved his capable loyalty to both his Church and to his country and there was no reason why this should not continue for the benefit of both London and the Vatican.[62]

On his arrival in Rome in 1917, Hinsley had become immediately involved in the diplomatic exchanges between the British government and the Holy See in connection with Pope Benedict XV's peace proposals. The Papal Court would have noticed the successful handling of such a delicate matter. His subsequent transformation of the English College further enhanced his reputation.[63] His six years in Africa demonstrated that he had the capacity to handle major issues across a huge geographical area, was firm enough to impose convergent Vatican and British imperial policies on disparate missionary institutes and was also sensitive to the needs of local communities. His absolute loyalty to both earned the admiration of his Church and his country.[64]

In its appreciation of his African ministry *L'Osservatore Romano* had referred to Hinsley's advanced age and the appointment of an old man, referred to by Gilley as 'an elderly stop-gap candidate',[65] gave the Vatican time to reflect on the future composition and leadership of the episcopal bench. Bishops of this era emerged, like Hinsley himself, from careers as bishops' secretaries, administrators, papal diplomats or rectors of colleges but, unlike Hinsley, most had extensive diocesan experience. Their collective experience was unevenly spread, however. Eight bishops had been raised to the episcopate before Hinsley but ten, including Downey, had less than ten years episcopal experience. None had Hinsley's international experience; none had come into contact with senior Vatican and senior British government officials as often as Hinsley; and all were members of a Hierarchy that under Bourne had caused much anxiety and frustration in Rome.

The roles of the very influential English cardinals, Aidan Gasquet and Rafael Merry del Val, who were admirers of Hinsley, must also be considered. Gasquet had observed Hinsley's firm anti-Modernist stance in the 1890s and had been favourably impressed by the young priest's zealous defence of orthodoxy. Working in Rome as Amigo's agent during the acrimonious dispute with Archbishop Bourne during the first decade of the century, Hinsley again came to the notice of Gasquet who was acting on the Pope's behalf. In 1917 Gasquet, as Cardinal Protector of the *Venerabile,* recommended that Hinsley be appointed its Rector and, in 1926, that he be raised to the episcopate. Before his death in 1929, therefore, Gasquet had already substantially enhanced Hinsley's career.[66] Merry del Val, Secretary of State to Pope Pius X, had been a student with Hinsley at Ushaw and was a frequent visitor to the *Venerabile.* Before his sudden death in 1930, he was a confidant of popes and a major figure in papal politics. He too had promoted Hinsley's cause.[67] As a missioner in Southwark, a professor at Wonersh, and as his agent in Rome, Hinsley had also gained the respect and friendship of Bishop Amigo. Fr Michael Clifton claims that during Bourne's final illness, Amigo suggested to Pope Pius XI that Hinsley should be appointed to Westminster.[68]

Heenan felt that a deciding factor in convincing the Pope of Hinsley's suitability might have been the final stage of the process to canonise Bishop John Fisher and Sir Thomas More in 1935. Bishop Amigo had attested the case for martyrdom to the Pope and the assembled cardinals on 10 February. On 3 March, Hinsley, who had been the Postulator of the cause before his appointment as Apostolic Visitor to Africa, proposed that it was safe to proceed with canonisation. Monsignor Richard Smith reported that at the end of the Consistory, Archbishop Hinsley read the address of thanks to the Pope 'in a voice shaking with emotion. I noticed the whole Pontifical Court listening with enthusiasm to the rolling Italian of this eminent Yorkshireman's own writing. It was really eloquent, as it proudly recalled our Catholic past. . . .' As the Pope concluded the Consistory, 'he owned he found it difficult, especially after Monsignor Hinsley's penetrating appreciation of his two great countrymen'.[69] Pius and his advisers obviously knew Hinsley and were well aware of his qualities, his experience, his patent loyalty to the Holy See and to his country. Such a man would be of value at Westminster. According to Archbishop Downey's panegyric on Hinsley, however, Pius XI's decision to translate Hinsley was not made on the spur of the moment. He is said to have told an English bishop that 'I have had had him in mind for Westminster for a long time. His fatherly warm-heartedness will do much for England'.[70] William Brown, Auxiliary Bishop of Southwark, who had known Hinsley for thirty years, also wrote that the Pope had been considering the translation of Hinsley to Westminster for some time:

> It came as a surprise to many, but not to me, because I knew that Pius XI thought highly of him. He told a friend of mine, after the appointment, that for a long time he had wanted Archbishop Hinsley to fill the vacancy, but had been afraid that his health would make it impossible. As, however, it had much improved, he had taken the matter into his own hands and made the appointment.

Brown added, 'I think it can be safely said that Cardinal Bourne never imagined that Arthur Hinsley would be his successor'.[71] Certainly, with Hinsley's appointment the chances of more Westminster students being sent to the *Venerabile* increased as did the likelihood of a more Roman spirit entering the diocese.

While still in a state of shock at the prospect of his forthcoming responsibilities, Hinsley had received the congratulations of the staff and students of the English College, Valladolid. The young priest who delivered the message of goodwill to the Archbishop in Rome was Fr Thomas Holland. He wrote:

> The Archbishop sat with me for about four minutes, awfully good of him with 'phones, etc, buzzing. . . . He was quite ingenuously sad at leaving Rome, and frightened almost of the job ahead.[72]

Mgr Richard Smith wrote that when Hinsley was resident in the

Canonry 'there was the finger of decay upon him, as one who has finished with life'. He wandered disconsolately to St Peter's for Office and even asked Mgr Godfrey for permission to walk the Cardinals Gallery at the English College. But when the full significance and importance of his appointment sank in and the Archbishop's immediate misgivings, which so obviously had caused him great distress, receded, his mood changed. Back came the determination so typical of Hinsley and students at the *Venerabile* noted a huge change in his physical and mental outlook.

> He had got a job to do again, and ten years seemed to have dropped from him. He stood erect, he stuck out his chin, his voice resounded – there was vigour and conviction and courage back in the man. Here indeed was resurrection.[73]

Heenan also wrote that the appointment to Westminster brought about a physical change in Hinsley: 'Hitherto he had been a ghost with memories. Now he was a man with a mission'. The dignified but tedious life of the *Canonica* was exchanged for one final challenge.[74]

Chapter Eleven

SETTLING IN

1935-1937

The New Archbishop

Despite his age and lack of diocesan experience, some sections of the Catholic community had high hopes and expectations of Hinsley. The editor of *Blackfriars* wrote that for the last 35 years English Catholics had looked for leadership to Westminster but never had there been a greater need for strong and sure leadership than at the present time. 'We can look for this with serene confidence form Archbishop Hinsley', he wrote, and thanked the Pope for 'his splendid choice of this worthy successor to our late revered and beloved Cardinal'. The new incumbent of Westminster faced many problems with many being the corollary of Catholics living in a non-Catholic land but Hinsley had the capabilities and experience to address them. He personified the great tradition of Catholicism that had taken root and kept the faith alive in the north of England:

> To have clear-cut ideas and principles, to act resolutely in accordance with them, to live deliberately and consistently, to be direct and where necessary dogged – these are the qualities that are part and parcel of that tradition and these are the qualities that should mark and do mark the leader of English Catholicism. It is surely not without significance that Archbishop Hinsley should come to his new appointment at the moment when those very qualities are being held up to us for our encouragement and our imitation by the approaching canonisation of the Blessed John Fisher and Thomas More.[1]

Many Catholics and non-Catholics had read reports of Hinsley's appointment and his arrival at Westminster but few had heard him speak. They got their chance when he delivered his first radio sermon from the BBC's Broadcasting House on Sunday 15 September 1935. The *Westminster Cathedral Chronicle* claimed that he had a natural gift for broadcasting and conveyed the feeling that he was speaking intimately to each person listening. He introduced himself to those who had not met him and made an honest attempt to reach out to both Catholics and non-Catholics. It was to be the first of many broadcasts that would bring Hinsley into homes across the British Isles and abroad.

The Archbishop began by preaching a short sermon based on John iii, 16: 'God so loved the world, as to give His only begotten Son. . .' and then proceeded to inform those who knew little of him about his background and his aspirations. It had been his 'happy lot', he said, 'to watch my fellow-Catholics, priests or laity, engaged in whole-hearted service in very many places from my dear native land of Yorkshire to the heart of Africa'. He told his listeners of his educational experiences at Ushaw, St Bede's, Wonersh, and at the *Venerabile* and of his pastoral ministry at Keighley, Sutton Park and Sydenham. 'And my very many African friends', he added, 'would be sorry if I did not affectionately mention the years I spent among them, when my duties took me to most parts of Africa. . . .' Throughout all this, he had seen and appreciated the efforts of those of other Christian denominations who had devoted their lives to the service of mankind. All, he said, were inspired by the grace of God.

He had obviously done much during his priesthood but modestly he admitted that he 'ought to have done much more in the service of souls and in imitation of my Master'. Then, returning to his text, Hinsley announced that just as Christ was for the whole world, he had not been appointed to Westminster simply to serve Catholics 'but all my fellow countrymen so far as I may'. It was a unique acknowledgement and his subsequent words indicated that he was very much attuned to social and economic problems in Britain and, as he saw it, the fallacious political alternatives being offered to cure these ills. 'We cannot confine our affection and energies', he said, 'to any one class, or language, or colour, or even creed' and just as Pope Pius XI had recently expressed social concern for all so too must he, having been appointed to Westminster, 'be of the same mind as the Holy Father'. His final blessing was not only to his fellow Catholics but to all who would accept it.[2]

Hinsley was the only bishop in the English and Welsh Hierarchy without diocesan experience. This, together with his advanced age, added urgency to the need to familiarise himself with both his archdiocese and the national Church. He could scarcely look forward to a long period in which to build up affection and respect among bishops, priests and people with whom he was unfamiliar. Moreover, he was not a junior bishop but the senior Catholic prelate in the British Empire. As Heenan wrote, 'it is hard to win spurs at the age of seventy – especially from the height of an episcopal bench'.[3] But Hinsley was not only engaged in national and international affairs: from his appointment in 1935 until his death, he was engrossed in the administration of his archdiocese, which included London north of the River Thames, Middlesex and Hertfordshire.

In 1935 there were 292,000 Catholics served by 363 secular priests and 241 priests from twenty-five religious orders in the Archdiocese of Westminster. Fourteen priests had been ordained for the diocese in 1934. There were 170 convents. The northern dioceses of Liverpool and Salford, traditional Catholic heartlands, both contained more Catholics than Westminster but had fewer priests. Liverpool had 393,700 Catholics and 555 secular and regular priests whilst Salford had 300,000 Catholics and 465 priests. Menevia was numerically the smallest diocese with a population of 15,324 Catholics, but with 139 priests had a larger proportion of priests per head of Catholic population than some other larger dioceses. In many dioceses there were more Catholics per head of population than there were in Westminster.[4]

Hinsley inherited a thriving diocese with 168 churches and chapels. Over 10,000 students were educated in eighty Catholic secondary schools and there were over 33,600 pupils in 108 Catholic primary schools. During 1935 there had been 7,158 infant baptisms, 3,070 marriages, and 1,486 conversions. As in other dioceses there were Catholic charitable institutions. There were Poor Law schools for boys at North Hyde and Mill Hill and for girls at Homerton, Totteridge and Walthamstow. There were schools for physically and mentally disabled children at Pinner, Buntingford, Much Hadham and Potters Bar. Additionally, there was a range of homes and refuges for mothers and babies, and working girls and working boys.[5]

Hinsley's enthronement address contained a brief but complimentary reference to his predecessor and also indicated the general way in which he saw his episcopate developing. He admitted that he did not possess the talents and attainments of Cardinal Bourne and doubted that he would be 'able to follow even afar off such a father and such a leader' but nevertheless he proceeded to outline his own programme and left no-one in doubt about his determination to accomplish it. In the fulfilment of this awesome task Hinsley stated that he would derive courage from reliance on the counsel and support of the Hierarchy, the suffragans and auxiliary bishops of Westminster, the Metropolitan Chapter, and the clergy of his diocese. Claiming to dislike the word 'policy', preferring instead a 'line of action', he stated very firmly that 'our home policy is Catholic Action, our foreign policy is Missionary Action'. 'Catholic Action' was defined by the Pope as 'the share and co-operation of the laity with the Hierarchy in the apostolate'. It was above party and sectional interests and was manifested in all Catholic organisations working together to promote peace and economic and social justice. The 'Schools Question' was one area where Catholic Action had to be mobilized and Hinsley appealed to Catholics to place their schools in 'an unassailable position' whilst requesting that government 'sanctioned a broad national settlement of the education question'. If education was to be the focus of his 'home policy' then, understandably given his recent ministry in Africa, the foreign missions were to be the focus of his 'foreign policy'. Supporting the missions, he reminded his congregation, was their duty and he promised aid and support to those extending the faith in foreign lands.

In addition to the two major proposed directions of his episcopate, Hinsley also referred to two other issues of contemporary significance. The power of the Catholic press 'was of the utmost importance' and 'was a mighty power for spreading the truth and for defending the faith'. It had 'a real apostolate and was second only to the preaching office of those who are divinely commissioned to teach in God's Church'. A Catholic press that worked in conjunction with the Hierarchy, he claimed, 'should be one of the strongest planks in the platform of Catholic Action'. And by intertwining the forthcoming canonisation of Blessed John Fisher and Blessed Thomas More with the celebration of King George V's silver jubilee, Hinsley emphasised the 'twofold loyalty' binding on Catholic citizens – 'our loyalty to God and our loyalty to King and country'. Fisher and More had proved by the shedding of their blood that their loyalty to God could not be usurped by unlawful obedience to the unjust claims of an earthy sovereign. In their martyrdom they were not only true to their God but also true to the proper nature of temporal kingship.[6] According to Ernest Oldmeadow writing in *The Tablet*, the allocution was a rallying cry which should have been termed 'Westminster Calling' because 'it may be taken as our new leader's marching orders'.[7]

Running the Archdiocese

With characteristic practical wisdom Hinsley did not propose any immediate or radical change. He did not arrive in London with a planned programme of reform but eventually introduced administrative procedures that were a gradual and logical result of his practical theology and his personal understanding of circumstances and his authority. To a great extent this was due to the efficient state in which the archdiocese had been bequeathed by Cardinal Bourne. There was no need to introduce sudden change or violent new departures. Westminster was a well-ordered diocese and there was little that needed urgent attention for Bourne had been a diocesan bishop who devoted much time to diocesan affairs. Although Bourne's public impact was relatively small, Bellenger and Fletcher claim that 'the development of a Catholic infrastructure of parishes and schools in his diocese and beyond marked the major achievement of his quiet episcopate'.[8] Hinsley was able to consolidate on this and one of his first diocesan engagements was to open the new church of Our Lady of Lourdes at Southgate in June 1935. In his first Pastoral issued in the same month he acknowledged that other churches were also needed and within the next four years churches were opened in Cockfosters (1936), North Harrow (1939), Perivale (1936), Redbourn (1936), Stanmore (1938) and Swiss Cottage (1938).[9]

Hinsley had to learn how to administer the diocese, become familiar with the issues confronting it, and gain the respect of priests and people. His lack of diocesan experience inevitably compelled him during the early part of his episcopate to spend a considerable amount of time on administration. Compared with his two immediate predecessors at Westminster, both of whom had previous diocesan experience, he was at a great disadvantage and in order to overcome this he had to move quickly. Mgr Elwes wrote that for some time after his enthronement Hinsley's approach was characterized by 'a certain impetuosity, a holy impatience underlying the outward calm that was certainly the work of grace and prayer'.[10] Archbishop Downey said that Hinsley felt frustrated by his age: 'It sometimes weighed upon him that he was so old, at a time when the good he could do was limited by nothing but his physical strength. He wished to be ten or five years younger, that he might do more'.[11] As Heenan remarked, 'he knew that he could hope to be spared to his diocese for very few years and was determined that the brevity of his reign in Westminster would be compensated by the intensity of his apostolate'.[12]

Unfamiliar with the running of a diocese, he relied upon the intimate counsels of a small inner cabinet and the deliberations of a wide range of advisory boards. Fr Heenan, one of Hinsley's personal advisers from among the ranks of his former students, claimed that by striving to avoid autocracy Hinsley inadvertently fell into the trap of generating bureaucracy:

> In addition to the Diocesan Council, which advises on clerical appointments and general affairs, he inaugurated a Diocesan Schools Commission and a Finance Board. There was set up also, a considerable number of minor boards to advise and guide the Archbishop. Moral welfare, youth, Catholic Action, art, music, – every aspect of diocesan activity, in fact, provided a sufficient reason for forming a committee usually composed of both priests and laymen.[13]

Mgr Elwes wrote that Hinsley was

> never a man who wanted things done only in his particular way. He would chose some priest or some layman for a particular responsibility, he would fire him with something of his own zeal for the task he had put upon him, but then he would always let that person do the job in his own way, giving him support and encouragement whenever necessary or when it was sought.[14]

Hinsley was fortunate in having two able and conscientious Auxiliary Bishops, Joseph Butt and Edward Myers. Joseph Butt was ordained priest for the Southwark Diocese in 1897 and in 1901 Bishop Bourne, then Bishop of Southwark, appointed him Rector of St John's College, Wonersh. Removed from that position in 1907 by Amigo, the unfortunate Butt found himself at the centre of one of the many disputes between Bourne and Amigo. The result was his incardination into Westminster where he became Chancellor in 1908. In 1909 he was appointed Vice-Rector of the Beda College and then in 1911 he was nominated as Auxiliary Bishop of Westminster with the titular see of Cambysopolis. He was an erudite priest with wide pastoral experience and was elected Vicar Capitular following Bourne's death.[15] Like Hinsley, Edward Myers was a Yorkshireman. Following an extensive education in Belgium, and at Christ's College, Cambridge, St Edmund's College, Ware, and Oscott he was ordained in 1902 for Westminster diocese. He had been a professor at St Edmund's for thirty years and was college president when he was appointed Auxiliary to Cardinal Bourne in 1932 with the title of Bishop of Lamus. A tall, dignified disciplinarian, Myers was a scholar of renown but also a man with a penchant for organisation and practical action. Hinsley relied heavily upon him.[16]

As national and international affairs began to dominate his episcopate Hinsley increasingly delegated routine administration to his Auxiliaries and his Vicars General. It appeared that Hinsley had learned that his managerial experiences of a small provincial grammar school, an exclusive Roman seminary and a papal legation could not simply be transmitted to a large diocese. It was the appointment as his personal secretary of Fr Valentine Elwes, his former student at the *Venerabile*, that really made Hinsley feel comfortable in organizing his affairs, however. As Cardinal Bourne did not send his seminarians to the English College in Rome there were no priests in the archdiocese who were close to Hinsley or who shared his Roman experience. He therefore turned to the Bishop of Northampton for the services of Fr Valentine Elwes as his secretary. The Oxford-educated Elwes, tall and handsome, had served in the Royal Navy during the Great War but had been an unconventional student at the *Venerabile* in Hinsley's time. Like many of men who came under Hinsley's tutelage, however, Elwes admired the former rector. For his part Hinsley recognised the many talents that Elwes possessed and brought to his side someone not of Westminster and someone he could trust. In 1936 Fr Elwes was incardinated into the Diocese of Westminster and made a Domestic Prelate with the title of Monsignor.[17] It cannot have been easy for the priests of Westminster to see their new Archbishop bring in his own man when he had over 350 diocesan clergy to choose from.

Hinsley had first approached Elwes on 5 May 1935 with the idea that he leave the Diocese of Northampton and move to Westminster as his secretary. He wanted, he told Elwes, a friend and 'one whom I could trust absolutely'. According to Hinsley, Mgr George Coote, Bourne's secretary was 'a good man and devoted' but 'not acceptable to many outside Archbishop's House'. Hinsley soon found out that Coote 'and a few others have complete knowledge of everything and nobody else knows what's what'. The new Archbishop wanted his own man: Coote left and Elwes arrived in August 1935. Elwes' task, according to his near contemporary Fr Heenan, was clear but by no means simple. He had to provide the atmosphere of the *Venerabile* in Archbishop's House. He had to 'interpret' Hinsley to his priests and he had to show that Hinsley's distaste of informality did not imply discourtesy or lack of dignity.[18] Hinsley also tried to enlist the services of Heenan but Bishop Doubleday of Brentwood was unwilling to part with such an able young priest. However, Hinsley consulted Heenan on many issues and his former student became an adviser and speechwriter for the Archbishop.[19]

Although most diocesan clergy would have been trained in their local or regional seminary, some would have been sent to one of the English colleges in Rome, Lisbon, Valladolid, or to St Sulpice in Paris for education and formation. But Westminster, alone of the English dioceses, did not send its seminarians to Rome and almost completely lacked a Roman tradition. Hinsley, therefore, as he had intimated to Cardinal Rossi, knew none of Westminster's clergy and on appointment immediately set about rectifying this deficiency. He systematically visited presbyteries throughout Westminster in order to establish personal contacts. It came as a shock to most priests to have the Archbishop call into the presbytery, check on their circumstances and smoke a cigarette with them, but his informal and personable approach soon won him the respect of most and the friendship of some. To consolidate on this approach he ordered a General Mission for the archdiocese in which he himself took full part by visiting the churches, unannounced, during the mission. However, according to Gordon Wheeler, himself a priest of Westminster, the priests were not entirely convinced that their Archbishop, faced with a myriad of issues, had his 'finger on the pulse of their activities' even though they liked his approachability and informality. Wheeler continued: 'The long and fatherly reign of Cardinal Bourne had made it difficult for anyone to take his place in that particular sphere'.[20] There were others, including Shane Leslie, who claimed that the unimaginative Bourne had made his clergy 'a body of meek and unremarkable yes-men'.[21]

One unfinished task left by Cardinal Bourne was the interior decoration of Westminster Cathedral.[22] Cardinal Herbert Vaughan, who succeeded Cardinal Manning as Archbishop in 1892 and who died in 1903, had commissioned John Francis Bentley to design a cathedral which would be the centre and showpiece of Catholicism in the capital. The resulting Byzantine edifice was opened in 1903 but though complete in all its essentials it was estimated that it would take years to complete Bentley's plans for its interior, central to which was the use of coloured marbles and mosaics to cover the walls, domes, arches and spaces in the vast building. Bourne commissioned work on the main architectural features and side chapels and, despite the shortage of money, some considerable progress had been made by the time of Cardinal Bourne's death in 1935. Much research was undertaken before any scheme was sanctioned but the Cardinal and the artists were subjected to harsh criticism and the choice of the recently-converted sculptor Eric Gill to design the Stations of the Cross did not meet with universal approval.

On his arrival in Westminster, Hinsley was persuaded by Edward Hutton and other luminaries in the artistic establishment to halt Gilbert Pownall's work on the mosaics above the sanctuary and the choir. The critics felt that Pownall was doing damage to 'Bentley's great church, the mother church of England's Catholicism', which was now one of London's significant building and a national monument. Hinsley immediately set up a committee to advise him on all artistic aspects of the cathedral and Pownall was paid off after threatening legal action. It soon became clear that although Hinsley had bowed to artistic pressure there were other reasons behind his decision. In December 1935 he told Bishop Myers that money ought not to be spent on 'unnecessary work' when Catholic schools called for almost every penny of the Church's income. How could the episcopate argue the poverty of Catholics, he asked, when money was being spent on luxuries for the cathedral? He called for simpler and inexpensive designs and found it unacceptable that huge sums of money were required for churches when 'the living stones' had nowhere to learn the faith. In 1936 there were 65 parishes in the diocese without elementary schools and Hinsley promised to rectify the situation.[23] Whereas Cardinal Bourne had been accused of neglecting school building, Hinsley took the opposite tack. No more financial appeals for the cathedral were allowed.

Nevertheless, Hinsley did allow the enhancement of the cathedral to continue as there was £27,600 still available for specific works and £23,000 for the completion of the cathedral in general. The advisory committee advised the Archbishop that Pownall's mosaics in the apse should be removed and Hinsley agreed to this. He also agreed to the hanging of Bentley's great crucifix over the sanctuary but decisions were deferred on the use and design of marble and mosaics on the walls and piers. Eminent architects, including Sir Gilbert Scott, were asked for advice but 'the issue of how far Bentley's intentions should be the guiding principle for later generations' continued to test the advisory committee.

In early 1939 Hinsley decided that the work for which ring-fenced donations had been given should proceed and released the necessary funds. St Joseph's Chapel was to be completed and so was the floor in St Paul's Chapel. It was also agreed that the north aisle should be lined with marble to match that of the south aisle and that new designs for the

choir apse and the tympanum should be commissioned. By April 1940
detailed work on the aisles was planned but in June steps had to be taken
to protect existing marbling from enemy bombs.

It was not Hinsley's vision and administrative achievements as a bishop
which ultimately made his reputation but his interest in international
affairs given focus by the Second World War. Heenan wrote that Hinsley's
methods of running the archdiocese were not 'typically episcopal', but
he went on to say that the healthy state of the diocese in 1943, and the
respect of his clergy, indicated the positive impact that Hinsley had made
as a diocesan bishop.[24]

The Catholic Community Outside Westminster

Hinsley's responsibilities went beyond his own diocesan boundaries and
the Catholic community outside Westminster was strong and vigorous.
In 1935 there were over 2.3 million Catholics in the eighteen dioceses
of England and Wales out of a total population of approximately forty
million.[25] The English and Welsh Hierarchy had been restored by Letters
Apostolic (*Universalis Ecclesiae*) of Pope Pius IX, dated 29 September 1850.
The Metropolitan See was fixed at Westminster and twelve suffragan sees
were established. Between 1850 and Hinsley's appointment in 1935 a
number of structural changes were made, mainly as a result of demographic
developments. The major alteration, by virtue of the Letters Apostolic
Si qua est, was the division of Westminster, in 1911, into the three new
provinces of Westminster, Liverpool and Birmingham but reserving
certain privileges to Westminster. In 1917 another province, Cardiff, was
created with the suffragan see of Menevia. During the same period,
the boundaries of other dioceses were re-arranged and new ones were
created. By Hinsley's time the Province of Westminster had suffragan sees
of Portsmouth, Southwark, Northampton, Nottingham and Brentwood.
The Province of Birmingham had suffragan sees of Shrewsbury, Clifton,
and Plymouth. The Province of Liverpool had suffragan sees of Salford,
Lancaster, Leeds, Middlesbrough and Hexham and Newcastle. The
Province of Cardiff had the suffragan see of Menevia. There was also
a bishop responsible for Army and Royal Air Force chaplains although
that position was vacant following the death of Bishop William Keatinge.
A number of bishops also had auxiliary bishops.[26]

When Hinsley was appointed to Westminster he was advised by Amigo
'to keep the Bishops united' and heal the divisions that had arisen during

Bourne's long episcopate. Amigo and other bishops had suffered from Bourne's aloofness and unwillingness to communicate or consult and it was hoped that the new Archbishop would change things. Hinsley was aware that he would have to rely upon the support of the episcopal bench and introduced a more collegial approach to meetings of the Hierarchy. At his first meeting with his brother bishops it was decided that they would meet three times a year rather than just once and that a standing committee of the four archbishops would be instituted to deal with matters of emergency. In this way Hinsley felt that he could gain trust and hear opinions but some bishops welcomed such changes as an opportunity to reject the methods of Bourne and maintain a check on Westminster.[27]

The dioceses varied tremendously with the majority of Catholics being in the northern and predominantly urban province of Liverpool. In 1937 Fr Philip Hughes published the results of a statistical survey he had undertaken in 1935 in attempt to plot the development of Catholicism in England and Wales. It illustrated the phenomenal growth of the Church during the eighty-four years since the Religious Census of 1851. In 1851 there were 596 Catholic churches and chapels; by 1935 there were 2,388. There were 739 priests in 1851; by 1935 there were 4,982. In 1851 there were sixty-two convents but in 1935 there were 984.[28] Additional information from the *Catholic Directory* also shows that in 1935 there were 1,382 Catholic elementary schools educating 403,917 children and 524 Catholic secondary schools educating 58,129 students. A succession of diocesan bishops, therefore, had presided over a unique period of expansion in buildings, infrastructure, and community.[29]

On the face of things, the Catholic community was loyal to its faith, its priests, its traditions and religious practices. It was, if anything, more overtly confident then at any time in its recent history but was still identified as a sub-culture by its churches, parish schools and outward signs of religion such as processions and confraternities. The Hierarchy had managed to negotiate massive concessions in the build up to the passing of the 1902 Education Act and could still muster huge support in its militant defence of Catholic schools. Led by their bishops, Catholics had played a full part in the national effort during the First World War and had made the same sacrifices as everyone else. The difficult waters of Irish independence had been successfully navigated without English Catholics being tainted with Irish nationalism and Bourne's condemnation of the General Strike of 1926 had won praise in government quarters. And although not entirely accepted throughout society, Catholics and their ecclesiastical, political and cultural leaders could at least claim a hearing in national councils.

The Catholic aristocracy and nobility were dominated by the Duke of Norfolk and his kinsmen the Fitzalan-Howards. There were 128 Catholic peers and baronets, and twenty-five Catholic Lords by Courtesy. In the House of Lords, where the senior Catholic members were the Dukes of Marlborough and Norfolk and the Marquis of Bute, there were thirteen earls, three viscounts, and twenty-seven barons. There were eleven Catholic members of the English Privy Council and twenty-two Catholic Members of Parliament representing mainly urban constituencies in England and Wales. Nineteen were Conservatives and three were Labour. In addition to Catholic spokesmen in Parliament there were also 119 Catholic knights from military, educational, medical, legal and political backgrounds. Some, like the Earl of Granard, Lord Howard of Penrith and Viscount Fitzalan were also members of the House of Lords.[30]

The loyalty of the faithful and the link with the Duke of Norfolk's family were very much in evidence when Hinsley visited the place of his birth on 15 January 1936, nearly sixty years after serving Mass for Canon Heptonstall and Mgr Goldie and over forty years since a brief visit following his ordination. His work at Ushaw and in Bradford, Southwark, Rome and Africa had obviously prevented him from visiting Carlton and to take full advantage of this rare occasion parishioners were bussed in from Selby, Goole and surrounding districts to see the Archbishop. Children lined the route as he approached St Mary's Church where he was welcomed by Fr Vos of Carlton, Fr O'Donnell of Selby, Fr O'Shea of Goole and his cousins Joseph and George Hinsley who had helped to carry the canopy held over the Archbishop. Meanwhile, a huge banner proclaimed *Ecce Sacerdos Magnus – ex Carlton*. Accompanied by Bishop Thomas Shine of Middlesbrough, Mgr Hall of St Charles's, Hull and his secretary Fr Val Elwes, Hinsley then went into the church to celebrate Benediction. 'It was a moving moment', recorded the *Leeds Mercury*, 'when this great man blessed his own people, who had seen his rise in the Church and wondering when they were to see him again. It was a solemn but not a stiff and formal occasion, because the Archbishop was obviously moved at being back among his own people'. In the churchyard Hinsley stopped by the grave of his parents but did not find time to visit either their house or those of his close relatives. As he left the church children sang *O Roma Felix* and from the door of the car the Archbishop said, 'It is a great privilege to me, and a pleasure to return to my native home after long wanderings. I bless all the people of Carlton and my friends and my few remaining relatives'. He then went for lunch with Baroness Beaumont at Carlton Towers.[31]

If Hinsley was circumspect in making changes to his diocese, his initiatives outside the diocese saw him take a very different approach from Cardinal Bourne. Foremost among these was his sale of *The Tablet*, a Catholic weekly magazine formed in the 1840s by Frederick Lucas and which had been bought in the 1860s by Fr Herbert Vaughan, later to become Archbishop of Westminster. On Vaughan's death in 1903 ownership of the weekly passed jointly to the Archbishop of Westminster, the Superior of the Mill Hill Missionaries (which had been founded by Vaughan) and the senior partner of Wortham Weld, the archdiocesan solicitors. By the 1930s, however, under the editorship of Ernest Oldmeadow, *The Tablet* had become a rather intolerant journal attracting few Catholic writers of note. Circulation had fallen and it was in financial difficulties. On 8 October 1935 after Hinsley and the Superior of the Mill Hill Missionaries 'expressed the view that they could not spend Diocesan funds and trust funds for the Missionary Society in running *The Tablet* at a loss, the Trustees passed a resolution to sell the paper. . . .' Hinsley's first intention was to sell the journal to the Hierarchy in equal shares and use it as an organ of Catholic Action but this met with a negative response. At their meeting in late October 1935 the bishops agreed that they were not disposed to undertake any responsibility for *The Tablet* or for *The Clergy Review* which was also in financial difficulty. Oldmeadow was offered *The Tablet* for £900 but was unable to raise the funds. Eventually, it was purchased by Tom Burns, an editor with Longmans Green, who made an offer of £500. At the bishops' prompting, Fr Joseph Keating SJ, editor of *The Month*, was assigned to the editorial board whilst the new directors, Burns and Douglas Woodruff, requested that Fr David Mathew, Chaplain at London University, and Fr Ronald Knox, the Catholic Chaplain at Oxford University, be ecclesiastical advisers. Under Woodruff's editorship, *The Tablet* adopted a less reverential style, attracted talented Catholic writers and commentators, and became an impressively designed and widely read and respected journal. According to Adrian Hastings, it was Hinsley's intention for *The Tablet* to pass into lay hands and thus become an example of lay freedom and enterprise but financial considerations were probably more influential.[32]

Before he became editor, Woodruff was certainly anxious that *The Tablet* should not be transmuted into the organ of Catholic Action and was, like Hinsley, but for different reasons, determined that it become detached from the see of Westminster. He wrote to Archbishop Williams on 23 July 1935 that the sudden removal of Oldmeadow might strengthen the impression that the editorship was in the personal gift of the Archbishop of Westminster. Each new holder of the see, he wrote, appointed the editor of *The Tablet* as he appointed his secretaries and therefore whoever went in as editor prior to a change of ownership would expect his tenure to be jeopardized whenever Hinsley, already advanced in years, died. Williams was of the view that *The Tablet* ought to have some semi-official status in order to keep episcopal tabs on it but Hinsley and others were of the opinion that the journal ought to interpret the Church to the world and the outside world to members of the Church.[33]

Ruffling Establishment Feathers

It was not long before Hinsley, a man of naive honesty, disturbed the delicate balance between the Catholic community and the British Protestant Establishment.

The cause for the canonisation of Bishop John Fisher and Sir Thomas More had been assiduously pursued by English and Welsh bishops who were anxious to secure the honour on the four hundredth anniversary of the martyrs' deaths and further substantiate the strong tradition of English Catholicism. It was felt that the canonisation of two Englishmen, the first since the Reformation, would confirm contemporary Catholic England's commitment to the universal Church and simultaneously reaffirm the loyalty of English Catholics to crown and country.

The efforts of Bishop Amigo and others to plead the martyrs' cause gained momentum throughout 1934 and 1935 and petitions flooded into the Vatican but there were inherent difficulties in pressing the claim too strongly and too publicly for the canonisation could be seen as an example of a foreign power sanctioning the illegal actions of two men in their own country. The bishops and postulators, including Hinsley, took great care therefore to define the loyalty and emphasise the Englishness of Fisher and More despite their execution for refusing to obey the King of England's will.[34]

Aware that the forthcoming canonisation might disturb Protestant sensitivities, Hinsley had stressed in his enthronement allocution that the martyrs' loyalty to God and to their King was not compromised by their refusal to obey the king's will. According to Hinsley they demonstrated that their primary loyalty to God could not be usurped by unlawful obedience to the unjust claims of a temporal sovereign. They died not because of disloyalty to an earthly ruler but because they were faithful to God and the true ideal of Christian citizenship. Their devotion to God and loyalty to their sovereign were, he urged his listeners, fine examples for all to imitate.

The British Delegation to the Holy See had warned London of a possible Protestant backlash yet the Foreign Office allowed British diplomatic participation in the build up to the canonisation. On 10 February 1935 the decree for canonisation was read in the presence of major British figures in Rome including the British Minister to the Holy See and the British Ambassador to Italy. It appeared that the Foreign Office regarded the canonisation simply as a Catholic event which was somehow complimentary to modern England and it appeared none too anxious about Hinsley's archiepiscopal motto. Later, however, the Foreign Office reacted rather differently. When Hinsley asked Sir Charles Wingfield if the King might be disposed to send an emissary to the canonisation ceremony in Rome on 20 May and when the King received a similar request from Viscount Fitzalan, the Southern Department of the Foreign Office reminded them that that the King could hardly be expected to send a representative to a ceremony which honoured two men who had defied royal authority, albeit in the sixteenth century. Wingfield was instructed to attend the canonisation alone while Hinsley was apparently bemused by the fuss he and others had caused. In the event there were only two objections from Protestant fundamentalists to Wingfield's presence: from the Scottish Protestant League and the Women's Protestant Union.[35]

In the summer of 1935 the Hierarchy decided to send a loyal Address to King George V and Queen Mary on the occasion of the Silver Jubilee of their coronation. The Home Office refused to countenance the Address and so Hinsley, short-circuiting usual channels, wrote directly to the King:

> May it please Your Majesty,
>
> I and my brother Archbishops and Bishops are much concerned lest You

think that they and their people are not truly loyal to Your Majesty as their King, for the reason that You did not receive an Address from them when You celebrated Your Jubilee.

We beg to say that we sent a loyal Address to Your Majesty on that occasion but we understand that for some technical reasons the Home Office would not allow this Address to be presented to you. May your Majesty be pleased to accept our most sincere feelings of loyalty and devotion, and an assurance of our fervent prayers at all times.[36]

A peremptory reply came not from the King but from the Home Office and again the loyal address was rejected. Hinsley was distressed that his personal loyalty and that of the Catholic community should be spurned so coldly and in an article in *The Dublin Review*, he wrote of his sadness. Being a Roman Catholic, he wrote, did not prevent him and others from being patriotic Englishmen: 'My faith tells me that genuine loyalty is due to my true and lawful king, and an enlightened patriotism adds to this a sense of duty. . . .' He complained that the King could call himself a Protestant but the name Catholic could not be used in a loyal address. People were no less loyal for being Catholic, he wrote. He then took the opportunity to itemize some of the disabilities still faced by Catholics despite Catholic Relief Acts, the last one being in 1926. The Royal Family had no Catholic advisers or Ministers; no Catholic could be Lord Chancellor yet an atheist could be the keeper of the nation's laws and the King's conscience; Catholics had served with distinction in the British armed services yet they could not present an address of loyalty to the sovereign on whose behalf they fought and died. Like his predecessors, Hinsley was the victim of circumstances dictated by centuries of ingrained anti-Catholicism and traditional constitutional etiquette but his sincere and forceful personal style began to disturb the accepted balance between the Catholic community and the British political establishment.[37]

Within months he was involved in another delicate situation which again involved the Royal Family and once more illustrated the awkward position of the Catholic Hierarchy in the official life of the nation. Just before the death of King George V at Sandringham on 20 January 1936, Hinsley wrote to the Hierarchy reminding them of the protocol which had been stipulated by the Vatican in 1929. This laid down that there could be Exposition of the Blessed Sacrament and prayers for the late King, his family and the new King but there could be no equivalent of the non-Catholic memorial Service nor a public Requiem Mass. Hinsley regarded the King's death as a personal loss. 'Our late beloved King', he said in Westminster Cathedral, 'was as fearless in the profession of his faith in God as in his attitude toward the difficulties and perils of his high responsibilities. . . . ' and he praised the monarch's devotion to duty, his quiet strength under pressure, and the dignity of his family life.[38]

While the Home Office had no jurisdiction in the spiritual affairs of the Catholic Church it did oversee relations between the Church and state and the Hierarchy's messages of condolence and loyalty which were sent directly to King Edward VIII definitely upset the accepted order of things. The Home Office responded by producing a heavy handed memorandum placing the relationship between Catholic Church and the British monarchy and government in the context of precedent and English constitutional law. The difficulty for Hinsley and the more enlightened occupants of government departments was that many in the Establishment continued to view the Catholic Church and the English and Welsh Hierarchy in a traditional and unchanging way and in consequence the spiritual leaders of over two million British subjects of the King were treated discourteously and disrespectfully. Not content with preventing the Hierarchy from presenting a loyal address to King George V, the Home Office subsequently rejected a letter of condolence from the Hierarchy to his son and forbade Hinsley from attending King George's funeral.[39] Despite these slights, Hinsley wrote to the Hierarchy on 16 July 1936 asking them to support the King George V Memorial Fund. Ever practical, he suggested that the Fund, designed to raise money for playing fields might be used to provide play grounds for Catholic schools. Money could not be collected in churches but could be collected at the church door. If Catholics were seen to contribute to the Fund, there might be a chance that they could benefit to a greater extent.[40]

In May 1937, in a further example of Establishment intransigence and its outdated views of Catholicism, no member of the Hierarchy was invited to the coronation of King George VI and Archbishop Guiseppe Pizzardo, the Pope's personal legate, was not allowed to take a place inside Westminster Abbey but had to sit in a special tribune outside the church. In the same month Hinsley and the Hierarchy submitted a loyal address to the new King but this was rejected by the Home Secretary, Sir John Simon, who felt that he could not accept or present an address which contained references to British territorial claims.[41] These claims of course referred to the episcopal sees of the Catholic bishops but it was a spurious and obstructive attitude which enraged the Catholic community. The *Manchester Evening News* reported Catholic indignation at the slight delivered by the Home Office while the *Daily Telegraph* called Simon's reasons 'pettifogging'.[42]

In another episode which provoked an official reaction, Hinsley again let his indiscretion get the better of him, or perhaps did not get anyone to check what he had written. During his early days as Rector of the *Venerabile*, Hinsley had been requested by Cardinal Gasparri, Papal Secretary of State, to write to the British representative at the Vatican asking for an official acknowledgement of Pope Benedict XV's Peace Note of August 1917. In a footnote to an article for *The Dublin Review* in July 1935,[43] Hinsley wrote that the Pope's Peace Note had not in fact been acknowledged by the British government but Stephen Gaselee of the Foreign Office was quick to point out that this was not the case and informed Hinsley that Count John de Salis, the British representative at the Vatican during the Great War had assured Pope Benedict of the King's appreciation and that the British government, would give due and close attention to his note. Gaselee suggested to the Archbishop that a speedy retraction would be welcome in order to rectify any false impression of the government that might ensue from his article.[44] Hinsley agreed but also went further by publishing an apology and Gaselee's letter in *The Dublin Review, The Tablet* and in all Catholic newspapers. Gaselee was impressed by Hinsley's frankness and wrote: 'This is honourable and decent on the part of the Archbishop. I think we should thank him and mention our appreciation of the action he proposes to take'.[45] Hinsley was deeply upset that his article had caused such distress. He was, of any, a man to check his facts and regretted that he had not been more careful. Gaselee takes some credit for minimizing the adverse impact such a mistake might have had but his measured yet firm actions subtly reminded Hinsley of the delicate nature of Anglo-Vatican relations and the need for vigilance.

Cardinal Priest

Like his four predecessors at Westminster, Hinsley was eventually raised to the Sacred Purple and created a Cardinal of the Catholic Church. It was claimed that this honour was delayed due to his public comments on the Italian invasion of Abyssinia and, as Archbishop Downey was to say later, Hinsley thought that his unconcealed criticism of the fascist regime in Italy would make it difficult for the Holy See to honour him without compromising its impartiality in political matters. *The Tablet*, however, felt that the honour had been bestowed comparatively quickly. In a comment reflecting as much on Hinsley's work as on his surprise appointment to Westminster it reported that Hinsley's career was quite unique. 'The new cardinal', it stated, 'will enter the Sacred College after a lifetime divided between parts of the Church's work seldom found together and seldom culminating in this way'.[46]

Pius XI's reaction to Hinsley's outburst against Italy's invasion of Abyssinia in 1936 is perhaps best illustrated by the fact that he later held two consistories to create cardinals but Hinsley was not included in either. It was only a question of time, however, before such a senior and loyal servant of the Church whom the Pope admired so much would be raised to the Sacred College. Within three years of his appointment to Westminster, and after the heat over Abyssinia had cooled, Hinsley received the red *galero* or 'red hat'. He became England's only cardinal and the third in the British Empire – the others being Cardinal Joseph MacRory of Armagh and Cardinal Jean-Marie-Rodrigue Villeneuve of Quebec.[47] His elevation was faster than that of Archbishop Manning, who was promoted to the Sacred College ten years after becoming Archbishop, and Archbishop Bourne who was created cardinal eight years after going to Westminster. Nicholas Wiseman had been created a cardinal-archbishop on the Restoration of the English and Welsh Hierarchy in September 1850 and Herbert Vaughan was elevated to the Sacred College nine months after going to Westminster.[48]

On 11 November 1937 *The Times* reported that Hinsley was about to be created a cardinal at a forthcoming consistory of the Pope and cardinals. A week later it officially announced that he was indeed to be elevated to the Sacred College and on 27 November Hinsley wrote to thank those who had already sent him congratulations and good wishes. He had already left for Rome by this time.[49]

When a new cardinal is created by the pope, he is not present at the Consistory and is 'officially' ignorant of the impending honour. The *biglietto* announcing the elevation is taken by the *Maestro di Camera* of the Cardinal Secretary of State to the new cardinal who, according to custom, is surrounded by clerical and lay friends. Upon receiving the *biglietto* the new cardinal does not read it but hands it to a prelate friend who then reads it aloud. Thus on 13 December, at the English College and in the presence of Mgr Heard, Mgr Duchemin, Dom Philip Langdon and the staff and students, Mgr Riberi, Hinsley's successor in Africa, read out the *biglietto*. In an address of great humility Hinsley compared his short career at Westminster with that of Cardinal Bourne. Unlike Bourne, he said, he could not look back on a lifetime of achievement in London. In his brief time there he had been unable to accomplish 'anything worthy of this high distinction which our Holy Father has conferred upon me'. But of course, as most knew, Hinsley was not simply accorded such a dignity for being at Westminster. In conclusion to a moving speech he said:

> My own personal debt can best, yet inadequately, be repaid to our great and beloved Father by the promise and dedication of what short span of life God allows me to the realization of the great aims and principles which Pius XI has set before the world in his masterly encyclicals: the place of Christ in the reign of Christ – peace in true Christian unity, peace in industry, peace among all peoples and in all social relationships – peace through the divine love of Christ our King.[50]

On Wednesday 15 December Pope Pius XI formally conferred the red galero on Hinsley and on the Thursday there was a public consistory in the *Aula della Benedizione* at which Hinsley made formal obedience to the Pope. Hinsley had got to this ceremony amidst some drama. The car in which he was travelling blew a tyre and Hinsley, in all his robes, had to disembark and get into the following but smaller car occupied by Mgr Elwes and Mgr Smith.[51] Eventually, flanked by Cardinals Cattani and Massini, with Graham Auckinleck, a Westminster student at the English College, holding his long train, and with Mgr Elwes and his *gentiluomo* Captain Frederick Sheedy in attendance, Hinsley was the third of the five new cardinals (Pellegrinetti, Gerlier, Piazza and Pizzardo being the others) to be presented to the Pope. After the singing of the *Te Deum* the new cardinals processed to the Sistine Chapel where they prostrated themselves on the altar steps before the Pope. There then followed the secret ceremonies of the *chiusura della bocca* and the *apertura della bocca* at which the new cardinals signified their duty of keeping and giving counsel to the Pope. Carrying the train of Cardinal Fumosoni-Biondi in the papal procession was an African student studying at the college of *Propaganda Fide*. Fr Birley noted this and commented that 'the flourishing condition of the Missions in British Africa is largely due to the great work of Cardinal Hinsley'.[52]

On Tuesday 21 December Hinsley took formal possession of his titular church, Santa Susanna, located on the Via Venti Settembre. It was an ancient foundation with a masterpiece of a facade by Carlo Maderno (1556-1629) and was the national church of the Americans in Rome. Coincidentally, until 1936 it had been the titular church of Cardinal Lepicier who had been Cardinal Protector of the English College between 1930 and 1936. Hinsley took the opportunity to praise the magnificent organisation and intense activity of Catholic America. From his titular church Hinsley proceeded to the Gregorian University where he and so many of his students had studied. Forsaking the use of a microphone, Hinsley 'filled that tremendous hall with his voice' and reminded his audience of the importance of loyalty to Rome – *Romanità* – and the courage and witness of the English and Welsh Martyrs.[53]

Douglas Newton wrote that even Catholics were astonished at the great crowds and the warmth of affection that greeted Hinsley on his return from Rome on 20 January 1938. He was met at Folkestone by Bishop Amigo, local clergy and their congregations, and a guard of honour formed by the Knights of St Columba. They were, it was reported, cheering him before the cross-Channel boat could reach the quayside. From the quay he was accompanied by the crowds to his railway carriage and similar scenes greeted him on his arrival at Victoria Station. 'Not only did crowds fill the station hall, but the more eager had invaded platform 8, so that as the Cardinal's train came in, it was caught and accompanied by a volume of cheers that seemed to carry it along to the Customs shed where it halted. Only stout barriers and many police kept the throng from swarming into this'. As it was, there was just enough space for the Earl Marshal of England, the Duke of Norfolk, to head a gathering of representative Catholic peers and MPs to greet the Cardinal. These included Lord Fitzalan, Lord Rankeillour, Lord Kenmare, and Lord Russell of Killowen. Members of Parliament included Sir Patrick Hannon of Birmingham, Colonel Sir John Shute of Liverpool, Mr R Grant-Ferris of St Pancras, and Mr Alfred Denville of Newcastle-upon-Tyne. With them were Mgr Collins, Master of Ceremonies, and Captain Sheedy.

When Hinsley appeared at the carriage door he cut an impressive figure, resplendent in scarlet from his broad hat to his buckled shoes. Camera bulbs flashed and the crowds responded cheerfully to Hinsley's waves. Two Queen's Scouts were signalled by Mgr Elwes to carry the box containing the red hat and the scarlet bundle of the *cappa magna* round to the cathedral. The short route from the station yard, across Vauxhall Bridge Road and down Ashley Place to the cathedral was lined by an estimated 10,000 people and the police had difficulty in controlling them. Through this throng the Cardinal was driven slowly in a car followed by a band of Irish pipers. At 6.30pm the large cheers from outside the vast cathedral informed the thousands of people inside that the Cardinal had arrived. The formal reception now began.

Hinsley took off his hat, cloak and *mozzetta* (a small hooded cape which covers the shoulders) and replaced them with the furred and great trained *cappa magna* (a voluminous hooded vestment covering the whole person). After kissing the crucifix presented to him by Bishop Butt he then blessed himself and to the singing of *Sacerdos et Pontifex* processed up the nave led by Captain Bell carrying the mace, Captain Sheedy and Mgr Elwes, the crossbearer and the Chancellor of the Diocese, Mgr Morrogh Bernard, carrying 'breast high a cushion bearing the multi-tasselled red hat'. Hinsley walked under a gold and white canopy carried by 'representatives of the great lay societies' and was described by Newton as 'tall, dignified and paternal'. The red hat was placed on the altar, prayers were said and the versicle *Protector Nostra* was intoned by Bishop Butt. Hinsley then addressed the congregation without using notes in a voice clear, strong and ringing. 'Once again', Newton reported, 'his deep, personal attachment to his flock was his chief emotion' but he was also anxious to convey the good wishes of the Pope whose affection for England was as strong 'as if it were his own personal joy'. It was 'a moving, very intimate, very noble speech, from a heart big with wisdom and experience. A deeper fervour touched it as he spoke of crucial things – Education, the children, Catholic Action, Peace'.

Hinsley then intoned the *Te Deum*, imparted a papal blessing and at the close of the proceedings left for his car. Outside, the crowd was so big that it took Hinsley's car twenty minutes to drive the very short distance from the Cathedral down Ambrosden Avenue to Archbishop's House. Although tired, Hinsley responded to this public show of affection by appearing on the balcony, waving to and blessing the kneeling crowds below. Newton ended his report by saying that it had been a unique and remarkable event and, 'even better, full of the happiest promise'.[54] Later, Hinsley wrote that he had been overwhelmed by the occasion and was both amazed and confused by it all. According to Archbishop Downey, Hinsley felt that his elevation was a wholly unexpected recognition of his value. Yet others could see that it was proof of the Holy See's high opinion of him and there is no doubt that his nomination as cardinal gave Hinsley an immense source of satisfaction. A working-class boy had become a Prince of the Church.[55] Meanwhile, *The Yorkshire Post* proudly proclaimed the first Yorkshire-born cardinal since St John Fisher in 1535.[56]

On 10 January 1938 the clergy of Westminster presented their new cardinal, sitting on a gilded chair in the Throne Rome at Archbishop's House, with an illuminated address and a cheque for £500. In expressing his gratitude Hinsley announced with his typically practical approach to his ministry that he hoped before long to put down before all the Catholic parishes in the diocese complete proposals for Catholic Action – the spiritual organisation of the Catholic laity.[57]

Chapter Twelve

INTERNATIONAL AFFAIRS

1935-1939

The First Test: Abyssinia

Hinsley may have been given the luxury of time in which to familiarize himself with his diocese and issues concerning the English and Welsh Church but there was no such allowance regarding international affairs. When he arrived at Westminster in 1935 Italy's dispute with the independent African country of Abyssinia (now Ethiopia) was the source of considerable international tension and it very soon developed into a crisis that was to place him at the centre of Anglo-Vatican diplomatic relations, strain his personal relations with the Holy See, catapult him into the public eye and severely test his political acumen. As Rector of the English College Hinsley witnessed the slow and careful forging of harmonious links between Great Britain and the Holy See but the Italian invasion of Abyssinia in October 1935 jeopardized these and confronted the newly-appointed Archbishop with the harsh political realities of high ecclesiastical office. Fr Heenan claimed that Hinsley's conduct throughout the Abyssinian crisis was a singular though not misleading example of his humble yet forceful demeanour when doing battle for the Holy See. Heenan was mistaken, however, in believing that the controversy over the Archbishop's actions simply arose over a speech he delivered at Golders Green in October 1935.[1] Its roots were deeper and more complicated.

Despite a treaty of 'perpetual friendship' signed in 1928, relations between Italy and Abyssinia had deteriorated as a result of Benito Mussolini's determination to revive the glories of imperial Rome. Among other tactics, this policy involved aggressive colonial expansion in Africa. The fascist dictator's request for territorial concessions from Abyssinia was refused by its emperor Haile Selassie and Mussolini concluded that only military force would bring the colony he so earnestly desired. Accordingly, Italy began preparations for military action against Abyssinia in 1932 and the financial arrangements were finalized two years later. In December 1934 Italian soldiers based in Italy's African colony of Somalia clashed with Abyssinian troops and investigators at the Wal–Wal oasis inside the adjoining Abyssinia. Mussolini demanded an apology from Abyssinia but one was not forthcoming. In January 1935 Haile Selassie requested that the League of Nations adjudicate in the dispute but Mussolini refused the League's involvement and his forces prepared to invade Abyssinia. In July 1935 the League banned arms sales to both sides and Britain proposed a collective security arrangement to protect Abyssinia. The League subsequently appointed a five-power committee to arbitrate in the dispute but both Haile Selassie and Mussolini refused this offer and on 3 October 1935 100,000 Italian soldiers invaded northern Abyssinia. With no alternative, the League announced Italy to be the aggressor and imposed economic sanctions on her. However, the democratic nations of Western Europe did little to enforce the sanctions, which excluded oil, and did nothing to assist Abyssinia. Moreover, it was revealed in December 1935 that earlier negotiations between Italy and France and France and Great Britain had actually concluded that Italy should receive up to two-thirds of Abyssinia. Italian aggression meanwhile continued unchecked. Through its use of modern weapons against a totally inadequate Abyssinian army and its barbarous tactics against a helpless indigenous population, the Italian army was able to complete the victorious annexation of large parts of the country by May 1936.[2]

Britain's scrupulous adherence to international treaties allowed Italian forces to sail through the Suez Canal and inflict military damage on Abyssinia. It also enabled Mussolini to begin annexing African colonies at a time when Britain itself was moving towards a more enlightened position regarding its imperial responsibilities. Relations between Italy and Great Britain worsened throughout 1935 as Italy ignored all entreaties to resist military aggression. Similarly, Anglo-Vatican relations were adversely affected for although Pius XI and some curial cardinals were apprehensive about Mussolini's militaristic intentions, Cardinal Alfredo Ildefonso Schuster of Milan and other Italian bishops supported Il Duce's aims and publicly declared that the invasion would open the gates of Abyssinia to the Catholic faith and civilization.[3] The Pope was conscious that an anti-Mussolini stance would be highly unpopular in Italy and would also threaten the Lateran Treaty of 1929 which had so recently regularized relations between the Holy See and the Italian government and established the Vatican City as an independent state on Italian territory. Under Article 24 of the Treaty the Vatican had also pledged to remain 'extraneous to the temporal competition between other States and to the international conferences summoned for such an object, unless the contending parties agree to its mission of peace. . . . '[4]

Hinsley was drawn into all this in the summer of 1935 when a surprised British government heard that the Archbishop wished to deliver a personal message from the Pope to King George V 'on the present situation'. This was an unusual form of diplomacy and would have created an awkward precedent had the King received Hinsley in audience. Sir Robert Vansittart, Permanent Under Secretary in the Southern Department of the Foreign Office, suggested that Sir Charles Wingfield, Ambassador to the Holy See and currently in London, should visit Hinsley to discuss the matter. Wingfield tactfully advised Hinsley that his direct approach to the King on behalf of the Pope was unorthodox although neither the King nor the government wished to be discourteous to His Holiness. Hinsley explained to Wingfield that Pius was appealing directly to King George in a sincere personal attempt to seek Britain's influence to prevent hostilities in Africa.[5]

From Rome, Hugh Montgomery, *chargé d'affaires* at the British Legation in Wingfield's absence, warned his political masters in London that English Catholics would deplore any efforts to prevent the Pope communicating with the King in an effort to preserve peace. He had little option, however, but to advise Cardinal Eugenio Pacelli, Papal Secretary of State, that Hinsley did not have diplomatic status and that his use by the Vatican in this way was both undesirable and possibly counter-productive. Pacelli's answer was that Hinsley was only used because there was no Papal Nuncio or Apostolic Delegate in England, a situation that prevented the Holy See from using normal diplomatic channels. Vansittart concluded that Pacelli had acted rather naively and he tried to defuse the situation by informing the Vatican that there was no objection to the Pope writing to the King via the Legation as long as copies of all correspondence were provided to the Foreign Office.[6] *The Tablet* later succinctly summarized the difficult problem facing Hinsley:

> As long as the diplomatic relations between the Vatican and the British government continue to be unique in that the Minister to the Holy See has no counterpart in a Nuncio in London, much will continue to fall

to the lot of the Archbishop of Westminster in the way of the formal and official representation of the Church, and even upon occasion in the way of diplomatic intercourse.[7]

The Vatican may have considered that the Pope corresponding directly with the monarch through Hinsley was the only route open to them but it obviously compromised the Archbishop and led him into relatively deep diplomatic waters. Yet Hinsley must have been aware of the diplomatic sensitivity of the situation. He recognised that his primary allegiance was to the Holy See and by acting on instructions from the Papal Secretary of State he was simply obeying the will of the Holy Father, but his love of Africa, his personal sense of natural justice and respect for the rule of international law also guided him. Carrying out the orders of the Pope was tempered by his humanity for the people of both Italy and Abyssinia and his understanding of the obligations of Britain and the League of Nations. Leading English Catholics, however, were more attuned to the traditional conduct of diplomatic affairs between the Vatican and London. On Lord Fitzalan's initiative and in order to prevent future misunderstandings and further deterioration in Anglo-Vatican relations, the Foreign Office provided Hinsley with guidelines for his dealings with the government. At a confidential meeting between the Archbishop and Sir Orme Garton Sargent, Assistant Under Secretary at the Foreign Office, Sargent informed Hinsley that although he could not be denied access to senior officials of the Foreign Office, he could not be regarded as a direct channel of communication with the Pope or as an unofficial diplomatic representative of His Holiness.[8]

This dialogue between Hinsley and the Foreign office had thus far been conducted in secret but in August 1935 Hinsley was drawn into a very public debate about the role of the Pope in the Abyssinian crisis. In a letter to *The Times* on 19 August George Lansbury, leader of the Labour Party, called upon Pope Pius to convene a peace conference to resolve the Abyssinian situation.[9] Four days later Hinsley replied in the same newspaper that the Pope had consistently condemned the arms race and had spoken out against war but the rulers of the world had seemingly rejected his words, actions and prayers. The Pope's earnest endeavours for peace had been 'met by the Powers with blind eyes and deaf ears'. It was not for the Pope to arbitrate, Hinsley concluded, but for liberal democracies and the League of Nations to act in the face of aggression.[10] Viscount Cecil, a leading figure in the League of Nations

Union thanked the Archbishop for 'his excellent and timely letter'.[11]

On 2 September Hinsley wrote another letter to *The Times* in which he interpreted a speech given by Pius XI to an International Congress of Nurses on 27 August. Hinsley addressed the temporal status of the papacy and in particular the role of Pius in the current Abyssinian situation. Drawing upon his African experience, he also set out his own views on colonial trusteeship. First, he stated that the papacy was an independent institution, that the 'fearless' Pope was not a subservient prisoner of Signor Mussolini (as the Bishop of Durham had asserted), nor was Mussolini in a position to intimidate the Pope. Secondly, the Pope had called for a period of calm reflection and prayer rather than military conflict but, contrary to Lansbury's request, the Pope was a teacher not an arbitrator. And finally, Hinsley called upon those civilized nations with responsibility for 'backward races' to understand the moral justification of their trusteeship and fulfil their sacred obligation to secure the moral and material betterment of mankind. The League of Nations advocated trusteeship and Hinsley proposed that Great Britain should revise its mandates to demonstrate its care for native peoples and avert, with other colonial powers, the 'growing distrust of the native peoples and the ultimate combination of the coloured against the whites. . . .'[12]

As the dispute dragged on Hinsley became more fearful of the association between the Italian Catholic Church and Mussolini's fascist regime. In particular, he was concerned how that association was being interpreted in England and felt that English Catholics were being asked unfairly to justify the relationship between the Church in Italy and Mussolini's colonial ambitions. On 23 September 1935, having received a memorandum from the Catholic Institute for International Relations, of which he was President, he wrote a remarkably frank letter to Cardinal Pacelli:

> The enclosed memorandum I send to your Eminence because it clearly expresses the anxiety of our Catholic people concerning the necessity of dissociating the Church from the action of the Italian government in refusing the good offices of the League of Nations for the settlement of its claims in Africa, and consequently in taking upon itself the grave responsibility of war. . . . For my part I endorse the statement of this organisation of the faithful . . . and I humbly express my sympathy with their desire to make clear to our fellow countrymen, already so hostile to the 'Roman Communion', that the Catholic Church is in no way associated with what outside Italy is considered a violation of an international agreements and

an act of aggression. I have also reason to know that my fellow Archbishops and Bishops in this country would recommend this appeal to the Holy Father.[13]

Pacelli did not reply to the letter and the Foreign Office, which received a copy, made no comment. The letter was unlikely to increase Hinsley's popularity in Rome.

Meanwhile Hinsley continued to make robust statements about the war. On 11 October he again wrote to *The Times* emphasizing that the Italians were inflicting every device of modern mechanical warfare on helpless Abyssinians who were almost entirely without medical aid. But he did not only castigate Italy. Christian charity, he continued, demanded that Great Britain as a leading member of the League of Nations, which had manifestly failed to prevent the war, should do all that was humanly possible to alleviate the misery and sufferings of Abyssinians.[14] In an article in the Jesuit periodical *The Month* he argued that if indeed Italy had grievances then warfare was not the way to address them. He was also critical of those European countries which exploited indigenous Africans by having them serve in their armed forces.[15]

Hinsley's trenchant comments and the Pope's role in the crisis aroused considerable interest and on Sunday 13 October, in a sermon preached at the Church of St Edward the Confessor in Golders Green, he took the opportunity to clarify the position as he saw it. 'I am told', he said, 'that the Catholic public and perhaps members of other religious bodies expect that ... I should express my thoughts and feelings on the Italian–Abyssinian situation as affecting the Pope and the Church'. Characteristically, he did not flinch and proceeded to speak his mind freely 'without fear of the favour or of the hostility of Extremists – whether they be Fascists, Nazis, Bolshevists or Imperialists of any type, whether they be Pacifists or Jingoists'. Fascism, he declared, was 'an example of the present day deification of Caesarism and of the tyranny which makes the individual a pawn on the chess board of absolutism'. He denounced those who would lead the world into a 'whirlpool of blood' and the ruination of civilization. 'Indignation has no bounds', he said, 'when we see that Africa, that ill-used continent of practically unarmed people, is made the focus and playground of scientific slaughter' and he warned that consequences would be wrought by future generations of Africans against the white man. But the crux of his sermon came in a passage that related directly to the Pope's position:

...what can the Pope do to prevent this or any other war? He is a helpless old man with a small police force to guard himself, to guard the priceless art and archaeological treasures of the Vatican, and to protect his diminutive state which ensures his due independence in the exercise of his universal right and duty to teach and to guide his followers of all races. Can he denounce or coerce a neighbouring power – a power armed with absolute control of everything and with every modern instrument of force? He could excommunicate and place under interdict! Yes! And thus make war with his dictator neighbour inevitable, besides upsetting the peace and consciences of the great mass of Italians with the result of a fierce anti-clerical outbreak. Spiritual penalties are for the correction of those who are knowingly guilty. And spiritual penalties for a world daily more godless are of little avail.

The Pope is not an arbitrator. Has he been invited by the contending parties in this dispute to be judge and arbitrator to settle the quarrel? He has not. I have insisted and I insist again that the Pope was expressly excluded by the secret Pact of London in 1915 from future deliberations in the Councils of Peace. Until he is invited to intervene by both sides, he cannot act as judge. But as an independent sovereign he has no grounds for intervention in this present case, not even those grounds enjoyed by a member of the League of Nations, to join which League, through Italy's express stipulation, he was not invited. The present Pope and his predecessors have made incessant and unavailing efforts to avert war and to instill some ordinary commonsense into the conditions of peace.

He pointed out that the Pope had been asked to unilaterally condemn Italy's action but yet the League of Nations could not decide which side was at fault in the dispute. The Pope had a duty to pontificate in cases of morality but could not castigate one side before the League made a decision on the same issue. On several occasions, Hinsley continued, the Pope had condemned aggression and branded self-defence as a pretext for guilty aggrandizement.[16]

Newspaper editors had a field day with Hinsley's comments, especially with his description of the Pope as 'a helpless old man'. The *Church Times* gleefully exclaimed that such a weak personage, 'terrorized into silence by wickedness in high places', was submitting to fascism and, as an Italian bishop, the Pope had little choice but not to upset the Italians. Hinsley, it claimed, had concluded that God's cause now seemed to rest on a rule which he described as 'the deification of Caesarism'. It regretted the silence of His Holiness but that regret had intensified now Hinsley had explained the reasons for it.[17] *The Times* was filled with letters condemning Hinsley's apologia for the Pope. One, from Charles

Warner, derided his argument that the Pope was guardian of priceless artifacts whilst making no mention of his guardianship of the great moral virtues sorely needed at the present time. Hinsley's remarks about the Pope and Italians, Warner continued, 'suggested the further displacement of expediency by treacherous compromise'. 'Principle dethroned by expediency degenerating into betrayal was not expected of the Roman Catholic hierarchy', he thundered.[18] There were few letters in support of Hinsley and the Pope. Hinsley was deeply disturbed by the reaction to his sermon and felt that his remarks were being misrepresented and taken out of context. Hinsley's reply to Warner simply reiterated the comments he had made at Golders Green, and before, and ended by writing that 'the pope is the best judge of his own duty'.[19]

The Golders Green sermon was indeed a remarkable public statement from a senior Catholic churchman. Writing after Hinsley's death, Bishop David Mathew, his Auxiliary Bishop in Westminster, observed that the Cardinal 'had only a diluted sympathy for other members of the Sacred College, unless they earned his friendship by some other title, and he was not drawn to the *majesty* of the Holy See'. This last fact, according to Mathew, went some way to explaining the sermon for Hinsley saw the person not the office and he spoke about the inability of the Pope as an individual to effect change in a world where nations did nothing to prevent conflict.[20]

Such an interpretation was not welcomed in Rome, however, from where Montgomery reported to the Foreign Office that Hinsley's words had made a 'a harsh impact' and the Pope had been very much upset by the reference to him as 'a helpless old man'. But, he continued, 'the real agent of the aggravation had been Hinsley's outspoken condemnation of the tyranny of fascism, a condemnation made expressly with the intention of dissociating English and Welsh Catholicism from any aura of Mussolini's state system. . .'[21] Cardinal Camillo Caccia-Dominioni, Prefect of the Pontifical Household, told Montgomery that although the sermon had made a bad impression in Vatican circles, he felt sure that the Archbishop had spoken sincerely with 'the intention of making it clear that English Roman Catholics were thoroughly English'.[22] However, Hinsley was not speaking on behalf of all English Catholics and certainly not the Hierarchy. Bishop Amigo of Southwark, for example, Hinsley's long-time friend and mentor, and Bishop John Kiely of Plymouth were public admirers of Il Duce and in February 1936 Amigo wrote of the danger to religion in Italy if Mussolini were to be overthrown by the policy of the League of Nations.[23] Nor was Amigo alone: eminent Catholic writers such as Hilaire Belloc and G K Chesterton were also fervent admirers of Mussolini.

Vatican officials thought that Hinsley had to be reined in before the delicate balancing act of Pius XI with the fascists was completely disturbed and the Pope severely compromised by an outburst of Italian anti-clericalism and fascist restrictions on Catholic life. Naturally, the Vatican could not summon Hinsley for a dressing down or it would reveal its own position, so other approaches had to be considered whereby the new man at Westminster might be restrained. The attempt to curb Hinsley's public utterances occurred through circuitous channels. Archbishop Paschal Robinson, an Irish Franciscan friar whose diplomatic postings for the Vatican included the Peace Conference at Paris in 1919, Apostolic Visitor to Palestine and Archbishop Delegate to Malta, became papal nuncio to the Irish Free State in 1929. In this capacity Robinson frequently travelled to Rome and told Montgomery at the British legation that senior Vatican officials considered that Hinsley was speaking and writing far too much about the Abyssinian crisis although they recognised that his sympathies were consistent with those of his compatriots. In the absence of a nuncio to England the Vatican thus alerted Hinsley, possibly through the Foreign Office via Sir Stephen Gaselee and then through Lord Fitzalan, that while acknowledging the sincerity of his remarks, silence might be the best policy.

His confidence shaken, Hinsley appeared to heed Fitzalan's advice and said little more about Abyssinia. Moloney observed that he gave a 'jagged and undiplomatic but clear lead' on an issue which threatened to divide English and Welsh Catholics from their government while Crichton remarked that his attempt to defend the Pope 'produced nothing but the gaffe of the century'.[24] Hinsley could hardly be blamed for being unable to fit into a diplomatic situation that was completely alien to him but his public utterances could have and should have been more politically astute. The Abyssinian affair demonstrated an incompatibility of interests between the British government and the Holy See and Hinsley was caught in the middle. In the absence of a nuncio Hinsley felt that it was his responsibility to protect the Pope and speak for the Church.

There can be little doubt that his opposition to fascism was overtly stronger than that of Pius but Hinsley was not living in a totalitarian state. Pius XI's silence on the crisis was taken as tacit approval of Il Duce's actions but the Vatican had taken some measures to distance itself from Mussolini. Before the Abyssinian crisis Pius had condemned the fascist transformation of the Italian state into an all-powerful determinant of the nature of public life. In 1929 senior officials of the Congregation for the Propagation of the Faith had negotiated directly with the Abyssinian government to enable Catholic missionaries to work in the country and Pius warned Italian missionaries that they must keep aloof from the spirit of nationalism. In 1930 the Pope publicly attacked Mussolini's policies and in 1931, in his encyclical *Non abbiamo bisogno*, he berated the fascists for their persecution of Catholic Action in Italy. Mussolini, therefore, did not receive automatic support from the Vatican. Yet the Pope's comments on the invasion of Abyssinia were so circumspect and couched in such generalities that it was impossible to discern his true feelings. He could not be expected to pass judgement on a case that had not been presented to him for arbitration but before hostilities commenced he issued a rather ambiguous statement of neutrality in which he stated that '. . .if the need for expansion is a fact, we must also take into consideration the right of defence, which also has its limits, and a moderation which must be observed if the defence is to remain guiltless'.[25] Fascist newspapers omitted the statement from their reports and were later to misinterpret and misrepresent his comments on the war. Some critics of Pius felt that despite his public pronouncements against fascism and his reservations expressed in well-written encyclicals, the authoritarian Pope failed to condemn fascism outright. In France and Germany some newspapers actually accused the Vatican of financing the Abyssinian War but a more prevalent view was that the Vatican considered fascism a better option than godless communism which would have overrun Italy had the fascists not brought stability and order. The Vatican, it seemed, preferred a diplomatic solution to the Abyssinian crisis for an Italian defeat might have led to Mussolini's collapse and domestic turmoil. The British Foreign Office considered the Vatican's policies to be opaque but in the event, the League of Nations, the Vatican and the major European democracies all came out of the Abyssinian crisis with blemished reputations.[26] For Hinsley it had not been a successful entry into public life. It also emphasised, as if he needed to be reminded, that the Hierarchy was not disposed or compelled to agree with his political sentiments.

Hinsley and The Spanish Civil War

Just over a year after Hinsley's arrival at Westminster civil war broke out in Spain and was to last until March 1939. It was another tortuous test for Archbishop Hinsley and if the case of Abyssinia could be regarded as a simple case of Mussolini's immoral and opportunistic politics, the situation in Spain was far more complicated and much closer to home. The war, between a coalition of the socialist Republican government and its communist and ultra left-wing sympathizers against the fascist Falange party and the Nationalists, was also brutal and vicious. The Holy See regarded the war as a struggle between Christianity and godless communism, a position adopted by the English and Welsh Hierarchy which issued a Pastoral against 'the anti-God forces ... sapping and mining the foundations of society in Spain'. It urged British Catholics to unite behind the banner of Catholic Action 'against the battalions of evil' and by implication, therefore, to support the Nationalist cause. Most Catholics were prepared to take this stance.[27]

Following the abdication of King Alfonso XIII in April 1931, a new constitution declared Spain a workers' republic, separated Church and state, secularized the schools and broke up large landed estates. It was also the signal for an outburst of anti-clericalism: the Society of Jesus was dissolved, religious processions were banned and churches were burnt, developments which outraged those Catholics who had voted for moderate republicanism. The Vatican was also extremely disturbed by these events and without supporting the restoration of the monarchy or condemning the republic, it spoke out against attacks on the Church and Catholic conscience. The predominantly Catholic people of Spain, however, again returned a coalition Republican government to power in the 1936 elections.

In July of the same year the Spanish army, under the conservative General Francisco Franco y Bahamonde, rose in rebellion against the Republican government and was joined by the majority of the Spanish army, large elements of the police, civil servants and diplomats, rich landowners and the clergy. The ensuing war was regarded as a conflict of ideologies competing not only for the political heart of Spain but also of Europe and both sides attracted military support from across the continent and beyond. The communist government of Soviet Russia sent men and materiel to the Republicans who also attracted an International Brigade of over 40,000 supporters including men from Britain, Europe and the United States. Franco and the Nationalists, on the other hand, received substantial military aid from Hitler's Germany and Mussolini's Italy. The German Luftwaffe's Condor Legion bombed Spanish cities whilst Italy sent 10,000 regular troops. From Ireland and from among the English-based Irish community General Eoin O'Duffy took 700 fascist Blueshirts to side with Franco.

Throughout the war both sides committed widespread atrocities. Anarchists, beyond the control of the Republican government, sacked churches and systematically waged a campaign of frenzied and brutal violence against the clergy and religious. Over 7,000 priests, monks and nuns were murdered in the war. Such actions served only to strengthen international Catholic support for Franco but the Nationalists were equally as murderous and it has been estimated that they killed Republican supporters in even greater numbers. Once again Pope Pius XI was compromised. Judged by some to be a tacit supporter of the Italian invasion of Abyssinia, he was now linked to the Nationalist and largely Catholic forces under Franco. While the Holy See had to be grateful to Franco in his fight against the communists and anti-clericalists, the *Caudillo's* reliance on Hitler and Mussolini presented the Pope with a difficult problem. Franco, meanwhile, skillfully bolstered his Catholic image by portraying himself as a Christian warrior fighting a crusade for the survival of the Universal Church.[28]

Hinsley and other bishops, of course, were sympathetic to the Vatican view that Spain was the battlefield between rampant atheistic Marxism and the traditional Christian culture of Europe. However, the Vatican consistently refused to support Franco openly even though it stood to benefit by his victory and the heads of the Catholic Church in France, Ireland and Austria all wrote to the Vatican expressing their sympathy and understanding with the Holy See and the Spanish Hierarchy. On home territory, the Hierarchies were not slow to publicly express their support for Franco. Archbishop MacRory and the Irish Hierarchy, supported by the Irish press, welcomed Franco's crusade.[29] On 20 October 1936 the English and Welsh Hierarchy expressed deep sympathy to the Spanish bishops but, like the British government, considered that military non-intervention was the best policy.[30] This did not, however, preclude support for Franco and Bishop Amigo again broke episcopal ranks as he had done in the Abyssinian crisis. At the beginning of the war in Spain he declared that 'we cannot side with the Communists. . .' and from the pulpit in St George's Cathedral said that if Franco was a 'rebel' then so was he. He continued: 'The people in Spain who are attacking the government were not rebels, they are fighting for the Church of God'. It was a pronouncement likely to cause a furore and it did. Catholics and non-Catholics alike attacked the bishop for his support of Mussolini and now Franco. Unbowed, Amigo fought his corner stridently and vigorously, gave support to organisations favouring the rebels and became Vice-President of The Friends of National Spain whose purpose was to procure material aid for those fighting on the Nationalist side and publicize their cause. To Amigo, Franco was a good Catholic fulfilling his duty on the side of God versus the Devil.[31]

The persecution of the Catholic Church in Spain meant that most British Catholics, like Amigo, openly supported Franco and those who opposed him, or his methods, were made to feel like 'a beleaguered minority in the face of the "corporate" outlook . . . of the hierarchy and priesthood'.[32] The popular Catholic press was totally behind the Nationalists and printed horrific stories of Red atrocities. The Catholic writer Hilaire Belloc called Franco 'the man who has saved us all' whilst Fr Cuthbert Lattey SJ held that the Nationalist leaders would one day be recognised 'as the saviours of Europe'.[33] Catholic peers, however, were reluctant to compromise Hinsley or embarrass the government and spoke judiciously on the Spanish situation. Some Catholic MPs, especially those with predominantly Catholic constituencies, were also circumspect about condemning Franco and the Hierarchy but others were openly critical of Hinsley's definition of Franco's rebellion as a crusade and accused the Hierarchy of browbeating Catholics into support for the Nationalists.[34] *Blackfriars*, the Dominican magazine, and *The Sower*, founded in 1919 by Fr Francis Drinkwater, whilst not overtly favouring the Republicans, called for a more thoughtful, restrained and non-partisan approach to the conflict.[35] Subtle philosophical and moral arguments were unlikely to gain Hinsley's favour in the face of the Republican onslaught against his Church but he refused to take sides publicly or be drawn into open debate on the war. The Irish Hierarchy enthused over the Nationalist cause but Hinsley was more prudent. When Eoin Duffy, a former leader of Fine Gael and organiser of the Irish Eucharistic Congress, asked if he could use the Archbishop's name to sanction appeals to Irish and Catholics who were resident in England to support Franco, Hinsley replied that his position 'precluded him from having anything whatever to do with military or political activities with regard to Spain. His position would be different were it a question of providing an ambulance to succour the wounded and sick no matter to which side of the struggle they belonged'.[36]

Some left-wing Catholics harboured sympathy for the Republicans and expressed it through liberal newspapers and journals. A tiny minority were members of *Pax* the largely-Catholic peace society which sought to strengthen Catholic support for the League of Nations. They and other predominantly Catholic intellectuals had difficulty with anyone who openly supported Franco, like some of the Hierarchy, or those who professed neutrality. But this neutrality was transparent and fooled few. The Catholic artist Eric Gill, for example, claimed that the Hierarchy supported the Nationalists and thus was prevented from publicly condemning Nationalist aerial attacks on Spanish towns. Like others, Hinsley may have regarded the artist as eccentric but he would allow for no flexibility of interpretation. He was characteristically blunt in his reply:

> You have no right or justification for stating that the Catholic Church in Great Britain has identified itself with the Nationalists.... But it is impossible to ignore the facts, and the comparison of the conditions prevailing in Government and Nationalist Spain is more than sufficient excuse for the present attitude of many Catholics in this country.... In fairness to the Bishops and myself you are under the obligation of sending or showing this letter to your fellow signatories, some of whom may then begin to use the right eye as well as the left.[37]

The Hierarchy's humanitarian assistance to those on the Nationalist side, however, added weight to those who considered the Catholic Church was biased in favour of Franco. In September 1936 the bishops had established a Committee for the Relief of Spanish Distress but although its aims were to relieve suffering for the wounded, refugees and the destitute in the whole of Spain, it could hardly be described as impartial. It was not intended to be, for the bishops sought to give evidence to their co-religionists in Spain that Britain contained some who actually sympathized with their cause. By 1937 over £8,500 had been raised by the Committee for dining rooms to feed necessitous children but most of it had gone towards the provision of mobile hospitals for the Nationalist army. Nevertheless, Hinsley and the Hierarchy could not surrender their apparent neutrality irrespective of their obvious support for those forces fighting for the Church against violent and savage secularism.

A small but significantly vocal group of Catholics challenged the Hierarchy's views that Franco was simply engaged in a holy war against the communists. Fr Francis Drinkwater, who had earlier called for a more balanced approach, eventually rejected the mainstream Catholic position and claimed that Franco should not be supported so vigorously. In an article in *The Catholic Herald* in June 1937 he contrasted the silence of the Catholic press on the nationalist bombing of the town of Guernica with its earlier outright condemnation of Red 'atrocities'. The Catholic press, he had long argued, had been far too militaristic. How could the Church teach peace, he asked, while supporting those who made war? Hinsley rounded on Drinkwater and wrote that 'your utterances were beyond explanation. I regret your imprudence, your own inaccuracy – and ill-timed, ill-placed outburst'. Drinkwater and others were not to be silenced easily, however. In 1938 a number of priests and laymen protested to the Hierarchy against the Nationalist bombing of civilians and claimed that

> the Catholic Church in this country has made the cause of the Insurgents its own, and authorities of the Church have identified the cause of the Insurgents with the cause of Christ. We respectfully submit that a grave responsibility rests on the authority of the Church to ensure that the methods employed by the Insurgents do not outrage the teachings of Christ.

Hinsley replied that the memo showed 'both a lack of discrimination and judgement and lack of loyalty and credulity given to Red propaganda'.[38]

Hinsley was especially, but privately, severe with Catholics who publicly questioned the Church's position, espoused the Republican cause or endeavoured to enlist left-wing Catholic support for it, but he was no less critical of those who sought to relate Catholicism unconditionally to the fascists and the Nationalists. In 1936 the Labour Trades Union Congress produced *The Drama of Spain* and *Catholicism and the Civil War in Spain*, two pamphlets which favoured the Republicans and condemned the Catholic Church's support for Franco. Hinsley wrote to Sir Walter Citrine, General Secretary of the TUC, and objected strongly that a political body which was supported by large numbers of Catholics should publicly and without evidence produce damning indictments of the Church. Such misrepresentations of the Vatican and the Catholic Church in Spain, he argued rightly, would rebound on the Party among

Catholics in England.[39] In August 1936 *The Catholic Worker*, based in Wigan and one obvious manifestation of Catholic Action, had already warned its readers against supporting the TUC's General Council in its call on behalf of the Spanish workers giving their lives for the preservation of democracy. According to *The Catholic Worker*, the Labour Party was deceptive in trying to justify the Republican government's cause by demonizing the Nationalists. While it did not completely vindicate the revolutionaries, the paper could not advocate the assistance of a government that was to make 'Spain free for Marxism, Freemasonry and Communism'. It argued that the rebellion was against a Republican government that had never governed but had been simply intent on establishing a left-wing dictatorship and had allowed a reign of terror to precipitate the Civil War. The attempts at pre-war Catholic Action in Spain had been dashed alongside the many palaces and churches which had been destroyed. The basis of social justice had been shattered but the paper did not attempt to hide the fact 'that a large proportion of Spanish workers is today inspired by a virulent hatred of the Church and her doctrines'.[40]

Hinsley's disenchantment with Labour's response to the war was matched by his growing alienation from the League of Nations Union of which he was a Vice-President. The L.N.U. worked for peace, was widely supported across the ecclesiastical and political spectrum, and included many members of the Catholic Social Guild. In October 1936 Hinsley learned that the L.N.U. was to become closer associated with the International Peace Campaign, a Moscow sponsored organisation. The possibility of the L.N.U. veering to the left seriously concerned Hinsley who was becoming increasingly pessimistic about the League's inadequacy in the face of military aggression. Fr David Mathew's advice to the Archbishop was that he should resign discreetly from the L.N.U.; Archbishop Downey had already done so having decided that it was riddled with communists. Fr Leo O'Hea, however, Hinsley's representative on the L.N.U.'s Christian Organisations Committee, argued against the Archbishop's resignation fearing that the loss of such a prestigious Vice-President would seriously weaken the L.N.U. and adversely affect the reputation of the remaining Catholic members. For Hinsley the last straw came in April 1937 when the L.N.U. voted in support of supplying the Spanish Republican government with food and munitions, thus contravening both the League of Nations sanctions and the British government's policy of non-intervention. He informed Lord Cecil that it was essential for him to detach himself from the political direction in which the L.N.U. was moving.[41] Cecil's reply failed to satisfy Hinsley and he placed the matter before a meeting of the Hierarchy in April 1938 at which the bishops dissociated themselves from any political resolutions passed by the Executive Council of the L.N.U. The Hierarchy's decision left Hinsley in an awkward position as a Vice-President of the L.N.U. but he resigned in December 1938 after being finally convinced that the L.N.U. was becoming more doctrinaire, increasingly influenced by the I.P.C. and more openly supportive of the Republican cause.[42] He instructed Mathew, O'Hea and other Catholic members of the L.N.U.'s Christian Organisations Committee to resign. *The Tablet* commented that the L.N.U. 'was not a body in which the Hierarchy can be expected to hold honorary offices'.[43]

Hinsley had access to information about the situation in Spain from Mgr Edwin Henson who had been Rector of the English College in Valladolid since 1924. Henson had an extensive network of friends and personal contacts and exerted considerable influence on Catholic opinion in England through his correspondence and accounts of Republican tactics. He had witnessed some of the atrocities committed against the Church in the early 1930s and predicted the leftward swing in the *Cortes*, the Spanish parliament, in the elections of Spring of 1936. In March of the same year the Hierarchy pledged to support the 'college which has done so much for the Church in England' by appointing Hinsley and Bishops Amigo and Doubleday as a 'Vigilance Committee' to keep a watch on the college's interests.[44] Henson's letters gave Hinsley a first-hand record of the war and also his insight on the predicament of the college, its staff and students and his interpretation of events as they affected the Church in northern Spain. The fighting around the college in the summer of 1936 had been light but it was felt prudent to move the students to the college's country retreat. 'All known communists', Henson reported, 'have been arrested and many of them shot after a summary trial'.[45] Hinsley was glad to hear that the students were safe but told Henson that the bishops wished to know how they could help the suffering. Bishop Amigo told Henson that he wished to have the students sent home[46] but they, Henson replied, wished to remain at Valladolid. Atrocities, Henson reported, were not taking place everywhere and life was 'normal' in Nationalist areas[47] but in September 1936, indicating another twist in the complexity of the war, Henson reported that the Archbishop of Valladolid, a Basque, was missing and had presumably returned home. Like other Basques, the Archbishop, was not necessarily a supporter of the Nationalist cause for the Republican government had indicated that the Basque region would gain autonomy.[48]

As the war progressed, conditions worsened for seminarians in Spain. By 1937 students were evacuated from the Irish College at Salamanca, the College in Valladolid was occupied by soldiers, and its country house had become a Nationalist convalescent home. Writing of the increasing intensity of the conflict, Henson wrote to Hinsley that 'the struggle here is between God and the devil represented by the international trinity of Financiers, Masons and Jews; and these three are one in Russia, the anti-Christ'. Franco's Spain, on the other hand, 'was blessed by God' but he feared that the people of England were being duped by their leaders who were plutocratic oligarchs. 'Jew and Masons', he continued, were the actual leaders of England. Such prejudice, however, unpalatable, was characteristic of the time.[49] Hinsley himself called 'The Reds . . . the most clever liars ever inflicted on the world' and was conscious that the British press was biased towards the Republicans.[50] The Hierarchy did not only have to contend with a largely antagonistic press. The Church of England was particularly detached from the Spanish crisis and regarded it as a distant and remote struggle. In the House of Lords in November 1936 Lord Rankeillour criticized Archbishop William Temple of York for his cold tone and lack of sympathy for the sufferings of fellow Christians in Spain. In Spring 1937 the Anglican Deans of Canterbury and Chichester and other clergy further complicated the divide between the Churches by publishing a belittling account of the attacks on Catholics in Spain. Their comments were received with shock and disgust by the Catholic establishment. Catholic peers supported the Nationalist cause but were careful, like Hinsley, not be drawn into open sponsorship of Spanish relief organisations; such actions would have compromised their stated position of neutrality. Peers like Rankeillour and Iddesleigh refused to patronize any fund.[51]

Just as the British press favoured the Republicans, the English and Welsh Hierarchy increasingly and heavily leant the other way. Bishop Amigo had openly sided with Franco from the beginning. In 1937 Archbishop Williams of Birmingham told the editor of the *Birmingham Post* that 'as he believed the only real basis for European civilization is Christianity, you may be able to appreciate my feeling that all Christians ought to unite against the threat to destroy Christianity and establish Atheism, for that is what is happening in Spain'.[52] As the war progressed the bishops became more partisan and their anti-communist statements became more strident as they heard accounts of Republican atrocities. Similarly, a strong anti-communist stance was generated by the publication in March 1937 of Pius XI's *Divini Redemptoris*, his encyclical on atheistic communism. On 9 May the encyclical was read at all Masses and the day declared one of public prayer for the salvation of the world from the menace of communism. And in July 1937 the Hierarchy publicly espoused the letter of the Spanish Hierarchy justifying Franco's military uprising.[53]

As Archbishop of Westminster, Hinsley's major task was to prevent misrepresentation of the Church's stance while doing whatever he could to alleviate suffering, but he fell foul of Mgr Henson when he called for the support of refugee children from the besieged city of Bilbao and annexed a letter from the Bishop of Vitoria to substantiate his plea.[54] Bilbao was a Basque city and according to Henson the Bishop of Vitoria, who had not signed the Joint Pastoral of the Spanish Bishops in July 1937, was responsible for the attitude of the Basques who did not support Franco but preferred to exploit the opportunity of war to secure Basque independence. 'Anyone who supports the refugee children from Bilbao', wrote Henson to Hinsley, 'indirectly supports the Communists in Spain. The removal of those children is an act of war. I am distressed beyond measure by this turn of events'.[55] Through his private secretary, Fr Joseph Halshall, Hinsley replied that his only desire was to see the refugee children placed in Catholic homes and that the letter of the Bishop of Vitoria, 'seemed to His Grace to contain nothing political but merely an appeal for the children's souls'.[56] Henson relented somewhat but feared that English Catholics were being manipulated by Basque separatists and it appeared in Spain that the Archbishop of Westminster was supporting a bishop whose political views ought to be better known in England.[57] Hinsley later admitted that he and others had been used in the evacuation of the children who, it was claimed by Republicans, were being removed from the Nationalist onslaught. No doubt Henson felt vindicated when he received a letter from Franco praising his stance and informing him that Hinsley's 'support' of the Bishop of Vitoria was unfortunate, 'but the Basque question seems to rouse the strangest feelings in British breasts.'

For good measure he added that the Pope labelling the Nationalists as fascists was an epithet which he felt was undeserved.[58]

Hinsley was compelled to write to Bishop Ambrose Moriarty of Shrewsbury to explain why he supported the Bishop of Vitoria's appeal for the evacuated children. He argued that though the Basque bishop 'may be an enemy of Franco, I do not think he is at enmity with the Holy See'. He had taken advice from Archbishop Guiseppe Pizzardo, President of the Roma Curia, whose opinion was that the Bishop, Matteo Múgica y Urrestarazu, was a victim of his efforts to conciliate the separatists and the Nationalist Basques. The letter that Hinsley had received from the bishop called only for the support for Spanish children evacuated to England. Hinsley had opposed the evacuation but once the children had arrived he did all he could to assist them. 'I see no reason', he told Moriarty, 'why we should hide the fact that the Bishop has appealed to us to see that the children do not get into the hands of the Reds'. This, he concluded, may give offence to the Nationalists but he was prepared to accept that. He also felt that Mgr Henson was unjust in his view of the Bishop of Vitoria and that his strong language displayed bias.[59] In an earlier letter to Moriarty, Henson's description of the bishop had been quite vitriolic and he also drew attention to the fact that by giving public assistance to such a man the British press, already viewed with great hostility in Nationalist Spain, would be further discredited. It had not reported, he told Moriarty, the communist bombing of Valladolid when 100 children were killed, nor did the British government offer any protest on that occasion.[60]

No doubt strengthened by Franco's positive sentiments, Mgr Henson wrote to Hinsley in November 1937 on the subject of Hinsley's intervention on behalf of a prisoner held by the Nationalists:

> I see those wretched Basque separatists have been wily enough to trick your Grace into lending your name to the suggestion that the Nationalist government is unjust to its prisoners – an appeal by the 'Primate of England' . . . can receive no other interpretation. The British and French governments some time ago interceded on behalf of the Austrian prisoners, and that action was very much resented in this country.

Henson concluded: 'we need no lessons from people who did nothing in the face of atrocities, martyrdom and sacrifice' and 'who failed to prevent the barbaric destruction of entire cities by the Reds'.[61]

In a letter that did not conceal his growing frustration, the Archbishop told Henson that he was grieved that so many people, including him, misunderstood all he said and did. He had spoken against the evacuation of the 4,000 Basque refugee children but when they arrived in England in May 1937 he had arranged, at the request of the Ministry of Health in London, for religious orders to care for over 1,200 of them at a cost of between £500 and £600 per week. He and others, like Archbishop Downey, had struggled to keep them out of the hands of non-Catholics and were working for their speedy repatriation. His efforts at Christian charity, he complained, had been misrepresented and misunderstood 'in the excited conditions of certain persons'. Again and again, he lamented, he had spoken and written in defence of Spain and the Church in Spain – and not without good effect. He had also let it be known how utterly ashamed he was of the British press, with one or two exceptions among the secular papers. 'A single word on world politics nowadays', he wrote, 'is twisted and worked beyond all possibility of rectification'. He was acutely aware from experience that any vagueness of language would be exploited by an unforgiving press and wrote that propaganda had done as much damage as aircraft. But he was particularly concerned that Henson seemed to consider him some form of traitor and would, he wrote, 'be glad to see you here and talk matters over with you quietly'.[62]

Hinsley continued to set out the Church's position in the face of what he regarded as common totalitarian and atheistic perils in Germany, Italy and Spain. On 26 July 1937, in a letter to *The Times*, he castigated those who felt that the Church in Spain was rich or sided with fascism and pointed out that Church land had been confiscated steadily since 1812. Nevertheless, priests and religious continued to look after schools and hospitals for the benefit of all Spaniards. Papal pronouncements, he pointed out, had stressed that the Church was not concerned with political systems and the Vatican maintained relations with any state which permitted Catholics to worship unmolested and provide Catholic education for their children. Hinsley's position, from a Catholic point of view at least, was strengthened by the publication of Pius XI's encyclical *Divini Redemptoris* which condemned communism outright as 'a pseudo-ideal of justice, of equality and fraternity in labour . . . which stripped man of his liberty, robs human personality of all its dignity, and removes all the moral restraints that check the eruptions of blind impulse'. But Pius did not propose fascism as an alternative for in 1931, in *Reconstructing the Social Order*, he had already described the fascist or 'corporative' state as excessively bureaucratic and political in character which, notwithstanding some benefits, tended to serve political aims rather than contributing to the initiation and development of a better social order. The Pope stressed the positive nature of the Church's social teaching demonstrated through a detachment from worldly goods, charity, true social justice and a life of prayer.[63]

Meanwhile in Spain Mgr Henson continued his support of the Nationalists as they moved towards victory. By 1939 the college's country house was named the 'Hospital Generalissimo Franco' and as the war drew to a close Henson informed the English and Welsh Hierarchy that there was 'every hope that Spain will soon return to her former grandeur as a great and powerful Catholic state'.[64] Bishop John McNulty of Nottingham was ecstatic at Franco's ultimate success and wrote to Henson in April 1939:

> How magnificently General Franco and his forces have carried out their tremendous work. God grant that he will now be able to solidify and crown his work and refashion Spain until it is worthy of its most glorious days.[65]

When Madrid fell and the Nationalist victory was assured in March 1939, Hinsley wrote to Franco:

> Your most kind action in sending to me, through Mrs Herbert, a signed photograph of yourself calls for my heartfelt thanks. I shall value this likeness as a treasure, for I look upon you as the great defender of true Spain, the country of Catholic principles where social justice and charity will be applied for the common good under a firm peace-loving Government.[66]

The termination of hostilities did nothing to weaken the strong public attitude in Britain that Catholics, in addition to their traditional allegiance to the Pope, were now associated with fascism and particularly with Franco, a view strengthened by the editorials of Catholic newspapers. In February 1939 Hinsley was told by Fr Samuel Gosling, editor of *The Sower*, that 'the suggestion is being made all over the country that the Catholic Church is backing fascism. This is doing untold harm; it is alienating the sympathies of our fellow countrymen'.[67] It was a depressing thought for Hinsley who could not bear the suffering Church in Spain nor accept the fact that British Catholics were associated with fascism or watch it advance in a Catholic country. For its part the British government was also in a dilemma. It could not publicly ally itself with Franco's regime yet it wished to support him in order to neutralize him and remarkably it responded positively to a request from Hinsley that it might help to refurbish damaged churches in Spain as part of a wider Hierarchy initiative. Conscious of a potential alliance between Franco and Hitler, the Foreign Office was of the opinion that Catholicism could perhaps moderate the course of Spanish politics and, among many other initiatives to prevent such an alliance, Britain contributed towards the repair of damaged churches. The money was accepted and added to that raised by British Catholics but, fearing that it would be seen as a propaganda stunt, Hinsley arranged for it to be taken to Spain in 1940 by Amigo and Sir Walter Maxwell Scott on behalf of the Hierarchy and not the Friends of Nationalist Spain.[68]

In Heenan's biography of Hinsley, there is absolutely no mention of the Archbishop's actions or pronouncements during the Spanish Civil War and there is no doubt that it was a difficult period for him. While he feared a communist victory, he was mindful of Franco's links with Mussolini and Hitler. Hinsley kept the photo of the *Caudillo* on his desk to remind him of the crusade against those who had attempted to destroy the Spanish Church and the persistent threat posed by the forces of irreligion and darkness. He had kept his counsel throughout the war but his heart and prayers were always with and for Franco. The survival of the Catholic Church in Spain, 'the martyred Church' as he called it, and the ideals of a Christian Europe were paramount to Hinsley.[69]

The Approach of the Second World War

Hinsley was unequivocally opposed to any form of political ideology that restricted the rights of the individual and threatened liberty of religious conscience. He had spoken out strongly against Mussolini's brand of fascism and the vicious secularism of the Republican movement in Spain but his letters and speeches denouncing German National Socialism before and during the Second World War earned him a reputation as a defender of freedom and a staunch opponent of Adolf Hitler.

In December 1935 Hinsley and the Hierarchy sent a message of fraternal support to the cardinals and bishops of Germany who were meeting at Fulda to discuss the problems presented by National Socialism.[70] The German bishops professed their loyalty to the Holy See and Pope Pius XI's response was the publication of his encyclical *Mit Brennender Sorge* ('With Burning Anxiety') in March 1937. The encyclical, which dealt with the problems of the Catholic Church in the Third Reich, was read in all Catholic churches in Germany. It warned of the Nazi regime's deification of nation, state and race and denounced Hitler for breaking the 1933 concordat which had promised freedom of religious conscience. In his 1937 Christmas Eve allocution the Pope was even more critical of Hitler's Reich and made a 'high protest' against the far-reaching, grievous and lamentable persecution of the Catholic Church in Germany, 'a fact that is as great in its geographical extension as in its moral gravity and seriousness'.[71] Hitler ignored all appeals for understanding.

In September 1937 Hinsley had written to *The Times* expressing concern that Hitler's Third Reich was pressurizing Catholic priests to revise the Catechism 'in a National Socialist sense'. It was a move, claimed Hinsley, designed to deny the principles of Christian faith. The introduction of pan-Aryan paganism based on, among other works, Alfred Rosenberg's pseudo-scientific theory of human worth, was forcing Germany towards racial intolerance. Afraid that all criticism was ruthlessly suppressed by the Nazis, he asked:

> Who shall be able to assure the present rulers of Germany that the seeds of hatred and of vile abuse for everything sacred may not bring forth on German soil fruits which must appal all true friends of the people of Germany?[72]

The plight of German Catholics was made more complicated by the German annexation of Austria through the *Anschluss* of March 1938. Cardinal Innitzer, the Primate of Austria, appeared to welcome the German invasion and his comments forced Hinsley to defend both Innitzer and the Vatican. The Holy See, he said,

> had no part in the action of the Austrian bishops by which they approved of union with Germany, just as it had no part in the political arrangement which insisted on the independence from the Reich of a diminished and crippled Austria.

He pointed to the resistance mounted by Cardinal Faulhaber of Munich against Nazi attacks on Christianity and claimed that Innitzer's words had been distorted and misconstrued by the German press. Sensitive to the uneasy and dangerous positions of the German and Austrian Hierarchies, he hoped that guarantees of religious freedom would be observed and that the Austrian bishops would be guided by the Holy See.[73]

In September 1938 France and Great Britain agreed to Germany's annexation of the German-speaking Sudetenland which lay within

Czechoslovakia and Neville Chamberlain's agreement with Hitler at Munich on 29 September appeared to guarantee peace in Europe and signal the end of Hitler's territorial ambitions. Many eminent politicians, including Winston Churchill and Anthony Eden, disagreed with this policy of appeasement but on 25 October the Hierarchy offered 'their heartfelt gratitude to the Prime Minister for his successful efforts in the cause of peace' and promised him their loyal support and prayers.[74] For some inside Germany, however, circumstances were increasingly hostile and on 1 December Hinsley took part, alongside Archbishop Temple of York, the Chief Rabbi and the Labour MP Herbert Morrison, in a demonstration at the Albert Hall against religious persecution in the country, particularly of the Jews. Hinsley, in his usual blunt style, said that the Roman Emperor Nero was 'a model of justice compared to the Führer of the German Reich'.[75] His contribution was singled out by the Nazi magazine *Der Angriff* which condemned the alliance of Catholics, Anglicans and Jews and asked 'How long can English people tolerate this?'[76] Hinsley was unperturbed and in the following week attended a meeting at the Mansion House with the Archbishop of Canterbury, Labour MP Clement Attlee and Lord Rothschild to express support for the increasingly persecuted Jewish population of Germany. He subsequently wrote to Cardinal Pacelli asking that the Pope make a declaration that all peoples 'are one in Christ'. Pacelli replied that the Pope was very busy and not in the best of health but Hinsley was authorized to interpret the Pope's mind and express His Holiness's approval of all charitable assistance given to those suffering unjustly. It was not exactly what Hinsley had expected or wished for but by the end of the month he had established the Catholic Committee for Refugees.[77]

In the midst of increasing political uncertainty Hinsley came out forcefully against the twin evils of fascism and communism when he addressed Catholics at Birmingham in January 1939 in a speech entitled 'Liberty – true and false'. Liberty and communism, he said, could not go together nor could liberty exist with pagan theories of state or race absolutism. Whereas nineteenth century liberals had accused the Church of opposing freedom, it was now recognised as 'the chief international bulwark of liberty'. He forbade Catholics to have any sympathy for or connection with the regimes of Italy, Germany and Russia warning then that communism was unnatural and anti-social and that Fascism and National Socialism destroyed the rights of the individual. It was true, he admitted, that fascists opposed the communists but it could not be deduced that because the Church also opposed communism it was therefore pro-fascist. He concluded by saying that all form of dictatorship and state-worship destroyed the common good.[78]

Circumstances changed dramatically with the death of Pope Pius XI on 10 February. Prime Minister Neville Chamberlain and Foreign Secretary Lord Halifax had visited Mussolini in Rome in January and had also met with the Pope. After the pontiff's death, Halifax commented favourably on his courageous stand against Nazi doctrines and anti-Jewish measures in Italy but Foreign Office officials commented that Hitler and Mussolini would be delighted at the Pope's passing and saw dangerous possibilities in a future Rome-Berlin axis. Cardinal Pacelli was favourite to succeed Pius XI and it was obvious that the 35 Italian cardinals would most likely vote for him but senior British diplomats wondered if any pressure could be exerted on the conclave to ensure Pacelli's election. Hinsley was the only English cardinal present at the conclave whereas there were four French cardinals. It was unlikely, therefore, that Hinsley could influence the election but he was not even disposed to participate in anything that would disturb his impartiality and sacred duty to operate only through divine guidance. Earthly motives did not affect Hinsley on such solemn occasions. Cardinal Pacelli was elected and took the name Pius XII.[79]

Throughout 1939 the European political situation deteriorated. Central to the situation were Hitler's designs on Poland, a country whose independence had been internationally recognised since the peace treaties of 1919. A complicating factor, and for Hinsley and all Catholics a very distasteful one, was the prospect of an alliance between France, Great Britain and Soviet Russia to counterbalance the threat of Germany. Not only was co-operation with the Soviets against Hinsley's principles, it was also contrary to Pius XI's encyclical of 1937, *Divini Redemptoris*, which had strongly condemned communism but the western democracies were drawn towards an unexpected rapprochement with the Soviets. In 1935 France had concluded a pact with Russia in order to protect France's borders against Germany – an agreement redolent of pre-1914 arrangements – and the British government made similar moves. In November 1936 Lord Rankeillour alerted the Lords to the morality of associating with regimes intent on spreading atheistic revolution but by 1939, as the prospect of an Anglo-Soviet alliance looked increasingly likely, Catholics were even more disturbed and Catholic newspapers and journals were full of letters and articles protesting against the government's strategy. Kevin Hayes wrote in *The Tablet* that the horror of an alliance with Russia could only be averted on condition 'that we powerfully and insistently demand a Christian foreign policy' while *The Month* was of the opinion that Catholics would scarcely need reminding 'that such co-operation is dangerous, unworthy and, to the Christian mind, indefensible'. Other commentators, whilst not supporting a British-Soviet alliance, touched a raw nerve when Catholics who had supported Franco were reminded of his alliance with the Catholic apostate, Hitler.[80]

Whatever his aversion to an association with atheistic Russia, Hinsley was very much aware of the pressures on Chamberlain's administration and wrote to Lord Halifax acknowledging the government's predicament. At the same time he was compelled to point out the dilemma facing him and other Catholics:

> The prospect of an alliance with Soviet Russia has filled a vast number of British people with the gravest alarm. . . .
>
> The pleas that Russia would be able to tie up large numbers of German troops, even if she is inefficient and untrustworthy, leaves out of count the question of the morality of using such people for our military and diplomatic ends.
>
> Personally, I consider my country has a claim on my whole-hearted loyalty, but I fear that many faithful adherents of the Church are troubled in conscience by a conflict between their religion and their loyalty to a Government allied with untrustworthy Soviet Russia. . . .
>
> My duty seems to require that I should give you information regarding the thoughts which many have expressed to me, while at the same time I wish to assure you of my fervent prayers and of my devotion to my country's cause.[81]

Halifax thanked Hinsley for approaching 'this difficult question' in a 'helpful spirit'. He appreciated that all Christians, including himself, regarded co-operation with the Soviets as abhorrent but such an alliance was less of an immediate threat to Christianity than Germany was to the cause of peace. At the Cabinet meeting of 3 May the Foreign Secretary, when outlining the permutations of military alliances, reminded his colleagues that it was well to remember that many in the country were hostile to communism and he added that he had received a long letter from Cardinal Hinsley expressing anxiety on the matter.[82]

Any apprehension harboured by Hinsley or anyone else about a British alliance with Soviet Russia was swept aside when Hitler and Stalin cynically signed a non-aggression pact on 23 August 1939. This agreement, which consolidated an earlier arrangement for the exchange of raw materials and goods, enabled Germany to attack Poland on 1 September without fear of a Russian military response. Hinsley's comments about an untrustworthy Russia had been justified. As Germany refused to withdraw its forces from Poland, Great Britain had no alternative but to declare war on Germany two days later.

Hinsley immediately issued a message calling for courage born of strong faith. The forthcoming conflict, he wrote, would entail sacrifices and trials which would bring people nearer to the Cross, 'the sign in which we shall finally conquer'. He urged prayer for the Pope 'who has spent himself in his efforts to avert war', for the victims of the horrible methods of modern warfare, and for 'Divine Wisdom to guide our government'. And he left Catholics in no doubt over their responsibilities:

> It is an obligation on all of us strictly to accept the restrictions and sacrifices which the civil power imposes for the general safety of the public. Moreover, we remind anyone who is able that it is a duty to give unstinted service to the country on behalf of the common good. We are bound also to foster unity and concord all around us and to have confidence in our King and his counsellors, our lawful rulers.[83]

The Hierarchy issued a similar declaration but it bears the mark of Hinsley. Entitled 'Poland's Claim', it referred to Pius XI's call for peace in his encyclical of 1932, *Caritate Christi Compulsi*, and stated that the British government had indeed laboured for international understanding. The conflict had been brought about by those who had 'no care for the world-wide unity of the Peace of Christ'. The bishops expressed their profound conviction in the justice of the nation's cause and urged upon the faithful 'at this time of trial and endeavour, the duty of loyal obedience to his Majesty the King, and of willing co-operation in every form of national service'. No country, the message continued, had a greater claim to support than Poland 'which has played through the centuries so great a part in the defence of our common Catholic heritage' but the bishops were careful to request prayers for France and the Dominions.[84] Meanwhile the Catholic Union of Great Britain assured the government of its unqualified support and confidently stated that the King's Catholic subjects would worthily play their part in the struggle ahead.[85]

Chapter Thirteen

DOMESTIC AFFAIRS

1935-1943

Catholic Action

One of the principal features of Vatican policy during the 1920s and 1930s was Catholic Action. In 1929 Pope Pius XI defined Catholic Action as the collaborative participation by lay Catholics in the hierarchical apostolate for the defence of religious and moral principles and for the development of beneficial social action. Catholic Action was to operate under the control of ecclesiastical hierarchies, transcend sectional and political interests, and restore Catholic life in the family and in society.[1] Throughout the mid- and late-1930s 'Catholic Action' became a rallying cry and Hinsley was one of its most fervent advocates.

The underlying principles of Catholic Action were not new. *Rerum Novarum,* Pope Leo XIII's encyclical on the Condition of the Workers, had warned that industrialisation was threatening the souls of men and that the Church had to address the plight of the economically and socially underprivileged. At the time of the promulgation of the encyclical in 1891, Hinsley was a student at the *Venerabile* and with Merry del Val pored over it when a copy arrived in the College. Both men – one of a distinguished Spanish lineage and the other a joiner's son from Yorkshire – immediately named it 'the Worker's Charter'.[2] Forty years later Pius XI issued the encyclical *Quadragesimo Anno*, on the Social Order, which confidently reaffirmed the social teaching of Pope Leo and gave shape to the idea of the social apostolate which had developed under Popes Pius IX, Pius X and Benedict XV. For Pius XI, however, the ideology of communism was an immediate and direct threat to Christianity and he warned that 'if Christian teaching is not accepted then atheistic communism will surely come'. His solution was Catholic Action, a movement in which the laity, under the leadership and control of the Apostolic Hierarchy, would unite and collaborate outside the limits of normal party politics in order to influence national

ABOVE: *From left: Fr Thomas Ronayne, Fr Patrick Whitney and Fr Thaddeus O'Connor CSSp with Bishop Joseph Shanahan at Maynooth, 1920. Frs Whitney and Ronayne were to found the Kiltegan Fathers.*

RIGHT: *Bishop Hinsley with Bishop John Campling of the Mill Hill Fathers, Vicar Apostolic of the Upper Nile, 1929.*

ABOVE: *Cardinal Francis Bourne, Archbishop of Westminster 1903-35.*

OPPOSITE: *Bishop Hinsley, Apostolic Visitor, with African leaders. To his left is Fr Engelbert Giersbach.*

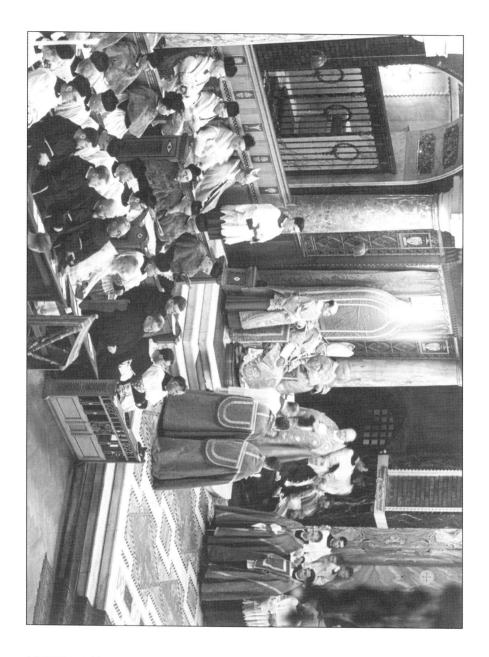

ABOVE: *Archbishop Hinsley's enthronement as Archbishop of Westminster on 29 April 1935.*

OPPOSITE: *Archbishop Hinsley waves to well-wishers from the balcony of Archbishop's House in April 1935, following his appointment as Archbishop of Westminster.*

ABOVE: *The coat of arms of Cardinal Hinsley on his appointment. The pallium is to the left, the dolphin from the shield of St John Fisher is to the upper right, and the cockerel from the shield of St Thomas More is to the lower right. The motto is 'Such are the defenders I invoke'.*

OPPOSITE TOP: *Archbishop on his visit to Carlton in January 1936.*

OPPOSITE BOTTOM: *Archbishop Hinsley stands over his parents' grave during his visit to Carlton, January 1936.*

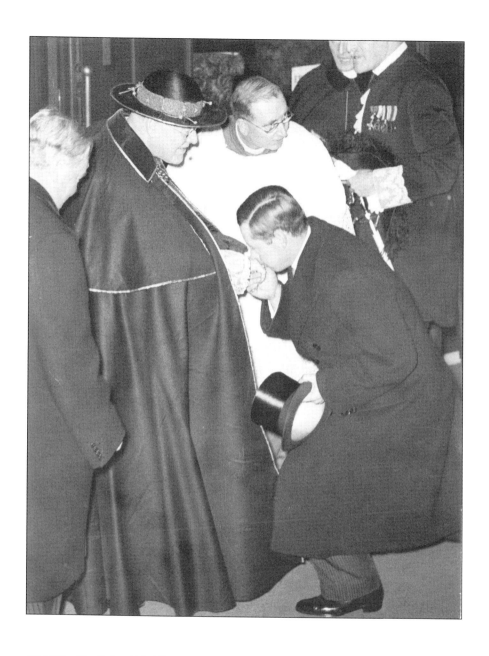

ABOVE: *The Duke of Norfolk greets Cardinal Hinsley on his return from Rome, January 1938.*
OPPOSITE: *Cardinal Hinsley receives the red hat from Pope Pius XI on 15 December 1937.*

ABOVE: *Cardinal Hinsley speaking in Westminster Cathedral, January 1938.*

OPPOSITE: *Cardinal Hinsley, January 1938.*

LEFT: *Cardinal Hinsley leaves for Rome to take part in the conclave following the death of Pope Pius XI in 1939.*

BELOW: *Cardinal Hinsley blesses the Knights of St Columba on a visit to a parish in London.*

LEFT: *Cardinal Hinsley with President Wladyslaw Raczkiewicz of Poland, August 1940.*

BELOW: *Cardinal Hinsley, Archbishop Godfrey, Bishop Radonski and members of the Polish government in exile, November 1942.*

The Archbishops and Bishops of England and Wales, Low Week, 1941. Back row, left to right: Daniel Hannon (Menevia); Thomas Flynn (Lancaster); John Francis McNulty (Nottingham); Ambrose Moriarty (Shrewsbury); William Lee (Clifton); John Barrett (Plymouth); James Dey (Army Bishop); John Henry Poskitt (Leeds); John Henry King (Portsmouth); Leo Parker (Northampton); Joseph McCormick (Hexham and Newcastle); Henry Marshall (Salford). Front row, left to right: Thomas Shine (Middlesbrough); Peter Amigo (Southwark); Richard Downey (Liverpool); Arthur Hinsley (Westminster); Thomas Williams (Birmingham); Michael McGrath (Cardiff); Arthur Doubleday (Brentwood).

LEFT: *Cardinal Hinsley, accompanied by Mgr Elwes, blessing the 'Cardinal's Cross' before its distribution to service personnel.*

BELOW: *Cardinal Hinsley with members of the Catholic Women's League at Aldershot in 1941.*

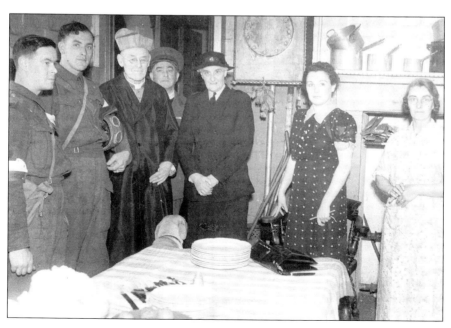

The funeral of Cardinal Hinsley.

life and resolve social problems. Catholic Action was intended to revive communities and refresh the endeavours of Catholics in parishes and dioceses. Existing diocesan groups and societies were encouraged to integrate and co-ordinate their efforts in order to deal more effectively with the ills of society at home and address the problems facing Catholics in countries which were threatened by or under the yoke of totalitarian communism.[3]

There was substantial Catholic political activity in early-twentieth century England and Wales. Following the tradition established by Cardinal Manning, Catholics were actively engaged in issues of social and economic concern but operated through the existing system of party politics rather than through a Catholic party with a distinctive political ideology. Urged on by bishops aware of Catholic electoral power, the clergy zealously activated and directed the Catholic vote, and organisations such as Catholic Federations, Catholic Poor Law Guardians' Association, Catholic Unions, the Catholic Evidence Guild, the National Confederation of Catholic Trade Unionists, the Catholic Social Guild, the Catenian Association and the Catholic Women's League demonstrated the willingness of Catholics to protect and further their religious and civic interests. A new and vibrant Catholic press with an increasing circulation supplemented established journals and the Catholic Truth Society's pamphlets brought the Church's teaching and history into Catholic homes. The laity was politically active, therefore, but as it attained a place in local and national politics it began to divest itself of clerical control. These developments, however beneficial they may have been to the Catholic community at large, were observed carefully by the bishops lest their influence be eroded, yet by the early 1920s external factors had already begun to loosen the bonds that had formerly tied Catholics together. The economic and social impact of the Great War had been pervasive, an extension of the franchise gave women political power, the growth of the Labour Party meant that the former equilibrium of British politics had been disturbed, and increasing secularism in British life, Parliament and the press challenged Catholic teaching.[4]

Recognising Catholic Action as a way to maintain episcopal control and also as a means of formulating a distinctive Catholic contribution to social questions, the English and Welsh Hierarchy took up Pius XI's initiative. In 1933 they discussed the possibility of establishing a National

Council for Catholic Action and whilst acknowledging that there was a great deal of Catholic activity which needed to be co-ordinated they admitted privately that the ailing Cardinal Bourne could not be expected to energise the process. In 1928 he had been approached by prominent Catholics calling for increased co-operation between clergy and laity but the Cardinal did not even favour them with a reply. Two years later he was again approached on the same issue but dismissed any such co-operation as unwise. Yet Bourne did not totally dismiss Catholic Action and in his Lenten Pastoral of 1934 he reminded his flock that the Westminster Federation of 1907 had been a form of Catholic Action but under clerical control. He emphasised that contemporary efforts remained subservient to ecclesiastical authority and that those involved must offer full submission and obedience to the bishops and those who represented them. His stance was in keeping with his traditional authoritarianism and the wishes of Pope Pius XI.[5]

Hinsley was an enthusiastic supporter of Catholic Action and his arrival at Westminster stimulated the development of the movement. In his letters to Archbishop Downey and Bishop McNulty, and in his enthronement allocution, he identified Catholic Action as his 'domestic policy'. Missionary Action abroad and Catholic Action at home, he said, were two fundamental phases of the living activity of the Church, the Mystical Body of Christ. Bishops, clergy and faithful, he continued, 'are bound to work in harmonious accord – as one organic force – for the good of the whole Body and for the salvation of all mankind'. He urged Catholics to put aside the narrowness of race and nationality, of parish and party and called upon them to co-ordinate their efforts to promote peace, charity, and social and economic justice. Catholic federations and other Catholic agencies had long been in the forefront of Catholic Action but circumstances now demanded a more systematic and cohesive approach to those evils which threatened social harmony and world peace.[6]

Aided by Archbishop Downey, Dom Ambrose Agius of Ealing Priory and Fr FitzGerald of Willesden, Hinsley outlined a scheme for Catholic Action in *The Clergy Review* in June 1936. He admitted that the notes had been hastily compiled but he hoped that they would provoke constructive criticism and suggestions. After progress had unfortunately been halted by the illness of Cardinal Bourne, Hinsley stated that it was now appropriate for the laity to participate in the Apostolate of the

Hierarchy and for all Catholic organisations to be co-ordinated in order to increase their effectiveness. 'Catholic Action', he wrote, 'is an official organisation which enables laymen to share more effectively in the work of the Bishops. . . . ' It was the outward expression of the energy or life of the Church, new only in name and organisation, and its objective was to uphold Catholic principles in every field of life and make them penetrate everywhere. Lessons could be learned from Catholic Action abroad but a cast-iron system was not to be imposed. Yet because of the importance of Catholic Action the Hierarchy must determine the exact nature of its organisation. Every sub-division of Catholic Action, therefore, was to be directed by the Hierarchy, the bishops or the clergy.[7] Such an approach would inevitably be ponderous and committee-driven.

In October 1936 Hinsley outlined his views on Catholic Action to the Hierarchy and promised to send an explanatory document. At the same meeting it was agreed that he and Downey would draw up a Joint Pastoral which would cover the press, the Catholic Truth Society, communism, Catholic Action, the Confraternity of Christian Doctrine and the spiritual dimension necessary for those participating in Catholic Action.[8] The Pastoral appeared in Advent 1936 as *The Apostolate of the Laity* but it was too wide-ranging and failed to explain fully the meaning of Catholic Action or how it might look in practice. The bishops acknowledged that Catholic social teaching had not influenced national life to any great extent and to remedy this they proposed a National Board of Catholic Action which would co-ordinate all Catholic organisations and societies in an attempt to address issues arising out of 'the social question'. They claimed that economic injustice and the increasing threat of communism could only be defeated by united Catholic efforts firmly rooted in spiritual renewal and the thorough education of apolitical 'lay apostles'. Recognising the value of the Catholic press as a means of keeping the Catholic community informed and being the first line of defence in time of attack, the bishops urged that it be supported as one of the most useful auxiliaries of Catholic Action.[9]

There was a good deal of activity which came under the umbrella term of Catholic Action but the overarching concept was interpreted and re-defined in many ways. When addressing the Westminster Catholic Federation and other diocesan societies in November 1936, Hinsley himself confused the issue by saying that a better term would be 'Catholic Unity'. On the other hand he hit the mark when he said that the biggest obstacle to the development of Catholic Action 'was the fear of the Hierarchy of a tendency on the part of the laity to interfere in the work of the clergy'. The bishops, of course, would ensure that clerical control of Catholic Action was undisputed.[10] The fundamental maxim of Catholic Action was *'Nil sine episcopo'*.

The scheme of Catholic Action which eventually emerged was cumbersome and top-heavy and reflected a mixture of caution and enthusiasm overtaking agreed understanding and sound management. Led and controlled by the bishops, its national structure included co-ordinating committees which would meet twice yearly, a Faith Committee, a League of Catholic Youth Committee, an Industrial Relations Committee, a Women's Committee for Moral or Social Work and for the Care of Girls in Domestic Service, all under the auspices of the National Board of the Apostolate whose members were appointed by the Hierarchy. At diocesan level the bishops would direct agencies operating within their jurisdiction and to ensure supervision of the movement in parishes the clergy would be spiritual directors. There were to be parish, diocesan and national councils with a special secretariat and financial organisation. Those who participated in Catholic Action had to be members of the Confraternity of Christian Doctrine and of the Guild of the Blessed Sacrament in order to emphasise the spiritual nature of Catholic Action. It was a highly bureaucratic scheme, likely to appeal to those with a taste for committees but unlikely to appeal to those either already involved in voluntary service or to those who had little interest in such affairs. Although Catholic Action was intended for all, the idea gained prominence that it was reserved for the more educated Catholics, a nucleus of trained apostles, and inseparably connected with study circles. The vast majority of Catholics were excluded from the direction and organisation of Catholic Action.

Other inherent weaknesses in the movement were the bishops arriving at an accepted definition of Catholic Action and the creation of a national organisation to bring together and co-ordinate the many existing diocesan activities. The practicalities of the undertaking were massive and beyond anything attempted by the Hierarchy before. There was also the tricky question of national structures conflicting with traditional diocesan independence. Consequently, the process of establishing Catholic Action as an effective movement was slow and laborious. As *The Tablet* commented on 19 December 1936, 'the development of Catholic Action under episcopal leadership cannot be a rapid business'.[11] Information had to be collected and collated and local and national boards and committees had to be established. Each diocese had its own culture and requirements and its propensity for action was largely defined by the leadership of its bishop and clergy and the involvement of its laity. Progress was so slow that in September 1937 Hinsley apologised to the Hierarchy for the delay in formulating a national scheme: 'I have found the extent of the field so great that I have been completely overwhelmed. My time and energies have been employed also in my proper work within the Diocese of Westminster'. He asked the Hierarchy what they understood by Catholic Action and offered to hand over national responsibility for it to any bishop willing to take it on and who had time to spare. No single definition emerged and none of the bishops accepted his offer.[12]

Born in a joiner's cottage, Hinsley had a natural affinity with working men and there is no doubting his social conscience. In his first radio broadcast he highlighted the plight of the unemployed and called for due respect for charity and social justice. Later, he said that work should be the normal means of serving God and not a positive obstacle to His service. Modern labour, he stated, was unmitigating in its physical demands on the worker, crushed the spirit and offered little possibility of a meaningful life beyond the factory, office or store. *The Catholic Worker* which, along with the Young Christian Workers, was a product of Catholic Action, described him as a true follower of Manning, referring to the famous nineteenth-century cardinal's support for the workers.[13] At a reunion held on 21 October 1936 of those who had been involved in the great London Dock Strike of 1889, he called himself a rebel, 'that is if trying to do good is being a rebel. . . .' His address to the survivors was remarkable. Calling them 'My Friends, My Comrades, My Sons', he proceeded to inform them that he had watched their strike as a young man 'keenly interested in the efforts of the workers to obtain just and reasonable conditions'. He was, he reminded them, 'a worker myself and the son of a working man, but I belong to the Church which offers to high born and to the lowly equal regard and equal opportunities. More readily, then, can I understand the spirit of sympathy which Manning had for the toilers in this country and the world over'. The British worker, he said – 'the real working man' – was not out for violence but was characterised by commonsense and was dogged and calm in his agitation for his rights. At the end of his address he was toasted by Ben Tillett and all present.[14] Speaking to the Westminster Catholic Federation in November 1936 Hinsley came out strongly against unjust wage systems, price fixing, and artificial scarcities. Nor, he said, did one nation or group of nations have the prerogative to subjugate and exploit others. The solution to such problems, he averred, was not to be obtained through parliaments and protocols but through the actions taken by men of good character.[15]

At a huge rally at the Royal Albert Hall on 30 September 1937, Hinsley addressed 'The Catholic Church and the Social Question'. His primary object was to explain the Church's social teaching and meet head-on the menace of communism. Other speakers included Archbishop Williams of Birmingham and the President of the Catholic Social Guild and such was the demand for tickets that the proceedings were relayed to the Brompton Oratory. In his opening remarks Hinsley asked the audience if they were prepared to suffer and die for Christ. The answer was a roar in the affirmative but when he asked his listeners if they were prepared to live for Christ the answer, although still in the affirmative, was rather muted.[16]

His Advent Pastoral for 1937 was devoted to the study of the mutual rights and duties of workers and employers. It was certainly his longest pastoral and some regarded it as his most important. Man did not work, he wrote, for the purpose of keeping the leisured class in comfort and no Catholic could regard the efforts of another as a commodity. He reminded his diocesan flock that it was the Christian's duty to relieve distress wherever it might occur and that many Catholic organisations existed for the betterment of social conditions. However, the effectiveness of such organisations was impaired as they failed to recruit sufficient Catholics who by reason of their education and position were best fitted to be leaders within the Catholic community. In particular he castigated those who were well-off for doing so little and for shrinking from association with Catholics of a lower degree. He wrote that those for whom Catholicism ought to be their proudest boast appeared not to have the true welfare of their weaker brethren at heart. Despite the efforts of Pope Leo XIII and Cardinal Bourne in England, many Catholics failed to recognise the evils which surrounded them and consequently did so little to eradicate them. It was the duty of educated Catholics and employers not only to be aware of the Church's social teaching but to put it into practice. Charity, he urged, was the best means of establishing social unity and abolishing the war of the classes. In Westminster the Catholic Social Guild was presenting a series of lectures to inform people of their Christian responsibilities but it was down to priests and parishes to establish Confraternities of Christian Doctrine and Guilds of the Blessed Sacrament in order to prepare, in prayerful way, for a true understanding of the issues confronting society and for adopting appropriate solutions through Catholic Action.[17]

On 26 October 1937 the Hierarchy met to finalise a national programme for 'The Lay Apostolate of Catholic Action' which was then submitted to Cardinal Pizzardo for approval. It was heavily bureaucratic. Each parish had a Parochial Council; a diocese had a Diocesan Board; the Boards were co-ordinated by a National Board which included one representative from the four provinces; the members of the National Board received their appointments from an executive group of bishops; and Councils and Boards had to be composed of laymen with at least one ecclesiastical assistant. It was further decided that the activities of all tiers should be directed towards the preservation of the Faith, the extension of the Faith, and the solution of social problems.[18] Cardinal Pizzardo approved the scheme on 6 January 1938.[19]

Hinsley meanwhile moved forward with plans for his own diocesan programme. Sensibly, he had delegated the matter to his Auxiliary Bishop, David Mathew, and in July 1937 an advisory committee produced a report which reflected the twin difficulties of maintaining existing parish societies and encouraging new initiatives and increasing lay responsibility without compromising episcopal control. There was also a heavy emphasis on the spiritual aspect of Catholic Action. In mid-1938 Hinsley submitted the *Scheme for Catholic Action in Westminster* to Cardinal Pizzardo. The Westminster Catholic Federation ceased to exist and became Westminster Catholic Action with branches in every parish. Parochial Councils were established and the Guild of the Blessed Sacrament and the Confraternity of Christian Doctrine became responsible for formation of candidates for the Councils. In a way round the problem of existing diocesan societies, they became 'Associated Societies' and were seen as an integral element of Catholic Action. In an attempt to co-ordinate the work of all constituent groups, a Diocesan Board of Direction was set up with seven lay members nominated by the Archbishop. By January 1939 there had been steady progress in the archdiocese with 57 parishes having established councils and the *Westminster Catholic Chronicle* contained monthly reports from the parishes and other organisations. But having gone through the laborious task of setting up the machinery of Catholic Action, Hinsley was not to see its fruits. The outbreak of the Second World War greatly slowed its momentum. In September 1939 he advised Henry Hope to 'keep a skeleton organisation going' and to ensure that all administrative and financial matters were in order. In February 1940 Hinsley wrote to the Diocesan Board of Direction to say that whilst practical work would inevitably be curtailed he hoped that united, spiritual work would continue through prayer, sacrifice and self discipline.[20]

Other than Hinsley, Archbishop Downey of Liverpool was perhaps the only bishop who really accepted the challenge of Catholic Action. He had convened a Catholic Action Congress in 1937 and established a lay Pro-Deo Commission to overcome communist influence among the Catholic working class. Republican Spain became the main target of the Commission which was supported in prayer by the League of Our Lady Immaculate. Branches of the Young Christian Students were established and courses in Catholic Action were provided. Among other developments, 130 Parish Councils were set up, Enquiry Bureaux helped people deal with unemployment and related issues, and houses of hospitality were opened to serve those in need. One of Downey's biggest achievements was the Catholic Action College, an ambitious attempt to train the lay apostles who would become leaders of the movement.[21] In the Diocese of Leeds Bishop Poskitt set up a Diocesan Committee for Catholic Action 'to associate and unite Catholic organisations in the common cause of restoring, defending, expanding and consolidating the Kingdom of Christ and the Church without interfering with the distinctive characteristics, objectives and qualities of such organisations. . . .'[22] In an effort to stimulate activity and exchange views, each organisation could send two delegates to the Diocesan Committee.

In most dioceses progress was slow. Catholic Action was neither properly understood nor particularly welcomed by clergy and laity set in traditional ways. It was also rendered less effective than it might have been because the bishops failed to adopt a unified stance in response to social issues such as unemployment and poor housing where a concerted effort may have had beneficial results. Ever mindful of their independence, it was left to individual bishops to take a lead or express a view on the relationship between Catholicism and politics. A distinctively Catholic contribution to political and social issues did not materialise due to the episcopacy's inability or unwillingness to formulate central policies to which they would all subscribe and implement. The Hierarchy appeared to be galvanised only by a threat to their schools. Catholic Action was not seen by all the Hierarchy as the challenge it really was and Hinsley's abstract and bureaucratic approach was ill-fitted to the practicalities of parish life however noble his aim may have been. Catholic Action may have helped ordinary Catholics to carry Christianity into secular life and for some it was an enlightening force but as an ecclesiastical organisation it offered nothing in place of the social and political structures it was attempting to change. There was also considerable vagueness about its aims.[23] As Dom Christopher Butler wrote, 'Catholic Action was primarily concerned with the diffusion of Christian principles, the formation of consciences, and the activation of vital forces at a profounder level than direct political action. . . .'[24] Strict episcopal control, bureaucratic structures and a lack of Catholic political institutions meant that Catholic Action could not replicate the European model and it remains an important but largely unfulfilled dimension of Catholic life in 1930s Britain.

The Fight For The Schools: 1936

The most obvious manifestation of organised Catholic Action in England and Wales was the coordinated and consistent attempt to protect and develop Catholic schools. With the other bishops Hinsley was to participate in the struggle and, in Archbishop Downey's words, became 'a firm centre of united action fortified no doubt by recollections of the similar crisis through which he had steered the bishops in Africa'.[25]

Unlike his predecessors at Westminster and many of his contemporaries on the episcopal bench Hinsley had substantial educational experience. He had taught at three major seminaries, he had been the headmaster of an urban boys grammar school and a manager of a mission elementary school. He had inspected the Church's educational provision in British colonial Africa and had supervised the introduction of new educational ordinances. None of the previous incumbents of the see of Westminster could lay claim to such a background but Hinsley was well aware that it counted for little in England and Wales where he faced a situation that was the outcome of the best part of a century's acrimonious negotiations between the British government, local councils and the Catholic bishops. Politicians at all levels had consistently attempted to restrict the influence of religion over education and in particular deny the right of Catholics to control their own schools and have them paid for out of the public purse. In Africa Hinsley had worked where a centrally formulated educational policy was implemented by colonial administrators who relied heavily on missionary schools. In England and Wales, where elementary education had been publicly-funded for nearly seventy years, there were alternatives to voluntary provided schools and local politicians did not always adhere to either the spirit or the letter of the law as it affected Catholic schools.

Hinsley's first public statement on Catholic education was included in his enthronement allocution. It was uncompromising. 'The school question', he said, 'presents the most pressing problem for Catholic Action. Our attitude in regard to our school must be action, and not apathy, and it must be Catholic'. He acknowledged that the faithful may have different political allegiances but was adamant that there could only be one undivided policy on the school question. In his own archdiocese, he admitted, there were thousands of Catholic children still without access to a Catholic school. Reflecting perhaps on his time in Bradford, Sydenham and Africa, he called upon his fellow countrymen – 'with their usual sense of justice – and even of generosity towards minorities' – to sanction a settlement of the education question that allowed for educational progress while giving religion its due place. His firmness of intent would undoubtedly have fortified those who had been struggling with the schools question for so long and who continued to face frequent difficulties in the provision of Catholic education.[26]

Hinsley's first problem concerning education emanated not from the government but from the inadequacy of the Hierarchy's own working arrangements. Since the establishment of the Hierarchy in 1850 the major and ever-present stumbling block to joint effective action was episcopal independence. Hinsley may have been permanent President of the English and Welsh Hierarchy but he was only *primus inter pares*. Each bishop ruled supreme in his own diocese and, as Hinsley had earlier found out from Archbishop Downey, the bishops were sticklers for protocol especially when it related to their own power and status. He was to confront a similar situation in the autumn of 1935 when, following a Hierarchy meeting, the bishops agreed to seek the educational views of prospective parliamentary candidates prior to a general election. Hinsley wrote to the Catholic Educational Council (C.E.C.) requesting advice on the best way to undertake the survey but in November he was informed by Archbishop Francis Mostyn of Cardiff that although the bishops had consented to undertake the exercise in their own dioceses they did not ask him, on their behalf, to seek advice from the C.E.C. They were therefore under no obligation to accept whatever counsel the C.E.C. might offer.[27] Such an interpretation was quite correct but it begged the question of having professional advisers if bishops were unprepared either to seek advice or act on it when given. Hinsley tactfully ignored Archbishop Mostyn's intervention and simply replied that the C.E.C. had advised that the question to prospective M.P.s may have been worded differently. The propensity of members of the Hierarchy to act independently and the bishops' failure to develop a systematic relationship with the C.E.C. seriously affected their room for manoeuvre during the build up to the Education Act of 1936. The majority of bishops continued to see state-supported Catholic education as something to be gained by direct confrontation rather than by negotiation and discussion and some, including Amigo of Southwark and Downey of Liverpool, saw themselves as proud inheritors of the militant prelates of former days when the battles for Catholic schools were fought to the bitter end. During the discussions Bishop McNulty of Nottingham had written to Bishop Cowgill of Leeds telling him that 'it is good for me to return to the fighting north'.[28]

But the political situation had changed and in May 1935 the Hierarchy established a Standing Committee of Archbishops Hinsley, Mostyn, Williams and Downey to enter into high-level negotiations with the government over the proposed Education Bill. The Bill, consequent upon the Hadow Report of 1926, proposed the raising of the school leaving age and the opening of senior schools. Both Local Authorities and the voluntary sector could claim building grants but such a development, whilst welcomed by the bishops, was likely to be exorbitantly expensive and therefore almost impossible for Catholic dioceses to implement.[29]

It became obvious as the discussions progressed that Hinsley's African experience was to the fore in both his interpretation and handling of the educational situation. He insisted that he was accompanied by the other Metropolitans in Church-state discussions, ensured that both sides were heard courteously, and saw to it that the Hierarchy was fully briefed.[30]

He was anxious to ensure that the Church was seen to be co-operating but he would not cede the Catholic position. On 5 February 1936 he informed readers of *The Times* that a provision in the proposed Bill which allowed un-denominational teaching in Catholic schools according to parental wishes was contrary to the 1902 Education Act and was not reciprocated by the provision of separate Roman Catholic teaching in Anglican or Council Schools. The reorganisation of schools to provide senior departments, he contended, would seriously jeopardise the ability of Catholic students to be given instruction in their faith if they were compelled to attend non-Catholic senior schools. He also argued that the costs of providing senior schools were so great that Roman Catholic dioceses would not be able to participate in the new development and only more generous government grants would facilitate this.[31] Speaking at Birmingham later in the month he stressed that although Catholics were as eager as any section of the nation to promote and support every effort for the advancement of education, they would not suffer any inequality or discrimination which would penalise Catholic students, hold back their schools or prevent them from giving the best to the nation.[32]

Hinsley wanted Catholics to benefit from progressive educational developments while being able to retain their confessional rights but unfortunately the plenipotentiary power which he possessed in Africa was not matched in England. An example of this came while the Education Bill was being debated in Parliament. At its meeting on 28 February 1936 the Hierarchy reiterated Hinsley's previously expressed concern over the provision in the Bill that allowed Local Authorities to place Catholic students in non-Catholic senior schools where there was no Catholic alternative.[33] Oliver Stanley, President of the Board of Education, was mortified when Hinsley and the other Archbishops made their feelings known to him. They had not, he reminded them, alerted him to this objection in previous discussions although they must surely have been aware of the Bill's provisions and he questioned whether they had indeed read the Bill or taken professional advice on it.[34] For Hinsley it was an embarrassment. He had publicly questioned the Bill's provisions. He was the leader of the Hierarchy but possessed no power unless it was delegated by the Hierarchy to him. The Hierarchy's corporate failings and Hinsley's limitations were compounded by the government's political authority and financial might.

He could not even consult the C.E.C. on behalf of the Hierarchy unless he was given permission to do so and wrote to his suffragan Bishop John McNulty of Nottingham lamenting the lack of 'parliamentary procedure' at Hierarchy meetings. He despondently told McNulty that although the bishops could press for amendments to the Bill they were otherwise powerless.[35] As in former days, some bishops were disposed to act independently and agitate more strongly for the rights of Catholics. Mgr William Hawkswell wrote on behalf of Bishop Cowgill of Leeds to Bishop Henshaw of Salford in March 1936 to complain that no direction had been given at the Bishops' meeting in February. Cowgill was delighted at the strong attitude Henshaw had taken in agitating against the Bill and suggested that if the Board of Education failed to make satisfactory concessions then Catholics throughout the country should rise up in protest.[36] Hinsley and Archbishop Williams, however, felt that co-operation rather than confrontation was needed and Hinsley wrote to Bishop McNulty chastising him for denouncing the Board of Education's proposals. He suggested that calmness and discretion were necessary rather than a fierce public campaign against advances in education.[37]

What became more evident as negotiations progressed was that the Bishops appeared to be adopting a more professional rather than a simply confessional approach to educational problems. At their meeting on 20 October 1936, for instance, the Bishops heard that their representatives had been invited to meet with Board of Education officials and the Local Education Authorities' Advisory Committee to discuss the recent Act. The Bishops accepted the invitation and proposed a deputation under the leadership of Bishop Brown of Pella, Auxiliary Bishop of Southwark. It was further decided that the deputation would report back through Hinsley and that a written report would be forwarded to all Bishops seeking their comments. More significantly, the Bishops also adopted at the same meeting a report from the Catholic Education Council Executive regarding agreements with Local Education Authorities and a proposal that each diocese establish a Schools Commission to advise on all aspects of diocesan education. Both developments were watersheds in the administration of Catholic education at the local level.[38]

Eventually, the bishops had to accept the new Act but remained concerned over its implementation. In July 1938 Hinsley, the three Archbishops and representatives of the C.E.C. presented a Memorandum to the Board of Education summarizing the Catholic experience since the passing of the Act. Like the government, the deputation was aware that the recent Act was but a step towards finally settling the problem of non-provided schools but the bishops claimed that only considerable legislation could effect that. Their main concerns related to problems surrounding the implementation of the 1936 Act, the provisions of which were not mandatory. Catholic dioceses had discovered that the reorganisation of schools unearthed all kinds of difficulties such as different patterns of reorganisation in neighbouring Councils, the relationship between ownership of land and building grants, existing trust deeds and leases, the acquisition of land in urban areas and the recovery of building costs from the Board. In Liverpool and Wales local Councils would not give discretionary grants to Voluntary schools. In rural areas Local Authorities would not pay travel allowances to Catholic children travelling to the nearest Catholic senior school. Such was the pessimistic mood of the Bishops that the Memorandum conceded that it would be better to leave Catholic students at the top end of an all-age school rather than go through the bureaucratic and political minefield of reorganisation which despite its advantages was still optional. Hinsley's own archdiocese had over sixty parishes without primary schools and he and other bishops could be forgiven for seeing this deficiency as a priority. As ever, it boiled down to money: the bishops' final request was for the Board to alleviate the financial burdens placed on Church authorities.[39]

The Board's reply conceded nothing and contained no promise of more money. Local Authority grants to Voluntary schools were optional and Church land held before the passing of the Act could not be classed as part of the claim for a building grant. The nature of the Act meant that the Board could not compel Local Authorities to reorganise their schools; Local Authorities were under no obligation to provide travel allowances for Catholic children; and the inability of Catholic schools to accommodate senior pupils was not a problem for the Board. Parents, the Board stated, had every right to expect that Catholic schools were of the same standard as Council Schools. It was up to the religious bodies to provide adequate accommodation. The Board was bound to have regard to parental wishes but it had also to be mindful of the interests of secular instruction and the economy of the rates.[40] The bishops' memorandum produced no beneficial effect but if nothing else its structure and content indicates that it was prepared by the professional officers of the C.E.C. and not by the Hierarchy. Despite there being no successful outcome to the bishops' negotiations with the government over the schools, Hinsley can at least be credited with attempting to modernise the organisational and administrative machinery of the Hierarchy and introducing a less confrontational approach to ministers and officials.

The Apostolic Delegate

Although Great Britain had been officially represented at the Holy See since early in the Great War, there was no reciprocal arrangement for Vatican representatives to reside in London. Anglo-Vatican diplomatic relations were a politically sensitive and emotionally charged issue in Great Britain for there were serious constitutional ramifications. To extreme and vocal Protestants any kind of relationship with the papacy was anathema but the absence of satisfactory diplomatic mechanisms caused difficulties for officials in both London and the Vatican. It was a practical problem that required a solution as each attempt at a dialogue between Great Britain and the Holy See had the potential to lead to damaging confusion. The appointment of an Apostolic Delegate to London could partially solve the problem but such a role was purely ecclesiastical and a Delegate would not possess diplomatic status. The appointment of an Apostolic Nuncio, with ambassadorial rank and the highest grade in the papal diplomatic service, remained out of the question as Great Britain and the Vatican had severed formal diplomatic relations in 1534 (though briefly restored in James II's reign). The Vatican was represented in over seventy countries throughout the world but not in Great Britain nor, for different reasons, in the United States of America. Rectifying such deficiencies would facilitate communications, increase the flow of useful information and strengthen the papacy's position in the face of Fascist Italy and Nazi Germany.

On a number of occasions Cardinal Bourne had acted as mediator between the Holy See, Buckingham Palace and Whitehall but the Foreign Office regarded the practice as unorthodox and therefore likely to cause diplomatic difficulties. Hinsley too had been used in this way by the Vatican to deliver a message from the Pope to King George V during the Abyssinian Crisis and, as we have seen, he also attempted to present loyal addresses which were rejected. The Home and Foreign Offices were hamstrung by legislation that did not allow direct correspondence between the monarch and the Pope, did not recognise the word 'Catholic' as opposed to 'Roman Catholic', and did not officially authorise the use of ecclesiastical titles by prelates of the Catholic Church in Great Britain.[41] As liaisons between the Holy See and Whitehall increased during the early-twentieth century, these pedantic issues began seriously to affect the methods of communication between respective officials and prevent an improvement in Anglo-Vatican relations. The British government and the Holy See moved carefully towards resolving this confusing and very delicate situation. The appointment of an Apostolic Delegate offered a channel of communication without establishing formal diplomatic relations. It was a solution that appealed to Pius XI who had established five Apostolic Delegacies during his papacy, including one occupied by Hinsley, but for the British there were problems surrounding the functions of an emissary who did not possess diplomatic powers.

Cardinal Bourne was not entirely convinced by the suggestion of an Apostolic Delegate for it would have reduced what he thought was his influence on the British government and his role as unofficial intermediary between Rome and London.[42] The Vatican and Bishop Amigo, however, took a contrary view but for different reasons. Bourne was disliked and distrusted by the Vatican and Amigo did not wish Bourne to be the link between the Vatican and Whitehall and therefore be excluded from important exchanges.[43] It was an opinion shared by the majority of the Hierarchy who felt that Bourne had given himself some kind of primacy to which he was not entitled. Sir Charles Wingfield informed the Foreign Office that the suggestion of an Apostolic Delegate would appeal to Pope Pius XI's centralising tendencies and would be welcomed generally by the Hierarchy although they would have to pay for it. Hinsley had been a most effective Apostolic Delegate in British colonial Africa and to him the benefits of similar appointments across the Empire were manifest.[44]

The lack of clear dialogue between the Vatican and the British government during the Abyssinian Crisis appears to have convinced both sides that there was an urgent need for clearer liaison between them. In November 1936 Lord Fitzalan confidentially informed Archbishop Williams of Birmingham that unofficial steps were being taken to get an English cardinal in Rome and that the Foreign Office was 'keenly anxious for the appointment'. Fitzalan suggested that a way of influencing the Vatican was for British diplomats to let it be known that such an appointment would be greatly appreciated by the English laity and suggested Monsignori Duchemin, Heard and Godfrey as possibilities. The Archbishop, he wrote, was aware of the situation:

> I mentioned all these things to Archbishop Hinsley before he went to Rome as I felt he ought to know what is being done. But not with a view to him taking any action himself as it is felt that the best approach at present is along the lines indicated above.[45]

Throughout 1937 the Holy See raised the question of representation in London not simply as a means of easing communication and understanding but also to recognise the political importance of the growing Catholic community in England and Wales, indicating perhaps that Fitzalan's suggestions had been accepted. There were further developments throughout 1938 and the British Legation to the Vatican reported that the Holy See had made tentative approaches to the British government to see if the appointment of a Nuncio to the Court of St James would be agreeable. Failing that, the appointment of an Apostolic Delegate might facilitate relations between Whitehall and the Vatican. The Vatican moved cautiously and in May 1938 Mgr William Godfrey, Hinsley's successor as Rector of the English College in Rome, notified the Foreign Office that he had been appointed Apostolic Visitor to inspect the seminaries and ecclesiastical colleges in England, Scotland and Malta.[46] It was a Vatican ruse to see how such a papal appointment might be received in London. Godfrey informed the Foreign Office that he had been requested by the Pope to discuss how an Apostolic Delegate might be received. Godfrey wrote:

> The Holy See feels that there is a great need of a Vatican representative in London, who can speak authentically the mind of the Vatican on those questions which are of common interest to the Church and State. No diocesan Bishop can suitably act in this capacity. The representative must be above and outside diocesan interests. . . .

> Naturally, the Holy See would desire a representative with diplomatic status but failing that, His Holiness would hope that, by appointing a Delegate Apostolic for Great Britain (a purely ecclesiastical appointment) the British government might permit him (the Delegate) to have such friendly contacts with Ministers and Government officials as would enable the Holy See to contribute by its councils and experience to the welfare of Europe and the Empire and the whole of Christendom.[47]

It was rather a pretentious statement and one which failed to address the distinction between an ecclesiastical and diplomatic representative. To the untrained eye the Delegate appeared to be both. Notwithstanding these difficulties, the Foreign Office continued throughout 1938, in the context of a worsening political situation in Europe, to negotiate with the Vatican for the appointment of a Delegate. On 21 November 1938 Godfrey himself was named as the Apostolic Delegate to Great Britain and raised to the episcopacy as titular Archbishop of Cius.[48]

The whole diplomatic process had taken place without reference to Hinsley or the Hierarchy. Only when Hinsley wrote to the Bishops in August 1938 did they become aware of how far and how fast developments had moved. Hinsley told them that negotiations had been carried out through the Nuncio to the Irish Free State and informed them that Godfrey had told him casually and confidentially of the development. He had received no official notification from either Rome or London.[49] At their meeting on 25 October 1938 the Bishops heard from Archbishop Amigo (he had been given the title *ad personam* in December 1937) that the appointment had recently been discussed by British diplomats in Rome and he had been informed that an Apostolic Delegate was to be sent to London.[50] It was understandably more than the episcopacy could stomach and they decided to send a letter of courteous protest to Cardinal Eugenio Pacelli, Papal Secretary of State. In the event, the letter which was drafted by Hinsley was never sent to Rome but it contained some fairly pointed comments and ones which demonstrated his knowledge of the English Protestant mind and the sensitivity of the European political situation. There were those, he wrote, who saw the Pope as tool of Italian fascism and the supporter of rebels against a lawfully elected Spanish government. The Rome-Berlin axis he argued would simply reinforce the view among Protestants that the Pope was in league with fascist dictators. 'Such an appointment', he wrote, 'would be dangerous to the cause of the Church in Great Britain'.[51]

Archbishop Amigo had already been in contact with Pacelli indicating therefore that he probably knew more than he had admitted to his confrères in October. His earlier predisposition for an Apostolic Delegate to come between him and Bourne had waned with Hinsley's appointment to Westminster as the two had been on good terms for over thirty years. After all, Hinsley had been a priest of the Southwark Diocese and presumably would not threaten diocesan boundaries or Amigo's status as Bourne had done. In July 1938 Amigo wrote to Pacelli citing examples of anti-Catholic prejudice which existed in Protestant

England. He informed the Cardinal that as an Apostolic Delegate would have to be Italian, the appointment would further inflame such sentiment. In Amigo's view, the presence of Hinsley at Westminster obviated the need to send a Delegate:

> We have a cardinal at Westminster who not only is deeply attached to the Holy Father and to all that breathes of Rome, but who at the same time is becoming daily more and more influential with Government officials. He is thoroughly English and esteemed as such, while his loyalty to the Vicar of Christ can never be called into question. He can help the Holy See better than an Apostolic Delegate could do. He has the whole Hierarchy with him and he is gaining ground continually with all . . . I therefore strongly feel that the interests of the Holy See in England are perfectly secured at present without the danger of rousing prejudice by appointing an Apostolic Delegate.[52]

The Vatican ignored Hinsley, Amigo and the rest of the Hierarchy and surprised them by appointing an Englishman. It was an appointment that brought relief to the Hierarchy and satisfied the Foreign Office. Godfrey arrived in London in February 1939 and wrote to the Hierarchy in grandiloquent tones similar to those contained in his letter to the Foreign Office in May 1935.[53] It was not likely to endear him to an independent bench formed in missionary days. Archbishop Hinsley, conscious of his own authority, reluctantly accepted the Vatican's decision and adjusted to the new arrangements. On 18 April 1939 the Hierarchy officially welcomed Godfrey at a dinner in his honour at Archbishop's House, Westminster.

For the Foreign Office, appointment of an Apostolic Delegate 'was a concrete expression of the respect and admiration for Great Britain and her Sovereign which the Pope so frequently voiced to British visitors'.[54] British officials hoped that it would strengthen the links between the papacy and Great Britain and prevent Italy from falling into the arms of Hitler's Germany. For the Vatican it was an acknowledgement that its interests in London were inadequately represented by the Hierarchy and 'that Britain was too important to be left in the hands of the Archbishop of Westminster – too frigid in the case of Bourne, too impulsive in the case of Hinsley'.[55] But Foreign Secretary Lord Halifax ensured that unofficial contact was maintained with Hinsley.[56]

Godfrey's promotion meant that a new Rector had to be found for the English College. When the terna was drawn up Hinsley suggested that Mgr R L Smith, Vice-Rector since 1932 and the Cardinal's former student, was 'the most suitable candidate'. He was overruled and Fr John MacMillan, a professor at Upholland College and another of Hinsley's students, was appointed.[57]

Translations

A number of important liturgical developments were introduced by the Hierarchy during Hinsley's episcopate. From 1936 until the Cardinal's death, committees appointed by the bishops revised the *Manual of Prayers*, produced a new edition of *The Westminster Hymnal* and began a new translation of the Bible. In all of these undertakings Ronald Knox was the fulcrum and Hinsley was his patron. Hinsley derived great pleasure from the scholarly pursuits of others and Knox found refuge in an ecclesiastical organisation which, despite its apparent discipline, gave rein to his talents.

Born in 1888, Ronald Knox was from an Anglican family. His father was the Bishop of Manchester and his maternal grandfather had been Bishop of Lahore. Educated at Eton and Balliol College, Oxford, Knox was an outstanding scholar. He became President of the Oxford Union in 1909 and on graduation was elected a Fellow of Trinity College, Oxford. In 1912 he received Holy Orders in the Church of England and until 1917 he remained in Oxford as the Chaplain of Trinity College. In 1917 Knox was received into the Catholic Church by Abbot Fernand Cabrol OSB of St Michael's Abbey, Farnborough, and two years later he was ordained as a Catholic priest after theological studies at St Edmund's House, Cambridge. From 1926 until 1939 Knox served as chaplain to Catholic men at Oxford University but he acquired a reputation that extended well beyond the confines of the university.[58] Through his secular and religious literary activities, Knox became one of a younger generation of Catholic writers and intellectuals who was to influence Catholic thought in the inter-war years. John Carmel Heenan regarded Knox as 'perhaps the greatest figure in the Church of the twentieth century'.[59]

Hinsley identified Knox as a priest of proven literary talent and doctrinal orthodoxy and saw him very much as a modernizer and a man for the future. In 1936 he began to advance Knox's career by successfully petitioning the Pope to create him a Prelate of Honour with the title of 'Monsignor' and in the same year appointed him to a committee set up by the Hierarchy to revise *The Westminster Hymnal*.[60] Such was Knox's prodigious input that he subsequently translated 47 out of 107 hymns and composed four originals. The new edition, published in 1940, led to much criticism as it departed in content, verse and music from the version which most Catholics had grown up with and had used so often. Yet, although the committee introduced some French Church melodies and Old Psalter tunes and revived devotional expressions which were centuries old, the new hymnal contained nearly all the hymns that English congregations commonly and comfortably sang. Knox and his co-compilers were anxious to preserve hymns which they considered part of a permanent tradition of Catholic worship, determined to root out poor verse, and introduce modern translations and original hymns. Their efforts were not going to please everybody nor did they.[61]

In 1937 Knox was appointed to another committee convened by the Hierarchy whose remit was to modernize the *Manual of Prayers* compiled in 1886 and last revised in 1922. It was a commission that was to give him no little trouble. The prayers, some of which were long-winded and insensitive, were for use on public occasions and Knox was required to translate texts whose originals were in either Latin or Italian. Under the chairmanship of Bishops Moriarty and Dey the committee set about revising them to match the requirements of the contemporary Church rather than one which looked back to penal times. Although technically just a member of the committee Knox again dominated the work. His efforts included translations of traditional prayers such as *Pange Lingua*, *Te Deum, O Salutaris* and *Tantum Ergo* but others such as the *Angelus* and the *Salve Regina* were left unchanged.[62] It was just as well he left some prayers and hymns untouched for his translations almost inevitably attracted criticism from within episcopal ranks. Hinsley was delighted with Knox's efforts and in November 1938 wrote to him to say that 'I have been ranting and raving to hurry up the publication of your revision of the *Manual of Prayers* on which you spent so much labour'.[63] But when the proofs of the new *Manual* were circulated to the Hierarchy in early 1939 there was opposition to Knox's revisions. Archbishop Amigo took advice from his *Censor Deputatus* who was highly critical of the revised *Manual*. Amigo posted on the comments from his Censor to Knox who replied that it was not the intention to make superficial amendments to the *Manual* but to go much deeper and change the idiom of the vernacular devotions used in the Catholic Church so that it corresponded more favourably with the dignity of Anglican prose. Knox also explained that in order to make the prayers meaningful to modern ears and facilitate the conversion of England the language would, of necessity, have to be changed.[64]

Knox was aware that Hinsley could not compel the Hierarchy to adopt the revised the *Manual* in their dioceses and despite his temperate words to Knox, Amigo so objected to the new edition that he informed Burns, Oates and Washbourne, the book's publishers, that 'I shall not have the *Manual of Prayers* in my Diocese'.[65] He was not alone in rejecting Knox's efforts: Bishop Poskitt of Leeds and Bishop McCormack of Hexham and Newcastle were of a similar opinion.[66] Knox wrote to Lady Acton: 'I can only hope that when the bishops meet again the Cardinal will tell him (Amigo) to go and make up his own *Manual*'.[67] In May 1939 Amigo told Knox that the 'the English of our prayers is not so much the cause of lack of conversions as our neglect of prayer and mortification'.[68]

When the time came for the *Manual* to be published there was a distinct lack of clarity over funding it. In June 1941 Christopher Hollis of Burns, Oates and Washbourne told Bishop Moriarty what the Bishop already knew, that Hinsley had not received a mandate from the Hierarchy regarding financial responsibility nor had it been discussed at the bishops' meetings. The Cardinal proposed to Hollis that the bishops share out the liabilities between them but Hollis did not feel that making such a suggestion was within his province.[69] Elwes told Moriarty that Hinsley was anxious that Hollis did not 'drag Birmingham or the Archbishop-Bishop (Amigo) into this question' and that each bishop should be made aware of the situation and promise to guarantee his quota of any deficit that might accrue. Such was the Cardinal's confidence in 'Ronnie' that he felt the *Manual* would be 'a good if not a best seller'.[70] His optimism, however, was misplaced for the new edition of the *Manual* did not appeal to the all the clergy. Errors of fact and translation combined with clerical hostility to compel the bishops to buy the book from the publishers and withdraw it from circulation.[71]

On 10 June 1938 Hinsley had offered Knox the Presidency of St Edmund's College. 'No-one whom I know', he wrote, 'could or would fulfil the post as you and no one would give so much prestige to the grand old college which you have already served so admirably'.[72] But after consulting Fr Martin D'Arcy, the Jesuit Principal of Campion Hall in Oxford, Knox declined the Cardinal's offer on the grounds that he wished to remain as Chaplain at Oxford, that he was thinking of translating The Vulgate, and that he wished to continue his chaplaincy to Lord and Lady Acton at Aldenham in Salop where he now resided for most of the time. Hinsley graciously and generously accepted Knox's reasons:

> I do completely agree with you that you should have time and opportunity to write. If I can do anything to secure this – either by releasing you from distractions, or by finding you a place somewhere where you can the great work of the pen apostolate, you will please let me know, and I will do my best.[73]

Hinsley's backing gave Knox the confidence to proceed with his revision of the Douai version of the Bible and he was also strengthened in his resolve by Archbishop Williams of Birmingham who proposed that he should commence the work. In October 1938 Archbishop Williams informed the Hierarchy that the bishops of the United States had invited Knox to prepare a new translation of the Bible for them and on hearing this news Hinsley and the bishops immediately commissioned him to begin a translation of the New Testament. On 8 November 1938 Hinsley wrote to Knox: 'We have confidence in you as the one man who can give us an English that is readable and understood by the people'.[74] The Cardinal offered Knox every facility in Westminster but Knox wished to sequester himself away in the comfortable home of his secular patrons at Aldenham. In April 1939 the Hierarchy set up a committee under the chairmanship of Bishop Flynn of Lancaster and whose members included Fr Cyril Martindale SJ, Mgr J M T Barton, the Dominican scholar Fr Hugh Pope, Fr T E Bird of Birmingham, and Dom Christopher Butler of Downside. The Hierarchies of Scotland and Ireland were asked to appoint representatives and the Hierarchy guaranteed to find the funds for the publication of the translation. The committee, however, rarely met and Bishop Flynn himself 'ventured to wonder whether any precise directions had been given'.[75] In 1939 Knox resigned his chaplaincy at Oxford and set about his task of translating the Vulgate Bible with the expectation that the committee would correct and advise. But this proved not to be the case and there were soon open disagreements and public controversy surrounding the project. The translation was, of course, a huge undertaking both linguistically and theologically and Hinsley, the Hierarchy, Knox and the committee were under no illusions about the complexity of the undertaking. The potential for confusion, misinterpretation and controversy was enormous and there were also many converts who had a greater respect and indeed a greater love for the Anglican Authorised Version of the Bible rather than the Douai version.[76]

At the Low Week meeting of the Hierarchy in 1940 Hinsley and Williams supported the work already completed by Knox and Williams, especially, urged him to modernize the language and use 'the best twentieth-century style'.[77] Archbishop Amigo, however, remained unimpressed by Knox and in 1941 wrote to him regarding his translation of St Matthew's Gospel. He had not expected such wholesale changes and warned Knox that 'I regret that your labours may be in vain as far as my diocese is concerned'.[78] Knox was deeply distressed by Amigo's letter and the Archbishop made matters worse by expressing his views to a priest in Hinsley's diocese. It was an episcopal *faux pas* and Hinsley wrote to Amigo complaining of his action and defending Knox. Amigo was compelled to back down in the face of Hinsley's obvious wrath and he wrote to Knox to urge him to continue with his work. His views, he admitted, were not those of the Hierarchy and he was happy to contribute towards Knox's expenses. Knox showed the letter to Hinsley who then felt compelled to apologize to Amigo for his outburst: 'Your letter has made me ashamed of having lectured you. I felt deeply for Mgr Knox because I could tell from his answer to you how keenly he was disappointed'.[79]

Knox continued with his translation and in October 1942 the Bishops approved 'the issue of a limited edition of Monsignor Knox's work, at his own risk and for private use'.[80] It was hardly a ringing endorsement of his efforts but Hinsley continued to support him and arranged for 1,500 copies of excerpts from the translation to be published and sold but not advertised. 9,500 copies had been sold by January 1943. Knox was personally well able to handle his scholarly and episcopal critics but his revisions of the *Manual* and the translation of the New Testament experienced mixed fortunes. Bishop Poskitt instructed his clergy to withdraw the *Manual* 'on account of the number of errors found in the text'. In May Bishop McNulty of Nottingham did the same.[81] However, Hinsley's successor, Archbishop Bernard Griffin, gave Knox's translation of the New Testament his *imprimatur* in 1944 and it was published in October 1945.[82] It was received enthusiastically.

Chapter Fourteen

A BISHOP IN WARTIME

1939-1943

The Impact of War

The normal pattern of Church life, especially in the crowded urban areas where the majority of Catholics had traditionally settled, was severely disturbed by the war and Hinsley's diocese, like many others, was affected by air raids, blackout restrictions, daily privations and the loss of priests to military chaplaincy. Children were evacuated; families suffered separation and the loss of loved ones; schools, houses, convents and churches were destroyed; and the liturgical routine was disrupted.

Through his Auxiliaries, Hinsley had to immediately oversee a plan dealing with casualties from possible air raids. It was arranged that casualty stations would be manned by the priests in whose parishes they were located and that all priests would ensure visits to casualty stations and hospitals when a raid had ended. A system was also introduced whereby priests would be sent from Archbishop's House to first aid posts and casualty stations in areas which had suffered heavily and where extra spiritual comfort was needed. An air raid post was set up at Archbishop's House and from there a system of messengers would communicate between the centre of the diocese and parishes in the event of raids. Services could not be held after sunset because of blackout restrictions, the Forty Hours Devotion was suspended, prayers in 'time of war' were introduced, and the faithful were dispensed from the laws of fasting and abstinence. It was ironic that as the first air raid warnings sounded in London shortly after the declaration of war, the new church of St Madeleine was being opened in St Quintin's Park.

Where possible, the pre-war round of diocesan activities continued but not without difficulty. The cost of printing and distributing notices from Cathedral House to the clergy, for example, became so expensive that Hinsley resorted to publishing information in the Catholic press. The efforts to reduce parish debts continued and collections were held for schools, ecclesiastical training and for poor missions in the diocese. Visitations to parishes continued and the Sacrament of Confirmation was administered in Westminster Cathedral on a monthly basis although these were rarely undertaken by Hinsley who increasingly lived for most of the time at his Hare Street residence.[1]

The Westminster diocese which included London north of the River Thames, Middlesex and Hertfordshire had a population of 300,000 Catholics. A large proportion were children and their evacuation during the early months of the war to areas less likely to be bombed caused an alarming problem for Hinsley and other bishops whose flocks were normally concentrated in urban parishes. Children were dispersed to areas where Catholics were few and where liturgical, pastoral and educational provision was scanty. There was, therefore, the strong possibility that the spiritual needs of the evacuees would not be addressed and at the outbreak of war Hinsley asked parents and teachers whose children and schools had been evacuated to keep him informed of any problems in this regard.[2] The bishops into whose dioceses the children were sent faced the influx of newcomers with equal trepidation for they did not possess the manpower and resources to cater for their needs. Hinsley's own parishes received schoolchildren and mothers and children from London's East End who were evacuated to Hertfordshire at the northern end of Westminster diocese. Due to the large number of evacuated children arriving from London into his diocese, the Bishop of Northampton gave permission for priests to say two Masses on Sundays and holydays. When the fear of a German invasion intensified in 1940 another wave of evacuation began as families were moved inland from coastal areas in the south of England.[3]

Nor did Hinsley and Amigo trust the London County Council's and Board of Education's assurances that Catholic evacuees would be placed with Catholic families and in Catholic schools. In theory this involuntary migration may have presented the opportunity for further pastoral work but the reality was very different. Bishops were reluctant to spare priests to either accompany evacuees or minister to them on their arrival. Evacuees were not always accommodated in Catholic homes or Catholic schools and there was an inevitable weakening of the bond between the family, school and Church. In his Pastoral of Trinity Sunday 1940 Hinsley was critical of those parents who were less than watchful over their children's spiritual welfare:

> We are grieved to have to say that the evacuation of children last September revealed to us the indifference of not a few Catholic parents regarding the religious training and practice of their children. We trust and we think that these indifferentists were the exception. They cannot have realised the dread responsibility of allowing the charges God has entrusted to them to attend non-Catholic schools, and to grow up without a knowledge of their religious duties.[4]

He could have been equally critical of those bishops who did not face up to the challenges presented by evacuation. He himself made every effort to assign priests to evacuation duties and by 1941 seven Westminster priests were ministering to evacuees.[5] The evacuation of Catholic children to homes overseas increased the Cardinal's concern for their spiritual welfare. In allowing their children to be evacuated to countries such as Canada, parents had to sign over guardianship to the government which in turn signed it over to reception authorities overseas. For Hinsley, who protested against these arrangements on behalf of the Hierarchy, this was dangerously akin to totalitarianism and he commented to Bishop McNulty that such temporary measures could easily become permanent.[6]

If the dispersal of Catholics raised serious issues for the bishops so too did the German Luftwaffe's intensive bombings of the cities. By 1940 London had suffered extensively from German air raids and in his Advent Pastoral of that year Hinsley referred to those in his diocese who had been rendered homeless by the barbarous cruelty of modern aerial warfare. Yet, he continued, the losses inflicted on them and the horrors they had suffered had not cowed their spirit and fortitude and he was especially grateful to those who had offered hospitality and charity.[7] Churches, schools and convents as well as homes and commercial buildings were destroyed in the attacks on London and other towns and cities and there was great concern among the episcopate that they and religious orders should receive full compensation for damaged Church property. By October 1940 twelve of Hinsley's own churches were damaged. Our Lady of Victories in Kensington was completely burnt out in September 1940. It had only recently been restored. As the blitz on the capital continued through late 1940 and into 1941, other diocesan churches were left in ruins. St John the Baptist at Hackney, the Church of the Five Precious Wounds at Stanebridge Park, Our Lady and St Joseph at Poplar, St Mary's Chelsea, the Holy Apostles in Pimlico, St Edmund's Whitton, and the Most Holy Redeemer in Chelsea were all damaged by enemy bombs. When the Church of the Holy Redeemer was bombed many people sheltering in its crypt were killed. The nearby convent and the Chapel of Perpetual Adoration in the former house of St Thomas More were also completely destroyed. Other churches, schools and presbyteries were damaged at Bow Common, Lincoln's Inn Fields, Limehouse and Milwall. Hinsley's cathedral, with walls between three and six feet thick, suffered extensive if minor damage. Every effort was made to protect the building and internal scaffolding was erected to protect the baldachino. Incendiary devices fell within the cathedral precincts and bombs falling nearby shattered the cathedral windows. An incendiary bomb pierced the cathedral roof but was extinguished before damage could spread. Clergy House and the throne room of Archbishop's House, meanwhile, were damaged in October and December 1940. Hinsley visited the bombed areas in London's East End to see the damage first hand and console the victims.[8] The priests were under intense pressure and in October 1940 Hinsley was encouraged to send an *Ad Clerum* to soothe troubled nerves and offer some respite:

> Dear Reverend Father,
>
> I have seen for myself the trouble which you have endured through a month of intense bombing. To say that I deeply sympathize with you and with your people is all too cold an expression. I long in some way to prove my feelings of affectionate concern for priests and people so sorely tried. At the same time I cannot withold my admiration for the courage shown in such appalling circumstances.
>
> I know that you and so many of our London priests are suffering from sleepless nights owing to the noise of the barrage and the dread anticipation of peril from the air. I know also that many of you are going the rounds of your parishes night after night or are kept wakeful and alert for any call that may come.
>
> My anxiety prompts me to propose that some respite should be arranged, some period of rest if only for a night or two, to allow of regard for health. I have asked, therefore, Mgr Morrogh Bernard, VG, to make it known that I would welcome at Hare Street two priests at a time who need the change and possibility of undisturbed sleep. The President of St Edmund's is also ready to offer hospitality at the College to those priests who are sorely tried by overwork and overwrought. . . . [9]

Hinsley commiserated with Bishop Doubleday of Brentwood whose diocese, containing large parts of the East End of London with its docklands, had been severely bombed. Hinsley told Doubleday that he had used his New Schools Fund to aid stricken missions but a more permanent solution was required.[10] Archbishop Amigo's Cathedral of St George was destroyed in an air raid and other dioceses suffered extensive damage to churches and ecclesiastical property.[11] Financial assistance was urgently needed and in March 1941 Hinsley wrote to Archbishop Edward Mooney of Detroit, whom he had known in Rome, on behalf of the Hierarchy asking for help from the American bishops. Mooney was informed that 58 churches had been destroyed and over 130 schools, convents and other church buildings. 'The list of our losses is a long one', wrote Hinsley, but he assured Mooney that spirits were high: 'Do not, however, think that we are dispirited. This country stands erect. . . . '[12]

To recompense the churches for damage caused by enemy action, the government introduced a War Damage Bill which offered some financial assistance for the rebuilding and repair of war damaged churches, schools and presbyteries. The Hierarchy liaised with the Anglicans and other denominations in order to present a united front and a sub-committee of Archbishop Amigo and Bishops Brown and Mathew represented the Hierarchy in negotiations with government officials. In January 1941 the Hierarchy's deputation, together with representatives from the Regular Orders, met with the Chancellor of the Exchequer to discuss the provisions of the Bill. The value of properties had been fixed at March 1939 prices and the government had promised to restore that value only if it was in the public interest to do so. The bishops were naturally concerned at the discretionary nature of the Bill and objected to the stipulation that a block grant was to be given to the Church for damaged property rather than compensation for each building. They also wished to have compensation for the contents of damaged buildings. The government modified its position only slightly by insisting that all claims be settled on a diocesan basis but the issue was further complicated by the possibility that a ruined church might be in an area which was to be redeveloped after the war and its congregation to be re-housed. The onus would then be on a diocese to use the compensation to build another church in a more expensive area. The fact that materials would be scarce in the post-war world also worried the bishops for future government controls would ensure that rebuilding ecclesiastical property was would not be a priority. The Anglican acceptance of the government's modifications did not help the Catholic position.[13]

In the midst of war the government set about the formulation of social policies which would facilitate post-war reconstruction and in 1942 the *Report on Social Insurance and Allied Services* was published. The *Report* was the outcome of a commission established under the chairmanship of Sir William Beveridge to consider ways of abolishing known causes of social wants and paved the way for the introduction of a post-war welfare state. It was very likely that the material and monetary benefits proposed by Beveridge would be welcomed by Catholics suffering from the wants he had identified but the Hierarchy were not altogether in favour of increased state interference into people's lives. They had frequently called for a new social order but the leftward swing of Beveridge's proposals presented them with a challenge. Hinsley and Archbishop Williams of Birmingham, although both deplored ever-increasing state interference, were generally in favour of the Report's proposals but others in the Hierarchy feared that a state bureaucracy would replace diocesan voluntary agencies as the arbiter and provider of welfare to Catholics in need. The *Beveridge Report* promised social security to many Catholics and Hinsley was realistic enough to welcome the document rather than condemn it out of hand. He was aware, wrote Heenan, that it was better to curtail liberty than permit licensed injustice.[14]

Immersed as he was in the social encyclicals of the popes, Hinsley had regularly addressed the theme of 'Christian social justice' rather than merely 'social justice'. For him it was a critical distinction and he emphasised it consistently. In his first broadcast he had referred to the fear that occupied the minds and hearts of those affected by combinations of sickness, unemployment and poverty. People such as these, he said, bewildered by the complexity of trying to relieve their distress, would easily fall prey to unscrupulous politicians ready to promote violent means to alter the social order. The best way forward, he proposed, was to think of alleviating social injustice 'as a co-operative task; as something in which we hope to work together with all men of good will'. In 1936 he had spoken of the abuses of capital and the *laissez-faire* economic system which 'preached rigid economic laws and gave no heed to moral and social rights and duties. . . .' With other bishops he castigated the inherent injustice of extreme capitalism no less than he did the alternative of atheistic material communism which sought to replace it through class war. As Heenan wrote, the Cardinal 'ardently desired to remedy injustice but was not prepared to do so at the cost of worse injustice'.[15] In September 1937, at the Royal Albert Hall, he had dismissed the principles of communism and instead proposed the practice of Christian justice in social and domestic life. His ensuing Pastoral of November was devoted to a study of mutual rights and duties of working men and employers. In it he stressed the need for fraternal charity and laid out his genuine belief that the rights of man could only be acknowledged and his duties fulfilled through a belief in God and adherence to the teachings of His Son. In particular, he was concerned that Catholics recognised their social responsibilities:

> No Catholic . . . can regard with indifference a state of affairs in which work is considered as a commodity and the worker merely as a "hand" and not, as he primarily is, an immortal soul. He must *want* those conditions to be changed into something Christian and he must do what he can to bring about the change. He must not apathetically acquiesce in them.[16]

But Catholics did not have a monopoly on critiques of the social and economic order. The famous letter in *The Times* from Hinsley and other Christian leaders in December 1940 had not dwelt solely on the Pope's Five Peace Points. There was an important and often overlooked rider to it that introduced ' . . .five standards by which economic situations and proposals may be tested. . .' The joint statement called for the abolition of extreme inequalities of wealth, equal opportunities in education, the primacy of the family, the sense of Divine vocation in daily work, and the equitable use of the earth's resources for present and future generations.[17] In his Advent Pastoral of 1941 Hinsley had emphasised the need to promote a fairer and more caring society through the 'divine precept of charity' rather than through a system that simply addressed material needs. 'The obligations of justice are mainly negative', he wrote, 'and their fulfilment can bring little more than a negative peace'. The over-emphasis on 'rights', although needing to be acknowledged, had obscured due attention to 'duties' which each had for his fellow-man. This concept applied to the state:

> While it is the duty of citizens to recognise and respect the rights of others, it is likewise the duty of the state to acknowledge and protect the rights of the individual and of the family, and to secure the equitable distribution of both goods and burdens.[18]

Where it could be seen that the state was acting in accordance with these precepts and in a manner likely to alleviate social distress rather than enslave the populace, Hinsley would not reject its attempts at social improvement. He told a priest that 'The Beveridge Report aims at helping the poor and aged. Therefore it is a good thing. I hope Parliament will pass it'.[19] Other prominent Catholics, however, considered that the *Beveridge Report* fell short of Catholic ideals. Some bishops and laymen warned that it was major step towards 'the servile state' but few priests and even fewer poor Catholics felt inclined to reject Beveridge's proposals entirely. In this they caught the mood of the nation for if the state were doing nothing to prepare for post-war reconstruction then it would be accused of self-complacency and inertia. There was an expectation that the problem of social welfare would be addressed and that legislation would remove the fear of social insecurity. Correspondents to *The Clergy Review* felt that the *Report* contained nothing contrary to papal teaching but much that supported it.[20]

Students, Chaplains and Combatants

As war approached, the government introduced Military Training and Military Service Acts and in May 1939 Hinsley wrote to the bishops asking them to agree on a common policy relating to exemption for clerical students and male religious. He had already been pressed by Archbishop Amigo and the Superiors of religious orders to intercede with the War Office and was anxious that the Hierarchy took early action.[21] With Hinsley's consent Amigo visited the War Office on 1 June 1939 to see if any concessions could be made for Church students. Amigo used the argument that if war came more military chaplains would be required. If seminarians were not allowed to complete their studies then there would be no future chaplains. It was an argument that was to rebound on Amigo.[22]

Using the precedent of the Great War, Hinsley suggested to the bishops that rather than ask for an exemption clause to be inserted into the Acts, the government should be approached to pass an Administrative Act which would allow exemption for all seminarians and teaching and nursing male religious. He therefore proposed to seek a general exemption but if a man left the seminary or religious life then the ecclesiastical authorities would inform the War Office. In this way no one who would be of future value to the country in a military capacity would gain exemption. If war did occur, however, then the requirements for military service would obviously have to be reconsidered. Chamberlain, in a letter thanking the bishops for their message of loyalty on the outbreak of war, agreed with the general principles and Hinsley informed the Hierarchy of the Prime Minister's decision on 6 September 1939.[23]

The bishops, however, were not of one mind and once again Hinsley was placed in the unenviable position of having to contend with a disunited Hierarchy – a delicate situation compounded by the differing views of the religious orders. Archbishop Amigo wished only students in philosophy and theology to be exempted whilst Archbishop Downey and Bishop McCormack of Hexham and Newcastle wished all their students to be exempted. The Jesuits, Redemptorists and Salesians were all in favour of exemption but the Oratorians were not and Mgr Bickford of St Edmund's College, Ware, wanted his students to undergo military training without exemption. Hinsley, who had asked Lord Fitzalan to explore the situation with the government, shared Bickford's view but could not set aside the requests of other bishops and the regulars. Bishop Mathew told Archbishop Williams that as a last resort the Cardinal would agree to students who were not in orders being taken for service.[24] The Archbishop confessed to Mathew that the business of military training for Church students was 'all a bit difficult' but felt that a short spell of military discipline and physical training would do his students no harm at all. He also saw compulsory training for all men as a way of ending snobbishness and class distinctions. He did, however, appreciate the difficulties facing the seminaries and religious orders and agreed with Hinsley's approach.[25] Amigo meanwhile continued to lobby the War Office for some concessions and in September, after war had been declared, Hinsley was informed that clerical students who had already embarked on seminary courses would be added to the list of reserved occupations.[26]

Throughout the war priests found themselves ministering to their parishes, evacuees and displaced persons, and to service personnel stationed in the many temporary military camps which sprang up all over the country. Like others in reserved occupations, priests under the age of 65 were also required to undertake civilian duties such as fire-watching and fire fighters. These demands inevitably interrupted the normal tempo of their spiritual duties and placed them under incessant pressure but the loss of ordained ministers to military chaplaincy was an even greater source of anxiety for the Hierarchy. Bishop James Dey, Bishop in Ordinary of the British Army and Royal Air Force, was keen to enlist as many chaplains as possible in order to cater for the spiritual needs of those in the armed forces but diocesan bishops and the Superiors of religious orders did not always support him. Some bishops were not disposed to losing their priests to the authority of another bishop, see them risk death and injury and at the same time deny the civilian population an adequate ministry. It led to an unfortunate situation where Dey was treated as extraneous to the Hierarchy.

The origins of this unhappy state of affairs lay in a similar dispute over military chaplains in the Great War. In 1917, against the wishes of Cardinal Bourne, the Vatican appointed Mgr William Keatinge, a contemporary of Hinsley at the *Venerabile*, as the first *Episcopus Castrensis* or Bishop of the Army and Royal Air Force with authority over all chaplains ministering to those services. Catholic chaplains for the Royal Navy remained under the control of the Archbishop of Westminster and the Admiralty. Whereas the discipline and organisation of army chaplains was maintained under bishops who had spent their careers with the military, the ecclesiastical control of naval chaplains was never firm and Bourne took little subsequent interest in chaplains for the Senior Service. In pique and on the weak premise that the *Episcopus Castrensis* was a neutral office with no diocesan jurisdiction Bourne also excluded Keatinge from Hierarchy meetings. Ironically, Bourne, who was responsible for temporary non-commissioned Royal Navy chaplains, had a place in the Hierarchy while the Army Bishop who was responsible for many more commissioned chaplains was not. It was an unfortunate decision and one which left Keatinge isolated and did little for the morale of army chaplains.[27] But Bourne was not the only one to show discourtesy to Keatinge. In 1930 Amigo would not even see Keatinge to discuss the recruitment of chaplains from Southwark diocese.[28] After his translation to Westminster Hinsley lobbied other bishops on Dey's behalf and managed to extract from them the concession that the Army Bishop could attend Hierarchy meetings when chaplaincy issues were on the agenda of their meetings. It was as far as Hinsley got, however. When Cardinal Rossi of Consistorial asked him in January 1938 to place the issue of Dey's financial situation before the Hierarchy, the bishops refused to offer the Bishop of the Forces any assistance.[29]

On the outbreak of war there were 54 chaplains serving the Regular and Territorial Army, 10 with the Royal Air Force and 11 with the Royal Navy but the expansion of the armed services meant that many more would be required. Some of the religious orders released their men almost immediately but the dioceses were not as eager to see their men go off to war. Hinsley had two roles: first as an Ordinary he had to consider which priests he could afford to become chaplains; and secondly he was the ecclesiastical superior of naval chaplains and therefore responsible for their welfare. Before the war Hinsley had encouraged his priests to volunteer as chaplains for the Territorial Army and when his secretary, Mgr Elwes, applied for chaplaincy work in September 1939 the Cardinal wrote that he would be better as a naval chaplain than attending to 'an old crock' and 'licking stamps'. He continued: 'I do not want selfishly to absorb the energy and time of one who could do so much in the way of National Service, i.e. either as a chaplain to the forces or as a parish priest'.[30] But Hinsley had a surplus of priests; other Ordinaries were not in the same fortunate position.

As in the Great War the supply of naval chaplains was always insufficient and the Admiralty was always less than co-operative. In 1940 Hinsley warned the Admiralty that if it refused to assign sufficient Catholic chaplains and facilitate their work there would be serious and unwelcome consequences regarding naval recruitment:

> You must now understand how reluctant we shall be to encourage men to enter the Senior Service since their highest interests apparently are not regarded by the Authorities at the Admiralty. At this moment of grave crisis the British public would regard this seeming indifference in no very favourable light. . . .[31]

The Admiralty's response was that the situation was being rectified as quickly as possible but Hinsley, relying on letters from officers and men, refused to believe it and replied to the Permanent Secretary at the Admiralty:

> Regretfully I must say that we are not satisfied. . . . An instance I may quote is the case of hospital ships at Scapa Flow. We had complaints of the lack of R.C. chaplains. The matter received little or no attention from your Department.
>
> I have information from some reliable R.C. men who have been to Norway that our R.C. naval units . . . had no provision made for their spiritual needs.
>
> While your Department has been as you put it 'flogging out' the question of words or names, our R.C. naval men have been sent into the next world without that preparation and that spiritual ministration for which we know many of them clamoured.[32]

The Cardinal took the precaution of sending the correspondence to the First Sea Lord, Admiral Sir Dudley Pound. The Admiral was concerned and promised Hinsley that administrative obstacles in the way of providing Catholic naval chaplains would be speedily removed but Admiralty hostility to Roman Catholic priests was ingrained and it was not until 1944 that priests were commissioned as naval chaplains.

As the war progressed Bishop Dey became increasingly concerned to provide for the spiritual welfare of those under his jurisdiction and angry with the Hierarchy for failing to provide chaplains. At the Low Week meeting of the bishops in 1942 he not only had to fend off the criticisms of military chaplains but failed to convince the bishops of his needs to supply units at home and overseas. Fr Coughlan, the Senior Army Chaplain, had already supplied figures to the Hierarchy showing that chaplains were ministering on the front line and also in prisoner of war camps and military hospitals in the United Kingdom. It was more than Dey could stomach and in June 1942 he wrote an 'open letter' to the bishops and Rome and then went public with his frustration and annoyance. Amigo in particular came in for unprecedented episcopal criticism. Dey wrote that in 1939 the Archbishop of Southwark had requested clerical exemption from military training so that chaplains could be provided in wartime. Now, Dey contended, out of 435 secular priests in Southwark only seven were military chaplains.[33] It made no difference to Amigo who was not only reluctant to release his priests but readily criticized the work of military chaplains. Archbishop Downey and Bishop Lee of Clifton were also sceptical of the chaplains' contribution to service personnel and Dey felt compelled to respond to them, although not in public. Bishop Doubleday wrote to Amigo to say that officiating chaplains could be provided on home bases while commissioned chaplains could minister to overseas units. He felt that if Bishop Dey explained fully to the Hierarchy what his 680 chaplains were actually doing rather than complaining to the press then an accommodation could probably be reached.[34] Amigo had no problem in saying what his priests were doing and attempted to defend his position by writing a long letter to Hinsley with details of the work undertaken by all of his priests. Two of his priests had already been killed in air raids while others were acting as officiating chaplains to the thousands of troops billeted in his diocese.[35]

In early 1943 Hinsley wrote to the Hierarchy giving a breakdown of serving chaplains by diocese and religious order and what the number would be if each diocese gave 10% of its priests to the military. Cardiff, Hexham and Newcastle, Lancaster, Menevia and Middlesbrough already exceed this target and of the 680 military chaplains, 238 were from religious orders. Hinsley warned the bishops that 'many more chaplains are needed now' and told them that the matter had to be raised again at the next Low Week meeting. By 1943 Hinsley had allowed 34 of his 434 priests to be military chaplains and by the end of the war 45 out of 479 Westminster priests were serving as chaplains.[36]

Altercations with the Hierarchy and the Admiralty did not prevent Hinsley from attempting to fulfil his position of ecclesiastical superior of naval chaplains. It was another burden for a man increasingly weighed down by the responsibility of high office and the strains of war but Hinsley found time to visit chaplains and naval establishments around the country. His addresses to ships' companies were motivational and manifested that genuine desire for victory that he so desired. Speaking to the officers and men of H.M.S. *Raleigh* he denounced the 'bastard breed of pagan mythology' who were subjecting Europe to devastation and slavery and emphasised the important role of naval personnel:

> Men of the Royal Navy, you are taking a foremost part in a great conflict for truth and justice against the cruel enemies of the most sacred rights of mankind. All true liberty is at stake . . . We have had grievous setbacks and losses. We are suffering for our sins and foolish mistakes. But we are confident that, whatever may have been our shortcomings in the past, victory will finally crown our efforts if we turn to Almighty God who alone gives strength to conquer evil and secure lasting good. But we must banish evil from our own hearts and minds, we must keep our hands clean from selfishness and defilement, we must seek true peace with our Creator. Then we shall win the war and prepare the way for the triumph of real peace – yes, for the Peace of Christ. For Christ alone can give us true peace – that peace which the world cannot give – the peace promised to men of good will. . . .

And then with a final exhortation he exclaimed:

> . . .Forward to victory under the standard of the Cross of Christ our King wherein is the pledge of resurrection and life for all nations.[37]

The visit of a Catholic prelate had the potential to offend the religious sensibilities of some non-Catholic officers and men and so the Admiralty gave orders for attendance at Hinsley's addresses to be voluntary for non-

Catholic sailors. Hinsley took great care not to use the word 'Catholic' in his addresses for fear of embarrassing the religious convictions of others and only spoke to Catholic sailors after an address. Nevertheless, Admiral Jack Tovey, Commander-in-Chief of the Home Fleet, was so inspired by Hinsley's words that in 1942 he invited the Cardinal to speak on ships in northern waters. It was an engagement beyond the Cardinal's physical capabilities and Hinsley politely refused the invitation. Tovey replied:

> My dear Cardinal,
>
> Thank you so much for your letter of 12th August. It is a terrible disappointment to us that we are not to see you this year, but I am sure you are wise. There is no getting away from the fact that, even under the best conditions, it is a very tiring journey.
>
> I really feel ashamed of ever having tried to tempt you to undertake it, but for many years I hoped I might one day have the honour and pleasure of meeting you and I know what a tremendous lot it would have meant to everyone in the Fleet. So . . . I couldn't refrain from trying to persuade you.
>
> It was more that good of you to even contemplate it. May I be allowed to send you our love and duty and pray that we may always have your blessing.[38]

Hinsley did not overlook other military personnel and somehow found time in his busy schedule to visit military establishments of the Allied forces up and down the country. In September 1941 he addressed Canadian troops at Aldershot and in English and French he urged them to oppose the principles and methods of the enemy. 'Against such races', he said, 'defence of our oppressed and persecuted brethren is just and necessary'.[39] Where he could not reach in person he let his broadcasts do the work. These were as stirring and sincere as his personal addresses and had the same effect. The Sword of the Spirit may have been at the forefront of Hinsley's spiritual crusade but he realised that the military crusade was more important if 'the Sword' was able to fulfil its aims. His addresses and broadcasts to service personnel, therefore, always possessed a spiritual and moral dimension. When he reviewed and addressed the Irish Guards outside Westminster Cathedral in 1939 he bade them to go forth in the spirit of Christian crusaders.[40] Speaking to New Zealanders in 1940 he reminded those who had volunteered for military service that they, like himself, were convinced that the war was being waged for the sake of justice and freedom and for human and divine values.[41] To Australians he spoke of the unconquerable courage shown by the Anzacs during the Gallipoli campaign of the Great War. He told them they were fighting in the battle for freedom and in a cricketing analogy he said they were upholding the team spirit of humanity 'against the tyranny of cliques who seek to enslave the world by the use of brute force. . . . Keep your eye true, fixed on the triumph of right over might. A straight bat and vigorous driving will win us the victory'.[42]

In August 1940, in the first of a series of radio talks called 'Looking for Christ', Hinsley spoke to all British and Commonwealth forces with typical honesty and sincerity:

> Let me begin by saying that I look upon you as champions fighting in a good cause. You are defending not only the freedom and existence of the British Empire. You are fighting the good fight against evil things. . . . You are on the same side of the angels in the struggle against the same pride of rebellious Lucifer . . . fight this fight as Christian soldiers. . . .

Modern soldiers, he reminded his listeners, were no longer mercenaries nor were they regarded as wild animals. They were Christian men with immortal souls striving to save the world from becoming a savage jungle. They were resisting the onslaught of brutal violence directed against the Christian values on which European values were founded and the chances of restoring peace depended on the Empire and its forces looking for Christ and affording him his rightful place in their hearts. While they and their colleagues might die in the struggle, the victory would surely come. It would be the triumph of the spirit and the symbol of victory would be the Cross. Their motto, therefore, had to be: *In Hoc Signo Vinces ('In this Sign Conquer')*. 'During this time of intense trial', he had written in his Lenten Pastoral of 1941, 'your crucifix will inspire fearless confidence'. He hoped that it would be possible for all fighting men, 'Christian knights of the British cause', to wear under their tunics a little cross with the inscription: 'The Pledge of Victory; so that you may ever have present in your thoughts your noble crusade for Christian truth and justice'. This was the origin of 'The Cardinal's Cross'. Over 2½ million were subsequently given to those who wished to wear it during their military service. The Cardinal concluded in typical fashion:

> Men of His Majesty's Forces, you need more than patriotism in the mighty struggle that is before you. Patriotism is a noble thing, it is part of the new commandment of love which Christ has left as the test of His

genuine followers. Yes! You need religion! And religion is summed up in the complete duty of a Christian to love God above all things and our fellow-men for God's sake. Religion is the spirit of unselfish service and sacrifice. Patriotism is perfect when the soldier is fired with the love of the Heart of Jesus Christ.[43]

One mother whose son had been killed while serving with the R.A.F. wrote to the Cardinal to say that Hinsley's words reached into the hearts of many, especially those who were suffering. Thanking him for referring in one of his broadcasts to her son's last letter which had been published in *The Times*, 'Your Eminence', she wrote,

> It was with great pride that I listened to your broadcast on Sunday and heard your inspiring call to youth and your lovely references to my son's letter. All of us who heard it were very touched and I am glad to tell you that the head of my boy's school had all his scholars going back to the school chapel to listen in to your address. This is one school at least where Christian teaching is definite and thorough. . . .[44]

An R.A.F. officer and his bomber crew had heard one of Hinsley's talks on the importance of youth and wrote from Yorkshire to thank him for his inspiring words. As they flew over the North Sea the crew recalled Hinsley's words: 'God's greatest gift to us was the joy of youth, and the greatest gift we could offer to God was the service of our youth'. They remembered, the officer wrote, the Cardinal's 'great comforting message, which we recall when the way seems lonely and the path dark, and it cheers us'. As a non-Catholic the officer was unsure how to address Hinsley but his final lines were from the heart: '. . .my pals asked me just to write and say "Thank you" for your message was not in vain, We shall pray often for you, Sir'.[45]

'We cannot surrender our schools'

The 1944 Education Act, one of the most important pieces of English educational legislation in the twentieth century, was the culmination of successive government attempts to arrive at a coherent system of national education. The Act created junior schools for children between the ages of seven and eleven and secondary schools for those aged between eleven and fifteen. Secondary schools could be grammar schools, secondary technical schools or secondary modern schools with respectively an academic, vocational or generalist curriculum. Unlike the 1936 Education Act, by which Local Education Authorities were given the opportunity to establish senior schools, the 1944 Act made secondary provision compulsory. The implications of these changes, introduced in wartime by a coalition government with an eye to the post-war world, were enormous and once again the Catholic Hierarchy had reason to unite in order to protect Catholic interests.[46]

The popular idea that Britain was fighting fascism, and communism in the early part of the war, for the ideals of Christian civilization seemed strangely at odds with the government's pre-war attempts to reduce the influence of Christianity on the nation's schools but, as in the First World War, the concept of a Christian struggle against the forces of barbarism was a strong element in British propaganda. No doubt the government's claim that the war was being waged for Christian values against Godless dictatorships appealed to something innate in the British cultural psyche and in 1940 *The Times* went so far as to state that the life of the nation had to be based on spiritual principles, that Christianity was the nation's historic religion, and that education without religion was not really education at all.[47] These sentiments had wide support and when the White Paper on Educational Reconstruction was published in July 1943 it stated that there was a general wish that religious education based on Christianity should be given a clearly defined place in the life and work of the schools, springing from a desire to revive the spiritual and personal values in society and the national tradition.[48]

The build-up to the publication of the White Paper was protracted and involved religious leaders and politicians in long and acrimonious negotiations. In mid-1941 the Board of Education published a Green Book setting out a basis for the discussion of planned educational reform and it became the responsibility of R. A. Butler, President of the Board of Education from July 1941, to conduct negotiations with appropriate parties, arrive at some form of consensus and prepare for legislation. From the outset the Hierarchy were unhappy with many aspects of the government's proposals and subsequently expressed their concern loudly and vehemently. First, the bishops reminded the government, as if it could be forgotten, that they remained totally committed to the principle of Catholic schools for Catholic children and for this reason were against that part of the government's scheme which allowed L.E.A.'s to control schools whilst guaranteeing some form of denominational education. In this the bishops rightly saw no genuine safeguards for Catholic religious education. Secondly, the Hierarchy was opposed to an alternative option of 'aided' status under which denominational bodies would receive a 50% state grant for capital maintenance of schools but would receive no state funds for the erection of new secondary schools envisaged in the Green Book. As LEAs could also enforce modern building standards on those elementary schools which were built in Victorian times and were now outmoded, the bishops were thus confronted with having to bring their existing schools, including those damaged by enemy action, up to required standards and also find the money for new schools.[49]

The 'Dual System' of state-provided and voluntary schools which had developed since the introduction of government educational grants in the nineteenth century was opposed by many sectors of society including the Trades Union Congress, the National Union of Teachers, many local authorities, some Anglicans and all the Free Churches but it was unacceptable to the Catholic bishops for different reasons. Whereas other opponents of the Dual System rejected it for a variety of reasons ranging from denominational tests for teachers, 'closed' headships and the imposition of an Agreed Syllabus, the Hierarchy was presented, in the Green Book, with a take-it-or-leave-it situation that on one hand eliminated their control over religious education and on the other hand incurred prohibitive expense.[50] It was another occasion, therefore, when the bishops donned their armour and strode into battle. Bishop Joseph McCormack of Hexham and Newcastle said that 'We shall have our Catholic schools where our children shall be educated in a Catholic atmosphere by Catholic teachers approved by a Catholic authority. We cannot surrender our schools'. Archbishop Downey said that 'We shall continue to struggle for our denominational schools even though we have to fight alone'. The intransigent views of both bishops were representative of the Hierarchy.[51]

In June 1941 Hinsley and a deputation from the Hierarchy and the Catholic Education Council met with Butler and his advisers. Hinsley wanted full equality for Catholic schools and a Catholic voice in the development of the Dual System. He and other bishops were also concerned that the full effects of the 1936 Act had not yet been worked out before additional legislation was planned. Butler said that nothing would be settled without the advice of the religious bodies but nor did he promise anything.[52] The stand-off continued throughout 1941 and 1942. Nothing was ceded and tempers became frayed. Mgr John Vance of the Westminster Schools Commission called the Green Book 'a shame and an iniquity' and the Board's officials became concerned that they were dealing with clerics not lay people and that negotiations were unproductive. Hinsley himself thought the proposals would wreck the Dual System but was pleased to hear from Butler that there was no such intention on the part of government.[53]

In an effort to move things forward Hinsley invited Butler to visit him in June 1942 at Buntingford, the Cardinal's country house, where, supported by Mgr Elwes, the Cardinal expressed his views openly and frankly to the President of the Board. His major concern was that the Catholic community was unable to meet the financial requirements of the government's proposals to which Butler replied that Catholics had little difficulty in finding money for the new Liverpool Cathedral. Taken aback, Hinsley privately admitted that he disapproved of Downey's scheme and found it financially unsound but that did not vitiate his argument and added that the Church's substantial contribution to private education was never acknowledged. James Chuter Ede, Butler's Parliamentary secretary later conceded the meeting had cleared the air and had brought the Catholic position into focus. Like the Board's officials, Butler, Chuter Ede and the Catholic Hierarchy knew that the Catholics would have great difficulties in providing the extra secondary school places required.[54]

In September 1942 Butler again met a delegation of the Hierarchy at which the Cardinal argued for 100% state funding for Catholic schools. It was rejected and the meeting turned into another occasion where Amigo, Bishop Flynn of Lancaster, Bishop Brown and Lord Rankeillour restated the Catholic case. Brown argued that if no agreement could be reached then the matter should be made public. The threat was not to Butler's liking and he countered by saying that much could be achieved confidentially.[55] At this critical juncture Hinsley wrote to *The Times* on 2 November 1942 arguing that political parties which professed freedom of conscience and religion should accommodate Catholic views. Catholics had already proved their determination to promote educational progress and he hoped that they would not be obstructed in their wish to collaborate in further developments that were so important to the nation. The predominantly poor Catholic community had contributed substantially to the provision of education in England and Wales and he appealed for 'fair play' especially form political parties 'that profess to uphold the just claims of the workers and the rights of minorities. . . . '

His statement about the Catholic contribution to the nation's schools was borne out by the facts. As Archbishop Amigo and Bishop Brown had earlier informed Butler, Catholics had raised £3.5 million in the last twenty-five years for their schools. Catholic dioceses owned 12% of all voluntary schools and educated 8% of the total school population but their schools were often sub-standard and, like the Anglicans, they faced a difficult task in bringing these up to the Board's requirements. Hinsley's letter was immediately seized upon by Butler who felt that Hinsley had indeed gone public and telephoned Hinsley to express his concern. The Cardinal replied that his comments were not meant for Butler or the Board but were an attempt to allay the fears of the Catholic community regarding its unease at the TUC's anti-denominational comments at its recent Blackpool conference.[56]

Hinsley again wrote to *The Times* on 31 November 1942 emphasising that as a result of forthcoming legislation Catholics, as tax payers, were to be saddled with huge debts simply because of their religion and because they would not accept a syllabus of religious instruction agreeable to many but not to them.[57] In February 1943 he approved the Catholic Parents and Electors Associations set up on the Bradford model to support the Hierarchy in the schools crisis. To Hinsley this was a most useful and obvious form of Catholic Action although not all bishops agreed with this opinion as they felt the CPEA to be outside their 'direction'.[58]

Hinsley had privately clarified his views on the education debate in a statesmanlike paper shortly before his death. Present defects in Catholic school buildings, he wrote, were the consequences of previous Education Acts which favoured Council rather than Catholic schools and more immediately the result of war damage suffered by Catholic schools in urban areas. Government grants for all purposes were inadequate and no system acknowledged Catholic debts incurred in the past, the contribution of Catholic private schools, the dispersal of the Catholic community and plans for post-war urban renewal. He was against 'denominationalism', which he called 'a bogus slogan', for 'undenominational' teaching was essentially Protestant as Agreed Syllabuses in Council schools were drawn up mainly by Anglicans and Non-Conformists. He was prepared to admit that a 75% all-round grant for repairs and capital build might be acceptable but he was of the opinion that to exclude Catholics from building new schools because they could not afford them would be unfair. He was even prepared to make concessions regarding the appointment of teachers providing that the religious interests of Catholic schools were safeguarded but his strongest statement related to education and the principle of fairness to the former and present sacrifices of Catholics in the advancement of their country's interests. He demanded that the Catholic community be treated with respect and justice and alluded to its contribution to the war effort:

> Since religion is generally recognised as the essential element in education and Catholics have with immense sacrifice upheld this principle throughout, they are entitled to generous recognition. If they do not obtain such recognition they will fight for it as loyally and vigorously as they have fought in the Navy, Army and R.A.F. We are as patriotic as any other Britishers, and for that very reason we are determined to combat any educational scheme which might jockey us out of the National System by endowing any other religious body at the expense of the general community.

Although he sympathised with Butler's political problems he wished for the Catholic conscience to be respected. He concluded: 'We want only what we desire for all British citizens'.[59] His belief in the British spirit of justice never foundered. On 16 January 1941 he wrote to the editor of *The Times* who had acknowledged the necessity of the Christian formation of children:

> I have confidence in the spirit of fair play of my fellow countrymen that in this [education] question we shall receive the full measure of that just treatment which is due to the liberty of consciences of the Catholic minority. The above principles we can never sacrifice. Definite knowledge of Christ is essential to the continued existence of a Christian people.[60]

For Hinsley the task of leading the Hierarchy through the negotiations was made more difficult by his increasing infirmity and the consequence of more than one archbishop or bishop leading different delegations to the Board of Education or attending meetings with its officials. His dealings with Butler were genuine and honest but he could never persuade the government that the Catholic bishops were not fanatical. Further difficulties arose out of his broad-mindedness towards the Church of England and his recent contacts with Anglican clergymen through the Sword of the Spirit movement but what he could never do, as the Church of England had done, was to hand over Catholic schools to government control. For Catholics, their schools and churches were the visible signs of their religious identity in a country where they were still a suspect minority. To Hinsley it was crucial that the places of Catholic training and formation remained available and strictly under clerical control.[61] In December 1942 he was still urging people to 'resist to the last any system of state absolutism such as in other lands that captures the bodies and souls of the children, thus usurping the rights and duties of parents'.[62]

At a meeting in September 1943, this time at Ushaw College and after Hinsley's death, the bishops reduced their request for state funding to 75% or 80%, as Hinsley had earlier suggested, but Butler's problem was not simply related to finance for such concessions would alienate Protestants and Non-Conformists and threaten the success of his proposals. Butler later recalled that the Roman Catholics wanted to act independently and that there was no question of an alliance between them and the Church of England. He must have known that such an alliance was highly unlikely and the Hierarchy continued its singular determination to maintain the Catholic identity of its schools. Butler, not unnaturally, felt angry and frustrated at his failure to convince the bishops of his sincerity. For the bishops, however, the threat of an extension of public control of schools, unfair differentiation against Catholics, the impossible financial burden to be levied on dioceses if they opted for the voluntary aided status, and the fact that Catholic authorities would receive no aid to build new schools were insurmountable obstacles.[63]

Hinsley's death in March 1943 meant that it was left to others to continue the fight in the lead up to the White Paper, the Bill and the Act. Much later Butler recalled that following the Cardinal's death there was no 'special leader' among the bishops. 'Those at the summit', he wrote, 'were very old and it was difficult to establish any personal contact'. He continued, '. . .it is wrong to say that had Cardinal Hinsley lived he would have obtained a more easy settlement, though the dignity of those with whom one had to deal could never equal his'.[64] But the Hierarchy's readiness to do battle for Catholic interests certainly matched that of the late Cardinal and in their Joint Pastoral letter of Advent 1943 they wrote that were prepared to fight for Catholic principles 'by every legitimate means at our disposal and to go on fighting for it until we attain our end . . . whatever betides we shall never cede our schools or retire from the educational field'.[65]

Chapter Fifteen

THE CROSS AND THE FLAG

1939-1943

The Sword of the Spirit

The Sword of the Spirit was a campaign of prayer, study and action whose fundamental aim was the restoration of Christian principles to the conduct of public affairs and private life. Inspired by Hinsley, who was spurred on by prominent lay Catholics, it advocated a spiritual rationale for the military struggle against Germany, a robust response to anti-Catholic propaganda, and a humane approach to social problems. To overcome Britain's enemies and liberate conquered peoples, members of the Sword of the Spirit dedicated themselves to pray and fight for victory after which they would work for the rebuilding of a Christian Europe. Other Christian denominations were invited to participate in this crusade and 'the Sword' became an early, unique and transitory expression of ecumenism.[1]

Throughout the planning stages and the launch of the Sword, Hinsley moved with speed but unfortunately without sufficient appreciation of the movement's wider ramifications, either for his Communion or for other Christian denominations. As the Sword was initially a diocesan enterprise, Hinsley had no reason to inform other Ordinaries and consequently the bishops were not, at first, fully aware of the Sword's existence, purpose and structure.[2] But when the Sword's officers tried to enlist support in other dioceses Hinsley discovered that his brother bishops were variously ill-disposed to the Sword as a Catholic movement, uncertain of its aims, and questioned its relationship to Catholic Action. As the movement progressed, the Hierarchy also became increasingly anxious about its widening ecumenical dimension. For Hinsley, euphoria at the launch of an embryonic crusade of national Christian collaboration was followed by periods of disappointment and bouts of occasional anger.

Hinsley's first public mention of 'the Sword of the Spirit' was on 10 December 1939 when he delivered a BBC radio broadcast dealing with the spiritual issues of the war.[3] In this deep, wide-ranging and very moving personal address, originally called 'The Sword and the Spirit' but later changed to 'The Sword of the Spirit', Hinsley got right to the essence of the war, the reasons for fighting it and the principles which had to guide those who were united in the Allied struggle. He exhorted his listeners to recognise that spiritual values had to predominate in the war against Hitler and Stalin and that European civilization must be nourished by a Christian faith which acknowledged liberty and morality. He revealed his abhorrence at the thought of a devastating war that would result in the loss of life and material, spiritual and cultural destruction. He lamented that the sword, once the symbol of justice and the instrument of chivalrous defence of the weak against the strong, had been replaced by techniques of modern warfare and that the high achievements of science had been prostituted to serve barbarism. Material progress, he said, did not always improve the world and the battles now to be won were in the hearts and minds of men, resulting in the triumph of either good or evil in the outside world. He warned that the spiritual values of truth, justice and charity 'must prevail or else the material warfare will continue to spread ruin over the earth'. He was convinced that Britain had done all in its power to preserve peace and was now engaged in a war 'for the defence of the things of the spirit' and in the cause of justice and freedom. Britain had not taken up arms from lust of power or for racial or political aims but in the stark realisation that a political settlement could only be achieved militarily. 'Yet in the end', he said, 'the sword of the spirit will alone convert unjust assailants and recreate peace and good will'.

For the Cardinal, Britain's principal motives for entering the war were for upholding Christian values, the defence of religious, personal and corporate liberty, and for Poland, Finland and other vulnerable populations. In the circumstances, he argued, Britain had a just cause to wage war: 'By the spirit Britain will conquer and Britain will sheathe the sword the moment her opponents yield to the force of right and to the claims of freedom'. Britons, he said, valued their Christian inheritance and despite being tempted by secularism they were not indifferent to spiritual and moral values or to the sufferings of their fellow Christians across Europe. The twin evils of Soviet Russia and Nazi Germany threatened this very inheritance and precluded the true development of the spirit. Conquered lands, therefore, had to be rescued and in victory

Britain should aspire to a spiritual renaissance and participate in the renewal or resurrection of Europe. It was a broadcast that set Hinsley unequivocally behind Chamberlain's government and revealed his patriotism in a time of danger. 'I love my country', he concluded, 'with the reasonable loyalty which my faith enjoins, and which the example of Christ commends to us'.

Hinsley was aware that despite his broadcasts, speeches and letters, and the service of Catholic men in the armed forces, Catholics were still regarded as a potential fascist fifth column within British society. It was little wonder then that in early 1940 he accepted the views of a small group of Oxford-based Catholics who, inspired by his 'Sword of the Spirit' broadcast, considered that calumnies against British Catholics had to be rebuffed by expressions of loyalty manifested by a crusade of prayer and action aimed at restoring Christian principles to the conduct of social and international relations. Among the early members of what became the Sword's executive committee were Christopher Dawson, the eminent Catholic historian and editor of the *Dublin Review*, and A.C.F. Beales, a Catholic educationalist at the University of London. With others they had met in November 1939 and established a War Aims Committee to act as standard bearers for Catholics and the Catholic cause during the war. They suggested to the Cardinal that British Catholics needed something tangible to sustain morale and counteract damning propaganda which continually identified them as part of a Latin and fascist conspiracy.[4] In circumstances rendered more dangerous by the disaster of Dunkirk, a possible German invasion of Britain, the fall of France and the establishment of the collaborationist Vichy government in France under Marshal Philippe Pétain, Hinsley needed little convincing and was more than anxious that differences of political opinion within the Catholic community did not give ammunition to those who doubted Catholic loyalty. In July 1940 Hinsley wrote to Douglas Woodruff, editor of *The Tablet*, who was favourably disposed to Pétain:

> There is a serious warning that a clever propaganda campaign is starting to make Catholics appear to have adopted an anti-British attitude. I do counsel you not to publish statements or comments, even if they purport to come from Vatican sources, tending to support to the present government of France. Recent quotations from *L'Osservatore Romano* and the Vatican radio have given a wrong impression to many of our fellow countrymen – Catholic and Protestant – and to some loyal Frenchmen.

He similarly advised the Press Association and *The Times* that private suggestions emanating from the Vatican that the Pope supported the Pétain government were not official pronouncements.[5] The fall of France, a great Christian country, and Britain's isolation had a profound impression on Hinsley. At his first meeting with Prime Minister Winston Churchill, he is reputed to have said: 'I am glad we're alone'. When Churchill asked why, he replied that 'Englishmen fight best when they have their backs to the wall'. It was sentiment to be brilliantly exploited by Churchill.

Hinsley was convinced that unless the majority of Catholics demonstrated their loyalty, the words of a small number of Catholic commentators and editors would be distorted by enemy propagandists and even hostile groups in Great Britain and consequently make life difficult for the Catholic community. He therefore gave his wholehearted support to those who were determined to embark on a public crusade to resist Nazi absolutism and paganism and make known Catholic and Christian views. The crusade, envisaged by Dawson, Beales and the wealthy Manya Harari, took as its name the title of Hinsley's December broadcast – 'the Sword of the Spirit' – and in bringing the Sword to the public's attention, he wrote in *The Times* on 22 July 1940 that:

> Our war activities do not exhaust our responsibility. By a sincere Catholic crusade of prayer and penance, by an intelligent study of the events and facts, by a strenuous defence of the country's cause, we shall do our share to secure the triumph of justice truth and charity. . . . I strongly commend this crusade, which I trust all truly Catholic organisations will zealously promote.[6]

The predominantly lay officers of the Sword of the Spirit were nominated by Hinsley and were drawn from the ranks of Catholic intellectuals. They included those who were active in the Catholic Social Guild and at the Catholic Workers' College in Oxford. Often referred to as 'the apostles of Catholic principles of social justice and international order', they were the very people that Hinsley needed to articulate and organise the movement. Hinsley, as the President, was supported by an executive committee of four chaired by Paul Kelly, a Catholic employer who had been Grand President of the Catenian Association and who was active in the Catholic Workers' College in Oxford. Its secretary was Barbara Ward, the Oxford-trained foreign editor of *The Economist* who worked for the Ministry of Information, and among the 23 committee members were Lady Winefride Elwes (Mgr Val Elwes' mother); Mrs Bower of the Union of Catholic Mothers; Fr Eugene Langdale of the Catholic Social Guild and Young Christian Workers; Fr John Murray SJ of the Catholic Truth Society and *The Month*; Fr Herbert Keldany of the Catholic Social Guild; Christopher Dawson; Fr Gervase Mathew, the Dominican brother of Hinsley's Auxiliary Bishop; Fr Leo O'Shea SJ, Principal of the Catholic Workers' College in Oxford; A.C.F. Beales; John Eppstein of the Catholic Council for International Relations; Dr Letitia Fairfield of the London County Council and the Fabian Society; Richard Hope of the Ministry of Information; and Redmond Roche of the London Newman Society.[7]

The Sword of the Spirit was officially inaugurated by Hinsley at a meeting held at Archbishop's House, Westminster, on 1 August 1940 in the presence of Archbishop Godfrey and a 'number of representative Catholics'. It was, Fr Murray recalled, a warm afternoon and 'a drowsy air filtered through the window curtains form the sultry streets beneath'. It was an occasion when the Cardinal's rhetoric gave sincere expression to the depth of his faith and his genuine concern for the future:

> We are met to start a movement for a more united and more intense effort for a true, just and lasting peace. Our aim is Catholic. We mean by prayer, self-sacrifice and work to do our part in promoting the reconstruction of Europe. We are convinced that a better world can be built only on the foundations of faith, hope and charity. Our purpose is large and deep. We are not inspired by a narrow patriotism, which limits our Christian charity to the red patches on the world's map where waves the British flag. We have no hatred for any nation or race. On the contrary, we will never lose sight of that kinship and love which ought to bind human beings to one another.[8]

The crusade which he launched called for the unity of all Catholics which as one body had been given direction by the Pope's Five Peace Points. 'Unity through Charity' was the battle cry and, echoing St Paul's words to the Ephesians, 'The Sword of the Spirit' was the title of the campaign. The Cross was the campaign standard and the Cross was the pledge of victory. A week later he addressed the citizens of the United States of America: 'I declare that for me neutrality of heart is impossible in this struggle. . . . We are not fighting for the continuance of a disordered system, but to build a new one on just and moral foundations'.[9]

The Tablet welcomed the Sword but suggested that by embracing exiled

Catholics it could develop a European dimension, whilst Christopher Dawson recommended that the Sword should explore the possibilities of co-operation with other non-Catholic Englishmen.[10] In London the Sword gained momentum as British Catholics were joined by their expatriate allies at lunchtime sermons, at Benediction and at weekend study circles. Hinsley's words, meanwhile, were increasingly welcomed by the Ministry of Information which paid for copies of his 'Sword of the Spirit' broadcast to be printed and distributed via Catholic outlets.[11] In October 1940, speaking at a Sword weekend following the fall of Holland, he gave another clear exposition of the Sword's essence:

> Our crusade of the Sword of the Spirit is not in actual fact a new movement. We have not started a fresh political agitation but are defending by spiritual means our age-long Christian position, on the lines laid down by the Holy See, against the Nazi and Fascist doctrines and policy which are essentially anti-Christian or pagan. We have taken the Cross as our standard and symbol. Christians of all times have taken the Cross as the emblem and pledge of victory over the gates of Hell. We cannot see any hope of salvation in the tortured cross and the fasces. When the Son of Man shall appear in the heavens to make the final delimination of opposing camps we have every confidence that we shall be found with the sincere Christians of Holland and of all the world on the side of those who shall be saved by the Blood of the Cross.[12]

In the same month Hinsley and the Sword of the Spirit movement was attacked by the German controlled radio of Holland in the name of Dutch Catholics. The Sword had obviously come to the attention of many both at home and abroad.[13]

Hinsley informed the Hierarchy of 'the Sword's' existence, origins and purpose on 7 August 1940. 'On an impulse from the laity', he wrote, he had started the movement in his diocese 'to secure more united and intense prayer and study and work among Catholics in the cause of the Church and our Country'. The recent collapse of France, the entry of Italy into the war and the isolation of Britain had made it imperative, he felt, for Catholics to forestall British anti-Catholic propaganda and join with others to fight and pray for victory and prepare for the post-war world. He urged the bishops to approve and recommend the Sword in their dioceses and informed them that committee members would visit them in order to explain its purpose and nature. Hinsley reminded the Hierarchy that he and Amigo had delegated power to act on behalf of the Hierarchy 'in matters calling for urgency' and if the bishops gave their consent then the Sword might be considered 'official'. It was a statement that demonstrated his limitations as President of the Hierarchy.[14]

The letter led to unease among the Ordinaries. On 11 August Bishop McNulty of Nottingham wrote to Bishop Marshall of Salford to say that if the Sword was Catholic Action writ large then he would support it but if it was condemnation of governments not yet condemned by the Pope then the episcopal bench should oppose it. As for Hinsley's anxiety over anti-Catholic propaganda, he wrote: 'I think his Eminence is inclined to exaggerate the possible charge of disloyalty brought against the Catholics in this country because of the defection of France and Italy'. He considered it a pity that 'the bishops did not meet to discuss the matter with the Cardinal' and was against giving Hinsley *carte blanche* to speak for the Hierarchy.[15] A few days later Bishop Marshall wrote to Hinsley to say that although he was largely in favour of the Sword he was not happy about the methods which were to be adopted in order to achieve its aims. There was a danger with the laity, he felt, 'that the methods proposed may easily pass from the Christian ideal to political propaganda'. He was convinced that the Hierarchy should consider the aims and methods of the movement before the Ordinaries made a commitment.[16]

Marshall's misgivings were shared by other bishops. When Lady Elwes reported that her visit to Bishop McCormack of Hexham and Newcastle had been less than fruitful, her son wrote to McCormack on behalf of Hinsley to say that although each bishop was free to adopt or reject the Sword, the Cardinal was 'much disappointed by the lack of co-operation with his national endeavours in certain parts of the country'. He continued that the Cardinal 'feels acutely that his position of Ordinary of the Westminster Diocese, which is his essential function, makes his position of *Praeses Perpetuus* as difficult as it is too often disagreeable'[17]

McCormack explained to Elwes that whilst welcoming the Sword in principle, he was distressed that his clergy and diocesan bodies were receiving material from the Sword's offices before he, as Ordinary, had been given the opportunity to discuss its purpose and nature with a committee member or sanction its work in his diocese. He felt that though the Sword's aims were sound from a national and patriotic point of view, he considered that 'the procedure of the committee all appears very strange' and as it was run by Catholic citizens without the Hierarchy's consent he would not agree to supervise it in his diocese 'as an officially approved movement of the Catholic Church'. Yet he did not wish to be disloyal to the Cardinal or give rise to a public disagreement with him.[18]

Hinsley's reply to McCormack was blunt and full of pent-up frustration. He had made it clear that the consent of each Ordinary was required before the Sword's officers got down to work and he apologised for the unintentional lack of respect for McCormack's episcopal authority. But he felt that circumstances were so dire that this protocol could have been overlooked and so too could the lack of information coming directly from the Sword's offices. He had written to the Hierarchy, over 25,000 copies of his 'the Sword of the Spirit' broadcast had been distributed across the country, and he did not know what else could be done to publicise it. As for McCormack telling Lady Elwes that he was waiting for details of the movement to come from 'ecclesiastical sources', presumably Hinsley, he wrote:

> I am utterly tired of the expectations of my position as *Praeses Perpetuus* and have thought of throwing the impossible post up completely. The truth is I receive and have received too little sincere help from my Brethren – particularly of the North. Yet I have tried my best. If only we could be frank and friendly. I seek only the good of the Church. Regrettably, I see North and South still far from genuine harmony.

As a postscript he added that the bishops could discuss the Sword at their next meeting 'without my presence'.[19] McCormack was apologetic. He assured Hinsley of his loyalty but nevertheless expressed his doubts about the status of the Sword as an official Catholic movement. Hinsley simply thanked McCormack for his frankness and said that he wished to avoid any misunderstanding.[20]

Archbishop Williams of Birmingham was convinced of the need to combat Nazism and 'world revolution' and considered the Sword to be 'magnificent and full of possibilities', but he suggested that its aims needed clearer definition. He was also unimpressed by the number of women on the Sword's committee and complained of its reluctance to enlist those such as Douglas Jerrold, the author and publisher, who had spoken out strongly for Franco and attempted to explain the Catholic cause in Spain. Yet Hinsley had said that there were to be no extremists in the Sword's organisation and he considered Jerrold to be in that category.[21]

In an important point of departure Hinsley went beyond the Catholic

communion when, in late August 1940, he urged all Christians to
'...unite in formulating and working for the definite Christian
principles underlying the social and international order for which we are
fighting'.[22] Henceforth, the Sword's call for a Christian basis for peace
and the future gained the interest and support of other Christian leaders
and the movement was given a further stimulus by the publication of
an historic joint letter to *The Times* on 21 December 1940 by Hinsley,
Archbishop Cosmo Lang of Canterbury, Archbishop William Temple of
York and W.H. Armstrong, Moderator of the Free Churches. This letter,
most unusual in the context of contemporary inter-religious relations,
advocated that any future peace settlement should include Pope Pius XII's
Five Peace Points and reference to the Five Economic Standards which
had been the product of an Anglican 'Life and Work' conference held
at Oxford in 1937. The letter was unprecedented and seriously alarmed
some Catholics while encouraging others. According to Geoffrey Fisher,
Anglican Bishop of London, the letter 'greatly promoted a fermentation
among Christian people' and led to much active thought and discussion
about the relevance of Christianity to contemporary world problems.[23]
The letter was followed by another in the next week when Hinsley, Lang
and Armstrong appealed for assistance to evacuees and refugees.[24] And
in February 1941 Hinsley put his name to an appeal for People's Service
Patrols signed by the Bishop of Bradford and others.[25] Having signed such
significant documents, Hinsley's support for an ecumenical approach to
peace and a new social order moved on to a different plane.

   This expression of unity increased the impulse of non-Catholics to
join the Sword. In the van was the energetic Bishop George Bell of
Chichester, the most notable Anglican ecumenist of the time. Bell was an
experienced mediator with the Catholic Church and a prolific writer on
the role of Christians in international affairs. He had little difficulty in
persuading like-minded Anglicans of the Sword's ecumenical potential
and they flocked to the movement.[26] It was a development that alarmed
Hinsley, Catholic bishops and the Anglican leadership. By the end of
1940 there were a thousand non-Catholic 'associates' in the Sword
and whilst the Anglican leadership feared that Catholics might use
Anglican involvement in the Sword for propaganda purposes, Hinsley
and the Sword's officers became anxious lest an Anglican takeover of the
movement should occur and embarrass the Cardinal.[27]

   Yet whatever reservations there may have been among Christian leaders, support for 'the Sword' grew spontaneously and throughout the Spring of 1941 it moved almost inexorably towards greater co-operation between Catholics and other Christian communions in the sphere of social and political life. In February Archbishop Lang wrote to Hinsley that he had read about the Sword with interest and believed that it embodied

> a desire to co-operate in social and internal matter with members of other Communions, and your Eminence has shown your own desire in this direction by signing that letter to *The Times* embodying the Pope's Points of Peace. . .

He concluded:

> I have been requested to ask you whether you would wish the 'Sword of the Spirit' to co-operate in such matters with any similar movements within other Christian Communions. If so, with whom, on behalf of the 'Sword of the Spirit', ought these representatives of such other Communions to communicate?[28]

It could hardly be described as an enthusiastic commitment to ecumenical dialogue but Lang's remarkable letter was a significant recognition that there were forces beyond both the Cardinal and the Archbishop that were now pushing the Sword along with vigour and it continued to attract many non-Catholics inspired by its principles. Richard Hope tried to arrange for meetings of Sword members and associates in churches but Hinsley rejected the idea. He was not averse, though, to Catholics and non-Catholics meeting in civic venues and the most memorable of these occurred on 10 and 11 May 1941, in between German air raids, when two packed public meetings of the Sword were convened at the Stoll Theatre, Kingsway, in London where Hinsley and Archbishop Lang presided. At the first meeting Hinsley and Bishop Bell delivered major speeches on 'A Christian International Order' while Archbishop Lang addressed the second meeting on the theme of 'A Christian Order for Britain'. Yet if the sharing of a platform by major Christian leaders was unusual, the Cardinal's recitation of the Lord's Prayer with non-Catholics at The Stoll was even more striking.[29] *The Church Times* reported that the meetings were a remarkable demonstration of Christian unity where leading Anglicans and Nonconformists shared a platform with Jesuits 'and a cardinal in all the glory of his crimson'.[30] Hinsley, obviously carried away by the euphoria of the meetings, said:

> Our unity must not be in sentiment and in words only . . . it must be carried forward into practical measures. Let us have a regular system of consultation and collaboration such as his Lordship the Bishop of Chichester has suggested, to agree on a plan of action which shall win the peace when the din of battle is ended.

His appeal was met with a burst of applause. As he rose to leave Bell asked the Cardinal if they might say the 'Our Father'. Hinsley turned to the audience and intoned the Lord's Prayer. It was a defining moment in the history of Anglican and Catholic relations. It was also a moment, Hinsley told Bishop Parker, that he later regretted.[31]

The Stoll meetings were not the first contact between Lang and Hinsley. Lang had spoken against the Italian invasion of Abyssinia and had corresponded with and met Hinsley at the Athenaeum Club during the days of the Munich crisis. Through Hinsley, Lang entreated Pius XI to intervene with Hitler during the period of appeasement but once war broke out he considered, like his counterpart at Westminster, that Britain had to fight to the end. Most meetings and contacts between the Christian leaders had been behind the scenes but a public expression of common ground had taken place in November 1938 when Hinsley shared the platform at the Albert Hall with Archbishop William Temple of York, the Chief Rabbi and the MP Herbert Morrison to alert the nation to the dangers of fascism.[32]

After Stoll it looked as if a new era of Christian dialogue had come into existence; the sentiments of the meetings were greeted warmly and similar events were held across the country. But there were many obstacles in front of the Sword and a united Christian front. Bishop Bell recalled that developments were too great and moving at too great a speed to escape criticism within the Roman Catholic Church and suspicion outside it.[33] The Hierarchy was quite unprepared for such a radical ecumenical departure and Beales noted that only one Catholic bishop and two auxiliaries attended the Stoll meetings and none were present to welcome the Archbishop of Canterbury. Beales considered that such discourtesy typified the Hierarchy's indifference to other faiths but Hinsley took a more sanguine approach and advised Beales:

> . . .as to the co-operation with non-Catholic bodies. This is a delicate matter. We have been living in partial isolation from national life. We cannot all at once throw off the habit, since we were largely forced by strong opposition to everything Catholic to keep apart and to hide our light under a bushel.

Now we have taken the lead in what promises to be not only a national but even an international movement.[34]

Catholic bishops were not alone in their suspicion of and even hostility to the remarkable events at the Stoll Theatre. The General Secretary of the Protestant World's Evangelical Alliance wrote that:

It is not 'the Sword of the Spirit', it is the sword of hypocrisy and deceit. . . . Cardinal Hinsley and the Roman Catholics in this movement, and in other clever moves at the present time, are out for two ends: (a) kudos for the Pope, and (b) the shelving of the question of religious freedom.

Hinsley and 'the Sword's' leaders were mistaken, he continued, if they considered the Pope to be the only author of Peace Points and the Alliance subsequently called on the British government to accept President Roosevelt's demand that liberty of conscience and worship should be essential to any peace settlement. According to the Alliance, the situation in Spain, where there was an alleged attempt to make Catholicism the only permissible religion, was an obvious example of a Catholic strategy to usurp control and restrict religious freedom.[35]

Hard-line Protestants were not the only critics and doubters that Hinsley had to contend with for his brother bishops were still uncertain of 'the Sword'. In a letter to Bishop Marshall in March 1941 Hinsley explained that he had called for immediate action in 1940 to offset the likely anti-Catholic propaganda which he feared would be caused by Italy's entry in to the war. This action gave rise to the Sword but he emphasised that the movement be confined to his own diocese unless other Ordinaries approved of its activities and admitted that the Sword had been formed in haste.[36] He eventually gave an official account of the origin, purpose and progress of the Sword of the Spirit movement to the Hierarchy in April 1941. The bishops' response was cautious although they accepted the Sword's draft constitution, with certain amendments, and promised to give it their full support as far as possible.[37] Episcopal support for the Sword, however, was at best lukewarm and at worst hostile. In spite of this, the Sword's Catholic officers and their Anglican associates carried on with their attempts to form a more lasting and practical religious alliance but Hinsley and Bell recognised that there were limits to collaboration. In June 1941, Archbishop Godfrey had asserted that there could be no question of reducing the teaching of Christ to a few fundamental propositions and it seemed essential to him that the use of the term 'common ground' by the Holy Father should be well understood as having no connection with any surrender of dogmatic principle or with the error of fundamentalism. It was a warning to Hinsley that the Sword was leading people down a dangerous path. From this point on, ecumenical dialogue slowed down considerably.[38]

The balanced approach which Hinsley had wished to impose on the executive of the Sword was compromised when Letitia Fairfield attacked those Catholics who favoured Pétain and objected to the distribution of leaflets on the Sword to General Charles de Gaulle's exiled French army on the grounds that they would not understand its principles. Such outbursts did little to help Hinsley bring together disparate views within the Catholic community and divided the Sword's committee. Dr Fairfield was unmoved by Hinsley's chagrin and Barbara Ward wrote to him to say that one of the major difficulties that the Sword faced was the lack of charity on both sides.[39] Beales, who was beginning to play an increasingly central role in the administration of the Sword, informed Mgr Elwes, and therefore Hinsley, that the infrastructure of the Sword was inadequate to service its growing membership and increasing activities and address the differences of opinions that were now emerging with its leadership. The active involvement of Catholic exiles and non-Catholic associates, each with their own views, alongside the friction generated by differences among the executive committee presented a combustible situation. Beales wished for a radical restructuring of the whole committee structure and Hinsley agreed.[40] This led in June 1941 to a new Executive Committee and a Council comprised of eight nominated by the Cardinal, eight selected by the Sword's membership, and eight representing Catholic societies nominated by the Cardinal. Hinsley's nominations included Bishop Bell, the Acting Moderator of the Free Church Federal Council, Bishop Mathew, Viscount Fitzalan and Lord Rankeillour. Ward and Beales became joint secretaries.[41]

Bishop Bell was also experiencing difficulties. Lang was interested but not enthusiastic about the Sword whilst extreme Protestant groups were violently opposed to it. Accordingly, he produced The Chichester Memorandum which proposed the Sword should be organised into Catholic and Anglican divisions.[42] Lang wrote to Hinsley and suggested that a 'consultative group' rather than a 'Consultative Council' be convened to receive opinion and discern a way forward.[43] In July 1941 with Hinsley's consent, plans were laid down for a Joint Council For Action to discuss an ecumenical approach to social issues but there were to be certain restrictions. There was to be to no shared worship or prayer and the Sword's leadership and ethos were to remain distinctively Catholic. But as the number of 'associates' within the movement continued to increase, a decision had to be made about their role and status. There were three alternatives for Hinsley and the Sword's leadership: non-Catholics could be fully integrated into the Sword's management and administration; they could be encouraged to form a non-Catholic Sword with its own leadership under an overarching joint committee structure; or they could institute a similar but distinct movement from the Sword. Hinsley was forced into a decision and on 9 August 1941, at the first Annual General Meeting of the Sword, he promulgated an amended constitution, placed the Sword firmly under episcopal control, and announced with some discomfort that non-Catholics may continue as 'associate' members but without voting rights. The announcement may have pleased the Hierarchy but it did not appeal to many in the Sword and disappointed non-Catholics. Yet in the context of contemporary Catholic theology and Canon Law, Hinsley's decision was almost inevitable. It was envisaged that in future the Sword would run parallel to an informal Anglican body which had been established in 1937 to mount 'Religion and Life' weeks and from which the Sword's officers had drawn inspiration. It was subsequently agreed that there would be separate campaigns but with a joint standing committee, shared literature and occasional meetings of both movements. Significantly, joint acts of worship or prayer were to cease.[44] *The Church Times* complained bitterly that a great ecumenical opportunity had been lost:

> ...'the Sword of the Spirit' movement might have become a national Excalibur. Instead, those who have forged it and are wielding it have decided that it shall have no more significance or striking power than any other weapon of exclusively Roman Catholic piety and propaganda.[45]

In October Hinsley met with Bishop Bell at Hare Street where the Cardinal spoke of Christian unity and of 'co-operation in applying traditions received from Christianity'. Hinsley, wrote Bell, had a strong belief in the value of personal relationships and in the coming together, as friends, of like-minded men and women who, whatever their differences, were animated by the same Spirit. For Bell the evening was 'a wonderful experience of charity, devotion and wisdom' and he left the next day 'richer spiritually as well as richer in wisdom'. Both men were full of conviction in the cause but were realistic enough to know that the inclusion of religious activities in the scheme of cooperation was too much for some Catholics to bear. They decided, therefore, that in the face of continuous objections and misunderstanding of the Sword among all Christian denominations, and particularly on issues surrounding joint worship, it was better if the Sword became exclusively Catholic and the 'Religion and Life' movement was formally constituted for the Anglicans and the Commission of the Churches. Hinsley told Bell that the Sword had been more popular than anyone had anticipated but there was no desire to capture converts.[46] Both men admitted that there was no prospect of unified action and in January 1942 an agreement was reached that separate movements would be the way forward. Henceforth there was low level co-operation 'in order to secure the effective influence of Christian teaching and witness in the handling of social, economic and civic problems, now and in the critical post-war period'. In 1942 there were 12 joint weeks of debate and study; in 1943 there were 24.[47]

Bishop David Mathew, who was intimately connected with the Sword but not entirely convinced by it, surmised correctly that while ecumenical collaboration may have been welcomed by some, the Sword was unable to prosper outside Westminster without the approval of the bishops and clergy and this was generally the case. Archbishop Michael McGrath of Cardiff said that the Sword would be 'a catastrophe for Wales', considered prayer with non-Catholics to be 'objectionable', and could not see it in his way 'to give any permission for any attempt to establish it in my diocese'. Bishop Thomas Shine of Middlesbrough felt that the Sword would undermine Catholic Action. Bishops Hannon of Menevia, Doubleday of Brentwood, Barrett of Plymouth and Lee of Clifton opposed it but not all bishops were as adamant. Bishop Mathew reported that Bishops McNulty of Nottingham and King of Portsmouth were pro-Sword but without any firm conviction.[48] In August 1940 Bishop Thomas Flynn of Lancaster wrote to Archbishop Williams of Birmingham to say that although he generally approved of the Sword he believed that nothing would come of it unless a man of Williams's stature and ability took charge of it.[49]

A year later Flynn wrote to Williams to say that while he believed that progress could only be made through co-operation, he feared that giving Anglicans full membership of the Sword might lead to loss of Catholic control. He reported that many people regretted the prayers said at the Stoll meetings but he was for letting the laity have their head over membership of the Sword 'as long as we keep a watchful eye on them'.[50] In September 1941 Downey told Flynn that he wanted nothing to do with the Sword but his misgivings were not an automatic rejection of anything that came from Westminster. He genuinely felt, like many others, that the Sword's aims were too vague and would interfere with his developing scheme of Catholic Action. Downey allowed the Catholic Society of Liverpool University to be involved in the Sword but only under the direction of the Catholic Action Board and he facilitated the distribution of 130,000 copies of the Cardinal's letter about the Sword within his diocese. He admitted that he did not fully comprehend what the Sword was supposed to do.[51] By 1942 he complained to Bishop Marshall that he 'was getting more and more alarmed' with the Sword's activities, especially co-operation with non-Catholics. He argued that the Sword's promoters were misinterpreting papal calls for co-operation with other Christians. Pius XII, he wrote, asked for 'concurrence of effort' rather than 'joint organisation'.[52]

Archbishop Amigo welcomed the reception given to the Sword by non-Catholics but was concerned that there was 'always the fear and danger that we should appear to recognise any other than the one True Church'. He advised Hinsley to keep the Sword under his personal guidance and allow non-Catholics to make whatever use of it they could but he pleaded with the Cardinal to avoid joint meetings and 'prayer in common'. He refused to allow Barbara Ward to circulate a letter about the Sword to his clergy and replied to Bishop Bell's request for Catholic co-operation in a Week of Christian Witness to be held in Brighton in October 1942, that despite his sympathy with the issues to be discussed, it was better for 'us to act separately'.[53]

Bishop Poskitt of Leeds wrote that if the Sword was to be interdenominational 'then our people will be scandalised and the Bishops, especially in the north, will no longer be able to support it'.[54] Yet both Poskitt and Catholics in his diocese supported the Sword. From September 1940 a small group of Christians in Sheffield, including Catholics, had been meeting to discuss the evils of modern society. Following the Stoll meeting they met weekly and eventually established the Association of Christian Communities in Sheffield with its own constitution. Poskitt was an *ex officio* member. At one point there were 36 interdenominational working groups which invited eminent churchmen and social commentators to address them. The Association ran alongside and with the agreement of the Sheffield Council for Catholic Action. Poskitt felt that the good will and cooperation arising out of the Association was of potential benefit and not a threat for the 'strength as exists springs from the clear recognition of doctrinal differences which cannot be compromised'.[55]

The Sword achieved limited success outside Westminster because the bishops were cautious in their response. Informed by Pius XI's encyclical of 1928 on 'True Religious Unity' (*Mortalium Animos*) which condemned anything remotely resembling a confederation of Christians, they were unlikely to transgress Church teaching. Nor was Hinsley but his leadership of the Sword was directed not towards a unification of Christians on dogmatic principles but more towards an improvement of social conditions based on the collaboration of all people of goodwill. In this he was adhering to Pius XI's later encyclicals *Caritate Christi* (1932) and *Divini Redemptoris* (1937) which invoked prayer and collaboration in an attempt to ward of the dangers of atheistic communism and fascism. The Pope called for energetic steps to prevent the enemies of religion achieving dominance and in 1940 Hinsley and other Christian leaders recognised that the time was ripe for a united proclamation of intent. Just as civic solidarity had been fostered by the exigencies of war, so too were religious leaders brought together by the need for common prayer and concerted action.

Bishop Bell was struck by the independence that each Catholic Ordinary possessed. It was the custom for each bishop to decide ecclesiastical policy in his own diocese and Heenan remarked that a spiritual renewal led by a national figure in the metropolis did not necessarily provide a pattern for the provinces to imitate. Although ready to applaud Hinsley's efforts in Westminster, his episcopal brethren felt that they knew what would suit their own particular circumstances. Heenan denied, however, that Hinsley's enthusiastic sponsorship of the Sword caused dissension among the Ordinaries. The Sword could not be imposed on dioceses and therefore bishops were at liberty to accept or reject it as they wished.[56] A minority of bishops attempted to introduce the Sword into their dioceses but with little tangible reward. Archbishop Williams and Bishop Leo Parker of Northampton allowed the Sword to function in their dioceses and despite his initial misgivings so did Bishop Poskitt.[57]

The Sword, however, prospered in the armed forces where young men and women, under great stress and away from home, looked to their faith. Under the guidance of Mgr Henry Beauchamp, it developed particularly in the R.A.F. where membership rose to 20,000. Through Moral Leadership Courses, lectures, and newsletters such as *The Sword* and *Catholic World,* service personnel were prepared for their return to civilian life as standard bearers of Catholic Action. There were also branches in the Royal Navy and in the army, especially in Egypt, Transjordan, Syria and Libya. To young men involved in the dangerous and deadly conduct of war, the Sword's idealism seemed to promise a brighter future. As Fr Murray wrote: 'their minds were enlightened and their outlook made firm'.[58] For similar reasons it attracted exiled Europeans and other allies living in London. Polish, French and Belgian communities adopted the movement and interest was shown in the United States, Canada, Mauritius and Singapore.[59]

In the dioceses the efforts of those who participated in the Sword usually became bogged down in endless meetings where well-meaning volunteers tried to understand social theories or decide how old diocesan structures related to the new. The range of clerical views also determined the Sword's progress. Some priests supported it whilst others, even in Westminster, had little enthusiasm for it. Mgr Barton Brown of Hanwell considered that Hinsley did not have the slightest idea of what he was dealing with. 'The desire to bring all religions together', he wrote, 'was a very clever piece of government propaganda and the Cardinal fell into the trap'. When Brown tried to point this out Hinsley snubbed him. To some, the Sword appeared to be Catholic Action all over again. Indeed, Fr Murray had actually defined the Sword as 'a lay society for Catholic Action'.[60] To many the Church was the last refuge of traditional morality and its teachings offered the solution to world and personal problems but in a country where there was no history of Catholic Action, the fervour inspired by the Sword did not easily take root. Against such odds, Hinsley had little chance of operating as a national religious leader let alone as the leader of an ecumenical movement. Nor could the Sword's intellectual elite find a secure place in the wider environs of Catholic life. They, the Cardinal and the Sword failed to triumph over the forces of hostility, tradition, uncertainty and misunderstanding.

For Archbishop Temple, a former Chairman of the World Council of Churches who succeeded Archbishop Lang at Canterbury in 1942, the attempt to collaborate with Catholics through the Sword merely confirmed his view that although inter-religious dialogue was to be encouraged it should always be on the understanding that Catholics adopted a different world view and that the theology and authoritarian structure of the Catholic Church did not easily facilitate ecumenical developments. This, however, did not prevent his active collaboration and there developed a notable but short-lived sympathy between Temple and Hinsley.[61]

At ground level, discussions and meetings seemed to proliferate, an inevitable consequence of two very different and hitherto antipathetic religious traditions coming together in a pioneering development. Some called for the Sword's organisers to be less nebulous in their aspirations. Many knew what the Sword was against but few appeared to know what it was actually supposed to do. The Ministry of Information, however, conveniently overlooked this important detail, saw the Sword as excellent propaganda and was prepared to finance its publications and those on related issues which could be distributed through Catholic channels.[62]

Hinsley may have opened a window on Christian collaboration and the Sword was a striking and shining example of Christian witness in the dark days of World War II but to the contemporary Hierarchy religious incompatibilities were so strong that joint action was bound to either disappoint Protestants or compromise Catholics. It was not that the bishops lacked charity towards the Sword, its principles, or non-Catholics but they were certainly not prepared to concede matters of doctrine or ecclesiastical authority. Nor was Hinsley but not for the first time his actions demonstrated that he was more than usually out-of-touch with the Hierarchy. As with Catholic Action, Hinsley's best endeavours regarding the Sword were weakened by his impulsiveness and his inability to communicate his ideas effectively, sufficiently weigh up the context in which he was working, and efficiently marshal the forces necessary for a successful outcome. He was also getting older and was increasingly affected by heart trouble. Although his mental capabilities were as acute as ever, his physical dynamism was draining away.

Animated by Christian principles, papal encyclicals and a genuine desire for a better world, the Sword's unique achievements were probably not as substantial as Hinsley would have wished or prayed for but he had broken down religious barriers, brought Catholicism directly into the mainstream of public and religious life, and considerably enhanced his reputation as a churchman of sincerity and understanding. The eminent theologians Canons George Smith and Edward Mahoney were asked by Hinsley and Downey to consider and report on the canonical status of ecumenical relations. They had to walk a very fine line and in their report of September 1941 they allowed for ecumenical collaboration and 'silent prayer' but advised against radical departures. After carefully studying papal pronouncements between 1895 and 1942 they observed that the directions of the Holy See had become progressively liberal, passing from mere tolerance to positive encouragement of association with non-Catholics without compromising belief. They concluded: 'The movement courageously initiated by His Eminence the Cardinal is, we believe, the first attempt to put the desires of the Holy See into practice'.[63]

For Hinsley the union of Christians through the Sword was a means of improving the social and international order rather than a forum to discuss divisive pastoral or theological issues. There was never any fear that he would allow the weakening of faith. As Heenan wrote, Hinsley never uttered anything that was incompatible with his faith 'but often he spoke not as a Bishop teaching his flock but as a Catholic Englishman testifying to his sense of spiritual communion with Englishmen outside the Fold'.[64] In other words, his theological orthodoxy never prevented the manifestation of his humanity. In 1942 he told the visiting American churchman C. P. Morehouse that

> While there was no possibility of an approach on doctrinal grounds, the Roman Catholic Church can and does welcome the co-operation of all men of goodwill in the application of fundamental Christian principles to the building of a better society. It is no longer this or that particular doctrine that is under attack; it is a question of secular and atheistic totalitarianism versus Christianity itself. In that struggle all Christians must be united.[65]

According to Moloney, the Sword was 'the most personal and characteristic expression of Arthur Hinsley's public life' but he added that it was 'splendidly ephemeral'.[66] When Hinsley died the Sword lost much of its impetus but it survived under a different guise.

'Awake or be Crushed'

From the outbreak of war until his death, Hinsley never flagged in his encouragement of others to pray, do their duty and fight for victory. In his crusade against the enemy his approach was uncompromising and his faith and loyalty were touchstones against which people could measure their own contributions to the cause. While the principle of 'turning the other cheek' may be applied in some circumstances, Hinsley told his flock in September 1939 that they now had no alternative: they could not stand idly by and allow Poland and other countries to be 'enslaved or ruthlessly done to death'. He reminded his diocese that everyone had a duty to give unstinted service to the nation and its rulers. It was a message that he was to emphasise throughout the next four years but as the war progressed political alignments and military circumstances were to change dramatically.[67] The fall of France and the British army's retreat from the beaches of Dunkirk in May 1940 were disasters which brought the reality of German might to Britain's shores and in a letter to *The Times* Hinsley exhorted the nation to 'Awake! or be crushed by the unleashed forces of evil'.[68]

A significant change in British politics occurred in May 1940 when Neville Chamberlain was replaced as Prime Minister by Winston Churchill. Chamberlain had been anxious to avert war with Germany but the agreement he reached with Hitler at Munich in 1938 and the consequent dismemberment of Czechoslovakia led to a vociferous condemnation of his policy of appeasement. To Hinsley, however, Chamberlain had worked for peace and he made no attempt to question the Prime Minister's political sagacity and his unwillingness to publicly discredit Hitler's amoral approach to international law. The Cardinal and other bishops admired Chamberlain's moral courage for attempting to spare mankind from the horrors of war and saw him as a man of honour and integrity. In October 1938, on his return from Munich, they had telegrammed him their congratulations on the success of his efforts in the cause of peace and assured him of their support and prayers.[69] That Hitler attacked Poland in September 1939, Hinsley argued, could not be blamed on Chamberlain. Shortly after the declaration of war Hinsley sent Chamberlain a copy of Pope Pius XII's encyclical *Summi Pontificatus (On the Unity of Human Society)* which condemned the religious policies of both Germany and the USSR and called for peace. The Prime Minster replied that it was his 'earnest hope that when we have put an end to terror and aggression we shall be able to establish such a peace in Europe'. He also thanked Hinsley for his sympathy and encouragement.[70]

When Chamberlain resigned and gave way to Churchill, Hinsley wrote to Chamberlain that:

> No man could have done more to save the world from this war. Your

efforts to secure peace gave to our cause a moral strength that can never be disregarded. For this all who have regard for Britain's honour must be profoundly grateful.

You saved us from war at a moment when we were unready, and if others had been sincere and faithful to their pledges you would have prevented hostilities in Europe perhaps for generations. You will surely receive the reward of those who are promised the blessings of the peace makers.[71]

It was a letter that inherently recognised that war could probably not have been averted but it was, nonetheless, a sincere and generous acknowledgement to one whose genuine attempts for peace were based on Christian principles. Chamberlain replied:

My Dear Cardinal Hinsley,

I am more than grateful to you for the very kind letter which you wrote to me on the 5th and, I would add, for the encouragement and support which you have given me on so many occasions.

I have greatly valued your good opinion and your approval of what I have endeavoured to do and I thank you very warmly for your good wishes now that my public career is finished.[72]

To those who were suffering from the onslaught of invading powers Hinsley offered support and prayers and his rallying cries were frequent and forceful. The first country to be subjected to the combined military might of Nazism and communism was Poland and in September 1939 Hinsley wrote to Fr Ladislaus Staniszewsky of the Catholic Polish Mission in London:

Poland has been, and is now, the bulwark of Catholic civilization. The indomitable spirit of the Polish people cannot fail to bring final success to a cause which is fundamentally just, since your people are defending their homes and their altars. They have the knowledge of the justice of their resistance to unwarranted violence. Prayerful goodwill and sympathy of the whole world is with you....

The attack on Poland, Hinsley said, had led to a sad and cruel martyrdom and without the resources to resist invasion the 'courage of Poland's people rests on supernatural and unshakeable confidence in Divine providence....'[73]

In November 1939 he broadcast directly to the Polish nation and assured them of support from British and European Catholics with whom they shared a common heritage:

The Catholics of England and France, convinced of the righteousness of your cause, are pledged to devote all their energies to bring nearer the day on which Poland, Catholic Poland, shall again take her place in the comity of nations.

Comparing the fate of Poland with Christ's darkest hour, he said that the 'soul of Poland cannot be slain'. No Catholic, he continued, could be unmoved by Poland's plight and 'men must denounce the mechanised butchery which threatened to finish civilized existence on earth'.[74] In December 1939 Hinsley likened Poland, crushed between Russia and Germany, to Christ being crucified between the two thieves of militant atheism and pagan slavery. 'I consider it my duty', he said, 'to protest aloud against any persecution of the Christians of Poland, any persecutions of the Catholics and orthodox, as I have protested in the past against the persecution of religious bodies in Nazi Germany. . . .'[75] By 1942 when details of German and Russian atrocities against the Polish Jews had become known in London, Hinsley was still pleading on their behalf and keeping their plight in the forefront of men's thoughts. 'Poland', he wrote, 'has witnessed acts of such savage race hatred that it appears fiendishly planned to be turned into a vast cemetery of the Jewish population in Europe'.[76] But he was in no doubt that the world would see 'the resurrection' of Poland. Its faith, he said, was stronger than the machines of barbarism. The day would come for Poland 'when the stone will be rolled away' and peace and freedom will be restored.[77]

Russia's attack on Finland in 1940 provoked Hinsley into a fierce condemnation of the Soviet Union and Finland's Minister in London wrote to the Cardinal to thank him for his words of support:

The people of my country have been deeply moved by your Eminence's thoughtful and generous reference to Finland. I would like to thank you for your bold call to the Church and Christian thought. As deeply religious, cultured and happy people, Finland is struggling for the same ideals of freedom and democracy as Great Britain.

The Cardinal replied:

The wicked injustice committed against Finland and the cruelty of bombing its civilian population must stir the indignation of everyone with any sense of humanity left in him. . . . Finland is fighting against a Godless tyranny for the Christian liberty of Europe and even of the world.[78]

Germany's westward expansion and the fall of France affected Hinsley very badly for he knew that the Nazi enemy was literally at the gate. In June 1940 he called for a Triduum of Intercession for 'heroic' France, 'fighting for her land, her culture and her saints', and prayers of thanksgiving for the successful evacuation of the British Expeditionary Force from the beaches of Dunkirk:

> For the third time in my lifetime the soil of that country is being ravaged and drenched in blood by an enemy without scruple and without pity. The fate of free peoples of the world hangs in the balance between these hordes and the unequal forces of our gallant allies aided by the British. . . . Our prayers have been answered in marvellous ways at Dunkirk. . . .[79]

After the fall of France Pope Pius XII and his Secretary of State Cardinal Luigi Maglione, gave serious consideration to Hitler's 'peace offer' but Hinsley would have none of it and left Archbishop Godfrey to liaise with the British government. 'His Eminence', Godfrey told Foreign Office officials, 'wished them to know that':

> . . .the Chancellor of the Reich's speech, being composed of insults, defiances and threats, is not only no peace offer but it does not contain any mention of guarantees or reparations in favour of invaded countries, according to the Holy Father's Five Peace Points (of December 1939).[80]

Hinsley's concern for France was not unconditional. When Sir John Reith of the Ministry of Information returned from France in early 1940 he asked Hinsley if the diocese could spare some French-speaking priests for service in France. Hinsley's reply was negative. He may have spare priests in his diocese, he told Reith, but there would not be a shortage of French priests if their government did not compel them to undertake military service. French clergy had been lost while serving as combatants in the Great War and that, he argued, was one of the reasons why there were now so few. He advised Reith to get the British government to pressurise its French counterpart to release priests from military duties.[81]

The prolonged siege of the island garrison of Malta enabled Hinsley in 1942 eloquently to combine reference to the sixteenth century Siege of Malta by the Turks with the successful resistance to sustained Italian and German aerial bombardment. His rhetoric was reminiscent of Churchill's:

> On Malta the gaze of the whole world is riveted in wonder. The spirit of its people, intrepid and unconquerable, surpasses all the records of resolute

courage and endurance of past generations. . . . On that island are enshrined undying memories of the past, but among all the tragedies and glories of Malta the story of the unbroken soul of its inhabitants in face of the most concentrated assault ever known in the annals of warfare will never fade while men still value the heroism of faith and loyalty. . . .

Maltese courage, patriotism and devotion, he continued, had won for their land the title of 'the shield of Christendom'. Only lately called to arms, Maltese men rivalled the bravery of the Knights of St John while women and children fought alongside them in the direst peril. 'In Malta today', he said, 'the fortitude of men women and children matches the courage of those heroes of the sixteenth century but under more frightful terrorism. The Cross prevailed then against the Crescent as the Cross will triumph over the Swastika. . . . '[82] C. P. Morehouse recalled that Hinsley had reportedly suffered a mild heart attack before the Mass for Malta but he insisted on carrying on and was anxious that the people of Malta heard his words. Hinsley entertained Morehouse after the Mass and their conversation covered the whole spectrum of international affairs and English religious issues. The Cardinal, wrote Morehouse, was 'a most impressive figure' and concluded that he was 'a great ecclesiastical statesman'. Hinsley also told Morehouse that if the Nazis invaded Britain he would be one of the first people to be shot.[83] In May 1942 the Council of Government of Malta resolved that their thanks be extended to the Cardinal for his inspiring leadership of Catholics throughout the British Empire and 'in particular for the courage and fortitude that his Eminence has helped to instil in the hearts of the Maltese people in their hour of severe trial by his constant remembrance of them in his prayers and in his utterances. . . . '[84] Malta, the Cardinal had said, was protected by 'the shield of Christendom' and its 'undiminished faith shall burn with a stronger flame and be as a beacon that every race and clime may look to for inspiration. . . .'[85]

The Ministry of Information regarded Hinsley's broadcasts to the United States of America as critical in the attempt to bring round American public opinion, and especially that of American Catholics, to the British cause. In September 1939 just after the outbreak of war Hinsley broadcast an address to the USA aimed at facilitating Anglo-American understanding. The isolationist spirit in the USA remained strong and Hinsley was aware of the need for Americans to appreciate not only the dangers of the European situation but also the advantages of the British Empire, traditionally suspect in American eyes. In October 1939 he had written to the editor of the American *The Catholic World* that sooner or later the USA would have to face the 'naked monsters' of Nazism, fascism and communism.[86] In February 1941, he wrote to Archbishop Edward Mooney of Detroit to ask him to publicise Great Britain's plight and asked him to make known the co-operation among Christians through the Sword of the Spirit.[87] In his broadcast of 1943 he was anxious to generate a spirit of collaboration that would help win the war and map out the future world order but his broadcasts appear naive and his glorification of both the Church and the USA seem rather simplistic. He overlooked, for example, racial segregation in the USA and called the Church a 'true democracy'. There were many in the Universal Church who would have taken issue with that statement. He saw the USA as the political equivalent of the Catholic Church – including every race and colour, teaching the value of all, and embracing democracy. The Church, he said, recognised the worth of all citizens while emphasizing their responsibilities to each other. Like the USA, the Church could give the world an object lesson in freedom and practical tolerance. The Founding Fathers of the USA, he told Americans, were men inspired by the fundamental principles of Christianity. They had regard to the laws of nature and to nature's God. Like the British who had worked hard through the Empire to unite men in spirit and truth, the Americans had also given men the right to the pursuit of happiness. Both nations, he said, had the opportunity to combine their different approaches to the implementation of similar social and political principles for the good of all:

After standing shoulder to shoulder in these dark days of war, we must face with one heart and soul the no less formidable task of building a new order which shall assure an era of freedom through a peace founded on universal justice. And by justice I mean no steel-cold calculating opportunism but the law of love which sees in our fellow-men images of God and souls precious in His sight, because redeemed by the sacrifice of Her Son. We are all the children of one Father. . . .

Away with the hatred and suspicions which divide us. Away with the unjust conditions of social life which destroy the security of the great family of mankind. America and the British Commonwealth of Nations have the opportunity of united action to realise in the world the laws of Christian morality which form the basis of our traditions, of our institutions, of our social well-being.[88]

Similar sentiments had been expressed by the Catholic writer and lecturer Christopher Hollis in June 1940. Hollis who had just returned from the USA alerted Americans especially to the threat posed by Hitler. Like Hinslcy, he argued that if the Americans did enter the war they would not be fighting to save Europe and the British Empire but to prevent the USA being threatened by Nazi imperialism. The German attack on Russia in 1941 and the subsequent Anglo-Soviet military alliance, however, caused unease in the United States for the European champion of democracy was now allied with a tyrannical dictatorship.

The Enemy

Hinsley reserved his fiercest comments for Britain's enemies and a recurring theme was that their political leaders had eliminated God from the conduct of human affairs. In June 1940, in a long address at Wimbledon Town Hall, he said that Hitler 'had swallowed his pride of race' to secure a partner in the assault on western democracy and 'the destruction of lower breeds'. 'Pride of race was the root of the Nazi gospel and', he wrote, 'there is no God but the German soul; no immortality but in pure Nordic blood: the new religion is the German race'. Fanatical racialism had become the driving force of the state and the state had become the servant of the race. The pseudo-scientific theories of Alfred Rosenberg, 'the appointed prophet' of Nazism, came in especially for Hinsley's wrath for attempting to replace true Christianity with 'a positive Christianity, the supreme test of which is Nordic race and blood must prevail'. In their twisted theories the Nazis were rejecting Christ and 'the teaching of the Fire Spirit will replace the crucifixion'. The victims of the National Honour, he said, were those whose land would be occupied for *lebensraum*, or living space, for the German race. But, he argued, the liberty to live was not a German prerogative: the 'right to live must be allowed to other nations, even to the smaller and weaker nations. The liberty of one nation . . . does not involve the slavery of a neighbouring nation. . . .' Instead of 'the deified idol of party, instead of the omnipotent secular State set by human caprice', man could only find peace, he said, in the centre of his being – the true living God who made him'. He urged men to follow the spiritual leadership demonstrated by Pope Pius XII working with President Franklin D. Roosevelt of the United States in an attempt to 'defeat the law of destruction forced upon us by wielders of brute force' and rediscover 'that faith without which the welfare of nations and the peace of the world cannot be rebuilt'.

Hinsley was under no illusions about the country's enemies. Nazism and Bolshevism were laws unto themselves. Both repudiated God and replaced him with idols of their own creation: for Moscow it was the material prosperity of one class; for Berlin it was the supremacy of race. Britain and her allies, he concluded, were 'resisting paganism united in unholy friendship with avowed atheism for the enslaving of those who are resolved to live and die rather than forsake Christ our King, and surrender the liberty of the sons of God'.[89]

Religion suffered the same fate in the Union of Soviet Socialist Republics (USSR). There had already been a stark warning in the Spanish Civil War that it was the communist intention to liquidate God, persecute believers and deify the state. To many Catholics the Soviets and their leader Joseph Stalin were a far bigger threat than the Nazis. The Labour MP Alfred Denville, for example, was of the opinion that the only difference for Catholics between Nazi paganism and Soviet communism was that they were not fighting the one which was the worst. In May 1940 *The Catholic Herald* echoed these sentiments:

> What sort of help can we expect from Stalin? Far better to go down with our honour intact than clutch at a filthy straw. . . . Would it not be infinitely more worthy of our cause to call Stalin's bluff, and, with the help of Turkey, to create a gigantic diversion which might well bring the Bolshevik superstructure tumbling down and release in Russia the forces that would prove to be our friends indeed? A mad plan? But consider where sanity has brought us.[90]

Hinsley, who had earlier expressed serious concerns about an Anglo-Soviet pact, now felt able to vent his spleen in public and without reservation. The tyrannical Soviet Union, he wrote, was imposed by violence, massacres, starvation, liquidation and unspeakable cruelties on one-sixth of the world 'and yet was called a *democracy*'. He derided Russian claims that it was 'a *liberator*' and not 'an *aggressor*' when it marched into the Caucasus, Outer Mongolia, Finland, Poland and the Baltic States. How, he asked, could the Russians be 'champions of *freedom*' when they bombed and machine-gunned ordinary working people? The Soviet Union, he argued, was like Germany, a Humpty Dumpty character living in a dangerous world of make-believe. Its political slogan of the dictatorship of the proletariat was not liberty for all but control of everyone and everything by an unscrupulous few. Liberty as perceived by the Soviet communists, he concluded, was not the kind of liberty 'which is our goal'.[91]

Germany's attack on Russia in June 1941 altered the political and military balance of power in the European war and seriously compromised Hinsley. While the opportunistic Churchill may have hailed the opening of another front against the Germans, Hinsley and others who had protested against close ties with the Soviets now had little alternative but to see them as 'co-belligerents'. It was an unwelcome and uncomfortable situation for the Cardinal who henceforth confined his utterances not to public support of the Soviet Union but to prayers for its people with reference to their Christian past now denied by Communist rule:

> For Russia we plead daily in our prayers after Mass. Let us redouble our prayers now, that the age-old devotion of the Russian people to the Mother of God, alive still – even though dormant – in so many of their hearts, may earn for them her special protection in these days and restore them soon to union with her Divine Son.[92]

For Hinsley this was the way around a distinctly uncomfortable position. He was in little doubt about Russia and wrote that 'all the world knows that Russia's past record is no less black than that of her German aggressors'. Prayerful and military support may be given to the Russian people, he said, but that 'cannot be transferred to support the communist system'.[93]

Sections of the independent Catholic press refused to toe the official line and continued to attack the USSR. The Soviet Ambassador in London, who had spoken of the new religious freedom and tolerance in the Soviet Union, came in for particular criticism. The newspapers were not fooled and they had a strong case: they had reported the extermination of religion in the USSR, Red atrocities in Spain, and the Soviet invasion of Poland, Finland and the Baltic States. They now witnessed their government in a mutual alliance with a communist regime and spoke out against it. Soviet diplomats requested the Ministry of Information to impose restraining orders on Catholic newspapers but the government was in a difficult position for even in the days of censorship it could not control opinion. The government was anxious to appease the Soviets and concerned that the English Catholic press would influence American public opinion against the Soviets, but it was averse to imposing greater restrictions on free speech and thus be tarred with the same brush as the Nazis and communists. The Foreign Office's News

Department reported that Hinsley was disturbed by the unhelpful stance taken by *The Catholic Herald*, *The Universe* and *The Catholic Times* but he could no more than advise them against being too aggressive.[94]

Hinsley had called the editors of the three main Catholic papers together at the beginning of the war in an attempt to get them not only to fall in with government propaganda but to present the Church's line on the international situation. It was not easy for him. The Hierarchy could only comment on matters of faith and morals. They could not control editorial freedom. Catholic editors had expressed their independence during the abdication crisis and during the Spanish Civil War and if the Ministry of Information considered that the views of Catholic newspapers were suspect or defeatist then there was little Hinsley and the bishops could really do other than dissociate themselves from editorial opinion.[95]

Nazi propaganda craftily exploited the anti-religious nature of the USSR as a pretext for its invasion. The spurious claim that the German invasion of Russia was a Christian crusade convinced some but not Hinsley and on 28 June he issued a statement condemning both Nazism and communism. He wrote that:

> ...no-one who knows how anti-Christian the ideas and the practices of the Nazis are will for one moment be deceived by Hitler's latest pose as the champion of European civilization, or think that it has become in any way less vital to resist his attempt to enslave the continent.[96]

Germany's attack on the bulwark of Bolshevism was welcomed in Italy, Spain and Latin America. While Italy made no secret of its support for Germany, Spain's position was more delicate and the Nazi invasion of Russia could easily have led to Spain abandoning her neutrality and entering the Axis coalition against the country that had supported the Republicans in the civil war. The British government, desperately anxious to keep Spain out of the war, attempted to enlist Hinsley's support but met his resistance. The Cardinal could not and did not condone the USSR's religious policy and would not be prevented from saying so in public. Nor would he attempt to portray the USSR as a nation fighting alongside those he considered to be Christian warriors fighting for the cause of Christian Europe. Despite a combined approach by Alec Randall of the Foreign Office, Richard Hope of the Ministry of Information and Douglas Woodruff, Editor of *The Tablet*, Hinsley absolutely refused to fall in with the government's position regarding the Anglo-Soviet alliance.[97]

Elsewhere, the Cardinal's total rejection of Germany's claim to have embarked on a Christian crusade against the USSR had a positive effect, especially in America where Catholic opinion had been profoundly disturbed by the Anglo-Soviet alliance. There was strong resistance in the USA to the USSR's restrictions on religious and other liberties and President Roosevelt needed much firmer guarantees of Soviet co-operation in this area before he could contemplate providing assistance to the alliance. It was important for the British government to keep the USA on side and Hinsley's unequivocal detestation of both Nazism and communism, while refraining from publicly opposing the alliance of 'co-belligerency' with the USSR, was welcomed by the British government. Mgr Elwes was officially asked to inform Hinsley '. . .that his Eminence's action, and in general the help he has so generously given on so many occasions, is deeply appreciated by the Foreign Office'. Foreign Secretary Anthony Eden claimed that Hinsley 'showed no anti-Russian bias' but Hinsley was choosing his words very carefully. On 7 September 1941, on a National Day of Prayer, the Cardinal said:

> Russia, or Russia's government, we know has been guilty of great wrongs to others and to Poland also. But a people whose rulers have done wrongs do not forfeit all its own rights. We pray that the defence of Russia's rights might help to repair Poland's wrongs. . . . [98]

The Foreign Office declared that Hinsley's broadcast to the USA was 'the best sort of Catholic propaganda' in that it made 'the distinction between 'the oppressive nature of Stalin's regime and the laudable struggle against Nazism of the Russian people'. Viscount Fitzalan, who maintained in the House of Lords that Britain had to support Russia in order to defeat the Nazis, supported Hinsley. Other English Catholics were not as understanding, however, and Richard Hope, a Catholic working in the Ministry of Information, reported that in spite of the mutual military interests of Britain and the USSR, Catholics in general tended to keep alive their opposition to communism. [99]

Russian demands to have their 1941 frontiers recognised and be free to annex the Baltic States and Eastern Poland embarrassed their newly-found British allies. They also disturbed Hinsley for he was acutely aware that any such agreements would inflame anti-British sentiment among expatriate Poles and Catholic countries in Europe. Soviet pressure on Britain to keep its press and media in check made it difficult for the government to maintain the equilibrium with the USSR but news of Russian massacres in 'liberated' Poland further exacerbated the situation.

The entry of Mussolini's Italy into the war alongside Germany cleared the way for to speak out more forcefully against the Italian regime. In June 1940 he wrote that Italian fascists had now clarified the issue: they were aligned with the Nazis and therefore deserved the same condemnation. There had been a chance of securing freedom of conscience in Italy, he wrote, but now the prospects of compromise had disappeared. The fascists whose paganism had been detected and denounced by Pius XI and Pius XII, had now openly broken with Christian principles. Fascism, he concluded, had become Nazism and aimed to pillage, dominate and enslave. Only an Allied victory would defeat their abominable system of religious and racial persecution:

> The disguise of temporising with religion has been cast aside. The leaders of Fascism have with brutal realism broken with the Christian civilization which built up Europe . . .If for a while there was a hope of securing freedom of conscience with the faithful under such a system, now there is no longer a possibility of a *modus vivendi* with this open enemy of the faith of the majority of Italian people.[100]

Hinsley asked for special prayers for the Pope, who was placed in 'an agonizing position'.

At their Low Week meeting in April 1942, the bishops, all immersed in the problems of their own war-torn dioceses expressed their sincere gratitude to the Cardinal

> . . .for the magnificent leadership he has shown us in the crisis which our nation has had to face, and for his fearless pronouncements in the cause of Christianity. We wish to tender to him our respectful homage, our loyal adherence and unswerving support in his uncompromising stand against the assaults on the freedom with which Christ has made us free.[101]

Two months before his death Hinsley spoke to an Empire Rally held at the Albert Hall. The address, subsequently broadcast on the various news bulletins of the BBC's European Service, was the Cardinal's final public statement and illustrated how his religion and his patriotism came together. It was not, however, an unconditional acceptance of the institutions of state and society. He said:

> The symbols of the our faith are the Cross and the flag. The Cross speaks to us of Resurrection through sacrifice. The flag reminds us of our duty to our country; for reasonable patriotism is the devotion we owe in due measure

to those who are nearest and dearest to us: *patriotism* is piety towards our kith and kin.

The flag, he continued, included that of St George denoting sacrifice; the white cross symbolising purity; and the cross of St Andrew which stood for victory over greed, pride, lust and hate. 'Faithful to that upright Cross and to our flag', he concluded, 'we face the new year undaunted, with the assurance of the final triumph of our cause. And when the war is over we will not slacken in united efforts to win the peace'.[102]

Chapter Sixteen

IRELAND, EXILES AND JEWS

1935-1943

Ireland

Following his arrival in Westminster Hinsley became involved in the dangerous complexity of Anglo-Irish relations. In the summer of 1935 there had been riots in Belfast and the National Council for Civil Liberties asked Hinsley to protest to Prime Minister Stanley Baldwin against the civil and social disabilities suffered by the Catholic minority in the Province of Ulster. The Archbishop refused to support the NCCL's protest but found it more difficult to ignore the pleas of Daniel Mageean, Bishop of Down and Connor, who told him that Loyalist pogroms against Catholics in Ulster were increasing in frequency and intensity. Mageean informed Hinsley that he had requested Baldwin to convene an independent tribunal to investigate Catholic complaints and urged him and the Hierarchy to take a similar course and enlist the support of Catholic MPs. Home Secretary Sir John Simon chose the obvious route and referred Mageean to the government of Northern Ireland but between November 1935 and June 1936 Mageean continued to lobby Hinsley on behalf of Ulster's Catholics.[1] The new Archbishop, initially reluctant to become embroiled in the matter, eventually sought the mediation of Cosmo Lang, the Anglican Archbishop of Canterbury:

> In the cause of Peace and of equal freedom for all members of the British Commonwealth, I venture to suggest to Your Grace that a word from you would induce the Authorities at Downing Street to give attention to threatening condition of affairs in Northern Ireland. . . .
>
> The wise intervention of the Imperial Government and an impartial enquiry would tend to put an end to a state of things which cannot fail to prejudice in many parts of the world the prestige of British rule.

Archbishop Lang promised to make discreet approaches to the government but Baldwin's administration ignored him as it had done Mageean.[2]

Before Hinsley received Lang's reply he had decided to write to

Baldwin himself. He addressed the Prime Minister with 'all the power of persuasion that I may have, and moved only by my concern for justice and the good name of my country'. He praised Baldwin's efforts for peace in Europe but added that 'could we do something more to bring peace to one special corner of the United Kingdom, we might seek peace abroad perhaps with greater serenity and confidence'. He added that 'all my brethren in the episcopate are with me in asking you to give this matter your personal consideration'. There is no record of the Prime Minister's reply.[3]

On his appointment to Westminster, Hinsley had been urged by Amigo 'to keep the bishops united here and let us make a good advance to the Irish Hierarchy'. In 1938 the English and Welsh Hierarchy invited its Irish counterpart to become involved in closer relations and address the spiritual needs of the thousands of Irish emigrants living in England and Wales. The Hierarchy feared that many of the 30,000 who annually left Ireland for England were detached from the strong bonds of their own indigenous communities and were leaving the faith. With the support of Hinsley and Cardinal MacRory, the Primate of All Ireland, the Hierarchies set up a committee of bishops to deal with the situation. Such was the commitment of the English bishops that Archbishop Williams of Birmingham promised Fr Charles McQuaid at Blackrock College that he would do all he could to alleviate the hardships of the exiled Irish and stated that 'my object is to try to get better relations between Irish and English Catholics. . . . '[4]

In June 1939 the Irish Republican Army (IRA) unleashed its violence on the streets of London and Hinsley condemned outright the explosions in the heart of his diocese:

> As Bishop of this Diocese of Westminster, I wish to make public my strong condemnation of such cowardly and atrocious outrages as it is reported have been committed last night in Piccadilly, Park Lane and in the Strand, outrages which would damage and discredit any cause. What I am about to say is inspired by no prejudice, but is dictated by my sense of duty as Chief Pastor of the Catholic Church in this area of England.

> There evidently exists a secret organisation (call it what you will – army, or lodge, or cell) which is plotting against the peace and order of this country, and by its insane methods exposing innocent persons to bodily injury and even, perhaps, loss of life. Such barbarism is in itself a crime, no matter how specious the pretexts advanced to make it appear less savage.

> The Church of God sternly and clearly condemns secret societies which plot against the Church or State. The members incur excommunication. Unless they repent and completely renounce their participation in such societies they cannot be admitted to the Sacraments. All simple and sincere Catholics of whatever nationality they may be should be deterred by this warning and should not allow themselves to be made the tools of designing extremists.[5]

Hinsley received no letters of support for this uncompromising stand. On the contrary he was accused by some Irish Catholics in England of being unsympathetic to the Irish nationalist cause.

A more threatening response came from Patrick Fleming of the Army Council of the IRA who told Hinsley in no uncertain terms that the Church's role was either to publicly support the natural justice of the IRA's cause or stay out of politics and remain silent. He and his colleagues had read Hinsley's statement 'with pained surprise' and accused him of 'reducing religion to the level of political diatribe'. They were quite certain that the Cardinal

> . . .was aware that the Cardinal Primate of Ireland has expressly stated that the occupation of our country by the armed troops of your country is an unwarrantable act of war and that as an immediate and direct result of that warfare the Catholics of Ireland have been subjected to recurring campaigns of murder, arson and despoliation beside which the London incidents you condemn are insignificant.
>
> Neither can we believe that you are ignorant or forgetful of the Teaching of the great Popes or the example of Cardinal Mercier when his country, like ours, was occupied by a foreign soldiery in the interests of another Empire.
>
> We are, however, sure that you have been malignantly misquoted in your references to the 'cowardly' activities of the Expeditionary Force in England. The adjective is so cheap, so offensive to the spirit of Catholicity which has suffered not from the soldier but from the judge; so repugnant to Catholic definitions, that it must have been inserted by someone who wished to reduce the pronouncements of the Church to the level of a vulgar altercation.
>
> Frankly Your Eminence, we feel that, if in your reported address you spoke for the Church, you misrepresented its spirit and its mission; that if you spoke as an English citizen you might with better effect have used the dignity of your position to say the simple truth: 'Our country England has no right or title to employ its army to occupy the territory of another nation and in our interests subsidise the subjection of its people.'

May we not expect from Your Eminence an assurance that you have been misquoted and that as a prelate of the Church you are prepared to use your influence to soften rather than render more acute the acerbities of a situation which is entirely the making of your own countrymen.[6]

There was no way in which Hinsley and the IRA could or would come together. The Cardinal would not modify his abhorrence of the IRA's violence nor would the IRA retreat from its military struggle for a united Ireland. Hinsley sent a copy of Fleming's letter to Eamon de Valera, Prime Minister of Ireland, but it was acknowledged without comment. He also sent a copy to Cardinal Joseph MacRory of Armagh, the Primate of All Ireland, explaining that:

I have considered it my duty to express my judgement on these incidents and on the secret organisation behind them because my Episcopal colleagues have declared openly their condemnation and because my clergy and my people are in agreement that this bombing campaign is doing very great damage to religion as well as to the material interests of our Catholic people. . . . Political questions do not enter into the motives of the action I have taken, and if these influence me at all in my official action it is solely because I see the methods adopted by the extremists discredit the cause which these men pretend to represent.[7]

MacRory's reply was as explicit as Hinsley's original statement of condemnation. He offered Hinsley his sympathy for 'the trouble my foolish countrymen have caused you' but firmly denied the allegation made by Fleming that he had called the British occupation of Northern Ireland an 'unwarrantable act of war'. Nevertheless, he felt very strongly about 'the injustice of England to Ireland, and not least the partition of our country'. While the action of the IRA in England was unjustified, it was perpetrated by men who believed they were acting from patriotic motives. 'They feel', he wrote, 'that England in her dealings with Ireland has never done justice except from fear or some sort of necessity, and they hope to terrorize her by the present campaign'. He ended: 'I am sorry for the worry and anxiety they may have caused Your Eminence and for the harm they have done so many Irish in Great Britain'.[8]

This difficult situation was exacerbated by some Irishmen imprisoned in English prisons for acts of terrorism embarking on hunger strikes until they were accorded political prisoner status. Hinsley and the Bishops of Brentwood, Leeds and Plymouth had prisons in their dioceses where the men were incarcerated and the Cardinal was anxious to arrive at a common policy on the issue. In his opinion the hunger strikers were morally wrong and they should be informed of this by prison chaplains who should also warn them that in the event of death (by their suicide) they would be debarred from the Sacraments and Christian burial. He hoped that he could trust the other bishops 'to act together on fixed principles and unflinching resolution'.[9] Archbishop Godfrey, who had been consulted by Hinsley, was in agreement with his position but the other three bishops expressed different views. Bishop Doubleday of Brentwood wished each case to be judged individually. Bishop Barrett of Plymouth agreed in general with Hinsley but was cautious about the denial of the Last Rites to a prisoner. Bishop Poskitt of Leeds stated that as the Holy See was still considering the case of Terence McSwiney, the Mayor of Cork, who had died as a result of a hunger strike twenty years previously, the English bishops could not pre-empt the Vatican's decision. He also thought it would be difficult to prove whether or not a prisoner remained un-reconciled right to the very end of his life. Poskitt's attitude was adopted by Canon Mahoney, a theologian of the Westminster Chapter, who advised Hinsley to proceed with caution. In the event, the IRA prisoners ceased their hunger strikes and the bishops were saved from having to make a decision.[10]

Some elements of society were eager to associate the Catholic community with the outrages committed by the IRA and Lord Fitzalan, President of the Catholic Union of Great Britain, drew the Cardinal's attention to the unfavourable repercussions of such allegations. He reported that the Irish and Irish Catholic priests in England were regarded as part of the IRA's campaign and he felt that Hinsley should make a public pronouncement denying these unsubstantiated claims. Archbishop Godfrey, he said, was willing to support this move. Hinsley, however, approached the problem with caution for he had a great distaste of ecclesiastics involving themselves in politics unless they had absolutely no alternative. While he was on firm ground in his condemnation of the IRA's violence, there was no such certainty about political involvement. Nor could he guarantee the unanimous support of the Hierarchy and he urged Godfrey to suggest some combined action on the part of the bishops. Hinsley was very much aware of his distinct lack of influence on the episcopate in this matter.

Despite his outspoken criticism of the IRA at the time of the London bombings, Hinsley pleaded for clemency for two IRA men who had been sentenced to death for their alleged complicity in an outrage which had left five dead in Coventry in August 1939. Their cause had been taken up by world leaders such as President Roosevelt of the United States and Prime Minister Jan Christian Smuts of South Africa and Hinsley wrote confidentially to Prime Minister Chamberlain to plead for the prisoners' lives not only out of compassion but also with regard to the consequences of their execution. It would, he claimed, defer any hope of reconciliation and peace with Ireland. The men would become martyrs and England would be considered to be no better than Germany which was 'animated by the spirit of Nazi frightfulness'. A reprieve, he argued, would demonstrate the goodwill of the British government and 'the people of our Sister Island would be rallied to our cause through the sentiment of lively appreciation of magnanimity'. But rescinding the death penalty should not be interpreted as excusing the crime and the Cardinal promised that 'I will renew in the strongest terms the condemnation I have already published of these cowardly methods of the IRA'. His appeal for clemency, and those of others, was unsuccessful and the two men were hanged.[11]

In October 1940 Hinsley wrote to Prime Minister Winston Churchill to complain about the embodiment of the Ulster Defence Volunteers as a branch of the 'B' Special Constabulary, itself a part of the Royal Ulster Constabulary. Ostensibly, the UDV was to guard against a possible German invasion but Hinsley protested that it would be seen by Catholics as a Protestant method of maintaining civil order. He suggested that 'for God's sake and for our great and just cause, the sake of bitter and sectarian differences should be removed' and the UDV be made into a force like the British Home Guard under the control of the War Office. He wrote:

> The danger is civil war in Ireland if this cause of religious and political bitterness is not by your wisdom removed. Surely it is not beyond the genius of statesmanship to effect such a change and to prevent disaster by adherence to the statute law which does not allow to the Government of Northern Ireland matters arising from a state of war.

He concluded: 'My support of this protest, made by so many prominent loyalists, is motivated by love for my country that springs from my faith as a Catholic'. As in the case of the two convicted IRA men, Hinsley's request was unsuccessful. For Churchill, the imminent threat of a German invasion overrode any feelings he may have had about the position of Catholics in Ulster.[12]

The neutrality of Eire during World War II caused further problems for the British government and Hinsley took great care to ensure that non-Catholics did not equate the English Catholic population with the stance adopted by the government in Dublin. He was, he said in 1941, a Home Ruler and stated that his time in Africa had convinced him of the benefit of close co-operation between the Catholic Church and state within the Empire. But the Irish situation was unique and remained a sensitive issue for the British government, for Hinsley and for the Hierarchy. In Eire, where the arch-conservative Archbishop John Charles McQuaid of Dublin had warned 'of the Sword of the Spirit confusion', Hinsley's outspoken and specific condemnation of the Axis powers were attacked and censored by the Irish government. Tommy Coyne, Secretary of the Department of Justice, considered his pronouncements to be jingoistic and described him 'as the most tactless member of the Sacred College, constantly identifying English interests throughout the world with the success of the British cause'.[13] The Minister of Defence, Frank Aitken, supported Coyne and called on the Irish Senate to ban the publication and broadcasts of Hinsley's letters and speeches. Archbishop McQuaid, meanwhile, refrained from commenting on Nazism and Bolshevism. A Polish visitor found him to be conversant with religious persecution carried out in Poland by the Germans and the Russians but the Archbishop steadfastly maintained his silence.

In September 1941 Hinsley wrote in his typically bullish way to ask McQuaid why he had been singled out by the Irish government: 'I am put down as a propagandist and one paid by the British Government to say things', he wrote, but 'personally I do not care a straw for what those who place politics before their religion say against me. I shall continue to defend religion, and to despise such calumny'. To Hinsley there was more at issue than his reputation. There was history to contend with and being half-Irish he was well aware of that. He wondered, he asked McQuaid, if his name had been blackened for speaking and acting throughout his life in the cause of a united Ireland. 'If I love England as the country in which I was born and educated', he wrote, 'I have had a great love for Ireland as the one-time home of my mother and as a Catholic land which has suffered for the Faith. . . . ' Was he also to be blacklisted in Eire, he asked, for rescuing children in England who had been abandoned by Irish parents? But more critically for McQuaid, Hinsley raised questions relating to the publication in Ireland of papal encyclicals and the pastoral letters of the German bishops and asked if these too were censored for criticizing the Nazis and Soviets. With a cutting edge he wrote: 'Is Eire under the sway of Berlin or Moscow?' It was obvious that he knew it was not for he concluded that 'the Nazi attack on the Archbishop of Westminster shall not quench the devotion I entertain for the Archbishop of Dublin and for my fellow Catholics in the land of my mother'.[14]

Hinsley's final involvement in Anglo-Irish affairs occurred in August 1942 when he intervened with the British government to commute the death sentence passed on six men found guilty of murdering a policeman in Belfast. On this occasion his intervention seems to have had some effect although it is difficult to ascertain the exact extent of his influence. Churchill wrote to him on 2 September 1942 to say that the Governor of Northern Ireland had spared the lives of the convicted men.[15]

Hinsley's influence on the course of Anglo-Irish affairs was limited by the weight of history and the polarized attitudes of others. The British and Ulster authorities were entrenched in their suspicious and hostile views of Eire and Irish Catholics, except when they wished them to join the British forces. The English and Welsh Hierarchy was influenced partly by personal heritage and partly by the social and ethnic composition of their dioceses. The Irish Hierarchy, all of whom had experienced the horrors of a people torn apart by civil war, wished only to see peace in their country but in honesty could not agree to its political division. And the murderous actions of politically motivated Green and Orange extremists on both sides of the Irish divide drove a bloody wedge between all. Hinsley, motivated by Christian love and a generous charity for all, could not hope to disentangle centuries of tortuous politics or dissolve ingrained sectarian hatred. He abhorred the terror inflicted by the Black and Tans and crimes committed in the name of British justice; he knew of the injustice perpetrated against Catholics in Ulster; and he was aware of the dangerous possibilities of Eire denying Britain the use of its ports in wartime. The intractable Irish problem was not to be solved by Hinsley's intervention and his silence on so many occasions indicated his recognition of the sensitivity of the situation and his own powerlessness. As ever, he was overcome by the suffering of people. In September 1941 Archbishops Williams and Downey were much exercised by the fact that two priests at the Travel Permit Branch of the Irish High Commission had reported that one of the two Archbishops had said that Hinsley was 'all bleeding heart and no bloody head' when it came to Irish matters. Williams was mortified, Downey claimed he was not responsible and it is not clear if Hinsley heard of the remark. Downey immediately informed Delahunty, the High Commissioner for Ireland, who may have been the actual perpetrator of the remark. Showing no remorse, Delahunty replied to Downey that he 'feared that the Cardinal had got even the Irish members of the Hierarchy solidly over to his somewhat limited view'. Neither Williams nor Downey refuted Delahunty's alleged comments.[16]

Exiles

The outbreak of war in Europe led to the establishment of exiled governments and expatriate Catholic communities in London. At times Hinsley became a fulcrum in their relations with the British government and found himself having to tread very warily through fragmented and sensitive European politics.

After the *Anschluss* of 1938, the case of Austrian emigrés was particularly difficult as the British government considered them to be both refugees and aliens. Following the fall of France in 1940 the remnants of the Hapsburgs, the former ruling dynasty of the Austro-Hungarian Empire, moved to London and among them were the Archdukes Robert and Otto, sons of the last Emperor Karl. Their wish was to return to central Europe and set up a federal system of nations modelled on the United States and their hopes were aired in columns of the Catholic press. The British government, however, would have little to do with them and Robert contacted Hinsley in October 1941 to solicit the Cardinal's support.

Hinsley, like Churchill, was of the opinion that Austria had not been a willing partner in the *Anschluss* but he would not be drawn into political machinations where he might be used by a foreign community against his own government's policies. The Cardinal therefore told the Archduke that to involve the English and Welsh Catholic Church would not only embarrass the Hierarchy but also compromise the government's plans for any future European settlement. Notwithstanding this cold reply, Robert continued to pressurize Hinsley. In turn, Robert was urged on by the Free Austria movement, a combination of diverse political groupings whose view, in his opinion, was dominated by 'these scoundrels of Jewish communists and freemasons'. In March 1942 the Archduke complained to Hinsley about an article which had appeared in *The Common Cause*, the paper of the Sword of the Spirit movement. The article, by an exiled Pole who advocated the restoration of the Polish monarchy as a stabilizing factor in central Europe, aroused Robert's ire. He asked the Cardinal to persuade the Poles to abandon 'this raving madness' and to stop attacking the Austrians and their alliance with Germany. Hinsley merely acknowledged receipt of the Archduke's complaint.

There were others besides the Poles and British government who observed the antics of the Free Austria coalition with suspicion. Exiled Yugoslavs and Czechs were concerned at Free Austria's designs on their homelands. The USSR too, with its driving ambition to subjugate central Europe, was ever watchful of a Hapsburg renaissance while the German propaganda machine simply exploited allied disagreements and Anglo-Soviet mistrust. To rid himself of some of the pressure, Hinsley delegated Bishop Mathew to liaise with the Austrian archdukes and hold meetings not at Cathedral House but at London University's Catholic Chaplaincy. The move may have got the Archdukes off Hinsley's back but it did not prevent the Austrians from lobbying the government for the re-creation of a greater post-war Austria. Churchill favoured the idea while Eden did not for fear of upsetting the USSR.

Hinsley had fewer contacts with the exiled Czech government in London but was caught up in their internal politics and their relations with the Slovaks by *The Catholic Herald's* rather maladroit publication of a letter from Peter Pridavok, who claimed to be the representative of the Slovak Catholic Populist Party. Pridavok's letter, which was supposedly written on behalf of Catholic Slovak leaders and bishops, attacked Dr Edvard Beneš, the Czech leader in London. The government, which had recently released Pridavok from internment on the understanding that he did not engage in political activity, was less than pleased that a Catholic newspaper allowed him free rein to inflame animosities among the Czech and Slovak exiles. At the Foreign Office the Catholic Alec Randall considered what could be done:

> I take it that there is no question of legal action against the paper, and that private persuasive action only is required in the first instance. I will consult Cardinal Hinsley about this, but I am not very hopeful of success, as *The Catholic Herald* is a well-known *enfant terrible* among the Catholic Press and has, I know, proved resistant even to the highest ecclesiastical pressure on one occasion. I hope the action with Pridavok will succeed in preventing further contributions to him by the paper, and I will see what can be done privately about the paper generally.[17]

Hinsley was not approached by the Foreign Office but the principal Czech chaplain in London, Fr Spacek, asked the Cardinal if he would intervene with *The Catholic Herald* to prevent further damaging comments about Beneš. The articles did stop but only after Pridavok was visited by officers of the government's security services. It was a welcome outcome for Hinsley who did not like having his position used by others to prevent free speech even though he knew that *The Catholic Herald* was dabbling in danger.

Before the war Hinsley had been an ardent supporter of Poland's freedom and a staunch admirer of its Catholic heritage, positions he maintained until his death. On 17 September 1939 he attended Mass at the Polish Catholic Mission in Islington where a letter from him was read in Polish to the congregation. He referred to Poland as the bulwark of civilization in Eastern Europe and expressed his great sorrow at the German occupation of Poland and its sacred and national shrine of Czestochowa, home of the Black Madonna. Poland's Cardinal Hlond, resident in Rome, wrote to thank Hinsley for his letter and particularly for his comments on the country's 'resurrection'.[18] It was a theme the Cardinal returned to in his broadcasts, letters and speeches. In 1941 he described the Nazi occupation of Poland as 'camouflaged paganism fiercely opposed to Christian civilization'. General Wladyslaw Sikorski, Prime Minister of the Polish government in exile and commander in Chief of the Polish Armed Forces, thanked the Cardinal 'in real emotion' for his condemnation of Germany's merciless control of Poland. By mid 1941 Hinsley knew the true extent of Germany's murderous regime in Poland and in particular the persecution of the Catholic Church.[19] The signing of the Anglo-Soviet alliance in summer 1941 altered the situation for Hinsley and Poland, as both Britain and Poland now found themselves on the same side as an erstwhile aggressor. The Cardinal carefully picked his way through the thicket of diplomacy and prayed that by defending the USSR Poland's unmerited wrongs would eventually be rectified. The test of sincerity in the cause of justice, he told the Russians, was concern for the resurrection of Poland.[20]

The course of official Anglo-Polish and indeed British-Catholic and Polish relations did not always run smoothly. Allegations of anti-Jewish attitudes in the Polish armed services compelled Sikorski to investigate. Again, *The Catholic Herald* was involved for in August 1940 it had supported the Polish weekly *Jestem Polakiem (I am a Pole)* in its defence against attacks by the *Evening Standard* that it was anti-Semitic. The Foreign Office, disturbed that the Catholic paper was once more intervening in sensitive issues and making matters worse, suspected that the Polish paper was receiving its newsprint from *The Catholic Herald*. It considered referring the matter to Hinsley but concluded that, as before, he would have no influence on the paper and its editor Michael de la Bédoyère. *The Catholic Herald* proposed that surplus Polish Jews be taken abroad.[21]

On 3 May 1942, Polish Constitution Day, the Cardinal repeated Polish claims for justice and restoration of its independent status in the international community. By this time he could count on the support of Polish Americans:

> I repeat the unquestionable truth that Poland is the test of justice and of the sincerity of British, American and Allied War aims. The persecution of religion in Poland, far from abating, continues ever more relentlessly. That state of things must be ended: the very soul of liberty is assailed in Poland.[22]

In July 1942 Hinsley devoted a broadcast to the memory of the 700,000 Polish Jews who had been slaughtered by the Nazis since 1939 and implored German Catholics and Christians to 'listen to the voice of reason and humanity and resist these black deeds of shame'[23] Dr Schwarzbarf, a representative of Polish Jews in the National Polish Council, expressed his gratitude to the Cardinal for his broadcast:

> In these terrible days when hundreds of thousands of Jews murdered by the Germans have added their sacrifice to that of other people for the cause of morality and justice, millions of my brethren will accept the words of Your Grace as encouragement to endure and fight until victory against barbarism is achieved.[24]

On 8 December 1942, a Day of Prayer for Poland, Hinsley again spoke out against the brutal persecution of the Jews and declared that the Nazis appeared intent on making Poland into one vast cemetery. Poland, he said, had earned the respect of other nations of the world for its heroic struggle and endurance. He demanded that Poland's rights and status be restored when victory was achieved. On a practical level Hinsley founded the Catholic Committee for Poland, an organisation established to provide for both the spiritual and material needs of exiled Poles. Its president was Bishop Mathew and it had an Anglo-Polish executive committee. In this way Hinsley hoped that the national and Catholic spirit would be sustained among the exiles.[25]

The evacuation of the British Expeditionary Force from Dunkirk in May 1940 was a serious military and psychological blow to Great Britain. Prime Minister Churchill, anxiously looking for ways of bolstering vulnerable France appealed to Hinsley to call upon the French Catholic Church to do whatever it could to resist the German advance. 'The Cardinal', he noted, 'is vigorous and tough, and I cannot see that it would do any harm if he made it absolutely clear to his brethren over the water that, whatever happened, we are going on to the end'. Lord Fitzalan acted as intermediary and Hinsley himself took the draft of the speech to Downing Street. The Cardinal conveyed to Cardinal Emmanuel Suhard, Archbishop of Paris, the deep admiration of all classes of English people for the French who were 'so worthy of the high Christian traditions of their saints and heroes especially St Jeanne d'Arc'. He assured the French Cardinal that Britain was determined to assist France in the recovery of its liberty and nationhood.[26] From 14-16 June a Triduum of Prayer for France was held at Westminster Cathedral and Hinsley appealed to the French to regain their inner spirituality and tradition of chivalry and resist the onslaught of pagan Nazism.[27] On 17 June the government of Marshal Philippe Pétain asked the Germans for an armistice and subsequently France was divided into a Nazi occupied area and an area administered by Pétain from the town of Vichy. On 23 June the Cardinal broadcast to the defeated French using the metaphors he had employed so effectively when speaking for Poland. France too had 'been crucified' but 'she will become greater when she has passed through the cleansing fires of agony and passion'. God, he said, 'would work through the sons of France when united among themselves by that strong Faith which shall renew her youth'.[28]

The Catholic Herald repeated its tendency to take a totally independent viewpoint and generate problems for Hinsley. It favoured Pétain, and his predominantly Catholic administration, and attacked M. Reynaud, the former Prime Minister of anti-clerical France. Richard Hope, Head of the Roman Catholic section at the Ministry of Information's Religions Division, informed Mgr Elwes that the paper was harming the cause of Catholicism in England and that the patriotism of Catholics was now doubted in some quarters of his Ministry. The Director of the Religions Division, although he was aware that Pétain's government was unrepresentative of France and French Catholics, thought that

English Catholics would mistakenly consider that the anti-clericalism of France would somehow disappear and France's Catholic identity be restored. While Hope admitted that German propaganda might exploit the idea of a Latin-Catholic bloc in Europe, he was of the strong opinion that the majority of Catholics in England were behind the war. *The Tablet* also held this view although it was not uncritical of the British government, but *The Universe* and *The Catholic Times* had expressed some support for Pétain. For the Ministry, however, the real problem was *The Catholic Herald* and in July 1940 strong representations were made to de la Bédoyère who was warned that the paper's future policy would be watched very closely. Hinsley could and did reprimand a French priest at the French Church in Leicester Square for his expressing his partisanship from the pulpit but it was more difficult for him to control the Catholic press.

Another source of concern for the Cardinal was the Vatican media offices lending their voices to the Pétain government, now installed at Vichy. Hinsley felt compelled to act swiftly in case the views of *L'Osservatore Romano* and the Vatican Radio convinced English Catholics that they were expressing a papal opinion that collaboration was acceptable. Confidentially he contacted the Press Association, all Catholic editors and the editor of *The Times* to share with them his specific and wider concerns:

> This is a serious warning that a clever propaganda campaign is starting to make Catholics as such appear to have adopted an anti-British attitude. I do earnestly counsel you not to publish statements or comments, even if they purport to come from Vatican sources, tending to give support to the present government of France. Recent quotations from the *Osservatore Romano* and the Vatican Radio have given a wrong impression to many of our fellow countrymen – Catholics and Protestants – and to some loyal Frenchmen. The *Osservatore Romano* and the Vatican Radio do not voice the judgement of the Pope; but people here regard these utterances as official Papal pronouncements. Please accept this warning as most urgent. The utmost caution is necessary in the existing confusion. Our loyalty to our faith and to our country is in question.[29]

To have both his faith and his loyalty questioned was of the utmost seriousness for Hinsley. In the event of doubt he asked the media to contact the Apostolic Delegate.

In France itself the situation grew more complicated. Some French bishops, for example, advocated French military collaboration with the Germans while Pétain rescinded some of his country's anti-clerical statutes and was happy to meet with Hitler. Such actions and events were exploited by Germany for propaganda purposes as was the concept of a European Latin-Catholic bloc. *The Tablet* was not fooled by these events and its editor Douglas Woodruff wrote: 'We trust to see a Christian and Catholic State in France again but France must first be free, and to that task . . . we shall bring all the help we can'. The restoration of Catholic France could not occur under German hegemony. Hinsley, meanwhile, attacked the exclusivity of a Latin-Catholic bloc and questioned how the identification of Catholicism could be confined to one group of European nations. This myopic view of the faith, he argued, excluded Poland, Ireland and other countries in Europe with sizeable Catholic populations. It also excluded Germany.[30]

Foreign Secretary Anthony Eden, like others, suspected the attitudes of French exiles and was of the opinion that the French Church was collaborationist. General Charles de Gaulle, leader of the Free French Forces in London, felt it necessary to protect the French in exile from such disparaging comments and spoke 'in the presence of Cardinal Hinsley about the attitude of Free France towards their Allies and the Vichy government'. Hinsley met with Eden in January 1941 to discuss how they could arrive at a more balanced view of the French position. Hinsley suggested that more trustworthy judgements on the French situation should be obtained. Eden agreed and reported that 'we were anxious to emphasise an increasing sense of solidarity between British and French Catholics in the common struggle against Nazi paganism'. Hinsley then sent Eden a list of French Catholics who might be trusted to broadcast to the Empire and the Allies. Some of these were missionary prelates whom Hinsley had met in Africa. From it, the Foreign Office chose Cardinal Jean-Marie Villeneuve, Archbishop of Quebec. British officials were of the opinion that Cardinal Villeneuve's words would carry particular weight with Pétain's followers who thought that collaboration with Germany was the only alternative to communism and also with the French 'higher clergy' who in their enthusiasm for the regeneration of France 'appear to gloss over the fundamental evils of the Nazi regime'. Hinsley agreed and with the Foreign Office formulated suggestions that might be put to the Canadian Cardinal. They were stressing that French freedom would only come with a British victory, the need for the clergy to keep alive 'the true French spirit', and that the Nazis had shown themselves to be the enemy of Christianity and the Catholic Church.

Hinsley then wrote to Villeneuve to ask for his assistance.[31]

As the prospect of France being fully integrated into a German Europe strengthened, Hinsley's spirits sank. At Westminster Cathedral on 7 December 1941, in the presence of de Gaulle and other Free French officers, he spoke of the agony and sufferings of France and of the two million of her sons held in captivity by the Germans. While there were encouraging signs that a spiritual regeneration had begun in France it was offset by the fact that it was occurring under a foreign rule that could not be trusted.

Hinsley and the Jewish Community

In 1936 *The Jewish Chronicle* took the opportunity:

> ...of congratulating Mgr Hinsley on his appointment to Westminster, and expressing the hope and belief that the cordial relations which prevailed between his predecessors and the Jewish community of this country will continue during his occupancy of his high and sacred office.[32]

This warm welcome from 'the Organ of British Jewry' was indeed sincere for although Cardinal Bourne opposed the extremism of the Zionist movement, he had spoken out against anti-Jewish atrocities and in favour of the Balfour Declaration of 1917 which pledged British support for the establishment of a Jewish home in Palestine.

Hinsley's position was soon to be tested. In February 1936, *The Catholic Gazette*, a magazine of the Catholic Missionary Society, contained an article which the Board of Deputies of British Jews regarded as 'redolent of the forgeries known as the Protocols of the Elders of Zion'. The Society was an evangelizing agency directly under the control of the Hierarchy and the Board made immediate representation to the Archbishop. Hinsley agreed with the Board's complaint and his response drew this comment from *The Jewish Chronicle*:

> We welcome his action heartily. Those who seek to drive Jews and Catholics into hostile camps are friends of neither community – especially in days when they are assailed by the common enemies of religious doubt and political enmity.[33]

The increase of anti-Jewish activity in Germany and other parts of Europe led Jews in Britain to seek sympathetic support from other religious groups. In early 1938 Hinsley was approached by the Agudas Israel World Organisation, an orthodox Jewish organisation, to protest against the Rumanian government which had compelled Jewish shops to open on the Sabbath. Hinsley took the line adopted by Cardinal Bourne, that if the Jews asked for and received support from Catholics then it should be reciprocated:

> All I can say is that my predecessors condemned such persecutions wherever they occur. I endorse their words. At the same time persecutions are going on and have been going on for some time against the Catholic Church. We should expect some condemnation of these outrages against humanity and religion.[34]

In the same month he received an appeal from the United Appeal for Jews in Poland for an expression of support and goodwill. He replied that all victims of persecution were assured of his compassion including 'the tens of thousands of my own faith who are undergoing similar trials and who have had to leave their native countries'. Hinsley was sympathetic to the needs of persecuted races all over the world but was wary of lending his name to a myriad of causes however laudable their aims. He declined a vice-presidency of the Friendly Discussion Circle for Jews and Christians but ordered prayers to be said for Jews and others being persecuted across the world.[35] In November 1938, through the pages of *The Times*, and with the Archbishop of Canterbury and the Moderator of the Church of Scotland, he called for the governments of Western Europe to adopt more liberal immigration policies regarding Jewish refugees from Germany. He urged the British government and imperial governments to profess their Christian duty and accept more refugees.[36] The Hierarchy, meanwhile, was doing what it could. At its Easter meeting in 1938 it established a Catholic Committee for Refugees from Germany and Austria under the Cardinal's presidency and this was given a further impetus later in the year when its remit was widened to include non-Catholic refugees.[37] On 1 December 1938 Hinsley appeared at the Royal Albert Hall with the Chief Rabbi and Archbishop William Temple of York to protest against the persecution of the Jews. There he denounced all forms of sectarianism and described the platform party as a demonstration 'of our common humanity'. He said:

> I stand here to uphold, as far as in me lies, the dignity and rights of human personality against the tyranny and persecution which have become the bane of the entire world, whether that persecution be inflicted on Jew or Gentile, whether on Catholic Christian or non-Catholic Christian; whether in Russia or Mexico or Spain or Germany or elsewhere.

He compared Hitler's persecution of the Jews with the Roman Emperor Nero's cruelty towards Jews and Christians. Both, he said, violated fundamental principles of humanity.[38] His words caused great resentment in Berlin and his aggressive tone was more than the German press could bear. His missionary work among 'the Negroes' in Africa, the editor of *Angriff* commented, accounted for his remarkable outburst. It continued:

> This explains the grotesque circumstances that a Roman Cardinal should enter the lists arm-in-arm with the heretical Archbishop of York and the English Chief Rabbi, to challenge the twentieth century.[39]

Hinsley did not restrict his demands for justice and charity to be extended only to the persecuted of Europe. In December 1938, at a meeting of the Royal Empire Society, he expressed his sympathy for the suffering Arabs of Palestine, emphasizing the need for justice, a proper implementation of League of Nations mandates and the unimportance of commercial interests in the face of a humanitarian problem. His words were taken up by anti-Zionist and Jewish groups alike. One side joyfully proclaimed that the Cardinal favoured the Arabs while the other faction was confused by his support both for Jewish refugees and justice for the Palestinian Arabs. And as Jewish demands for a homeland in Palestine increased Hinsley was faced with a political situation more complex than that in Ireland. Inevitably, he was approached by both Arab and Jewish supporters to lend his name to their cause but he had to exercise great caution. To one who tried to enlist his backing for the Arabs, he wrote:

> On the Palestinian question I fear that there is too much complication and excitement to allow me, in my position, to say anything. Every word in such circumstances is torn from its context and twisted to suit the caprice of partisans.[40]

In November 1938 he replied to an appeal from the Jewish Petition Committee for Immigration into Palestine in a similar vein. He would not sign the appeal because of its political character. Yet he would always support humanitarian appeals such as that in February 1939 on behalf of Arab orphans. In mid-1939 he was secretly working with representatives of the government to re-settle Jewish refuges in Latin America. It was an initiative based on the premise that transporting Jews to South American countries would not inflame Arab passions. In June 1939, after receiving a plea from the Bishop of Galilee, he intervened with the Colonial Office on behalf of a Palestinian Arab sentenced to death for terrorist activity. The man's sentence was commuted to life imprisonment.[41]

Fascist movements and anti-Jewish sentiment were not confined to Germany or Italy. Sir Oswald Mosley's British Union of Fascists was particularly strong in Hinsley's own diocese and there were anti-Jewish demonstrations and attacks on Jewish property in the East End of London. The rousing speeches of Mosley and the BUF's attempt to imitate the uniforms, banners and the strong arm tactics of the Nazis caused much unrest in areas where hitherto there had been harmony between the immigrant communities of Catholics and Jews. Hinsley ensured that the BUF would not be as successful as the Nazis by guiding parish priests into publicly denouncing Mosley and his message of hate. The priests then became the object of fascist wrath and were openly scorned in the fascist press. Despite clerical opposition some Catholics were drawn to the BUF and Hinsley was compelled to detach himself from their political opinions and actions. In September 1939, after hostilities with Germany had begun, he wrote to the Commissioner of Police highlighting another dangerous dimension to the problem:

> I have repeatedly dissociated Catholic membership and principles from these anti-Jewish agitators. Moreover, I strongly suspect that there is treasonable activity behind this smoke screen in order to blind simple sincere Catholics. I urge that this matter is taken up by the Police and efforts be made to stop this dangerous propaganda.[42]

During the war the British public eventually became conscious of the horrors of the Nazi concentration camps and the systematic liquidation of the Jews. In 1942 the Polish government in London published a White Book of German atrocities. It reported the murder of 700,000 Polish Jews. Hinsley could scarcely bear to contemplate the news percolating from Europe of the barbaric treatment of the descendants of Christ's own House of Israel. In a BBC broadcast on 8 July he said that 'their innocent blood cries out to the heavens for vengeance.[43]

In 1941 he had written to *The Jewish Chronicle* to assure its readers that 'We cannot forget that in every Mass we speak of "our Father Abraham" thus recognizing that we are *by faith* not anti-Semites but on the contrary we owe a moral debt that we should ever be ready to repay to the race of the Prophets and Apostles of our religion'. Nevertheless, he was anxious to remind the world that Catholics were also in Nazi concentration camps and that persecution was not the prerogative of the Jewish race nor were pogroms restricted to Germany. While he continued to protest against German treatment of Jews he was also mindful that the plight of persecuted Catholics in Germany and across the world should be known.[44] In January 1942 he wrote to *The Times*:

> Whatever can be done to save or to help the victims of Nazi persecution we most urgently support. Multitudes of Christians are among the victims but the Jews are singled out for extermination. Blind racial hate, as Cardinal Faulhaber has repeatedly declared, is the motive of these unparalleled barbarities. As he has said: "Christian love of men of every race is the fundamental commandment of our Lord. We must pray to remain always Christian". That should be the stimulus to action as well as to prayer, and that at once.[45]

In September 1942 *The Jewish Chronicle* gratefully acknowledged the intervention of the Vatican in Berlin and Vichy on behalf of Jews and added 'in the spirit of these profound verities, Cardinal Hinsley's voice has been raised with unexcelled eloquence and power'.[46] His public statements on behalf of the Jews earned him the epithet 'Friend of the Jewish People' from the Nazis and he was proud to own it. His prayerful and vocal support of the Jewish people was evident when he powerfully addressed the World Jewish Congress gathered in Madison Square Gardens, New York, in March 1943:

> In unison with the voice of indignant protest that cries aloud from all human hearts and in accord with the declarations of the Church, I denounce with utmost vigour the persecution of the Jews by the Nazi oppressors. From the most recent reports it is clear that the terrible situation facing the Jews in Europe shows no sign of improvement but is actually more terrible than ever. Words are weak and cold: deeds and speedy deeds are needed to put a stop to this brutal campaign for the extermination of a whole race. Justice must be done and quickly. It is little use uttering tirades against anti-Semitism. Jews and Christians are our fellowmen and brethren. If Christian mercy finds no place in the Nazi breast, then the lesson of stern retribution must be given in such wise that never again shall these hideous wrongs be possible. The blood of the innocent victims of savage hatred cries aloud from the earth to the highest heaven for vengeance. There is the Almighty God above who has said "Vengeance is mine". We are assured that the guilty will suffer in the measure of the cruelty they have perpetrated. Yet this thought gives little consolation to those who are at this moment suffering extreme torture of body and soul from their pitiless persecutors. To all who have the power to help or rescue them we appeal for immediate action. Meantime as individuals we are helpless to aid save by our prayers and by our protestations. . . .

I trust that the great demonstration . . . will stir public opinion the world over so that relief of every possible kind may be quickened to succour the victims of the appalling cruelty of the Nazis and to end the inhuman brutality.[47]

British Jews present at the rally thanked Hinsley for his 'eloquent message' and informed him that over 25,000 people had prayed for his speedy recovery from ill health. From nearer home he also received expressions of gratitude. One Jewish man told the Cardinal that 'you have inspired me and all our Jewish race by the way you have championed our cause. . . . Your true Christian spirit towards us Jews has certainly inspired me by the way you sacrifice and fight for freedom, liberty and justice to our race'. A Jewish woman from Cardiff wrote to Hinsley to tell him that his broadcasts 'have always touched me, especially the broadcasts relating to the enslaved peoples of Europe and my co-religionists. . . .' After listening to his broadcasts, she told him, 'I feel uplifted and look upon life more happily. . . .'[48]

The common antecedents of faith were an added impetus to Christian sympathy for Jewish suffering and Hinsley was not alone among the Hierarchy in his opposition to anti-Semitism. Before Hinsley's appointment to Westminster Archbishop Downey had spoken out against the Nazi treatment of German Jews. Bishop Henshaw of Salford had done the same as had Archbishop Williams. In another demonstration of ecumenical dialogue, Hinsley, Archbishop Temple and the Chief Rabbi were members of the British Council of Christians and Jews which was founded in 1942.[49]

EPILOGUE

Cardinal Hinsley died at the age of 77 on 17 March 1943, St Patrick's Day, fortified by the last rites of the Church he had served all his life. The American *Time* magazine reported that a sign requesting silence had been erected on the road leading past the rambling house at Buntingford where the Cardinal passed his final days following a series of severe heart attacks. United in sympathy, Catholics and the Church of England Synod prayed for his recovery. When news of the Cardinal's not unexpected death was announced there was genuine grief and sadness at the passing of this hard-working, honest, sincere and straight-speaking Yorkshireman who had so evidently touched the lives of many in his Church, in his country and across the world.

Obituaries testified to the huge contribution that Hinsley had made to securing the place of the Catholic Church in the mainstream of British public life. They also illustrated that he had become a figure of national and international stature. His reputation as a formidable and respected churchman was universally acknowledged and his substantial achievements were compared favourably with those of Cardinal Manning. But it was also his personality that had affected people. Hinsley's successor at Westminster, Archbishop Bernard Griffin, said that Hinsley was admired and loved for his deep sincerity, his outstanding courage, his championship of the oppressed nations, and his clear denunciation of persecution, irrespective of creed.[1] Prime Minister Winston Churchill wrote to Bishop Myers, Hinsley's Auxiliary Bishop and Vicar Capitular, to assure the Roman Catholic community of his deep sympathy in the loss of a leader of character and courage, a great patriot and a true lover of justice and freedom.[2] King George VI wrote to his mother, Queen Mary, to express his annoyance when protocol prevented him from attending the Cardinal's funeral at which so many eminent personalities were present:

> No one was more annoyed than I when I was 'advised' not to be represented at Cardinal Hinsley's funeral. I know how much he had done to bring his Church into line with our churches and I was going to see him and thank him personally . . . I feel it was a great chance missed when relations are definitely better.[3]

The British press was fulsome in its praise of the Cardinal's commitment

357

to his faith, the nation's cause, social and religious harmony, and the rights of man. *The Church Times* set the tone:

> Cardinal Hinsley must be numbered among the few men who have become national figures through sheer force of character when already in their seventies. . . . In character as well as in appearance Cardinal Hinsley remained until his life's end a typical Yorkshireman – tall, spare of figure, downright in speech, full of commonsense, uncompromising where principles were concerned but ready to associate as far as possible with non-Roman Christians. . . . The representation of the Archbishop of Canterbury and the presence of other high dignitaries of the English Church at Cardinal Hinsley's funeral seemed so right and proper that few people realised how great a departure from precedent it was. Such a thing has never happened before but then there has never been such an Archbishop of Westminster as Cardinal Hinsley.[4]

The Daily Telegraph stated:

> It should not be invidious to say that no English cardinal since Cardinal Manning has made a deeper impression on his own community and on the national life. His advancement with which he would have willingly dispensed had he not conceived it as his duty to shoulder the burden, was achieved from the humblest of beginnings. . . . No churchman has overcome with more transparent and convincing sincerity the embarrassments with which war necessarily inflicts sincere Christians.[5]

The Times was of the opinion that Hinsley 'without in any way abating his own belief in the significance of doctrine and observance by which his Church is divided from other denominations . . . held strongly that there is a righteousness that can be perceived by all who bear the name of Christians and through his steadfastness and loyalty to all who would extend a hand to him as a fellow soldier for that cause he leaves a happier relation between his communion and the national church than has been known since the Reformation'.[6]

The *Daily Mail* called Hinsley the greatest English cardinal since Wolsey 'and probably the best loved cardinal England has ever had'. It stated that he had 'gained the love and respect of all denominations' and had become 'one of the acknowledged leaders in his country'. The Socialist *Daily Herald* was of the opinion that had Hinsley been a younger man when he arrived at Westminster he would have achieved greater things but 'even as it was he did more in seven years than almost anyone else would have done in fifty'.[7] The Conservative M.P. Cuthbert

Headlam wrote that 'one read his speeches and pronouncements with such admiration and respect'.[8]

The exiled Polish community in London added its own tribute. They received news of Hinsley's death

> with deep and sincere grief. Seldom has the death of a high dignitary of the Church so affected so profoundly the people of a nationality other than his own. Since the day of our arrival in this island we have grown used to looking upon him as a true friend, a champion on whom we could implicitly rely. . . . The Poles will always keep fresh in their minds the memory of the great Prince of the Church. They will take it with them back to their country where it will live forever as the memory not of a stranger but as one of ourselves.[9]

General De Gaulle called him a great figure 'who was a source of inspiration for the entire Catholic world, and particularly for Fighting France which he honoured with his friendship'.[10]

Meanwhile the Nazis disclaimed Hinsley's attacks on them and their Führer and denounced him as a friend of Bolshevism: 'Cardinal Hinsley, like the Archbishop of Canterbury, regarded it as his supreme aim to further the spread of Bolshevism. As is well known, he recently issued a Pastoral Letter asking for daily prayers for the Soviets. Hinsley acquired world-wide notoriety for his violent hatred of the Germans and for his campaigning for Bolshevism'. The Holy See was not prepared to let German attacks on the dead Cardinal go unanswered. On 22 March Vatican Radio pronounced that:

> Cardinal Hinsley spoke for Russia and for the Russian people but not for Bolshevism. In doing so he based himself on the opinion expressed in Pius XII's customary prayer after Holy Mass. This concerns inner peace and religious freedom for the Russian people. . . . During the last few years of his life the fate of the suffering nations, particularly of Poland, greatly touched Cardinal Hinsley. In a number of utterances this high prelate of the Church energetically took the part of those persecuted and deprived of their rights because of their nationality or origin. He thus acted as an advocate and defender of the rights of men so little respected today.[11]

The Sunday Times reported that 'The German Radio has followed him with calumnies after death and it is not surprising for he was their formidable foe in life. He was formidable because he vibrated with a love of justice and a hatred of iniquity'.[12]

Many others added their tributes to a man who had only recently come among them yet had made such a profound impression. Archbishop Temple of Canterbury recalled that the Cardinal was eager to co-operate with other Christians and had nobly served the cause of Christian witness. 'All whose aspirations are set upon a Christian Britain mourn his loss', he said; 'many of us also mourn a most kindly and warm hearted friend'.[13] Rab Butler, President of the Board of Education and architect of the 1944 Education Act, had frequently come into contact with Hinsley and other members of the Hierarchy during the protracted and rancorous negotiations over the provisions of the Act. Following the Cardinal's death he wrote that although it would be wrong to say that had Cardinal Hinsley lived he would have obtained a different settlement for Catholic schools, he was convinced that the dignity of the other bishops could never equal Hinsley's.[14] Bishop Bell of Chichester, Hinsley's Anglican partner in wartime ecumenical collaboration, called him saintly and liberal-minded but not all Bell's co-religionists shared these sentiments.[15] Hedley Henson, the former Anglican Bishop of Durham, claimed that Hinsley was presumptuous in claiming that the Catholic Church alone was the champion of the Christian conscience and bulwark of Christian liberty. But contemporary leaders of the established church were dwarfed by Hinsley's forceful personality and Henson angrily questioned why the Church of England seemed to fade in the presence of the Cardinal's pontifical dogmatism and why ancient Canterbury yielded to modern Westminster.[16] But when looking for a successor to the late Archbishop Lang of Canterbury, Prime Minister Churchill is reputed to have said: 'Why can't we have the old man at Westminster?'[17]

Catholics also acclaimed Hinsley's episcopate, with some suggesting a much more complex character beneath a straightforward public persona. Evelyn Waugh claimed that following the long period of Bourne's dominance Hinsley's appointment was a refreshing tonic to English Catholics inside and outside the Diocese of Westminster.[18] Mgr Val Elwes, Hinsley's secretary and confessor, wrote that Hinsley's impetuosity and impatience underlying the outward calm was an understandable attitude for an old man with still much to accomplish.[19] David Mathew, Hinsley's Auxiliary Bishop in Westminster, wrote of the Cardinal's personal devotion to the papacy and the Pope but hinted at another, perhaps surprising, facet of his personality when he recalled that he was not drawn to the *majesty* of the Holy See.[20] Douglas Newton observed that Hinsley, a tall man of imposing physique, managed to mingle dignity and gentleness with impulsiveness and native shrewdness. In his faith and friendship, Newton wrote, Hinsley was the humblest of men, yet on principles he was unyielding. He hid a deep spirituality and sound learning under a fatherly simplicity.[21] Clifford Longley wrote that Hinsley was neither authoritarian nor remote and his approachable style made him popular, but when necessary he could be unyielding and outspoken.[22] To Adrian Hastings, Hinsley was a man of the people who had reached the top in old age. Of a naturally warm and fatherly disposition, he was a priest who had outgrown ecclesiastical fears and ambition and had come to see that Church windows needed to be opened, that the laity could be trusted, and that Christians of other traditions could be welcomed as brothers.[23]

From an insider's perspective, Bishop Brown of Pella offered a more practical judgement. He recalled that Hinsley was a man of strong impulses and emotional temperament which led him to initiate activities with great energy. Sadly, the Bishop continued, Hinsley's major weakness was that he was unable to sustain interest and momentum. In some things, he wrote, the Cardinal lacked 'determined and persistent application'. He conceded that Hinsley had reached a wide audience due to the war but, like others, doubted that Hinsley would have become such a notable figure without such an opportunity.[24] Bishop Mathew expressed the opinion that Hinsley's personality was his major weakness in a job that demanded so much more than a generous and understanding nature. Hinsley, wrote Mathew, could be impetuous and stern yet he was a very humble bishop who was unsparing of his time for his clergy. 'It may be held', he concluded, 'that this personal quality, which was invaluable as Rector of the English College and had its merits for certain aspects of his work in Africa, was a disadvantage in the administration, late in life, of a large archdiocese'.[25] Nevertheless, Bishop McNulty of Nottingham wrote that Catholics and non-Catholics, who saw Hinsley from a different vantage point, revered the late Cardinal 'as a national figure and a most loyal son of his King and country as he was of God's Vicar on earth who bestowed on him that princely dignity which he carried so worthily'. His reign as Archbishop, he concluded, 'has been short but abundantly fruitful and we may take a just pride in his memory and draw consolation in our sorrow from the confidence that he will speedily receive the reward of the Good and faithful Servant of His Lord and Master'.[26]

However fulsome and sincere these tributes and comments may have been, contemporaries in England and Rome tended to assess Hinsley's career only in the context of his time at Westminster or in Africa and to a large extent modern historians have adopted this approach. But an assessment based on these two periods, however important they may have been, does not do full justice to Hinsley's other achievements. Nearly 70 years after his death and with a wider range of evidence available, it is now possible to arrive at a more balanced judgement of Hinsley and what emerges is the picture of a priest who succeeded despite the odds usually being stacked against him. Only with the financial support of others was he able to go to Ushaw to study for the priesthood where he achieved high academic success. In Rome he studied in appalling conditions and under the eye of a rector who though able and affable was hardly a leader of men. He returned to Ushaw as an enthusiastic and conscientious minor professor but laboured in a theologically conservative seminary. His limited success as a headmaster was the more remarkable given the financial and personal difficulties which beset him and his governors. His twelve years on the mission in Southwark, however, were more successful. They enabled him to gain valuable pastoral experience whilst simultaneously allowing him to lecture at the diocesan seminary and gain the respect of Bishop Amigo while representing the interests of the Southwark Diocese in Rome. There he was drawn to the beneficial attention of Abbot Gasquet. He was appointed to the *Venerabile* in the face of episcopal opposition but managed to rescue the college's fortunes. In the teeth of missionary nationalism and self-interest he initiated educational reforms in British colonial Africa and set in motion the building of structures which facilitated the future development of the African Church.

In Westminster he consolidated on Cardinal Bourne's achievements whilst introducing reforms in diocesan organisation and, as Bishop Mathew commented, brought a much more fatherly approach to his priests without seeking to control them. He sought to extend lay participation in social and economic affairs through Catholic Action, he approached other Christian denominations through the Sword of the Spirit, and in time of war he reached out to his own countrymen and other nations through his confident use of the radio. Though his methods were never free from fault, he persisted in his attempts to bring unity to a Hierarchy long accustomed to diocesan independence. His frustration occasionally surfaced as it did in May 1940 when he told Bishop Doubleday that since his 'most unhappy arrival in Westminster' he had done his 'utmost' to improve communication and collaboration between the bishops but his efforts had met with little success.[27] His outspokenness, openness, and blunt and impulsive nature did not always endear him to his episcopal brethren and, according to Bishop Mathew, Hinsley had no real confidants among the Hierarchy.[28] Their approach to problems and to institutional and social structures, tempered by years of struggle and suspicion, did not easily match his.

On the day of Hinsley's Requiem Mass Bishop Myers wrote to the priests of the Westminster Diocese:

> We have all been deeply moved by the universal expression of esteem and affection for the late Cardinal, which found a fitting climax in today's wonderful ceremony at the cathedral. And while we rejoice in this stirring testimony to Cardinal Hinsley as bishop, statesman and patriot, we shall not forget our privilege and duty of Masses and prayers for the repose of his soul. Nor shall we forget to remind our people of this last duty of affection for a great Christian leader.
>
> As I write under the impression of the beautiful Requiem Mass, it is not possible to do justice to the Cardinal's outstanding qualities in a few words. He won the hearts of all by his inner holiness of life, by his simplicity, and by his warm-hearted love for his clergy, his people and their children. All who came into contact with him – and he was eminently accessible – felt the deep impact of a life dedicated with entire and self-effacement and humility to Christ Our Lord. His firm grasp of Christian principles led to his being heralded as a statesman of outstanding merit in these troubled days, and while he was prepared to champion any oppressed people with a mighty zeal and effectiveness, everyone realised he was a great English patriot. He loved his country devotedly, and believed that the spirit of her people, informed by Christian principles, was needed to lead the world into the paths of fairness, justice and freedom. His words rang through Europe and the New World and everywhere men caught the authentic notes of authority and sincerity. England is the poorer for his passing, and the race of men has lost a champion of freedom.
>
> But when that is said, we in this diocese mourn the loss of a friend of deep personal holiness, of an Archbishop of clear vision and power, and a zealous defender of the faith.[29]

In his Last Will and Testament Hinsley asked for the pardon of those whom he may have wronged and forgave those who had injured him.

'As to my funeral', he wrote, 'I desire as little pomp as possible. Let there be a Low Mass of Requiem and the least possible expense. Bury my body wherever most convenient. My Brother and Sister are buried at Kensal Green'.[30] But Hinsley was a Cardinal of the Catholic Church and the obsequies, as he would have known, were scrupulously observed. Following his Requiem Mass he was buried in St Joseph's Chapel in Westminster Cathedral. Inside his coffin was the *Rogito*, or outline of his life, which condensed into one page of Latin prose the story of a man who had given so much to his Church, his country and his fellow men and women. According to custom, his cardinal's red hat or *galero* was suspended above his coffin.[31]

NOTES

Introduction

1. See McReavy, 'Patriotism' in *The Clergy Review*, Aug. 1942, pp. 337-341. Pope Leo XIII issued two encyclicals relating to the origin of civil authority and the Christian's duty to the state: *Diuturnum illud* (1881) and *Immortale Dei* (1885).
2. In addition to McReavy see Farrell and Healy, *My Way of Life: The Summa Simplified for Everyone*, pp. 397-405.
3. Kensit, *The War and the Papacy: Mr. Kensit's Open Letter to Cardinal Hinsley*.
4. Beck, 'Cardinal Hinsley: A Memoir' in *The Clergy Review*, May 1944. The Augustinian George Andrew Beck became Coadjutor Bishop of Brentwood in 1948, Bishop of Brentwood in 1951, Bishop of Salford in 1955 and Archbishop of Liverpool in 1964.

Chapter One *From Boyhood to Priesthood 1865-1900*

1. Page (ed.), *The Victoria History of the County of York*, vol iii, p. 527.
2. Kaye (ed.), *The Parish Registers of Carlton-Juxta-Snaith 1598-1812*, pp. 88, 97, 99, 138. The name 'Hinsley' appears in 1797.
3. St Mary's Church, Carlton, *Parish Register*; Bellenger and Fletcher, *Princes of the Church: A History of the English Cardinals*, p. 154. On an index card among Hinsley's papers at the Venerable English College, Hinsley recorded that his father was born on 2 Aug. 1835. AVEC, Scritt. 86.3.
4. Heenan, *Cardinal Hinsley*, pp. 50-51.
5. Census Enumerators' Returns (1871), Carlton-juxta-Snaith.
6. Bence-Jones, *The Catholic Families*, (London, 1992), pp. 217-221; *Guide to Carlton Towers The Yorkshire Home of the Duke of Norfolk*.
7. Kenyon, *The Popish Plot*, pp. 226, 230, 246.
8. Heptonstall, *St Mary's, Carlton* (1875).
9. Hagerty, 'The Roman Diary of George Heptonstall' in *The Venerabile* (2004-2005), pp. 1-12.
10. The term *Venerabile* is derived from the college's full title: *Venerabile Collegium Anglorum de Urbe*. The college had been established in the sixteenth century to provide Catholic priests during penal times. St Mary's Church, Carlton, *Parish Register*.
11. Heenan, *Cardinal Hinsley*, p. 38.
12. Hinsley to Shattock, 11 Jan. 1938. I am grateful to Dr Mark Goldie for this reference.
13. Heenan, *Cardinal Hinsley*, p. 50.
14. Norman, *The English Catholic Church in the Nineteenth Century*, pp. 179-181, 287-301. See also Evenett, 'Catholics and the Universities' in Beck (ed.), *The English Catholics 1850-1950*, pp. 291-312.

15. Doyle, 'The Education and Training of Roman Catholic Priests in Nineteenth Century England' in *Journal of Ecclesiastical History*, vol. 35, no. 2, (April 1984), pp. 208-219.

16. Milburn, *A History of Ushaw College*, pp. 283 ff.

17. Milburn, *A History of Ushaw College*, pp. 284-302; An Old Alumnus, *Records and Recollections of St Cuthbert's College, Ushaw*, pp. 296-297, 332.

18. St Cuthbert's College, Ushaw, *Student Registers*.

19. Milburn, *A History of Ushaw College*, pp. 134-138, 144, 217-219, 290.

20. I am grateful to Fr Michael Sharratt of St Cuthbert's College, Ushaw, for this information.

21. LDA, St Cuthbert's College, Ushaw, file. See also Hagerty, 'Hinsley at Ushaw' in *Northern Catholic History*, no. 23, Spring 1986, pp. 27-34; and Bonney, 'Hinsley at Ushaw' in *Ushaw Magazine* (July 1898), pp. 34-37.

22. Wrennell to Cornthwaite, Nov. 1883, LDA, St Cuthbert's College, Ushaw File.

23. Bradley, 'The Leeds Seminary – An Experiment in Clerical Education' in Finnigan and Bradley (eds), *Catholicism in Leeds: A Community of Faith 1794-1994*, pp. 57-70.

24. St Cuthbert's College, Ushaw, MSS.

25. Forbes, *Rafael, Cardinal Merry del Val*, pp. 20-21.

26. St Cuthbert's College, Ushaw, MSS.

27. For details on the contemporary English College see Williams, *The Venerable English College*.

28. Hagerty, 'The Roman Diary of George Heptonstall' in *The Venerabile* (2004-2005), pp. 1-12.

29. Heenan, *Cardinal Hinsley*, pp. 29-30, 37.

30. Newton, *Dictionary of National Biography 1941-1950*, pp. 394-395.

31. *Ushaw Magazine*, (Dec. 1894), p. 374.

32. *Ushaw Magazine*, (March 1896), p. 86.

33. For a full analysis of the Modernist controversy see Reardon (ed.), *Roman Catholic Modernism*.

34. Quoted in Williams, *The Venerable English College*, p. 170.

35. For Gasquet's impressions of Hinsley's contribution see Leslie, *Cardinal Gasquet*, p. 197.

36. Leahy to Heenan, 10 April 1944, BDA, F3.

37. *Yorkshire Post*, 26 March 1935.

38. Dix, 'Memories of 1880-1886' in *Ushaw Magazine* (March 1950), pp. 5-11.

39. *Ushaw Magazine*, (Dec. 1898), pp. 290-291; Bonney, 'Hinsley at Ushaw' in *Ushaw Magazine* (July 1898), p. 35.

40. Heenan, *Cardinal Hinsley*, pp. 38-39.

41. Quoted by Bonney, 'Hinsley at Ushaw' in *Ushaw Magazine* (July 1898), p. 35.

42. Heenan, *Cardinal Hinsley*, p.40; *Ushaw Magazine*, (Dec. 1898), p. 290.

43. Berry, *Keighley Catholic Church 1835-1985*, pp. 16-19.

Chapter Two *The Headmaster 1900-1904*

1. Firth, *A History of Bradford*, p. 81.
2. Firth, *A History of Bradford*, chapter 7.
3. Firth, *A History of Bradford*, p. 106.
4. Jowitt, 'The Pattern of Religion in Victorian Bradford' in Wright and Jowitt, *Victorian Bradford*, pp. 43, 51.
5. Hagerty, *Bradford's Catholic Churches and Parishes 1825-1997*.
6. LDA, *Acta of the Diocese of Leeds*, Educational Statistics 1878-1900. The terms higher grade and middle class referred to educational rather than social divisions.
7. Hagerty, 'A New Century, A New School: St Bede's Grammar School, Bradford' in *Northern Catholic History*, no. 41, 2000, p. 61; *Catholic Directory* (1870 to 1900); LDA, *Acta of the Diocese of Leeds*, Educational Statistics 1878-1900.
8. See Bradley, 'Bishop Gordon' in Finnigan and Hagerty (eds), *The Bishops of Leeds 1878-1985: Essays in Honour of Bishop David Konstant*, pp. 65-69.
9. Earnshaw, *The Record and Reminiscences of St Patrick's Church, Bradford*, p. 207.
10. *Bradford Daily Telegraph,* 20 Jan. 1900.
11. Governors of St Bede's Grammar School, *Minute Books.*
12. *Yorkshire Observer,* 21 May 1900.
13. Governors of St. Bede's Grammar School, *Minute Books.*
14. Earnshaw, *Record and Reminiscences,* pp. 194-195.
15. Battersby, 'Secondary Education for Boys' in Beck (ed.), *The English Catholics 1850-1950*, pp. 322-336.
16. *The Tablet*, 4 Aug. 1900.
17. St Bede's Grammar School, *Trust Deed.*
18. Heenan*, Cardinal Hinsley,* p. 28.
19. Governors of St Bede's Grammar School, *Minute Books.*
20. St Bede's Grammar School, *Annual Reports* (1902-1903, 1904-1905).
21. City of Bradford Education Committee, *Co-ordination Report* (1905), p. 35.
22. LDA, *Acta of the Diocese of Leeds*, Educational Statistics 1903.
23. St Bede's Grammar School, *Admission Registers*; *Souvenir of the New School 1939* and *Golden Jubilee 1900-1950.*
24. Brown, *Through Windows of Memory*, p. 96.
25. *Report of the Seventh Annual Conference of Catholic Colleges (*1902), pp. 21-37.
26. *Report of the Eighth Annual Conference of Catholic Colleges* (1903), pp. 53, 59; *Report of the Ninth Annual Conference of Catholic Colleges* (1904), pp. 18, 31-32.
27. Governors of St Bede's Grammar School, *Minute Books.*
28. *The Tablet,* 9 Jan. 1904. When Cardinal Francis Bourne visited Bradford in 1925, he described the achievements in Catholic secondary education in the city as a 'constant source of encouragement'. 'The work which had been

accomplished so successfully', he said, 'had been almost totally the work of the laity'. See *The Tablet*, 20 June 1925.

29. Heenan, *Cardinal Hinsley*, p. 28.
30. Clarkson to Hughes, 6 June 1950, St Bede's Grammar School Archives.
31. Heenan, *Cardinal Hinsley*, p. 29.
32. Heenan, *Cardinal Hinsley*, pp. 28-29.
33. Heenan, *Cardinal Hinsley*, p. 28
34. St Bede's Grammar School, *Souvenir of the New School 1939.*
35. Governors of St Bede's Grammar School, *Minute Books.*
36. Hagerty, 'The Headmaster Who Became A Cardinal' in Bradley (ed.), *Yorkshire Catholics*, pp. 66-73; St Bede's Grammar School, *Souvenir of the New School 1939.*

Chapter Three *On The Mission 1904-1917*

1. Clarkson to Hughes, 6 June 1950. St Bede's Grammar School Archive. In the *Catholic Directory 1905*, p. 395, Hinsley is described as being 'on sick leave'.
2. Hinsley first appears as a priest of the Southwark Diocese in the *Catholic Directory 1906*, pp. 312, 403.
3. Taylor (ed.), *The Catholics Of Sutton Park*, p. 70.
4. Brown, *Through Windows of Memory*, p. 96.
5. Gaine, 'Hinsley, Arthur (1865-1943), Roman Catholic Archbishop of Westminster' in *Oxford Dictionary of National Biography*; *Catholic Directory 1906*, p. 312.
6. Taylor, *The Catholics Of Sutton Park*, p. 118.
7. Taylor, *The Catholics Of Sutton Park*, p. 179.
8. Brown, *Through Windows of Memory*, pp. 96-97.
9. Taylor, *The Catholics Of Sutton Park*, p. 70.
10. Brown, *Through Windows of Memory*, p. 97.
11. Taylor, *The Catholics Of Sutton Park,* pp. 70-71; Brown, *Through Windows of Memory*, p. 97.
12. Kieran-Hyland, 'Arthur Hinsley – Parish Priest' in *The Venerabile,* vol. xiii, no. 1, 1946, pp. 25-28.
13. Taylor, *The Catholics of Sutton Park*, p. 71.
14. Brown, *Through Windows of Memory*, p. 97.
15. McKeown, *A Beacon of Hope: A History of Sydenham Parish*, pp. 16-17.
16. McKeown, *A Beacon of Hope*, pp. 18, 47-50.
17. McKeown, *A Beacon of Hope*, p. 19.
18. Leahy to Heenan, 10 April 1944. BDA, Heenan Papers.
19. The dispute is dealt with in Clifton, *Amigo – Friend of The Poor*, pp. 42-45.
20. Gasquet to Amigo, 14 June 1914. DAA, Gasquet Papers, P 3805, vii, A.3.F. Boundary disputes between Bourne and the other bishops continued well into the next decade. Bishop McIntyre, the Rector of the Venerable English College, Rome, warned Bishop Ilsley of Birmingham that when in Rome

Bourne was arguing for a division of the Birmingham Archdiocese. McIntyre referred to 'our Westminster friend . . . a diabolical twister'. McIntyre to Ilsley, 6 Feb 1917. ABA, McIntyre Papers, D3742.

21. Williams, *The Venerable English College, Rome*, p. 151. Dom Aidan Gasquet was close to Cardinal Herbert Vaughan and had, like Merry del Val, been tipped to succeed Vaughan as Archbishop of Westminster. Gasquet had been created a cardinal in 1914 and became very influential in the Roman Curia. See Bellenger, 'Cardinal Gasquet (1846-1929): An English Roman', in *Recusant History*, vol. 24, no. 4, Oct 1999, pp. 552-560.

22. Williams, *The Venerable English College*, p. 153; Heenan, *Cardinal Hinsley*, pp. 29-30.

23. Ilsley to Vannutelli, n.d. 1913, ABA, D 3049; Ilsley to Hierarchy, 13 Dec. 1913, ABA, Ilsley Papers, D 3055; Ilsley to de Lai, 16 Dec. 1913, ABA, Ilsley Papers, D 3067. See also McInally, *Edward Ilsley: Archbishop of Birmingham*, pp. 331-333.

24. Amigo to Gasquet, 3 June 1917. DAA, Gasquet Papers, 917A.

25. Bird to Heenan, 17 March 1944. BDA, Heenan Papers.

26. O'Keefe to Rope, 10 Oct. 1915, in *The Venerabile* (Winter, 1965), vol. xxiii, no. 3, p. 185.

27. Williams, *The Venerable English College*, p. 151.

28. McIntyre to O'Toole, 20 May 1916. AVEC, Scritt. 84:12. Canon O'Toole of St Joseph's, Birkenhead, was Treasurer of the Roman Association, the association of former students of the English College.

29. O'Toole to Gasquet, n.d. 1916. AVEC, Scritt. 84:12.

30. Gasquet, Diary, 5 Oct. 1917. DAA, Gasquet Papers.

31. Gasquet to English and Welsh Bishops, 26 Feb. 1917. DAA, Gasquet Papers; Williams, *The Venerable English College*, pp. 151-153. Pope Benedict XV transferred responsibilities for seminaries from Consistorial to the Congregation of Seminaries in 1915.

32. Williams, *The Venerable English College*, pp. 151-152.

33. *Acta* of the Annual Meeting of the Bishops, 17 April 1917. ALA, Whiteside Papers, S1/VII B/1.

34. O'Connor to Dunn, 13 April 1917. NDA, Dunn Papers, G – 01.

35. Amigo to Gasquet, 21 June 1917. DAA, Gasquet Papers.

36. McIntyre to Gasquet, 27 Aug. 1917. DAA, Gasquet Papers.

37. Gasquet, Diary, 5 Oct. 1917. DAA, Gasquet Papers.

38. Amigo to Gasquet, 20 July 1917. DAA, Gasquet Papers.

39. Cardinal Bourne to the Bishops, 6 Sept. 1916. AAW, Bo 1/16.

40. Amigo to Gasquet, 12 Sept. 1917. DAA, Gasquet Papers.

41. Whiteside to Singleton, 22 Sept. 1917. DSA, Singleton Papers.

42. Amigo to Gasquet, 25 Sept. 1917. DAA, Gasquet Papers.

43. Bourne to Gasquet, 26 Sept. 1917. DAA, Gasquet Papers.

44. *Catholic Directory 1917*; FitzGerald–Lombard, *English and Welsh Priests 1801-1914*, pp. 55, 87, 107.

45. Whiteside to Gasquet, 24 Sept 1917; Cotter to Gasquet, 3 Oct. 1917; Singleton to Gasquet, 10 Oct. 1917. DAA, Gasquet Papers.

46. Gasquet to Amigo, 18 Oct. 1917. DAA, Gasquet Papers.

47. The Vatican informed Gasquet on 30 October 1917 of Hinsley's appointment to the *Venerabile*; see Gasquet, Diary, 30 Oct. 1917. DAA, Gasquet Papers. See also Hinsley to Gasquet, 8 Nov. 1917. DAA, Gasquet Papers; Williams, The Venerable English College, p. 153.

48. Williams, *The Venerable English College*, p. 153; Heenan, *Cardinal Hinsley*, p. 28. Heenan commented that the appointment of that new Rector to the English College 'was a minor affair not only to the Roman authorities but even to the English Bishops'. The correspondence does not bear out the validity of this statement.

49. Singleton to Whiteside, 11 Nov. 1917. ALA, Early Bishops' Correspondence, S2vA/42.

50. Amigo to Ilsley, 7 Jan. 1917. ABA, Ilsley Papers, AD3721. For the dispute over the appointment of the Episcopus Castrensis see Johnstone and Hagerty, *The Cross On The Sword: Catholic Chaplains in the Forces*, chapter 14.

51. Casartelli to Gasquet, 10 Nov. 1917. DAA, Gasquet Papers, 889.

52. Ilsley to Cardinal de Lai, 13 May 1917. ABA, D3380.

53. Sheehan to Gasquet, 20 June 1916. DAA, Gasquet Papers, 888.

54. Amigo to Gasquet, 21 June 1917. DAA, Gasquet Papers, 888.

55. Cambourne to Heenan, 14 March 1944. BDA, Heenan Papers.

56. Hinsley to Gasquet, 8 Nov. 1917. DAA, Gasquet Papers.

57. Amigo to Gasquet, 26 Nov. 1917. DAA, Gasquet Papers, 917A.

58. Williams, *The Venerable English College*, p. 154.

59. AVEC, Scritt. 86.2

60. *Ushaw Magazine* (Dec. 1918), p. 251.

61. *The Tablet*, 1 Dec. 1917.

62. Roughneen to O'Riordan, 22 Nov. 1917. PICA, O'Riordan Papers.

Chapter Four *The Rector 1917-1930*

1. AVEC, Membranae 436. Gasquet had requested this honour from the Pope on 31 October 1917, the day after Hinsley's appointment to the *Venerabile*. Gasquet Diary, 31 Oct. 1917. DAA, Gasquet Papers, 902.

2. Meagher, 'Early Years As Rector of the English College' in *The Ushaw Magazine*, July 1943, pp. 37-38. Meagher contributed to a collection of commemorative articles on Hinsley.

3. Gasquet to Amigo, 27 Nov. 1917. DAA, Gasquet Papers, 902. See also Rolls, 'A Troubled Transition – The Roman Association and the English College, 1913-1922', in *The Venerabile*, vol. xxix, no. 2, 1988, pp. 59-63.

4. Gasquet to Amigo, 6 Dec. 1917. DAA, Gasquet Papers, 3805.

5. Gasquet to Amigo, 24 Dec. 1917. DAA, Gasquet Papers, 3805.

6. *The Tablet*, 22 Feb. 1919.

7.	Smith, 'Cardinal Hinsley: An Appreciation', in *The Venerabile*, vol. xi, no. 2, May 1943, p. 106.

8.	Quoted in Williams, *The Venerable English College*, p. 153. San Calisto was Gasquet's Roman residence.

9.	Amigo to Gasquet, 12 Dec. 1917. DAA, Gasquet Papers, 917A.

10.	Williams, *The Venerable English College*, pp. 154-155.

11.	O'Toole to Singleton, 22 Sept. 1917. SDA, Singleton Papers.

12.	Ward to Gasquet, 1 July 1918. DAA, Gasquet Papers, 889.

13.	*Acta* of the English and Welsh Bishops, 9 April 1918. ALA, Whiteside Papers, S1/VII B/1.

14.	Gasquet Diary, 30 Dec. 1918. DAA, Gasquet Papers, 902. Amigo to Gasquet, 27 April 1918, DAA, Gasquet Papers, 917A. Williams, *The Venerable English College*, pp. 154-155.

15.	Gasquet Diary, 28 Dec. 1918, 30 Dec. 1918, 16 March 1919, 18 March 1919, 21 March 1919. DAA, Gasquet Papers, 902.

16.	*The Rector's Annual Report on the English College, Rome* (1918-1919), ABA, Ilsley Papers.

17.	Williams, *The Venerable English College*, p.155; Hinsley to Gasquet, 4 April 1918. DAA, Gasquet Papers. The Congregation of Seminaries was not too happy with the introduction of the nuns but the practice was later copied by other houses of study. See 'Some Reminiscences given by Bishop Edward Ellis of Nottingham to R. Ashton and A. Laird, during the Fourth Session of Vatican II' (n.d.). AVEC, Scritt. 86.2.

18.	Domira de Zolfi, 'Nova et Vetera' in *The Venerabile*, vol. xxiii, no. 1, Summer 1968, pp. 188-190.

19.	Hinsley to Gasquet, 2 July 1918. DAA, Gasquet Papers. AVEC, Libre 619, *Consiglio di Administrazione del Venerabile Collegio Inglese*, (1918).

20.	Hinsley to Gasquet, 5 Aug. 1918. DAA, Gasquet Papers.

21.	Hinsley to Gasquet, 16 Sep. 1918. DAA, Gasquet Papers.

22.	Hinsley to Gasquet, 6 Nov. 1918. DAA, Gasquet Papers.

23.	Williams, *The Venerable English College*, p. 156.

24.	Hinsley to Ward, 21 Dec. 1919. BDA, Ward Papers.

25.	*The Universe*, 22 Jan. 1926; *The Times*, 11 Feb. and 27 Feb. 1926.

26.	Hinsley to Doubleday, 31 March 19126. BDA, K2, *Venerabile.*

27.	Hinsley to McIntyre, 8 Jan. 1926. ABA, McIntyre Papers, D5540.

28.	Hinsley to McIntyre, 7 July 1927. ABA, McIntyre Papers, D5547.

29.	Williams, *The Venerable English College*, p. 156; *The Universe*, 20 Aug. 1926.

30.	Gasquet Diary, 26 April 1917. DAA, Gasquet Papers, 902. Hinsley to Gasquet, 18 Nov. 1918. DAA, Gasquet Papers. I am grateful to Fr Nicholas Schofield for information on the sale of Monte Porzio.

31.	Hinsley to Gasquet, 29 March 1920. DAA, Gasquet Papers.

32.	*A Short History of Palazzola*, p. 19. I am very grateful to Fr Nicholas Schofield for information on the purchase of Palazzola.

33.	Hinsley to Gasquet, 28 April 1918. DAA, Gasquet Papers.

34. Hinsley to Gasquet, 27 July 1919. DAA, Gasquet Papers.
35. Hinsley to Gasquet, 6 Aug. 1920. DAA, Gasquet Papers. *The Rector's Annual Report on the English College, Rome* (1919-1920). DAA, Gasquet Papers.
36. *The Rector's Annual Report(s) on the English College, Rome* (1922-1923) and (1927-1928). DAA, Gasquet Papers.
37. *Acta* of the English and Welsh Bishops, 29 April 1919. ALA, Whiteside Papers, S1/VII B/1.
38. Bourne to Hinsley, 4 May 1919. AVEC, Scritt. 86.4
39. Bourne to Hinsley, 1 May 1924 and 30 April 1927. AVEC, Scritt. 86.4.
40. Williams, *The Venerable English College*, p. 157. For a student view of life under Hinsley see Smith, 'One Man in His Time . . . Memories of a Monsignore', TLP, pp. 11-83.
41. Smith, 'Cardinal Hinsley: An Appreciation', in *The Venerabile*, vol. xi, no. 2, May 1943, p. 111.
42. Hinsley to Gasquet, 6 Aug. 1920. DAA, Gasquet Papers.
43. Hinsley to Gasquet, 17 April 1923. DAA, Gasquet Papers.
44. Williams, *The Venerable English College*, pp. 158-159.
45. Casartelli to Gasquet, 24 Sept. 1923. DAA, Gasquet Papers.
46. Hinsley to Whiteside, 12 April 1918. ALA, Early Bishops' Collection, Series 2, S2 II H/40.
47. Hinsley to Whiteside, 12 April 1918. ALA, Early Bishops' Collection, Series 2, S2 II H/41-44.
48. Ward to Hinsley, 28 April 1919. BDA, Ward Papers.
49. Hinsley to Ward, 3 May 1919. BDA, Ward Papers.
50. Ward to Hinsley, 28 April 1919. BDA, Ward Papers.
51. Hinsley to Ward, 3 May 1919. BDA, Ward Papers.
52. Hinsley to Ward, 16 May 1919. BDA, Ward Papers.
53. Ward to Hinsley, 13 June 1919. BDA, Ward Papers.
54. Hinsley to Fr Wareing, n.d., (1921). AWA, Hi 45.
55. *The Tablet*, 25 Feb. 1922; Hachey, *Anglo-Vatican Relations*, p. xxvii.
56. *The Tablet*, 29 Aug. 1924.
57. de Wiel, *The Catholic Church in Ireland 1914-1918*, pp. 261-289.
58. Hachey, *Anglo-Vatican Relations*, p. 23. The diplomat James Rennell Rodd reported that 'certain members of the Irish College made no secret of their open hostility to the Allies'. See Rennell Rodd, *Social and Diplomatic Memories, 1902-1919*, pp. 214-215.
59. Hagan to Hinsley, 17 Dec. 1918. PICA, Hagan Papers.
60. Hagan to Hinsley, 26 Dec. 1920. PICA, Hagan Papers.
61. Hachey, *Anglo-Vatican Relations*, p. 25.
62. *The Venerabile*, vol. i, no. 1, 1922, p. 76.
63. Hachey, *Anglo-Vatican Relations*, p. 25.
64. Browne to Hagan, 2 Dec. 1926. PICA, Hagan Papers.
65. 'Some Reminiscences given by Bishop Edward Ellis of Nottingham to R. Ashton and A. Laird, during the Fourth Session of Vatican II', n.d., AVEC,

Scritt. 86.2

66.   Smith, 'Cardinal Hinsley: An Appreciation', in *The Venerabile*, vol. xi, no. 2, May 1943, p. 105.

67.   Hinsley to Ward, 26 Oct. 1919. BDA, K2, *Venerabile*.

68.   See Rolls, 'A Troubled Transition – The Roman Association and the English College, 1913-1922', in *The Venerabile*, vol. xxix, no. 2, 1988, pp. 59-63.

69.   See Heenan, *Cardinal Hinsley*, pp. 32-36; Heenan, *Not The Whole Truth*, pp. 52-54.

70.   Moloney, *Westminster, Whitehall and the Vatican*, p. 21.

71.   Smith, 'Cardinal Hinsley: An Appreciation', in *The Venerabile*, vol. xi, no. 2, May 1943, p. 105. See also Smith, 'One Man in His Time . . . Memories of a Monsignore', TLP, pp. 255-258.

72.   MacMillan, 'Cardinal Hinsley' in *The Venerabile*, vol. xi, May 1943, p. 104.

73.   *The Tablet*, 27 March 1943.

74.   Williams, *The Venerable English College*, pp. 157-158.

75.   *The Tablet*, 13 Feb. 1926.

76.   Hinsley to Doubleday, 15 July 1927. BDA, K2, *Venerabile*.

77.   Williams, *The Venerable English College*, p. 161.

78.   For biographical details of these bishops see Plumb, *Arundel to Zabi*.

79.   Williams, *The Venerable English College*, p. 161.

80.   *The Venerabile*, vol. i, no.1, pp. 80-81.

81.   Leslie, *Cardinal Gasquet*, p. 257. Hinsley's name had been mentioned for the vacant see of Hexham and Newcastle in 1924 but it was decided that it would better for him to remain at the *Venerabile* until his work was complete. See Williams, *The Venerable English College*, p. 161.

82.   AVEC, Membranae M437, 26 Nov. 1926; Plumb, *Arundel to Zabi*.

83.   *The Venerabile*, vol. iii, no. 2, April 1927, p. 105.

84.   *The Tablet*, 21 and 28 Aug. 1926.

85.   Smith, 'The Rector's Consecration' in *The Venerabile*, vol. iii, no. 2, April 1927, pp. 105-113.

86.   Moloney, *Westminster, Whitehall and the Vatican*, p. 22.

87.   *The Venerabile*, vol. iv, no. 4, April 1930, pp. 315-316.

88.   *The Venerabile*, vol. v, no. 1, Oct 1930, pp. 72-73.

89.   *The Venerabile*, May 1942, vol. x, no. 3, p. 24.

90.   Heenan, *Cardinal Hinsley*, p. 25.

91.   *The Venerabile*, vol. iv, no. 4, April 1930, pp. 315-316.

Chapter Five *Catholic Missions and Colonial Policy*

1.   Leslie, *Cardinal Gasquet*, pp. 214, 224-231. Gasquet was not the only one to be concerned at Great Britain's lack of influence in the Vatican. See Rennell Rodd, *Social and Diplomatic Memories 1902-1919*, pp. 214-218.

2.   Leslie, *Cardinal Gasquet*, p. 227. In 1916 Howard was replaced by another Catholic diplomat, Count John de Salis. In 1922 he wrote that Gasquet's

influence and qualities 'have given prestige to his country', and that del Val 'commands support'. See Hachey, *Anglo-Vatican Relations: Confidential Reports of the British Ministers to the Holy See 1914-1939*, p. 15. See also Gaslee, 'British Diplomatic Relations With The Holy See' in *The Dublin Review*, vol. 204, no. 408, Jan.1939.

3. *The Tablet*, 30 March 1935.
4. Hachey, *Anglo-Vatican Relations*, pp. 43 and 99.
5. Hachey, *Anglo-Vatican Relations*, p. 99. For the percentage of missions in British colonial territory see Hinsley to Smith (n.d.). AAW, Hi 2, 139/1.
6. Hachey, *Anglo-Vatican Relations*, p. 99.
7. Sir Samuel Wilson to Sir H. R. C. Dobbs, 11 Feb. 1927, CO 323/966/7, CF 21417/1927.
8. Hachey, *Anglo-Vatican Relations*, p. 99.
9. Hachey, *Anglo-Vatican Relations*, p. 100.
10. Russell to Austen Chamberlain, 7 Nov. 1926. CO, C1191/622/22.
11. Hachey, *Anglo-Vatican Relations*, p. 115.
12. Randall, *Vatican Assignment*, pp. 29,79–80.
13. ASV, Scatt. I, Fasc. 2; Oliver, *The Missionary Factor in East Africa*, p. 274.
14. Hetherington, *British Paternalism in Africa 1920-1940*, p. 122.
15. Hetherington, *British Paternalism in Africa*, p. 112.
16. The reports were published as Jones, *Education In Africa* and Jones, *Education in East Africa*.
17. Lewis, *The Phelps-Stokes Report on Education in Africa*, pp. 6–10.
18. Jones, *Education In Africa*, p. 28.
19. Jones, *Education in East Africa*, p. xxviii.
20. Giersbach, 'H.E. Cardinal Hinsley's Journeys through Africa as Papal Visitor'. AAW, Hi 2, 139/2 (e), pp. 1-2. Dom Engelbert Giersbach OSB of St Otillien Abbey in Germany was Hinsley's secretary in Africa.
21. Boucher, *Petit Atlas des Missions Catholiques 1928*. See also Gramatica, *Testo e Atlante di Geografica Ecclesiastica 1927*, pp. 104-106.
22. 'Hinsley to RL', p. 6. AAW, Hi 2, /139/1/3. Hinsley to Smith at the English College, Rome.
23. *Catholic Directory 1927*, p. 45. See also Brady, *Princes of His People: The Story of Our Bishops*, p. 21 for details of the Dutch Dominican Gijlswijk. His career mirrors Hinsley's in that he was sent to report on the Dominican missions in South Africa and returned later as Apostolic Delegate.
24. The four Irish Vicars Apostolic were Henry Gogarty, C.S.Sp., of Kilima-Njaro; Ignatius Joseph Shanahan, C.S.Sp., Lower Niger; John Neville, C.S.Sp., Zanzibar; and Thomas Broderick, SMA, Western Nigeria. Peter Rogan, MHM, was the Irish Prefect Apostolic of Buea; Robert Brown, S.J., was the English Prefect Apostolic of Rhodesia; and John Campling, MHM, was the Prefect Apostolic of the Upper Nile. *Catholic Directory 1927*, pp. 45-46; *The Catholic Who's Who 1940*. See also Boucher, *Petit Atlas des Missions Catholiques*, for the regional deployment of missionaries in Africa.

25. Informal arrangements were not favoured by Propaganda. In January 1901 the Superior General of the Montfort Fathers, the Superior General of the White Fathers, and Bishop Dupont, Vicar Apostolic of the Shiré Vicariate, agreed a contract whereby the Montfort Fathers took responsibility for the Shiré region of Nyasaland. In June 1901 Cardinal Ledochowski, Cardinal Prefect of Propaganda, declared the contract null and void because he had not been previously informed. Propaganda then expelled three Montfort Fathers from Shiré. See Muyebe, *The Catholic Missionaries Within and Beyond the Politics of Exclusivity in Colonial Malawi 1901-1945,* pp. 196-199.

26. American Assistancy of the Society of Jesus, *The Selected Writings of Father Ledochowski,* pp. 662-663; Hallett, *A Catholic Dictionary,* p. 102.

27. Hastings, *Church and State: The English Experience,* pp. 38-40.

28. Holmes, *The Papacy in the Modern World,* pp. 23-27. See also Freemantle, *The Papal Encyclicals In Their Historical Context.*

29. Statistics collated from the *Catholic Directory* (1915, 1919, 1923, 1928).

30. Sundkler and Steed, *A History of the Church in Africa,* p. 626.

31. Statistics collated from *Catholic Directory* (1919, 1923, 1928); Boucher, *Petit Atlas des Missions Catholiques;* Gramatica, *Testo e Atlante di Geografia Ecclesiastica.*

32. Statistics collated from *Catholic Directory* (1919, 1923, 1928).

33. Sundkler and Steed, *A History of the Church in Africa,* p. 626.

Chapter Six *Apostolic Visitor 1928-1930*

1. *The Tablet,* 17 Dec. 1927. *The Times* subsequently referred to Hinsley's mission in Africa as being of 'peculiar delicacy and importance'; *The Times,* 18 March 1943.

2. Hinsley, *Diary,* 2-19 Dec. 1927. Hinsley to Smith in 'Letters from Africa to the English College'. This document is undated. AAW, Hi 2/139/1/3. The entries are spasmodic.

3. *IRM,* vol.14 (1925), p. 426; *Diary,* 22 Dec. 1927.

4. *Diary,* 21 Dec. 1927.

5. *Diary,* 24 Dec. 1927; I am grateful to Abbot Aidan Bellenger OSB for providing information on Fr Giersbach.

6. *Diary,* 18-20 Jan. 1928.

7. *Diary,* 18-26 Jan. 1928. For Spreiter's career see Brady, *Princes of His People,* p. 22. Spreiter had been in Africa since 1900. During the First World War he was compelled to leave Tanganyika. In 1921 he became the first Prefect Apostolic of Eshowe.

8. *Diary,* 3 Feb. 1928.

9. *Diary,* 20 Feb. 1928.

10. *The African Missionary,* no. 80, May-June 1928, p. 170.

11. *Diary,* 23 Feb.-5 March 1928; *Fides,* 4 May 1928.

12. *Fides,* 21 May 1928; Brown, *The Catholic Church in South Africa,* pp. 338-339.

13. *Fides*, 4 and 25 May 1928. For details of Cenez's career see Brady, *Princes of His People*, p. 17.

14. Sundkler and Steed, *A History of the Church in Africa*, p. 422.

15. *Diary*, 25 April 1928; *Fides*, 25 May 1928.

16. In 1939 the Catholic Truth Society published six pamphlets under the auspices of the Association for the Propagation of the Faith to celebrate the APF's centenary in England. One of the pamphlets, by Fr Herbert Keldany, Assistant National Director of the Pontifical Mission Aid Societies, was a brief description of Hinsley's extensive travels in Africa rather than an analysis of his work as Apostolic Visitor. The pamphlet was based entirely on *Journeys* which included Fr Giersbach's diary. See Keldany, *H.E. Cardinal Hinsley's Travels in Africa 1928-1929*, pp. 10-11.

17. Keldany, *Hinsley's Travels in Africa*, p. 13; *Diary*, 16-20 June 1928.

18. Sundkler and Steed, *A History of the Church in Africa*, p. 414.

19. *Diary*, 7 July 1928.

20. Keldany, *Hinsley's Travels in Africa*, pp. 13-15.

21. 'The Vicariate Apostolic of Zanzibar 1860-1924'. AAW, Hi Misc. 26B.

22. *Fides*, 10 Sep. 1928; Keldany, *Hinsley's Travels in Africa*, p. 18.

23. *Diary*, 2 and 15 Dec. 1928.

24. *Catholic Who's Who*, p. 430.

25. Keldany, *Hinsley's Travels in Africa*, pp. 20-21.

26. Keldany, *Hinsley's Travels in Africa*, p. 22.

27. Keldany, *Hinsley's Travels in Africa*, p. 23.

28. Giersbach to Mathew, 22 Feb. 1930, CO, C 29992/441/22; See Hachey, *Anglo-Vatican Relations*, p. 207.

29. Keldany, *Hinsley's Travels in Africa*, pp. 25-26; *Fides*, 22 July 1929.

30. Keldany, *Hinsley's Travels in Africa*, p. 27; *Catholic Who's Who*, p. 51.

31. *Fides*, 22 July 1929.

32. Keldany, *Hinsley's Travels in Africa*, p. 28; *Fides*, 7 Oct. 1929.

33. Keldany, *Hinsley's Travels in Africa*, pp. 21-29; *Fides*, 25 Nov. 1929.

34. *Fides*, 4 May 1928.

35. Brandsma to Schut, 17 Jan. 1928. AMHM, ROM 07.

36. Brandsma to Schut, Easter Sunday 1928. AMHM, ROM 07.

37. Brandsma to Schut, 8 May 1928. AMHM, ROM 07.

38. Rogan to Schut, 29 Jan. 1928, AMHM, ROM 97.

39. Rogan to Biermans, 12 Sept. 1928. AMHM, CAM 1.

40. *Missionary Annals of the Holy Ghost Fathers*, vol. x, no. 4, April 1928, pp. 74-74.

41. *The Zambesi Mission Record*, July 1928, p. 291.

42. *The Zambesi Mission Record*, Jan. 1929, p. 365.

43. Gavan Duffy, *Let's Go*, p. 451.

Chapter Seven *Imposing Vatican Policy*

1. Sundkler and Steed, *A History of the Church in Africa*, p. 641.
2. Hannecart, *'Intrepid Sowers': From Nyasa to Fort Jameson 1889-1946 – Some Historical Notes*, pp. 211-212. *Diary*, 20 June 1928.
3. *Fides*, 10 Sep. 1928. *Diary*, 3-9 Aug. 1928.
4. Pels, *A Politics of Presence: Contacts between Missionaries and Waluguru in Late Colonial Tanganyika*, p. 202.
5. Versteijnen, *The Catholic Mission of Bagamoyo*.
6. Keldany, *Hinsley's Travels in Africa*, p. 14.
7. *Fides*, 14 Dec. 1928.
8. Pels, *A Politics of Presence*, p. 202.
9. *Diary,* 15 Aug. 1928.
10. *Diary*, 16 Aug. 1928.
11. *Diary*, 6-7 Nov. 1928; 3 Jan. 1929. Hinsley described Scott as 'very straightforward, even blunt' but, he continued, 'he understands our position'. *Fides*, 17 Dec. 1928.
12. O'Neill, *Mission to the Upper Nile*, pp. 92-94.
13. Tourigny, *So Abundant A Harvest*, p. 129; O'Neill, *Mission to the Upper Nile*, pp. 134-135.
14. Tourigny, *So Abundant A Harvest*, pp. 132-133.
15. Campling to Bukedi Mission Superiors, 1 Nov. 1928. AMHM, UGA 22.
16. *Fides*, 8 April 1929.
17. *Journeys,* 21 March, 1 April, 3 April, 11 April 1929.
18. *Fides*, 15 July 1929.
19. *Fides,* 7 Oct. 1929. For Broderick see *Diary*, 21 Sep. 1929; Todd, *African Mission*, pp.154-155; and Society of African Missions, *One Hundred Years of Missionary Achievement* 1856-1956, pp. 12, 16, 56. It was claimed that Broderick recognised the school as 'the gateway to the Church' and that his idea of schools was adopted by Catholic missionaries 'all over Nigeria'.
20. ASV, Scat. II, Fasc. VIII; Omenka, *The School in the Service of Evangelization*, pp. 220-225.
21. Omenka, *The School in the Service of Evangelization*, p. 222.
22. Hastings, *The Church in Africa*, p. 562. The influx of Irish missionaries into Nigeria is discussed more fully in the chapter dealing with Hinsley's role as Apostolic Delegate.
23. *Fides*, 7 Oct. 1929.
24. *Fides*, 4 Nov. 1929.
25. *Fides*, 4 Nov. 1929; *The Catholic Directory* 1927, p. 46.
26. Omenka, *The School in the Service of Evangelization*, p. 221.
27. *Fides*, 25 Nov. 1929.
28. *Fides*, 25 Nov. 1929.
29. Groves, *The Planting of Christianity in Africa* (vol. 4, 1914-1954), p. 119.
30. Beidelman, *Colonial Evangelism*, p. 21.

31. Sundkler and Steed, *A History of the Church in Africa*, pp. 874–875.

32. Sundkler and Steed, *A History of the Church in Africa*, p. 641.

33. Smythe, 'The Creation of Catholic Fipa Society' in Spear and Kimambo (eds), *East African Expressions of Christianity*, pp. 129, 130, 144.

34. Stenger, *The White Fathers in Colonial Central Africa*, pp. 143–144. Gavan Duffy described the White Fathers as the 'only grown up missionaries in the field' but added 'they are so very static and entrenched and soberly devoid of our little experimental enthusiasms'. Duffy, *Let's Go*, p. 98.

35. Hannecart, *Intrepid Sowers*, p. 211.

36. Stenger, *The White Fathers in Colonial Central Africa*, pp. 143–144.

37. Stenger, *The White Fathers in Colonial Central Africa*, p. 147.

38. O'Neill, *Mission to the Upper Nile*, p. 137.

39. Sundkler and Steed, *A History of Christianity in Africa*, p. 74.

40. Ogudo, *The Holy Ghost Fathers and Catholic Worship among the Igbo People of Eastern Nigeria*, p. 93.

41. Ogubo, *The Holy Ghost Fathers and Catholic Worship*, p. 93.

42. Omenka, *The School in the Service of Evangelization*, pp. 151–152.

43. Bassey, *Missionary Rivalry and Educational Expansion in Nigeria 1885-1945*, pp. 64, 77. Hinsley's relationships with Shanahan and the Holy Ghost Fathers (the Spiritans) are discussed in the chapter dealing with his role as Apostolic Delegate.

44. Linden, *The Catholic Church and the Struggle for Zimbabwe*, p. 28.

45. Dachs and Rea, *The Catholic Church and Zimbabwe*, p. 80.

46. Sundkler and Steed, *A History of the Church in Africa*, p. 803.

47. Dachs and Rea, *The Catholic Church and Zimbabwe*, p. 83.

48. *The Zambesi Mission Record*, April 1929, p. 402.

49. Sundkler and Steed, *A History of the Church in Africa*, pp. 720–726.

50. Gray, 'Christianity', pp. 21–22.

51. Omenka, *The School in the Service of Evangelization*, pp. 219–220.

52. ASV, Scat. I, Fasc. VI; Burgman, *The Way the Church Started in Western Kenya*, pp. 143–145.

53. Chilton to the Foreign Office, 5 Dec. 1930, CO 323/1101/14, c9012/441/22.

54. Hachey, *Anglo-Vatican Relations*, p. 182.

55. Burgman, *The Way the Church Started in Western Kenya*, p. 146.

56. *IRM*, (1930), vol. 19, p. 69.

57. Report on the International Educational Conference held at Dar-es-Salaam on 11 March 1929, CO 822/18/7.

58. *Journeys*, 10 March 1929.

59. Rivers-Smith to the Colonial Office, 2 Nov. 1929, CO 323/1034/12, 60257/29.

60. Memorandum on principles to be observed in grants-in-aid to mission and denominational education (1929), CO 323/1034/12, 24422-35 J1.

61. *Fides*, 17 June 1929.

62. *IRM*, vol. 20, 1931, p. 229.

63. Hinsley to Thomson, 3 Oct. 1929. ASV, Scat I, Fasc. VIII.
64. Thomson to Hinsley, 27 Nov. 1929 and 6 Dec. 1929. ASV, Scat I, Fasc. VIII.
65. Hinsley to Thomson, 27 Dec. 1929. ASV, Scat I, Fasc. VIII.
66. Hinsley to Slater, 19 Oct. 1929 and 1 Feb. 1930. ASV, Scat I, Fasc. VIII.
67. *Fides*, 20 Jan. 1930.
68. Campling to Schut, 26 July 1928, 26 Sep. 1928. AMHM, ROM 07.
69. Brandsma to Schut, 25 March 1929. AMHM, ROM 07.
70. Brandsma to Biermans, n.d., (1930). AMHM, KEN 2.
71. *The African Missionary*, no. 99, Jan. 1930, pp. 14-15.
72. Brandsma to Schut, 8 April 1929. AMHM, KEN 2.
73. Linden, *The Catholic Church and the Struggle for Zimbabwe*, p. 26.
74. *Letters and Notices*, April 1928, p. 94.
75. *The Zambesi Mission Record*, Jan. 1927, p. 370.
76. Oliver, *The Missionary Factor in East Africa*, p. 276.
77. *IRM*, vol. 20, 1931, p. 75.
78. *The Times*, 18 March 1943.
79. Quoted in Kiggins, *Maynooth Mission To Africa*, p. 55.
80. Heenan, *Cardinal Hinsley*, pp. 63-72. Heenan's account confuses Hinsley's role as Apostolic Visitor with that of Apostolic Delegate.
81. ASV, Scat I, Fasc. VII.
82. ASV, Scat I, Fasc. VII.
83. *Fides*, 21 Jan 1930.
84. ASV, Scat I, Fasc. VII.
85. ASV, Scat II, Fasc. III.
86. ASV, Scat I, Fasc. VI.
87. ASV, Scat I, Fasc. II.
88. ASV, Scat II, Fasc. VIII.
89. *Fides,* 20 Jan. 1930.
90. Hachey, *Anglo-Vatican Relations*, pp. 132-133.
91. Moloney, *Westminster, Whitehall and the Vatican*, pp. 22-23.

Chapter Eight *Larger Fields and Wider Horizons 1930-1934*

1. *Diary*, 9 Jan. 1930; Hachey, *Anglo-Vatican Relations*, p. 182.
2. *Fides*, 20 Jan. 1930.
3. Heston, 'Papal Diplomacy: Its Organisation and Way of Acting' in Gurian and Fitzsimons, *The Catholic Church in World Affairs*, pp. 43-45.
4. Hallett, *A Catholic Dictionary*, p. 496.
5. Hallett, *A Catholic Dictionary*, p. 43.
6. *Fides*, 20 Jan. 1930.
7. Gray, 'Christianity' in *The Cambridge History of Africa*, p. 161. Gray contends that this was Hinsley's most important task.
8. Heenan, *Cardinal Hinsley*, p. 68; Gray, *Christianity*, p. 161.
9. Hinsley to Fumasoni-Biondi, 25 May 1934. ASV, Scat. I, Fasc. 1/2.

10. Quoted in Moloney, *Westminster, Whitehall and the Vatican*, pp. 22-23.

11. Hachey, *Anglo-Vatican Relations*, p. 182.

12. *Diary*, 6 Jan. 1930.

13. *Diary*, 8 Jan. 1930.

14. *Diary*, 9 Jan. 1930; *Fides*, 30 Jan. 1930.

15. *Fides*, 20 Jan. 1930.

16. *The African Missionary*, no. 101, (March 1930).

17. Toruigny, *So Abundant A Harvest*, p. 131.

18. *Fides*, 20 Jan. 1930.

19. *Fides*, 9 Dec. 1929; Campling to Biermans, 26 March 1929. AMHM, UGA 23.

20. Ogilvie-Forbes to Henderson, 13 Jan. 1930. CO, C 441/441/32.

21. Hachey, *Anglo-Vatican Relations*, p. 207.

22. *Fides*, 13 March 1930.

23. Huddleston to Foreign Office, 5 April 1930. CO, C2992/441/22.

24. For a history of the Catholic Church in the Sudan see McEwan, *A Catholic Sudan: Dream, Mission, Reality*.

25. *Fides*, 13 March 1930.

26. Hachey, *Anglo-Vatican Relations*, p. 207.

27. McEwan, *A Catholic Sudan*, pp. 185-186.

28. Report on the Visitation to the Anglo-Egyptian Sudan, 1 May 1930. ASV, Scat. II, Fasc. IX.

29. *Fides*, 28 Aug. 1930; Groves, *The Planting of Christianity in Africa,* p. 197; Hinsley to Fr Patrick Whitney, 28 Aug. 1930. SPMS.

30. *IRM.*, vol. 24, 1935, p. 108; Latourette, *Advance Through Storm*, p. 47.

31. Oliver, *The Missionary Factor in East Africa*, p. 232.

32. *Fides*, 3 March 1932; Cameron and Dodd, *Schools, Society and Progression Tanzania*, p. 43.

33. Barnes, 'Evangelizing where it is not wanted: Colonial Administrators and Missionaries in Northern Nigeria during the first third of the Twentieth Century' in *Journal of Religion in Africa*, vol. 25, 1995, pp. 412-413.

34. *Fides*, 29 Dec. 1932; 2 March 1933.

35. *Fides*, 7 May 1931; 29 Dec. 1932; *IRM*, vol. 21, 1932, p. 374.

36. Burgman, *The Way the Church Started in Western Kenya*, p. 145.

37. Tourigny, *So Abundant A Harvest*, pp. 132-133.

38. *IRM*, vol. 21, 1932, p. 376.

39. *Fides*, 3 March 1932.

40. *Fides*, 7 July 1932.

41. Tourigny, *So Abundant A Harvest*, pp. 131-132.

42. *Fides*, 7 July 1932.

43. Keldany, *Cardinal Hinsley's Travels in Africa*, p. 18; *Fides*, 7 July 1932.

44. Murray, 'The Church Missionary Society and the Female Circumcision Issue in Kenya 1920-1932' in *Journal of Religion in Africa*, vol. 8 (1976), p. 92; *Fides*, 7 July 1932; Hachey *Anglo-Vatican Relations*, p. 206.

45. Gottneid, *Church and Education in Tanganyika*, p. 46.

46. Cameron and Dodd, *Schools, Society and Progress in Tanzania*, p. 61.

47. Iliffe, *A Modern History of Tanganyika*, p. 359.

48. Listowel, *The Making of Tanganyika*, pp. 113-114.

49. Barnes, 'Catholic Evangelizing in one Colonial Mission: the Institutional Evolution of Jos Prefecture, Nigeria, 1907-1954' in *Catholic Historical Review*, vol. LXXXIV, no. 2, (April 1998), p. 251.

50. Omenka, *The School in the Service of Evangelization*, pp. 225-227; Barnes, 'Catholic Evangelizing', p. 248.

51. Oliver, *The Missionary Factor in East Africa*, p. 281.

52. Omenka, *The School in the Service of Evangelization*, pp. 225, 226-227.

53. Falola and Roberts, 'West Africa' in Brown and Louis (eds), *The Oxford History of the British Empire*, vol iv (*The Twentieth Century*), p. 521; Nduka, *Western Education and the Nigerian Cultural Background*, p. 47.

54. Barnes, 'Evangelization where it is not wanted', pp. 412-413; Omenka, *Schools in the Service of Evangelization*, p. 220.

55. 'Missionary Activities in Nigeria 1930'. CO, 583/176/15; Barnes, 'Catholic Evangelizing', p. 242;

56. 'Missionary Activities in Nigeria 1930'. CO, 583/176/15.

57. 'Missionary Activities in Nigeria 1930'. CO, 583/176/15.

58. Omenka, *Schools in the Service of Evangelization*, pp. 230-236.

59. Nduka, *Western Education and the Nigerian Cultural Background*, p. 47.

60. Omenka, *Schools in the Service of Evangelization*, p. 232.

61. *Fides*, 7 July 1932.

62. 'Colonial Course 1931-1932'. AMHM.

63. *The Catholic Who's Who*, p. 562.

64. 'Colonial Course 1931-1932'; Vernon to Fr Basil Gudgeon, 2 Dec. 1932. AMHM.

65. Hinsley to Fumasoni-Biondi, 25 May 1934. ASV, Scat. I, Fasc. 1/II.

Chapter Nine *Building The African Church*

1. *Fides*, 27 April 1933.

2. *Fides*, 23 Feb. 1935.

3. *Fides*, 20 Nov. 1930; 3 March 1932.

4. *Fides*, 27 April 1933.

5. *Fides*, 20 and 27 April 1933.

6. *Fides*, 23 Feb. 1935.

7. Barnes, 'Catholic Evangelization', pp. 248-249.

8. Walsh, *The Growth of the Catholic Church in the Diocese of Jos*, pp. 82-83.

9. *Fides*, 23 Feb. 1935.

10. *Fides*, 29 Dec. 1932.

11. Gottneid, *Church and Education In Tanzania*, p. 48.

12. Barnes, 'Catholic Evangelizing', p. 257.

13. Crocker, *Nigeria: A Critique of British Colonial Administration*, pp. 225-226.

14. Oger, *Where A Scattered Flock Gathered*, p. 71.

15. Quoted in Oger, *Where A Scattered Flock Gathered*, pp. 70-71.

16. Quoted in Oger, *Where a Scattered Flock Gathered*, p. 86.

17. Oger, *Where A Scattered Flock Gathered*, pp. 86-87.

18. *Fides*, 2 March 1933.

19. Rankine to Colonial Office, 24 March 1933. CO, 4079/33/EA.

20. Colonial Office to Rankine, 14 July 1933. CO, 4079/33/EA; Roman Catholic Missions Organisation (Memo) (Zanzibar and the Mainland). CO, 822/56/6.

21. *Fides*, 3 March 1932; 20 April 1933.

22. *Fides,* 27 April 1933.

23. *Fides*, 7 May 1931.

24. *Fides*, 3 March 1932.

25. *Fides*, 3 March 1932.

26. O'Neil, *Mission to the Upper Nile*, pp. 110-111.

27. Cameron and Dodd, *Schools, Society and Progress in Tanzania*, pp. 45-46, 61; *Fides*, 29 Dec. 1932.

28. Jordan, *Bishop Shanahan of Southern Nigeria*, p. 140; Okwu, 'The Beginning of the Maynooth Movement in Southern Nigeria and the Rise of the St Patrick's Missionary Society 1920-1930' in *Journal of Religion in Africa*, vol. x (1979), p. 45.

29. Okwu, 'The Beginning of the Maynooth Movement', pp. 24-26. St Patrick's College, Maynooth was established in 1795. In the 1920s it was the major Irish seminary for secular priests and was a constituent college of the National University of Ireland. It was controlled by the Irish Hierarchy.

30. Quoted in Okwu, 'The Beginning of the Maynooth Movement', p. 28.

31. See Hogan, 'The Motivation of the Modern Irish Missionary Movement 1912-1939' in *Journal of Religion in Africa*, vol. x (1979), pp. 157-173.

32. Okwu, The Beginning of the Maynooth Movement', pp. 4-41; Kiggins, *Maynooth Mission To Africa*, p. 55. See also Fox, 'Lord That I May See' (unpublished biography of Bishop Shanahan, Dublin, 1971), p.29. (I am grateful to Fr Raymond Barry C.S.Sp. for this reference).

33. Hinsley to Whitney, 28 Oct. 1929. SPMS.

34. Hogan, *The Irish Missionary Movement*, p. 130.

35. Okwu, 'The Beginning of the Maynooth Movement', pp. 37-38.

36. Hinsley to Whitney, 1 Jan. 1930. SPMS; *Diary*, 8 Jan. 1930.

37. Hinsley To Whitney, 16 April 1930. SPMS. Hinsley writes of the proposed division of the Vicariate; *Fides*, 30 Oct. 1930.

38. Okwu, 'The Beginning of the Maynooth Movement', pp. 42-43.

39. Hogan, *The Irish Missionary Movement*, p. 105. The first three members of St Patrick's Missionary Society were Fr Patrick J Whitney, his cousin Fr Patrick F Whitney, and Fr Francis Hickey. They professed their vows on St Patrick's Day 1932. The new institute was given property and land at Kiltegan in

County Wicklow and became known as the Kiltegan Fathers. See Kiggins, *Maynooth Mission To Africa*.

40. Ozigboh, *Roman Catholicism in South East Nigeria 1885-1931*, p. 253. See also Obi 'The Missionary Contribution of Bishop Joseph Shanahan C.S.Sp. 1902-1932' in Obi, *A Hundred Years of the Catholic Church in Eastern Nigeria*, p. 169. Obi maintains that Shanahan had offered to resign in 1926 because of failing eyesight and poor health but was refused. Instead, he was offered an auxiliary bishop.

41. Okwu, 'The Beginning of the Maynooth Movement', p. 41; Kiggins, *Maynooth Mission To Africa*, pp. 56-57; Hinsley to Whitney, 28 Aug. 1930, SPMS.

42. O'Neil, *Mission to the Upper Nile*, pp. 110-111; 'Spiritual Returns 1927-1932'. AMHM.

43. 'Spiritual Returns 1932'. AMHM.

44. Brandsma to Schut, 31 July 1928. AMHM, ROM 07.

45. Burgman, *The Way The Church Started in Western Kenya*, p. 169; Brandsma to Schut, 20 Feb. 1929. AMHM, ROM 07.

46. Brandsma to Schut, 29 Dec. 1928; Brandsma to Schut, 8 April 1929. AMHM, ROM 07.

47. Hinsley to Biermans, 18 July 1931. AMHM, KEN 2.

48. Biermans to van Rossum, 2 Oct. 1931. AMHM, KEN 2.

49. Doyle to Hinsley, 10 Aug. 1931; Hinsley to Doyle, 18 Aug. 1931. AMHM, KEN 2.

50. Doyle to Brandsma, 16 Feb. 1932; Doyle to van Rossum, 17 March 1932. AMHM, KEN 2.

51. Schut to Biermans, 2 May 1932. AMHM, ROM 07.

52. van Rossum to Biermans, 17 March 1932. AMHM, KEN 2.

53. Schut to Biermans, 2 May 1932. AMHM, ROM 07.

54. Brandsma to Schut, 12 Jan. 1933. AMHM, ROM 07.

55. Schut to Biermans, 1 June 1933. AMHM, ROM 07; O'Neil, *Mission to the Upper Nile*, p. 113.

56. *Fides*, 3 March 1932; 27 April 1933. See also Boucher, *Petit Atlas des Missions Catholiques*; Grammatica, *Testo e Atlante di Geografica Ecclesiastica*; *Annuario Pontificio*; *Catholic Directory*. The dates given in each source do not always correspond. An *Abbey nullius dioeceseos* belongs to no diocese.

57. Ogez, *Where It All Began*, pp. 89-90.

58. *Fides*, 23 Feb. 1935.

59. *Fides*, 7 May 1931.

60. *Fides*, 6 Aug. 1931.

61. *Fides*, 3 March 1932; Waliggo, *A History of African Priests*, p. 132.

62. *Fides*, 3 March 1932.

63. *Fides*, 27 April 1933.

64. *Fides*, 28 April 1934.

65. *Fides*, 20 April 1933.

66. *Fides*, 3 March 1932.

67. *Fides*, 27 April 1934.

68. *Fides*, 28 April 1934.

69. Quoted in Linden, *The Catholic Church and the Struggle for Zimbabwe*, pp. 29-30.

70. Bodkin, *Memoriale of the Visitation of the Zambesi Mission 1924-1925; Letters and Notices,* vol. CCLV111 (Oct. 1930), p. 297; Barr, *Archbishop Aston Chichester 1879-1962*, p. 40.

71. Compiled from *Fides*, 31 May 1933 and *IRM*, vol. 23 (1934).

72. *Fides*, 3 March 1932.

73. *Fides*, 29 Dec. 1932.

74. *Fides*, 3 March 1934.

75. *Fides*, 23 Feb. 1935.

76. *The Clergy Review,* vol. vxii, no.3 (Sept. 1939), p. 204.

77. Heenan, *Cardinal Hinsley*, p. 69.

78. Hastings, *The Church in Africa*, p. 561.

79. Quoted in Heenan, *Cardinal Hinsley*, p. 70.

80. Gottneid, *Church and Education in Tanzania*, p. 49.

81. Heenan, *Cardinal Hinsley*, p. 73.

82. Hachey, *Anglo-Vatican Relations*, pp. 267-268.

83. *L'Osservatore Romano*, 25 May 1934.

84. Newton, *DNB*, p. 394.

Chapter Ten *'Habemus Ducem': Archbishop of Westminster 1935*

1. Hinsley to Amigo, 1 Jan. 1935. ASA, Amigo Papers, Correspondence with Hinsley, C4.

2. Hachey, *Anglo-Vatican Relations*, pp. 295-6.

3. Amigo to Archbishop Williams, 14 Jan. 1935. ABA, Williams Papers, AP/C28/2 APB5.

4. See for example, Bishop Casartelli to Gasquet, 10 Nov. 1917; Bishop Ward to Gasquet, 17 Jan. 1918. DAA, Gasquet Papers, 889.

5. Plumb, *Arundel to Zabi.*

6. Plumb, *Arundel to Zabi*; Moloney, *Westminster, Whitehall and the Vatican*, p. 18.

7. *Perth Daily News*, 3 Jan. 1935.

8. *Melbourne Star*, 8 Jan. 1935.

9. *Northern Star*, 5 Jan. 1935.

10. *Melbourne Herald*, 11 Jan. 1935.

11. *Brisbane Mail*, 13 Jan. 1935.

12. *Illustrated Weekly News*, 27 Jan. 1935.

13. *Ceylon Daily News*, 30 Jan. 1935.

14. *Times Of Ceylon*, 31 Jan. 1935.

15. *The News*, 23 Feb. 1935.

16. *Birmingham Daily Mail*, 20 Feb. 1935.

17. *Evening Standard*, 22 March 1935.
18. *Daily Express*, 23 March 1935; *Sunday Dispatch* 24 March 1935.
19. *Cork Examiner*, 19 March 1935.
20. Hinsley to Amigo, 1 Jan. 1935. ASA, Amigo Papers, Correspondence with Hinsley, C4.
21. Elwes, 'Cardinal Hinsley' in *The Clergy Review*, June 1943, pp. 241-247.
22. Heenan, *Cardinal Hinsley*, pp. 17-18.
23. Hachey, *Anglo-Vatican Relations*, p. 296.
24. *The Catholic Who's Who 1940*, p. 142.
25. *The Catholic Who's Who 1940*, p. 225.
26. Hachey, *Anglo-Vatican Relations*, pp. 296-297. Wingfield was obviously unaware that Hinsley's father was English and his mother Irish.
27. Hinsley to Downey, 25 March 1935. ALA, Downey Papers, Series 1, II B63.
28. Hinsley to Downey, 27 March 1935. ALA, Downey Papers, Series 1, II B63.
29. Hinsley to McNulty, 25 March 1935. DNA, McNulty Papers, H.01.01.
30. Smith, *John Fisher and Thomas More: Two English Saints*, p. v; I am grateful to Mgr John Dunne for his advice on Hinsley's coat of arms. Another interpretation of *Tales Ambio Defensores* is 'I gird myself with such defenders'.
31. *The Tablet*, 20 March 1935.
32. *The Venerabile*, vol. vii, no. 3 Oct. 1935.
33. Heenan, *Cardinal Hinsley*, p. 17.
34. *The Times*, 2 Jan. 1935.
35. Wheeler, 'The Archdiocese of Westminster' in Beck (ed.), *The English Catholics 1850-1950*, p. 181.
36. Brown, *Through Windows of Memory*, pp. 98-99.
37. Heenan, *Cardinal Hinsley*, p. 14.
38. Moloney, *Westminster, Whitehall and The Vatican*, pp. 24-25.
39. *The Universe*, 1 March 1935.
40. Sydney *Bulletin*, 3 April 1935.
41. *Yorkshire Post*, 26 March 1935.
42. *The Month*, vol. CLXV, May 1935, p. 386.
43. *The Tablet*, 30 March 1935.
44. *Church Times*, 29 March 1935.
45. Lang to Hinsley, 26 April 1935. AAW, Hi 1/7.
46. *The Times*, 26 March 1935.
47. *Cork Examiner*, 19 March 1935.
48. *Sunday Times*, 31 March 1935.
49. *Manchester Evening News*, 15 April 1935; *Daily Express*, 15 April 1935.
50. *South Wales Echo and Evening Press*, 3 April 1935.
51. *Manchester Evening Chronicle*, 20 Aug. 1935.
52. *Bulletin*, 3 April 1935.
53. *The Times*, 30 April 1935; *The Tablet*, 4 May 1935; *Westminster Cathedral Chronicle*, May 1935, no. 5.
54. *The Tablet*, 11 May 1935.

55. Smith, *John Fisher and Thomas More,* pp. v–vii.
56. *The English Churchman*, 4 April 1935.
57. ALA, Downey Papers, S1 II, B 64.
58. *The Tablet*, 15 June 1935.
59. Beck, *The Clergy Review* (May 1944). Beck was reviewing Fr Heenan's recently published *Cardinal Hinsley*.
60. *Catholic Directory 1935*, pp. 59–64; Moloney, *Westminster, Whitehall and The Vatican,* pp. 26–28; Bellenger and Fletcher, *Princes of the Church*, pp. 153–156.
61. Hinsley to Elwes, 6 and 20 July 1935. AAW, Hi MSC.
62. Hachey, *Anglo-Vatican Relations*, p. 296.
63. Williams, *The Venerable English College,* chapter 8, 'The Hinsley Tradition'.
64. Hagerty, 'The Politics of Presence'.
65. Gilley, 'The Years of Equipoise' in McClelland and Hodgetts (eds), *From Without the Flaminian Gate: 150 years of Roman Catholicism in England and Wales 1850-2000*, p. 52.
66. Leslie, *Cardinal Gasquet*, pp. 197, 257.
67. Buerhle, *Rafael, Cardinal Merry Del Val*, pp. 231, 290.
68. *Amigo: Friend Of The Poor*, pp. 50, 116.
69. Smith, 'Report From Rome' in *The Clergy Review*, April 1935.
70. *The Tablet*, 27 March 1943.
71. Brown, *Through Windows of Memory*, pp. 98–99.
72. Holland to Mgr Henson, 27 March 1935, ACSA, Henson Papers, 122.1. Fr Thomas Holland later became Bishop of Salford.
73. Smith, 'Cardinal Hinsley', *The Venerabile*, vol. xl, no. 2, May 1943, pp. 105-116.
74. Heenan, *Cardinal Hinsley*, p. 16.

Chapter Eleven *Settling In 1935-1937*

1. *Blackfriars*, May 1935, p. 325.
2. *Westminster Cathedral Chronicle,* Oct. 1935, pp. 168–171.
3. Heenan, *Cardinal Hinsley*, pp. 18, 21.
4. *Catholic Directory* (1935), p. 621.
5. *Catholic Directory* (1936), p. 110.
6. *Westminster Cathedral Chronicle,* May 1935, pp. 72-73, 76.
7. *The Tablet*, 4 May 1935.
8. Bellenger and Fletcher, *Princes of the Church*, p. 153.
9. *The Times*, 19 June 1935; *Catholic Directory*.
10. Elwes, 'Cardinal Hinsley' in *The Clergy Review*, June 1943, p. 243.
11. *The Tablet*, 27 March 1943.
12 Heenan, *Cardinal Hinsley*, p. 83.
13. Heenan, *Cardinal Hinsley*, p. 79.
14. Elwes, 'Cardinal Hinsley' in *The Clergy Review*, June 1943, p. 244.
15. Plumb, *Arundel to Zabi; The Catholic Who's Who 1940*, p. 60.

16. Plumb, *Arundel to Zabi*; *The Catholic Who's Who 1940*, pp. 362–363.

17. Heenan, *Cardinal Hinsley*, p. 223; *The Catholic Who's Who 1940*, p. 154.

18. Hinsley to Elwes, 5 and 21 May 1935; 20 June 1935. AAW, Hi/Misc.

19. Hinsley to Heenan, 12 Aug. 1935. BDA, Doubleday Papers.

20. Wheeler, 'The Archdiocese of Westminster' in Beck (ed.) *The English Catholics,* pp. 182–183.

21. Allitt, *Catholic Converts: British and American Intellectuals Turn to Rome*, p. 210.

22. This and the following paragraphs are based on Doyle, *Westminster Cathedral 1895-1995*, pp. 80-83, 85-86; and Markham, *Keeping Faith: 700 Years of Catholic Life in Hull*, pp.121-123. Markham cites correspondence between Hinsley and Joseph Henry Hirst, a distant cousin of the Cardinal and an architect, in which Hinsley stresses the importance of not building 'costly churches'.

23. Archbishop Hinsley, *Pastoral Letter on The Urgent Need of Catholic Schools*, Lent 1936. AAW, Hi Pastorals.

24. Heenan, *Cardinal Hinsley*, p. 80.

25. *Catholic Directory* (1935), p. 622.

26. See Albion, 'The Restoration of the Hierarchy 1850' and Hughes, 'The Bishops of the Century' in Beck (ed.) *The English Catholics 1850-1950*, pp. 89, 187-188.

27. Quoted in Aspden, *Fortress Church*, p. 202.

28. *The Tablet*, 2, 9 and 16 Oct. 1937.

29. *Catholic Directory* (1935), p. 622.

30. *Catholic Directory* (1935), pp. 63-64.

31. *Yorkshire Post*, 16 Jan. 1936.

32. *Acta* of the Bishops' Meeting, 22 Oct. 1335. LDA, Poskitt Papers. See Walsh, *The Tablet: A Commemorative History 1840-1990,* pp. 42-43 and Aspden, *Fortress Church*, p. 107.

33. Hinsley to Williams. 23 July 1935. ABA, Williams Papers, AP/28/47. Walsh, *The Tablet: A Commemorative History 1840-1990*, p. 49.

34. Moloney, *Westminster, Whitehall and The Vatican*, pp. 32-41.

35. Hachey, *Anglo-Vatican Relations*, pp. 333-334; Moloney, *Westminster, Whitehall and The Vatican*, p. 41.

36. Quoted in Heenan, *Cardinal Hinsley*, pp. 5-6.

37. *The Dublin Review*, July 1935, pp. 1-6.

38. Hinsley to the Bishops, 20 Jan. 1936. ABA, Williams Papers, AP/W3.

39. Moloney, *Westminster, Whitehall and The Vatican*, pp. 84-85.

40. Hinsley to the Bishops, 16 July 1936. ABA, Williams Papers, AP/W3.

41. Moloney, *Westminster, Whitehall and The Vatican*, pp. 84-86.

42. *Manchester Evening News*, 21 May 1937; *Daily Telegraph*, 22 May 1937.

43. *The Dublin Review*, Jan. 1939, pp. 1-19.

44. Gasalee to Hinsley, 23 Sept. 1935. AAW Hi, 2/86/1.

45. Quoted in Moloney, *Westminster, Whitehall and The Vatican*, p. 42; *The Tablet*, 5 Oct. 1935.

46. *The Tablet*, 20 Nov. 1937.

47. *Yorkshire Post*, 13 Dec. 1937.

48. For details of their careers, see Plumb, *Arundel to Zabi*.

49. *The Times*, 11 and 27 Nov. 1937.

50. *The Times*, 18 Dec. 1937.

51. *The Venerabile* (April 1938), vol. iii, no. 4, pp. 292-299.

52. Birley, 'The Consistories' in *Westminster Cathedral Chronicle*, Jan. 1938, pp. 10-11.

53. *The Venerabile* (April 1938), vol. iii, no. 4, pp. 292-299.

54. Newton, 'The Cardinal's Return' in *Westminster Cathedral Chronicle,* Feb. 1938, pp. 41-42.

55. *The Tablet*, 27 March 1943.

56. *Yorkshire Post*, 18 Nov. 1937.

57. *Westminster Cathedral Chronicle,* Feb. 1938, pp. 37-38, 40.

Chapter Twelve *International Affairs 1935-1939*

1. Heenan, *Cardinal Hinsley*, p. 55.

2. Kent, *The Pope and the Duce*, pp. 40, 124-125, 149, 171.

3. Hastings, *A History of English Christianity*, pp. 314-315.

4. Quoted in Sturzo, *Church and State*, pp. 501-502.

5. Moloney, *Westminster, Whitehall and The Vatican*, pp. 44-45.

6. Moloney, *Westminster, Whitehall and The Vatican*, pp. 45-46.

7. *The Tablet*, 20 Nov. 1937.

8. Moloney, *Westminster, Whitehall and The Vatican*, pp. 46-47.

9. *The Times*, 19 Aug. 1935.

10. *The Times*, 23 Aug. 1935.

11. Quoted in Moloney, *Westminster, Whitehall and The Vatican*, p. 48.

12. *The Times*, 2 Sept. 1935.

13. Quoted in Moloney, *Westminster, Whitehall and The Vatican*, p. 49.

14. *The Times*, 11 Oct. 1935.

15. Quoted in *The Tablet*, 12 Oct. 1935.

16. Heenan, *Cardinal Hinsley*, pp. 55-58.

17. Quoted Heenan, *Cardinal Hinsley*, p. 55.

18. Quoted in Heenan, *Cardinal Hinsley*, p. 59.

19. *The Times*, 17 Oct. 1935.

20. Mathew, *Catholicism in England*, pp. 264-265.

21. Quoted in Moloney, *Westminster, Whitehall and The Vatican*, p. 51.

22. Hachey, *Anglo-Vatican Relations*, p. 298.

23. Clifton, *Amigo: Friend of the Poor*, p. 141; Aspden, *Fortress Church*, p. 227.

24. Moloney, *Westminster, Whitehall and The Vatican*, pp. 51-53; Crichton, '1920-1940: The Dawn of a Liturgical Movement' in Crichton, Winstone and Ainslie (eds), *English Catholic Worship: Liturgical Renewal in England Since 1900*, p. 34.

25. Quoted in Fontenelle, *His Holiness Pope Pius XI*, p. 252.

26. Hastings, *A History of English Christianity*, pp. 314-315.

27. *Acta* of the Bishops' Meeting, 20 Oct. 1936. LDA, Poskitt Papers. The Hierarchy had sent a similar letter of support to the Spanish bishops on 4 July 1933. AAW, Hi 139/2 (b)

28. Holmes, *The Papacy in the Modern World*, pp. 98-100; Atkin and Tallett, *Priests, Prelates and People*, pp. 210-211.

29. Burleigh, *Sacred Causes*, p. 157.

30. *Acta* of the Bishops' Meeting, 20 Oct. 1936. AAW, Hi 139/2(c). The Hierarchy had sent a message of support to the Spanish bishops in July 1933 during previous attacks on the Church. AAW, Hi 139/2 (b).

31. Quoted in Clifton, *Amigo: Friend of the Poor*, pp. 142-143. See also Hale, 'Fighting Over The Fight in Spain: The Pro-Franco Campaign of Bishop Peter Amigo' in *The Catholic Historical Review*, vol. XCI, no. 3, July 2005, pp. 462-483.

32 Buchanan, 'Great Britain' in Buchanan and Conway (eds), *Political Catholicism in Europe, 1918-1965*, p. 269.

33. Quoted in Aspden, *Fortress Church*, p. 216.

34. Moloney, *Westminster, Whitehall and The Vatican*, pp. 68-70.

35. Aspden, *Fortress Church*, pp. 218-223.

36. Quoted in Moloney, *Westminster, Whitehall and The Vatican*, p. 64.

37. Quoted in Allitt, *Catholic Converts: British and American Intellectuals Turn To Rome*, p. 227.

38. Aspden, *Fortress Church*, pp. 217-223.

39. Moloney, *Westminster, Whitehall and The Vatican*, p. 66.

40. *The Catholic Worker*, Aug. 1936.

41. Aspden, *Fortress Church*, pp. 207-208.

42. *Acta* of the Bishops' Meeting, 26-27 April 1938; Moloney, *Westminster, Whitehall and The Vatican*, pp. 77-82; Birn, *The League of Nations Union*, p. 174.

43. *The Tablet*, 17 Dec. 1938.

44. *Rector's Annual Report*, Lent 1936. AAW, Hi/53; Williams, *St Alban's College, Valladolid*, pp. 206-211.

45. Henson to Hinsley, 31 July 1936. ACSA, Henson Papers, 127.1.

46. Hinsley to Henson, 22 Aug. 1936. ACSA, Henson Papers, 127.1.

47. Henson to Hinsley, 30 Aug. 1936. ACSA, Henson Papers, 127.1.

48. Henson to Hinsley, 17 Sept. 1936. ACSA, Henson Papers, 127.1.

49. Henson to Hinsley, 31 Aug. 1937. ACSA, Henson Papers, 127.1.

50. Hinsley to Henson, 30 March 1937. ACSA, Henson Papers, 127.1.

51. Moloney, *Westminster, Whitehall and The Vatican*, pp. 67-70.

52. Quoted in Aspden, *Fortress Church*, p. 217.

53. *The Times*, 3 March 1937 and 26 July 1937.

54. Williams, *St Alban's College, Valladolid*, p. 214.

55. Henson to Hinsley, 10 May 1937. ACSA, Henson Papers, 127.1.

56. Hinsley to Henson, 14 May 1937. ACSA, Henson Papers, 127.1.

57. Henson to Hinsley, 1 Nov. 1937. ACSA, Henson Papers, 127.1.
58. Franco to Henson, 12 May 1937. ACSA, Henson Papers, 127.1.
59. Hinsley to Moriarty, 20 May 1937. SHDA, Moriarty Papers.
60. Henson to Moriarty, 14 May 1937. SHDA, Moriarty Papers.
61. Henson to Hinsley, 1 Nov. 1937. ACSA, Henson Papers, 127.1.
62. Hinsley to Henson, 8 Nov. 1937. ACSA, Henson Papers, 127.1.
63. *The Times*, 26 July 1937.
64. Henson to the Hierarchy, 27 March 1939. ACSA, Henson Papers, 127.1
65. McNulty to Henson, 1 April 1939. ACSA, Henson Papers, 127.1
66. Hinsley to Franco, 28 March 1939. AAW, Hi 2/217.
67. Quoted in Moloney, *Westminster, Whitehall and The Vatican*, p. 60.
68. Hinsley to Moriarty, 29 Jan. 1940. SHDA, Moriarty Papers. *Acta* of the Bishops' Meeting, 3 April 1940. LDA, Poskitt Papers.
69. *The Times*, 24 May 1937. In April 1941 the Hierarchy sent its congratulations and thanks to Henson in recognition of his devoted and successful work as Rector of the English College, Valladolid. Bishop McNulty proposed that he be created a Protonotary Apostolic. AAW, Hi 2/217.
70. Moloney, *Westminster, Whitehall and The Vatican*, p. 124.
71. Holmes, *The Papacy in the Modern World*, pp. 111-113, 125.
72. *The Times*, 23 Sept. 1937. Hinsley had addressed the issue of 'the radical equality of human beings' in his Advent Pastoral of 1937. See *The Sword of The Spirit*, p. 3.
73. Quoted in Moloney, *Westminster, Whitehall and The Vatican*, p. 124.
74. *Acta* of the Bishops' Meeting, 25 Oct. 1938. LDA, Poskitt papers. See also Feiling, *Neville Chamberlain*, p. 462.
75. *The Times*, 2 Dec. 1938.
76. *The Times*, 3 Dec. 1938.
77. Holmes, *The Papacy in the Modern World*, p. 153.
78. *The Times*, 3 Feb. 1939; Heenan, *Cardinal Hinsley*, pp. 100-102.
79. Moloney, *Westminster, Whitehall and The Vatican*, pp. 121-124; Rhodes, *The Vatican in the Age of the Dictators*, p. 225.
80. Flint, 'English Catholics and the Proposed Soviet Alliance, 1939' in *Journal of Ecclesiastical History*, vol. 48, no. 3, July 1997, pp. 471-472; *The Tablet*, 22 April 1939.
81. Quoted in Moloney, *Westminster, Whitehall and The Vatican*, p. 128.
82. Moloney, *Westminster, Whitehall and The Vatican*, p. 129.
83. *The Times*, 8 Sept. 1939.
84. *The Bond of Peace and other Wartime Addresses*, pp. 5-6.
85. *The Tablet*, 16 Sept. 1939.

Chapter Thirteen *Domestic Affairs 1935-1943*

1. MacDonald, *Catholic Action: The Notion and England*, p. 178. In 1930 the British Minister in Rome reported that one of the principal features of

papal policy was the constant advocacy of Catholic Action. See Hachey, *Anglo-Vatican Relations*, p. 196.

2. Heenan, *Cardinal Hinsley*, p. 153.

3. *Joint Pastoral Letter of the Hierarchy of England and Wales on The Apostolate of the Laity*, Advent 1936. SDA, Henshaw Papers, 203/145.

4. Aspden, *Fortress Church*, pp. 156-157, 198-199; Atkin and Tallett, *Priests, Prelates and People*, p. 229.

5. Moloney, *Westminster, Whitehall and The Vatican*, pp. 149-151.

6. *Westminster Cathedral Chronicle*, May 1935, p. 73.

7. Archbishop Hinsley, 'Regale Sacerdotium:The Participation of the Laity in the Apostolate of the Hierarchy' in *The Clergy Review*, Jan.-June 1936, pp. 181-191.

8. *Acta* of Bishops' Meeting, 22 Oct. 1935. LDA, Poskitt Papers.

9. *Joint Pastoral Letter of the Hierarchy of England and Wales on The Apostolate of the Laity*, Advent 1936. SDA, Henshaw Papers, 203/145.

10. *The Tablet*, 7 Nov. 1936.

11. *The Tablet*, 19 Dec. 1936.

12. Hinsley to the Hierarchy, 18 Sept. 1937. NDA, McNulty Papers, Catholic Action file; Aspden, *Fortress Church*, p. 201.

13. *The Catholic Worker*, Jan. 1936.

14. Heenan, *Cardinal Hinsley*, pp. 157-161.

15. *The Tablet*, 7 Nov. 1936.

16. Heenan, *Cardinal Hinsley*, p. 164.

17. *Westminster Catholic Chronicle*, May 1935, p. 73.

18. *Acta* of the Bishops' Meeting, 26 Oct. 1937. LDA, Poskitt Papers.

19. *Westminster Catholic Chronicle*, Feb. 1938, pp. 38-39. The monthly magazine kept priests and congregations fully informed of developments in Catholic Action.

20. Hinsley to Hope, 9 Sept. 1939. AAW, Bo 1/141; Aspden, *Fortress Church*, pp. 199-200.

21. Doyle, *Mitres and Missions in Lancashire:The Roman Catholic Diocese of Liverpool 1850-2000*, pp. 272-284; Aspden, *Fortress Church*, p. 211. Downey used the pages of *The Catholic Worker* to describe how Catholic Action operated in his diocese.

22. Diocese of Leeds, Report of the Diocesan Advisory Committee for Catholic Action, 30 Jan. 1938. LDA, Poskitt Papers.

23. De La Bédoyère, *Christian Crisis*, pp. 123-124.

24. Quoted in Moloney, *Westminster, Whitehall and The Vatican*, p. 152.

25. *The Tablet,* 20 Mar. 1943.

26. *Westminster Catholic Chronicle*, May 1935, p. 73.

27. *Acta* of the Bishops' Meeting, 22 Oct.1935. LDA, Poskitt Papers. Moloney, *Westminster, Whitehall and The Vatican*, p. 157.

28. McNulty to Cowgill, 22 March 1936. LDA, Cowgill Papers. Moloney, *Westminster, Whitehall and The Vatican*, p. 158.

29. *Acta* of Bishops' Meeting, 1 May 1935. LDA, Poskitt Papers.
30. Moloney, *Westminster, Whitehall and The Vatican*, p. 159.
31. *The Times*, 3 Feb. 1936.
32. Quoted in Moloney, *Westminster, Whitehall and The Vatican*, p. 159.
33. *Acta* of Bishops' Meeting, 28 Feb. 1936. LDA, Poskitt Papers.
34. Moloney, *Westminster, Whitehall and The Vatican*, pp. 159-160.
35. Hinsley to McNulty, 3 May 1936. NDA, McNulty Papers, H02-01.
36. Hawkswell to Henshaw, 9 Mar. 1936. SDA, Henshaw Papers, Box 41, File 7.
37. Moloney, *Westminster, Whitehall and The Vatican*, p. 158.
38. *Acta* of Bishops' Meeting, 20 Oct. 1936. LDA, Poskitt Papers.
39. *Acta* of the Bishops' Meeting, 27 April 1938. LDA, Poskitt Papers. *Memorandum presented to the Board of Education by a Deputation of the Catholic Archbishops of England and Wales and representatives of the Catholic Education Council.* SDA, Henshaw Papers, Box 41, File 7.
40. Board of Education to the C.E.C., 25 July 1938. SDA, Henshaw Papers, Box 41, File 7.
41. Moloney, *Westminster, Whitehall and The Vatican*, pp. 85-86.
42. Clifton, *Amigo: Friend of the Poor*, pp. 116-117.
43. Moloney, *Westminster, Whitehall and The Vatican*, pp. 85-86.
44. Hachey, *Anglo-Vatican Relations*, pp. xxii-xxiii; Heenan, *Cardinal Hinsley*, pp. 226-228; *The Tablet*, 26 Nov. 1938.
45. Fitzalan to Williams, Nov. 1938. ABA, Williams Papers, AP/C28/18.
46. Moloney, *Westminster, Whitehall and The Vatican*, p. 90.
47. Quoted in Moloney, *Westminster, Whitehall and The Vatican*, p. 90.
48. Hachey, *Anglo-Vatican Relations*, p. 390; *The Catholic Who's Who*, 1940, p. 197.
49. Quoted in Moloney, *Westminster, Whitehall and The Vatican*, pp. 94-95.
50. *Acta* of the Bishops' Meeting, 25 Oct. 1938. LDA, Poskitt Papers.
51. Quoted in Moloney, *Westminster, Whitehall and The Vatican*, pp. 96-97.
52. Quoted in Clifton, *Amigo: Friend of the Poor*, pp. 116-117.
53. Godfrey to the Hierarchy, 24 Mar. 1939. AAW, Hi 2/5.
54. Hachey, *Anglo-Vatican Relations*, p. 386.
55. Hastings, *Church and State: The English Experience*, p. 44.
56. Moloney, *Westminster, Whitehall and The Vatican*, p. 100.
57. Hinsley to Doubleday, 11 Dec. 1938. BDA, Doubleday Papers, D2/Westminster.
58. *The Catholic Who's Who 1940*, p. 274. See also Drumm, *The Old Palace: The Catholic Chaplaincy at Oxford* for a full treatment of Knox's work at the university.
59. Quoted in Norman, *Roman Catholicism in England*, p. 125.
60. Hinsley to Godfrey, 8 Aug. 1936, AVEC, Scritt. 86.6. Hinsley spoke of Knox as 'a great writer who cleverly and effectively defends the Catholic cause. In this respect he is second only to G.K. Chesterton'.
61. Bainbridge, 'French Church Melodies in *The Westminster Hymnal*' in *The*

Clergy Review, April 1943, pp. 167-171; and 'Old Psalter Tunes in *The Westminster Hymnal*' in *The Clergy Review*, July 1943, pp. 301-305.

62. Thompson, 'Second Thoughts on *The New Westminster Hymnal*' in *The Clergy Review*, Feb. 1943, pp. 74-76.
63. Waugh, *The Life of Ronald Knox*, p. 256.
64. Clifton, *Amigo: Friend of the Poor*, pp. 120-122.
65. Quoted in Waugh, *The Life of Ronald Knox*, p. 256.
66. Quoted in Waugh, *The Life of Ronald Knox*, p. 256.
67. Waugh, *The Life of Ronald Knox*, pp. 256-257.
68. Quoted in Clifton, *Amigo: Friend of the Poor*, p. 123.
69. Hollis to Moriarty, 26 June 1941. SDA, Moriarty Papers.
70. Elwes to Moriarty, 1 July 1941. SDA, Moriarty Papers.
71. Crichton, '1920-1940: The Dawn of a Liturgical Movement' in Crichton, Winstone and Ainslie (eds), *English Catholic Worship: Liturgical Renewal in England Since 1900*, p. 37.
72. Quoted in Waugh, *The Life of Ronald Knox*, p. 264.
73. Quoted in Waugh, *The Life of Ronald Knox*, p. 268.
74. *Acta* of the Bishops' meeting, 25 Oct. 1938. LDA, Poskitt Papers; Quoted in Waugh, *The Life of Ronald Knox*, p. 269.
75. Quoted in Waugh, *The Life of Ronald Knox*, p. 285. *Acta* of the Bishops' Meeting, 18-19 April 1939. LDA, Poskitt Papers.
76. Knox, 'Some Problems of Bible Translation' in *The Clergy Review*, Feb. 1940, pp. 95-103; Pope, 'Some Omissions in the Douay-Rheims Version' in *The Clergy Review*, Aug. 1940, pp. 112-121.
77. Quoted in Waugh, *The Life of Ronald Knox*, p. 287.
78. Quoted in Clifton, *Amigo: Friend of the Poor*, p. 124.
79. Quoted in Clifton, *Amigo: Friend of the Poor*, p. 124.
80. *Acta* of the Bishops' meeting, 29 Oct. 1942. LDA, Poskitt Papers.
81. Waugh, *The Life of Ronald Knox*, p. 290.
82. Waugh, *The Life of Ronald Knox*, pp. 298-302.

Chapter Fourteen *A Bishop In Wartime 1939-1943*

1. *The Tablet*, 16 Sept. 1939.
2. *The Bond of Peace and other Wartime Addresses*, p. 3.
3. Gwynn, 'The Flight from the Cities' in *The Clergy Review*, Dec. 1939, pp. 471-480; and 'Evacuation and its Opportunities' in *The Clergy Review*, March 1940, pp. 211-223.
4. *Pastoral Letter of Cardinal Hinsley, Trinity Sunday 1940*. AAW, Hi Misc.; Clifton, *Amigo: Friend of the Poor*, pp. 156-157.
5. *Westminster Cathedral Chronicle*, Oct. 1940, p. 223; Aug. 1941, p. 183.
6. Hinsley to McNulty, 16 Oct. 1940. NDA, McNulty Papers, H37.
7. *Pastoral Letter of Cardinal Hinsley, Advent 1940*. AAW, Hi Misc.
8. *Westminster Cathedral Chronicle*, Oct. 1940, p. 222; Nov. 1945, pp. 219-221.

9. Hinsley, *Ad Clerum*, 9 Oct. 1940. AAW, Hi 2/147.
10. Hinsley to Doubleday, 19 Sept. 1940. BDA, Doubleday Papers.
11. Hinsley to Doubleday, 19 Sept. 1940. BDA, Doubleday Papers. Clifton, *Amigo: Friend of the Poor*, pp. 163-164.
12. Hinsley to Mooney, 30 March 1941. AAW, Bo 1/141.
13. Clifton, *Amigo: Friend of the Poor*, pp. 159-160.
14. Aspden, *Fortress Church*, p. 251; Heenan, *Cardinal Hinsley*, p. 171.
15. Heenan, *Cardinal Hinsley*, p. 162.
16. *Pastoral Letter of Cardinal Hinsley, Advent 1937*. AAW, Hi Misc.; Heenan, *Cardinal Hinsley*, pp. 164-172.
17. *The Times*, 21 Dec. 1940.
18. *Pastoral Letter of Cardinal Hinsley, Advent 1941*. AAW, Hi Misc.
19. Heenan, *Cardinal Hinsley*, p. 172.
20. Watt, 'The Beveridge Report Summarised' in *The Clergy Review*, April 1943, pp. 146-154.
21. Hinsley to the Hierarchy, 8 May 1939. ABA, Williams Papers, AP/W3.
22. Clifton, *Amigo: Friend of the Poor*, pp. 154-155.
23. *Acta* of the Bishops' Meeting, 6 Sept. 1939. LDA, Poskitt Papers.
24. Mathew to the Hierarchy, 14 May 1939. ABA, Williams Papers, AP/W3.
25. Williams to Mathew, 15 May 1939. ABA, Williams Papers, AP/W3.
26. Clifton, *Amigo: Friend of the Poor*, p. 156.
27. Johnstone and Hagerty, *The Cross on the Sword: Catholic Chaplains in the Forces*, pp. 185-189.
28. Clifton, *Amigo: Friend of the Poor*, p. 158.
29. Johnstone and Hagerty, *The Cross on the Sword: Catholic Chaplains in the Forces*, pp. 192-193.
30. Hinsley, *Ad Clerum*, 30 Jan. 1939. AAW, Hi 2/168; Hinsley to Elwes, 11 Sept. 1939. AAW, Hi Misc. Elwes became a Royal Navy chaplain in 1943. See Drumm, *The Old Palace: The Catholic Chaplaincy at Oxford*, p. 90.
31. Quoted in Moloney, *Westminster, Whitehall and the Vatican*, p. 146.
32. Quoted in Moloney, *Westminster, Whitehall and the Vatican*, pp. 146-147.
33. Dey to Doubleday, 1 June 1942. BDA, Doubleday Papers. Coughlan to Hinsley, 31 March 1942. AAW, Bo 1/142. Dey wrote in a similar vein to *The Tablet* on 24 August 1942 when he complained that 'the producers', i.e. the bishops, would not respond to 'supply the need'.
34. Doubleday to Amigo, 19 Jan. 1943. BDA, Doubleday Papers.
35. Clifton, *Amigo: Friend of the Poor*, p. 159.
36. Hinsley to the Hierarchy, Jan. 1943. BDA, Doubleday Papers.
37. Heenan, *Cardinal Hinsley*, p. 121.
38. Heenan, *Cardinal Hinsley*, p. 119.
39. *The Times*, 2 Sept. 1941.
40. Heenan, *Cardinal Hinsley*, p. 115.
41. *Westminster Catholic Chronicle*, March 1940, pp. 55-57.
42. *The Bond of Peace and other Wartime Addresses*, p. 141.

43. *The Bond of Peace and other Wartime Addresses,* pp. 103-108.
44. Heenan, *Cardinal Hinsley*, p. 126.
45. Heenan, *Cardinal Hinsley*, p. 127.
46. See Chadwick, *Shifting Alliances: Church and State in English Education*, pp. 25-39; Cannon, 'The Influence of Religion on Educational Policy, 1902-1944' in Musgrave (ed.), *Sociology, History and Education*, pp. 162-173.
47. *The Times*, 20 Jan. and 17 Feb. 1940.
48. Chadwick, *Shifting Alliances: Church and State in English Education,* p. 26.
49. Chadwick, *Shifting Alliances: Church and State in English Education,* pp. 30-33.
50. Davies, ' "L'Art du Possible": the Board of Education, The Catholic Church and Negotiations over the White Paper and Education Bill, 1943-1944' in *Recusant History*, vol. 22, no. 2, Oct. 1994, pp. 231-250.
51. Quoted in Chadwick, *Shifting Alliances: Church and State in English Education*, p. 31.
52. NAEd. 136-271, 13 June 1941. These references are taken from Davies, 'The Catholic Church and the 1944 Education Act' in *Catholic Archives*, 1998, no.18, pp. 43-54.
53. NAEd. 136-271, 19 Nov. 1941.
54. NAEd. 136-226, 25 June 1942.
55. NAEd. 136-226, 15 Sept. 1942.
56. *The Times*, 2 Nov. 1942.
57. *The Times*, 31 Nov. 1942.
58. Elliott, ' "A very pushy kind of folk": Educational Reform 1944 and the Catholic Laity of England and Wales' in *History of Education*, vol. 35, no. 1, (Jan. 2006), pp.92-93.
59. Heenan, *Cardinal Hinsley*, pp. 129-131.
60. *The Times*, 16 Jan. 1941.
61. Heenan, *Cardinal Hinsley*, p. 132.
62. *The Times*, 8 Dec. 1942.
63. Davies, ' "L'Art du Possible": the Board of Education, The Catholic Church and Negotiations over the White Paper and Education Bill, 1943-1944', p. 240.
64. Quoted in Cannon, 'The Influence of Religion on Educational Policy, 1902-1944', pp. 13-14.
65. *Joint Pastoral Letter of the Hierarchy of England and Wales on The Schools Question.* LDA, Poskitt Papers. This contained a summary of the Church's huge contribution to the provision of education.

Chapter Fifteen *The Cross and the Flag 1939-1943*

1. See Walsh, *From Sword to Ploughshare: Sword of the Spirit to Catholic Institute for International Relations 1940-1980*; Mews, 'The Sword of the Spirit: A Catholic Cultural Crusade of 1940' in Sheils (ed.), *The Church and War*,

(Studies in Church History, no. 20, 1983), pp. 409-430; and Beales, 'The Sword of the Spirit' in *The Month*, vol. CLXXVI, no. 916, Oct. 1940, pp. 203-208.

2. Hinsley to Marshall, 25 March 1941. SDA, Marshall Papers.

3. Hinsley, *The Sword of the Spirit: An Address broadcast on December 10, 1939*. Tom Burns of the Ministry of Information told Elwes that the Cardinal had 'made a tremendous hit' and that the Ministry wanted to put the broadcast 'to the best possible use'. Burns to Elwes, 12 Dec. 1939. AAW, Hi 2/13.

4. Moloney, *Westminster, Whitehall and the Vatican*, pp. 188-189.

5. Quoted in *Westminster Cathedral Chronicle*, Aug. 1940, p. 173.

6. *The Times*, 22 July 1940.

7. Moloney, *Westminster, Whitehall and the Vatican*, p. 189.

8. Murray, 'Some Successful Experiments in Christian Formation in the British Army and Royal Air Force', *Lumen Vitae*, vol. ii, no.1, 1947, p. 138; Hinsley, *Bond of Peace*, p. 87.

9. *The Times*, 6 Aug. 1940.

10. Moloney, Westminster, Whitehall and the Vatican, p. 189.

11. Burns to Elwes, 15 Dec. 1939. AAW, Hi 2/13.

12. Quoted in Heenan, *Cardinal Hinsley*, p. 189.

13. Heenan, *Cardinal Hinsley*, p. 93.

14. Hinsley to Bishops, 7 Aug. 1940. SDA, Marshall Papers, 183/74.

15. McNulty to Marshall, 11 Aug. 1940. SDA, Marshall Papers, 183/76.

16. Marshall to Hinsley, 13 Aug. 1940. SDA, Marshall Papers, 183/79.

17. Elwes to McNulty, 5 Nov. 1940. ADHN, McNulty Papers, OF/162.

18. McNulty to Elwes, 7 Nov. 1940. ADHN, McNulty Papers, OF/162.

19. Hinsley to McNulty, 12 Nov. 1940. ADHN, McNulty Papers, OF/162.

20. McNulty to Hinsley, 20 Nov. 1940; Hinsley to McNulty, 24 Nov. 1940. ADHN, McNulty Papers, OF/162.

21. Mews, 'The Sword of the Spirit: A Catholic Cultural Crusade of 1940', pp. 421-422.

22. *The Times*, 27 Aug. 1940.

23. *The Times*, 21 Dec. 1940.

24. *The Times*, 28 Dec. 1940.

25. *The Times*, 7 Feb. 1941.

26. Aspden, *Fortress Church*, pp. 234-237.

27. Walsh, 'Ecumenism in Wartime Britain: The Sword of the Spirit and Religion and Life, 1940-1945 (1)', p. 243 in *The Heythrop Journal*, July 1982.

28. Quoted in Moloney, *Westminster, Whitehall and the Vatican*, pp. 190-191.

29. Heenan, *Cardinal Hinsley*, pp. 190-193.

30. Walsh, 'Ecumenism in Wartime Britain: The Sword of the Spirit and Religion and Life, 1940-1945 (1)', p. 245.

31. Quoted in Heenan, *Cardinal Hinsley*, p. 193; Aspden, Fortress Church, p. 242.

32. Iremonger, *William Temple, Archbishop of Canterbury: His Life and Letters*, p. 385.

33. Bell, *Christian Unity: The Anglican Position*, p. 79.

34. Quoted in Moloney, *Westminster, Whitehall and the Vatican*, p. 192.

35. Quoted in Mews, 'The Sword of the Spirit: A Catholic Cultural Crusade of 1940', p. 425.

36. Hinsley to Marshall, 25 March 1941. SDA, Marshall Papers, 183/80.

37. *Acta* of the Bishops' Meeting, 22-23 April 1041. LDA, Poskitt Papers.

38. Quoted in Moloney, *Westminster, Whitehall and the Vatican*, p. 198.

39. Mews, 'The Sword of the Spirit: A Catholic Cultural Crusade of 1940', pp. 422-423.

40. Heenan, *Cardinal Hinsley*, p. 194; Moloney, *Westminster, Whitehall and the Vatican*, p. 203.

41. Moloney, *Westminster, Whitehall and the Vatican*, p. 194.

42. Jasper, *George Bell, Bishop of Chichester*, pp. 252-253.

43. Moloney, *Westminster, Whitehall and the Vatican*, p. 199.

44. Heenan, *Cardinal Hinsley*, pp. 193-198; *A Champion of the Spirit*, p. 8.

45. Quoted in Heenan, *Cardinal Hinsley*, pp. 199-200.

46. Jasper, *George Bell, Bishop of Chichester*, pp. 252-253.

47. Jasper, *George Bell, Bishop of Chichester*, p. 254.

48. Aspden, *Fortress Church*, pp. 244-245.

49. Flynn to Williams, 20 Aug. 1940. ABA, Williams Papers, AP/C28/20.

50. Flynn to Williams, 3 Aug. 1941. ABA, Williams Papers, AP/C28/20.

51. Doyle, *Mitres and Missions in Lancashire: The Roman Catholic Diocese of Liverpool 1850-2000*, pp. 106-109.

52. Downey to Marshall, 20 March 1942. SDA, Marshall Papers, 183/85.

53. Clifton, *Amigo: Friend of the Poor*, pp. 167-170.

54. Moloney, *Westminster, Whitehall and the Vatican*, p. 202.

55. *The Tablet*, 11 April 1942.

56. Heenan, *Cardinal Hinsley*, pp. 194, 209.

57. Moloney, *Westminster, Whitehall and the Vatican*, p. 202.

58. See Murray, 'Some Successful Experiments in Christian Formation in the British Army and Royal Air Force', *Lumen Vitae*, vol. ii, no. 1, 1947, pp. 138-158; and Mayne, 'Lay Apostles in the Forces', *The Month*, March-April 1943, vol. CLXXIX, no. 932, pp. 107-115.

59. Moloney, *Westminster, Whitehall and the Vatican*, p. 195.

60. Brown to Heenan, 3 March 1944. BDA, Heenan Papers; Murray, 'Some Successful Experiments in Christian Formation in the British Army and Royal Air Force', *Lumen Vitae*, vol. ii, no. 1, 1947, pp. 138-158.

61. Lowry, *William Temple: An Archbishop For All Seasons*, p. 54; Iremonger, *William Temple, Archbishop of Canterbury: His Life and Letters*, pp. 423-424.

62. Moloney, *Westminster, Whitehall and the Vatican*, pp. 189-190.

63. Mahoney, 'Christian Co-operation' in *The Clergy Review*, July 1942, pp. 294-311.

64. Heenan, *Cardinal Hinsley*, p. 209.

65. Morehouse, *Wartime Pilgrimage*, pp. 112–113.

66. Moloney, *Westminster, Whitehall and the Vatican*, p. 186; Bell, *Christian Unity: The Anglican Position*, p. 79.

67. *The Times*, 8 Sept. 1939.

68. *The Times*, 22 May 1940.

69. *Acta* of the Bishops' Meeting, 25 Oct. 1938. LDA, Poskitt Papers.

70. Heenan, *Cardinal Hinsley*, pp. 113–114.

71. Quoted in Feiling, *Neville Chamberlain*, p. 462.

72. Quoted in Heenan, *Cardinal Hinsley*, p. 114.

73. *The Times*, 20 Sept. 1939.

74. Cardinal Hinsley: *Friend of Poland*, p. 10.

75. *A Champion of the Spirit*, p. 12.

76. *The Times*, 9 Dec. 1942.

77. *Westminster Cathedral Chronicle*, Jan. 1943, p.10.

78. Finnish Ambassador to Hinsley, 14 Dec. 1939; Hinsley to Finnish Ambassador, 15 Dec 1939. AAW, Hi 2/13.

79. *The Bond of Peace and Other Wartime Addresses*, pp. 75–76.

80. Quoted in Moloney, *Westminster, Whitehall and the Vatican*, pp. 143–144.

81. Reith to Hinsley, 15 Feb. 1940 and Hinsley to Reith, 16 Feb 1940. AWA, Bo 1/141.

82. Quoted in Heenan, *Cardinal Hinsley*, pp. 218–221.

83. Morehouse, *Wartime Pilgrimage*, pp. 110–116.

84. Quoted in Heenan, *Cardinal Hinsley*, pp. 218–219.

85. *Westminster Cathedral Chronicle*, May 1942, p. 100.

86. Hinsley to Editor, *The Catholic World*, 13 Oct. 1939. AAW, Hi 2/173. Like others in England, Hinsley was conscious of the fact that a few significant Americans 'in high places' were favourably disposed to the Nazis. Hinsley to Sheehy at the Catholic University of America, 16 Sept. 1940. AAW, Bo 1/141.

87. Hinsley to Mooney, 23 Feb. 1941. AAW, Bo 1/141.

88. *A Champion of the Spirit*, pp. 4, 11–12.

89. *The Bond of Peace and Other Wartime Addresses*, pp. 57–71.

90. *The Catholic Herald*, 31 May 1940.

91. *The Bond of Peace and Other Wartime Addresses*, pp. 57–71; Flint, 'English Catholics and the Proposed Soviet Alliance, 1939' in *Journal of Ecclesiastical History*, vol. 48, no. 3, July 1997, pp. 468-484.

92. *The Tablet*, 13 March 1943.

93. *Westminster Cathedral Chronicle*, July 1941, pp. 145–147.

94. Flint, 'English Catholics and the Proposed Soviet Alliance, 1939' in *Journal of Ecclesiastical History*, vol. 48, no. 3, July 1997, p. 469.

95. See Hinsley's Press Statement on the Abdication, 14 Dec. 1936; Catholic Newspapers Committee to Hinsley, 22 Jan. 1940; and Ministry of Information to Hinsley, 24 June 1940. AAW, Hi 2/173.

96.   Quoted in Moloney, *Westminster, Whitehall and the Vatican*, p. 226.

97.   Moloney, *Westminster, Whitehall and the Vatican*, pp. 228-232.

98.   *The Times*, 8 Sept. 1941.

99.   *Moloney, Westminster, Whitehall and the Vatican*, pp. 232-233.

100.   *The Catholic Herald*, 16 June 1940.

101.   *Acta* of the Bishops' Meeting, 14-15 April 1942. LDA, Poskitt Papers.

102.   *Westminster Cathedral Chronicle*, Feb. 1943, p. 26.

Chapter Sixteen *Ireland, Exiles and Jews 1935-1943*

1.   NCCL to Hinsley, 21 Aug. 1935 and 22 Aug. 1935. AAW, Hi 2/190 D. *Acta* of the Bishops' Meeting, 22 Oct. 1935. LDA Poskitt Papers.

2.   Hinsley to Lang, 21 June 1936 and Lang to Hinsley, 23 June 1935. AWA, Hi 2/190 D.

3.   Hinsley to Baldwin, 23 June 1936. AAW, Hi 2/190 D.

4.   Quoted in Aspden, *Fortress Church*, pp. 202-203; Hinsley to McNulty, 5 Jan. 1939. NDA, McNulty Papers, H 36, on 'Leakage'.

5.   *The Tablet*, 1 July 1939.

6.   Fleming to Hinsley, 1 July 1939. AAW, Hi 2/190 D.

7.   Hinsley to MacRory and De Valera, 5 July 1939. AAW, Hi 2/190 D.

8.   MacRory to Hinsley, 8 July 1939. AAW, Hi 2/190 D.

9.   Hinsley to Bishops Doubleday, Barrett and Poskitt, 6 July 1939. AAW, Hi 2/190 D.

10.   Godfrey to Hinsley, 7 July 1939; Hinsley to Mahoney, 8 July 1939; Poskitt to Hinsley, 8 July 1939. AAW, Hi 2/190 D.

11.   Canning, *British Policy Towards Ireland, 1921-1941*, p. 259.

12.   Hinsley to Churchill, 4 Oct. 1939. AAW, Hi 2/190 D.

13.   Quoted in Cooney, *John Charles McQuaid, Ruler of Catholic Ireland*, p. 143.

14.   Cooney, *John Charles McQuaid, Ruler of Catholic Ireland*, pp. 142-144.

15.   Heenan, *Cardinal Hinsley*, pp. 98-99.

16.   Williams to Downey, 28 Sept. 1941; Delahunty to Downey, 8 Oct. 1941; Downey to Williams, 14 Oct. 1941. ABA, Williams Papers, AP/C28/15.

17.   Moloney, *Westminster, Whitehall and The Vatican*, pp. 168-172.

18.   Moloney, *Westminster, Whitehall and The Vatican*, p. 172.

19.   Moloney, *Westminster, Whitehall and The Vatican*, p. 173; see also *The Persecution of the Catholic Church in German Occupied Poland*.

20.   *The Times*, 8 Sept. 1941.

21.   Moloney, *Westminster, Whitehall and The Vatican*, pp. 172-174.

22.   *The Times*, 4 May 1942.

23.   Moloney, *Westminster, Whitehall and The Vatican*, p.174.

24.   Schwarzbarf to Hinsley, 9 July 192. AAW, Hi 1/25.

25.   *The Times*, 9 Dec. 1942.

26.   Moloney, *Westminster, Whitehall and The Vatican*, p. 175; Hinsley to Suhard, 4 June 1940. AAW, Bo 1/141.

27. Hinsley's prayer for France was reprinted in *A Champion of the Spirit*, pp. 12-13.

28. 'Heroic France' in *The Bond of Peace and other Wartime Addresses*, pp. 75-77.

29. Moloney, *Westminster, Whitehall and The Vatican*, pp. 176-178.

30. Moloney, *Westminster, Whitehall and The Vatican*, pp. 179-181.

31. Hinsley to Eden, 7 Feb. 1941. AAW, Bo 1/141.

32. *The Jewish Chronicle*, 4 Jan. 1935, quoted in Moloney, *Westminster, Whitehall and The Vatican*, p. 208.

33. *The Jewish Chronicle*, 29 May 1936, quoted in Moloney, *Westminster, Whitehall and The Vatican*, p. 209.

34. Quoted in Moloney, *Westminster, Whitehall and The Vatican*, p. 206.

35. Moloney, *Westminster, Whitehall and The Vatican*, p. 206.

36. *The Times*, 17 Nov. 1938.

37. *Acta* of the Bishops' Meeting, 25 Oct. 1938. LDA, Poskitt Papers.

38. *The Times*, 2 Dec. 1938.

39. *The Times*, 3 Dec. 1938.

40. *The Times*, 17 Dec. 1938.

41. Moloney, *Westminster, Whitehall and The Vatican*, pp. 213-215.

42. Moloney, *Westminster, Whitehall and The Vatican*, p. 211.

43. Rhodes, *The Vatican In The Age of Dictators 1922-1945*, pp. 346-347; Moloney, *Westminster, Whitehall and The Vatican*, p. 219.

44. Heenan, *Cardinal Hinsley*, p. 224.

45. *The Times*, 26 Jan. 1942.

46. Quoted in Moloney, *Westminster, Whitehall and The Vatican*, p. 219.

47. Heenan, *Cardinal Hinsley*, pp. 221-222.

48. Heenan, *Cardinal Hinsley*, pp. 223-224.

49. Aspden, *Fortress Church*, pp. 245.

Epilogue

1. Griffin, *Seek Ye First*, p. 3.

2. *The Times*, 22 March 1943.

3. Wheeler-Bennett, *King George VI*, p. 743.

4. Heenan, *Cardinal Hinsley*, pp. 4-5.

5. Heenan, *Cardinal Hinsley*, p. 9.

6. Heenan, *Cardinal Hinsley*, p. 10.

7. Heenan, *Cardinal Hinsley*, pp. 8-9.

8. Quoted in Bellenger and Fletcher, *Princes of the Church: A History of the English Cardinals*, p. 156.

9. Heenan, *Cardinal Hinsley*, p.12.

10. *Westminster Cathedral Chronicle*, May 1943, p. 2.

11. Heenan, *Cardinal Hinsley*, pp. 2-3.

12. Heenan, *Cardinal Hinsley*, p. 10.

13. *Westminster Cathedral Chronicle*, May 1943, p. 2.

14. Butler, 'The Art of the Possible' in Fowler et al, *Decision Making in British Education*, p. 14.
15. Jasper, *George Bell, Bishop of Chichester*, p. 249.
16. Henson, *Retrospect of an Unimportant Life*, p. 191.
17. Quoted in Bellenger and Fletcher, *Princes of the Church: A History of the English Cardinals*, p. 156.
18. Waugh, *Ronald Knox*, pp. 243-244.
19. Elwes, 'Cardinal Hinsley' in *The Clergy Review*, June 1943.
20. Mathew, *Catholicism in England*, p. 265.
21. Newton, 'Cardinal Hinsley' in *Dictionary of National Biography 1941-1950*, pp. 394-395.
22. Longley, *The Worlock Archive*, pp. 25-26.
23. Hastings, *A History of English Christianity*, p. 273.
24. Brown, 'Cardinal Hinsley' in *Through Windows of Memory*, p. 101.
25. Mathew, *Catholicism In England*, p. 265.
26. McNulty to Payne, 18 March 1943. NDA, McNulty Papers HO2 /01.
27. Hinsley to Doubleday, 12 Aug. 1940. BDA, D2 Westminster.
28. Mathew, *Catholicism In England*, p. 268.
29. Myers: *Ad Clerum*. NDA, McNulty Papers, HO2/01.
30. Heenan, *Cardinal Hinsley*, p. 239.
31. *Westminster Cathedral Chronicle*, May 1943, p. 8.

SOURCES AND BIBLIOGRAPHY

Ecclesiastical Archives

Archivio Segreto Vaticano: Archivio della Delegazione Apostolica in Mombasa; Archivio della Delegazione Apostolica in Nigeria
Archdiocese of Birmingham: Ilsley Papers; Williams Papers
Archdiocese of Liverpool: Whiteside Papers; Downey Papers
Archdiocese of Southwark: Amigo Papers
Archdiocese of Westminster: Bourne Papers; Hinsley Papers
Diocese of Brentwood: Ward Papers; Doubleday Papers; Heenan Papers
Diocese of Hexham and Newcastle: Thorman Papers; McCormack Papers
Diocese of Leeds: Cornthwaite Papers; Cowgill Papers; Poskitt Papers
Diocese of Nottingham: Dunn Papers; McNulty Papers
Diocese of Salford: Henshaw Papers; Marshall Papers
Diocese of Shrewsbury: Moriarty Papers
Downside Abbey: Gasquet Papers
St Joseph's Society For Foreign Missions, Mill Hill, London: Roman Papers; African Mission Papers
St Patrick's Missionary Society, Kiltegan, County Wicklow: Whitney Papers
The Pontifical Irish College, Rome: O'Riordan Papers; Hagan Papers
The Royal English College, Valladolid: Henson Papers
The Venerable English College, Rome: Membranae, Libri e Scritture (ii), vols. 51-130

National Archives

Colonial Office Papers:
CO 96: (690/14) Activities of the White Fathers' Mission in the Northern Territories of the Gold Coast, 1929
CO 323: (959/4) Recognition of Missionary Societies, 1926; (966/7) Roman Catholic Ecclesiastical Appointments Within the British Empire, 1926-1927; (1034/12) Advisory Committee on Grants in Aid to Mission and Denominational Education; (1101/14) Great Britain's Attitude to Roman Catholic Missionary Schools; (1128/16) Missionaries: Training of Roman Catholics for Educational Work in the Colonies, 1931-1932; (1175/12) Training of Roman Catholic Missionaries for Educational Work in the Colonies, 1932-1933; (1214/4) Training of Roman Catholic Missionaries for Educational Work in the Colonies, 1933-1934
CO 536: (156/2) Role of Missions in Southern Sudan, 1929
CO 583: (1176/15) Mission Activity in Nigeria, 1927-1928
CO 628: (26) Kenya: Register of Correspondence
CO 822: (18/7) International Education Conference, 1929; (56/6) Roman Catholic Missions Organization in Zanzibar

Rhodes House, Oxford

African Manuscripts:

Marshall, J.R, 'Reminiscences of a Career in the Education Service in West Africa, 1928-1950, MSS.Afr.s.1755 (20); Tregear, P.S., 'Experience in the Education Services of Northern Rhodesia and Sierra Leone', MSS, Afr.s.1755 (89)

St Bede's Grammar School, Bradford

Governors' Papers; Annual Registers; Annual Reports, 1900-1913; Commemorative Magazines

Talbot Library, Preston

Mgr R A L Smith, 'One Man in His Time . . . Memories of a Monsignore'

Printed Primary Sources

Published Documentary and Statistical Information

(a) British Government

Colonial Office, Memorandum by the Advisory Committee on Native Education in the British Tropical African Dependencies, 1924–25. Cmd. 2374, XX1, 27
Colonial Office, Report of the East African Commission, 1925. Cmd.2387, 1X, 855
Colonial Office, Higher Education in East Africa (London, 1937)

(b) Catholic Publications

Annual Report of the Conference of Catholic Colleges
Annuario Pontificio
Catholic Directory
The Catholic Who's Who

(c) Others

Boucher, A, *Petit Atlas des Missions Catholiques* (Paris, 1928)
Buell, R.L., *The Native Problem in Africa* (London, 1965 edn.), 2 vols.
City of Bradford Education Committee, Co-ordination Report (Bradford, 1905)
Gramatica, L., *Testo e Atlante di Geografia Ecclesiastica* (Bergamo, 1927)
Hachey, T.E., *Anglo-Vatican Relations 1914-1939: Confidential Annual Reports of the British Ministers to the Holy See* (Boston, Mass., 1972)
Hailey, Lord, *An African Survey* (London, 1938)
Jones, T.J., *Education In Africa: A Study of West, South and Equatorial Africa by the African Education Commission* (New York, 1922)
Jones, T.J., *Education In East Africa* (London, 1924)
Mair, L.P., *Native Policies in Africa* (London, 1936)
McLeish, A., *Light and Darkness in Africa – A Missionary Survey of Uganda, Anglo-*

Egyptian Sudan, Abyssinia, Eritrea and the three Somalilands (London, 1927)
Reports of the Annual Conferences of Catholic Colleges (1902-1904)
Streit, R., *Catholic World Atlas* (New York, 1929)

NEWSPAPERS AND PERIODICALS

Blackfriars
Catholic Missions
Fides Service
International Review of Missions
Letters and Notices (Society of Jesus)
Missionary Annals of the Holy Ghost Fathers (The Spiritans, Dublin)
St Joseph's Advocate (St Joseph's Society For Foreign Missions, Mill Hill, London)
The African Missionary (Society of African Missions, Cork)
The Catholic Herald
The Catholic Times
The Clergy Review
The Dublin Review
The Month
The Review of the Churches
The Tablet
The Times
The Universe
The Ushaw Magazine
The Venerabile
The Zambesi Mission Record (Society of Jesus)
Westminster Cathedral Chronicle
Yorkshire Post

CONTEMPORARY WORKS

Ahaus, H., 'Pope Pius XI and Foreign Missions' in *The Clergy Review*, May 1932
———— 'Missionary Progress' in *The Clergy Review*, Sep. 1939
American Assistancy of the Society of Jesus, *The Selected Writings of Father Ledochowski* (Chicago, 1945)
Anthology, *King and Country: Selections from British War Speeches 1939-1940* (London, 1940)
Beck, G.A., 'Cardinal Hinsley: A Memoir' in *The Clergy Review*, May 1944
Bell, G.K.A., *Christian Unity: The Anglican Position* (London, 1948)
Bouniol, J., *The White Fathers and Their Missions* (London, 1929)
Brown, S.J., *Catholic Mission Literature: A Handlist* (Dublin, 1932)
Brown, W.F., *Through Windows of Memory* (London, 1946)
Crocker, W.R., *Nigeria: A Critique of British Colonial Administration* (London, 1936)
D'Eliah, P.M.D., 'When the Storm Had Blown Over: How the Catholic Church in China Emerged from the Nationalist Revolution' in IRM, vol. 23, 1934

de la Bédoyère, M., *Christian Crisis* (London, 1940)

Duffy, T.G., *Let's Go* (London, 1928)

Earnshaw, J., *The Record and Reminiscences of St Patrick's Church, Bradford* (Bradford, 1903)

Elwes, V., 'Cardinal Hinsley' in *The Clergy Review*, June 1943

Fontenelle, R., *His Holiness Pope Pius XI* (London, 1938)

Forbes, F.A., *Rafael, Cardinal Merry del Val* (London, 1934)

Fraser, D., 'Reviewing African Missions' in *The Review of the Churches*, April 1929

Friis, F.T.B., 'Mandates and Missions' in IRM, vol. 18, 1929

Gaselee, S., 'British Diplomatic Relations With The Holy See' in *The Dublin Review*, vol. 204, no. 408, Jan. 1939

Gasquet, A., *A History of the Venerable English College, Rome* (London, 1920)

Gordon, A., *Security, Freedom & Happiness* (London, 1944)

Goyau, G., *Missions and Missionaries* (London, 1932)

Heenan, J.C., *Cardinal Hinsley: A Memoir* (London, 1944)

Henson, H., *Retrospect of an Unimportant Life* (London, 1950)

Hinsley, Cardinal, *The Bond of Peace and other War-Time Addresses* (London, 1941)

———— *A Champion of The Spirit: A Selection from the Speeches of Cardinal Hinsley* (London, 1942)

Hlond, A., *The Persecution of the Catholic Church in German Occupied Poland* (London, 1941) Iremonger, F.A., *William Temple* (Oxford, 1948)

James, Fr, *African Adventure* (Dublin, 1936)

Jordan, J.P., *Bishop Shanahan of Southern Nigeria* (Dublin, 1949)

Keldany, H., *H.E. Cardinal Hinsley's Travels Through Africa 1928-1929* (London, 1939)

Latourette, K.S., *Advance Through Storm (A History of the Expansion of Christianity*, vol. vii), (London, 1945)

Lockhart, J.G., *Cosmo Gordon Lang* (London, 1949)

Mathew, D., *Catholicism in England* (London, 1948)

Newton, D., 'Cardinal Hinsley' in *Dictionary of National Biography* 1941–1950 (London, 1950)

O'Leary, M., *The Catholic Church and Education* (London, 1943)

Oldham, J.H., 'Educational Policy of the British Government in Africa' in IRM, vol. 14, 1925

Oxford University Summer School on Colonial Administration, Summary of Lectures (Oxford, 1937)

Premoli, O.M., *Contemporary Church History 1900-1925* (London, 1932)

Rennell Rodd, J., *Social and Diplomatic Memories 1902-1919* (London, 1925)

Ritson, J.H., 'The British Government and Missions of Alien Nationality' in IRM, vol. 8, 1919

Schmidlin, J., *Catholic Mission Theory* (Techny, Illinois, 1931)

Simnett, W.E., *The British Colonial Empire* (London, 1942)

Smith, R.A.L., *The Catholic Church and Social Order* (London, 1943)

Smith, R.L., 'Report from Rome' in *The Clergy Review*, April 1935

Smith, R.L., *John Fisher and Thomas More: Two English Saints*, (London, 1935)

Sturzo, L., *Church and State* (London, 1939)

Teeling, W., *The Pope in Politics: the Life and Work of Pope Pius XI* (London, 1937)

Walker, E.A., *The British Empire: Its Structure and Spirit* (London, 1943)

Whitney, P., *An Irish Missionary in Central Africa* (Dublin, 1923)

Bibliography

(a) Books

Abernathy, D.B., 'Nigeria' in Scanlon D.G. (ed.), *Church and State and Education in Africa* (New York, 1966)

Agbeti, J.K., *Church Missions and Theological Training 1842-1970* (Leiden, 1991)

Allen, C. (ed.), *Tales From The Dark Continent* (London, 1979)

Allitt, P., *Catholic Converts: British and American Intellectuals Turn To Rome* (Cornell, 1997)

Arim, N.O., 'Ghana' in Scanlon, D.G. (ed.), *Church and State and Education in Africa* (New York, 1966)

Aspden, K., *Fortress Church* (Leominster, 2002)

Atkin, N., and Tallett, F., *Priests, Prelates & People: A History of European Catholicism Since 1750* (London, 2003)

Aubert, R. (ed.), *The Church in a Secularized Society* (London, 1978)

Baeta, C.G., *Christianity in Tropical Africa* (Oxford, 1968)

Bane, M., *Catholic Pioneers In West Africa* (Dublin, 1956)

———— *The Popes and Western Africa: An Outline of Missionary History 1460s-1960s* (Dublin, 1968)

Barrett, D. (ed.), *African Initiatives in Religion* (Nairobi, 1990)

Bassey, M.O., *Missionary Rivalry and Educational Expansion in Nigeria 1885-1945* (Lewiston, New York, 1999)

Beck, G.A., *The English Catholics 1850-1950* (London, 1950)

Beidelman, T.O., *Colonial Evangelization* (Bloomington, 1982)

Bellenger, D.A. and Fletcher S., *Princes of the Church: A History of the English Cardinals* (Stroud, 2001)

———— *The Mitre and the Crown: A History of the Archbishops of Canterbury* (Stroud, 2005)

Birn, D.S., *The League of Nations Union 1918-1945* (Oxford, 1981)

Bloun, F.X., (ed.), *Vatican Archives: An Inventory and Guide to Historical Documents of the Holy See* (Oxford, 1998)

Booth, B.F., *Mill Hill Fathers in West Cameroon: Education, Health and Development* (Ottawa, 1995)

Boylan, H., *A Dictionary of Irish Biography* (Dublin, 1988)

Brady, J.E., *Princes of His People: The Story of Our Bishops 1800-1951* (Johannesburg, 1951)

Briggs, A., *The History of Broadcasting in the United Kingdom*, vol. 3, *The War of Words* (London, 1970)

Broadley, M.J., *Louis Charles Casartelli: A Bishop in Peace and War* (Bury, 2006)

Brown, J.M. and Louis W.R. (eds), *The Oxford History of the British Empire* (Oxford, 1999)

Brown, W.E., *The Catholic Church in South Africa* (London, 1960)

Bruls, J., 'From Missions to "Young Churches" ' in Aubert, R. (ed.), *The Church in a Secularized Society* (London, 1978)

Buchanan, T. and Conway, M., *Political Catholicism in Europe 1918-1965* (Oxford, 1996)

Buerhle, M.C., *Rafael, Cardinal Merry del Val* (London, 1957)

Burgman, H., *The Way the Church Started in Western Kenya* (London, 1990)

Burke, T.J.M., *Four Great Missionary Encyclicals* (New York, 1957)

Burleigh, M., *Sacred Causes* (London, 2006)

Butler, R.A., 'The Art of the Possible' in Fowler, G. et al. (eds), *Decision Making in British Education* (London, 1973)

Cameron, J. and Dodd, W.A., *Schools, Society and Progress in Tanzania* (Oxford, 1970)

Carmody, B., *Conversion and Jesuit Schooling in Zambia* (Leiden, 1992)

Chadwick, O., *Britain and the Vatican during the Second World War* (Cambridge, 1986)

Chadwick, P., *Shifting Alliances: Church & State In English Education* (London, 1997)

Charles, R., *An Introduction to Catholic Social Teaching* (Oxford, 1999)

Cleary, J.M., *Catholic Social Action in Britain 1909-1959* (Oxford, 1961)

Clifton, M., *Amigo: Friend of the Poor* (Leominster, 1987)

Cooney, J., *John Charles McQuaid, Ruler of Catholic Ireland* (Dublin, 1999)

Coppa, F.J., *The Modern Papacy Since 1789* (London, 1998)

Coventry, J., 'Roman Catholicism' in Davies, R. (ed.), *The Testing of the Churches 1932-1982* (London, 1982).

Crichton, J.D., Winstone, H.E. and Ainslie, J. R. (eds), *English Catholic Worship: Liturgical Renewal in England Since 1900* (London, 1979)

Dachs, A.J. and Rea, W.F., *The Catholic Church in Zimbabwe 1879-1979* (Gwelo, 1979)

Dah, J.N., *One Hundred Years of the Roman Catholic Church in Cameroon* (Buea, 1988)

Delavignette, R., *Christianity and Colonialism* (London, 1964)

De Wiel, J.A., *The Catholic Church in Ireland 1914-1918: War and Politics* (Dublin, 2003)

de Vries, J., *Catholic Mission, Colonial Government and Indigenous Response in Cameroon* (Leiden, 1998)

Doyle, P., *Mitres and Missions: The Roman Catholic Diocese of Liverpool 1850-2000* (Liverpool, 2005)

Drumm, W., *The Old Palace: The Catholic Chaplaincy at Oxford* (Dublin, 1991)

Duffy, E., *Saints and Sinners: A History of the Popes* (New Haven and London, 1997)

Dunn, E.J., *Missionary Theology: Foundations in Development* (Lanham, Maryland, 1980)

Easton, S.C., *The Rise and Fall of Western Colonialism* (London, 1964)

Ehler, Z. and Morrall, J.B. (eds), *Church and State Through the Centuries: A Collection of Illustrative Documents* (London, 1954)

Falola, T.(ed.), *Nigeria in the Twentieth Century* (Durham, North Carolina, 2002)

Falola, T. and Roberts, A.D., 'West Africa' in Brown, J. and Louis, W.R. (eds), *The Oxford History of the British Empire*, vol. iv *The Twentieth Century* (Oxford, 1999)

Farrell, W. and Healy, M.J., *My Way of Life: The Summa Simplified for Everyone* (New York, 1952)

Fitzgerald-Lombard, C., *English and Welsh Priests 1801-1914* (Stratton on the Fosse, 1993)

Freemantle, A., *The Papal Encyclicals in Their Historical Context* (New York, 1963)

Gaine, M., 'Hinsley, Arthur (1865-1943), Roman Catholic Archbishop of Westminster' in *Oxford Dictionary of National Biography* (Oxford, 2004)

Gannon, T.M., *World Catholicism in Transition* (London, 1988)

Garvey, B., *Bembaland Church: Religious and Social Change in South Central Africa* (Leiden, 1994)

Gilley, S., and Sheils, W., *A History of Religion in Britain* (Oxford, 1994)

Gottneid, A.J., *Church and Education in Tanzania* (Nairobi, 1976)

Gray, R., 'Christianity' in *The Cambridge History of Africa*, vol. 7, 1905-1940 (Cambridge, 1986)

———— 'The Planting of Christianity in Africa in the Nineteenth and Twentieth Centuries' in Baeta, C.G. (ed.), *Christianity in Tropical Africa* (Oxford, 1968)

Groves, C.P., *The Planting of Christianity in Africa*, vol. 4, 1914-1954 (London, 1958)

Hagerty, J.M., *The Centenary History of St Bede's Grammar School, Bradford* (Bradford, 2000)

———— *Bradford's Catholic Churches and Parishes 1825-1997* (Bradford, 1997)

Hallett, P.E., *A Catholic Dictionary* (London, 1954)

Hannecart, K., *'Intrepid Sowers': From Nyasa to Fort Jameson 1889-1946. Some Historical Notes* (Rome, 1991)

Hansen, H.B., *Mission, Church and State in a Colonial Setting: Uganda 1890-1925* (New York, 1984)

Hastings, A., 'Vocations for the Priesthood in Eastern Africa' in Barrett, D. (ed.), *African Initiatives in Religion* (Nairobi, 1971)

———— *A History of English Christianity 1920-1985* (London, 1986)

———— *Church and State: the English Experience* (Exeter, 1991)

———— *The Church in Africa 1450-1950* (Oxford, 1994)

Hebga, M.P., 'The Evolution of Catholicism in Western Africa: the Case of Cameroon' in Gannon, T.M., *World Catholicism in Transition* (London, 1988)

Heenan, J.C., *Not The Whole Truth* (London, 1971)

Henkel, R., *Christian Missions in Africa* (Berlin, 1989)

Heston, E.L., 'Papal Diplomacy: Its Organization and Way of Acting' in Gurian, W. and Fitzsimons, M.A., *The Catholic Church in World Affairs* (Notre Dame, Indiana, 1954)

Hetherington, P., *British Paternalism and Africa 1920-1940* (London, 1978)

Hickey, R., *The Catholic Church in Gongola Sate* (Yola, 1989)

Hogan, E.M., *The Irish Missionary Movement* (Dublin, 1990)

Holmes, J.D., *More Roman than Rome: English Catholicism in the Nineteenth Century* (London, 1978)

————— *The Papacy in the Modern World* (London, 1981)

Iliffe, J., *A Modern History of Tanzania* (Cambridge, 1979)

Isichei, E., *A History of Christianity in Africa from Antiquity to the Present* (London, 1995)

Jasper, R., *George Bell* (London, 1967)

Keating, J., 'Discrediting the "Catholic State": British Catholics and the Fall of France' in Tallett F. and Atkin, N. (eds), *Catholicism In Britain and France Since 1789* (London, 1996)

Kent, P.C., *The Pope and the Duce* (London, 1981)

Kiggins, T., *Maynooth Mission to Africa* (Dublin, 1991)

Kirk-Greene, A., *On Crown Service: A History of H.M. Colonial and Overseas Civil Service, 1837-1997* (London, 1999)

————— *Britain's Imperial Administrators 1858-1966* (Basingstoke, 2000)

Kittler, G.D., *The White Fathers* (London, 1957)

Latourette, K.S., 'Ecumenical Bearings of the Missionary Movement and the International Missionary Council', in Rouse, R. and Neill, S.C. (eds), *A History of the Ecumenical Movement 1517-1948* (London, 1954)

Leslie, S., *Cardinal Gasquet* (London, 1953)

Lewis, L.J., *Educational Policy and Practice in British Tropical Areas* (London, 1954)

————— *The Phelps-Stokes Report on Education in Africa* (London, 1962)

Listowel, J., *The Making of Tanganyika* (London, 1965)

Linden, I., *The Catholic Church and the Struggle for Zimbabwe* (London, 1980)

Longley, C., *The Worlock Archive* (London, 2000)

Machin, G.I.T., *Churches and Social Issues in Twentieth Century Britain* (Oxford, 1998)

Makuzi, A.O. and Afolabi, G.J. (eds), *The History of the Catholic Church in Nigeria* (Lagos, 1982)

Markham, J. (ed.), *Keeping Faith: 700 Years of Catholic Life in Hull* (Beverley, 1999)

MacLaine, I., *Ministry of Morale* (London, 1970)

MacDonald, J., *Catholic Action: The Notion and England* (London, 1949)

McClelland, V.A., *English Roman Catholics and Higher Education 1830-1903* (Oxford, 1973)

McClelland, V.A. and Hodgetts, M. (eds), *From Without the Flaminian Gate: 150 Years of Roman Catholicism in England and Wales 1850-2000* (London, 1999)

McCracken, J., *Politics and Christianity in Malawi 1875-1940* (Cambridge, 1977)

McEwan, D., *A Catholic Sudan: Dream, Mission, Reality* (Rome, 1987)

McGlade, J., *A History of Irish Catholicism*, vol. vi, *The Mission: Africa and the Orient* (Dublin, 1979)

McInally, M., *Edward Ilsley, Archbishop of Birmingham* (London, 2002)

McKeown, A., *A Beacon of Hope: A History of Sydenham Parish* (Sydenham, 2001)

Meagher, P.K., O'Brien, T.C. and Aherne, C.M. (eds), *Encyclopedic Dictionary of Religion* (Washington, 1978)

Mews, S, 'The Sword of the Spirit: A Catholic Cultural Crusade of 1940' in Sheils, W. (ed.), *The Church and War*, (Studies in Church History, no. 20, Oxford, 1983)

Milburn, D., *A History of Ushaw College* (Ushaw, 1964)

Mobley, H.W., *The Ghanaian Image of the Missionary* (Leiden, 1970)

Moloney, T., *Westminster, Whitehall and the Vatican: the Role of Cardinal Hinsley 1935-1943* (London, 1985)

Murphy, J., *Church, State and Schools in Britain* (Oxford, 1976)

Muyebe, H.W., *The Catholic Missionaries Within and Beyond the Politics of Exclusivity in Colonial Malawi 1901-1945* (Lewiston, New York, 1999)

Neill, S., *A History of Christian Missions* (London, 1964)

Nduka, O., *Western Education and the Nigerian Cultural Background* (Ibadan, 1965)

Newton, D., 'Cardinal Hinsley' in *Dictionary of National Biography* 1941-1950 (London, 1950)

Norman, E., *The English Catholic Church in the Nineteenth Century* (Oxford, 1984)

———— *Roman Catholicism In England from the Elizabethan Settlement to the Second Vatican Council* (Oxford, 1986)

Obeng, P., *Asante Catholicism* (Leiden, 1996)

Obi, C.A., *A Hundred Years of the Catholic Church in Eastern Nigeria* 1895-1995 (Onitsha, 1985)

Oger, L., *Where A Scattered Flock Gathered* (Ndola, Zambia, 1991)

Ogez, J.M., *Where It All Began* (Rome, 1991)

Ogudo, D.E.O., *The Holy Ghost Fathers and Catholic Worship among the Igbo People of Eastern Nigeria* (Paderborn, 1988)

Oliver, R., *The Missionary Factor in East Africa* (London, 1952)

Omenka, N.I., *The School in the Service of Evangelization* (Leiden, 1989)

O'Neil, R., *Mission to the Upper Nile* (London, 1999)

O'Neill, R.J., *Mission To the British Cameroon* (London, 1991)

Ozigboh, I.R.A., *Roman Catholicism in South Eastern Nigeria 1885-1931* (Onitsha, 1988)

Pearson, J. (ed.), *A Guide to Manuscripts and Documents in the British Isles Relating to Africa*, (London, 1993, 1994)

Pels, P., *A Politics of Presence: Contracts between Missionaries and Waluguru in Late Colonial Tanganyika* (Amsterdam, 1999)

Plumb, B., *Arundel to Zabi: A Biographical Dictionary of the Catholic Bishops of England and Wales (Deceased) 1623-1987* (Warrington, 1987)

Pollard, J.F., *The Unknown Pope: Benedict XV (1914-1922) and the Pursuit of Peace* (London, 1999)

Porter, A., *Bibliography of Imperial, Colonial and Commonwealth History Since 1600* (Oxford, 2002)

Randall, A., *Vatican Assignment* (London, 1956)

Randolph, R.H., *Report to Rome* (Gwelo, 1978)

———— *Dawn In Zimbabwe* (Gweru, 1985)

Rhodes, A., *The Vatican In The Age Of The Dictators 1922-1945* (London, 1973)

Roberts, A. (ed.), *The Colonial Moment in Africa* (Cambridge, 1986)

Rockett, J., *Held in Trust: Catholic Parishes in England and Wales 1900-1950* (London, 2001)

Rotberg, R.I., *Christian Missionaries and the Creation of Northern Rhodesia 1880-1924* (Princeton, 1965)

Rouse, R. and Neill, S.C. (eds), *A History of the Ecumenical Movement 1517-1948* (London, 1954)

Scanlon, D.G. (ed.), *Church, State and Education in Africa* (New York, 1966)

Schofield, N. and Skinner, G., *The English Cardinals* (Oxford, 2007)

Smith, H.L. (ed.), *War and Social Change: British Society and the Second World War* (London, 1985)

Smythe, K.R., 'The Creation of a Catholic Fipa Society: Conversion in Nkansi District, Ufipa' in Spear, T., Snelson, P.D., *Educational Development in Northern Rhodesia 1883-1945* (London, 1970)

Society of African Missions, *One Hundred Years of Missionary Achievement 1856-1956* (Cork, 1956)

Spear, T. and Kimambo, I.N. (eds), *East African Expressions of Christianity* (Oxford, 1999)

Stenger, F., *White Fathers in Colonial Central Africa* (Hamburg, 2001)

Sundkler, B., *The Christian Missionary in Africa* (London, 1960)

Sundkler, B. and Steed, C., *A History of the Church in Africa* (Cambridge, 2000)

Taylor, B. (ed.), *The Catholics of Sutton Park* (Guildford, 2005)

Tittmann, H.H., *Inside The Vatican Of Pius XII* (New York, 2004)

Todd, J.M., *African Mission* (London, 1961)

Tomkins, O.S., 'The Roman Catholic Church and the Ecumenical Movement, 1910-1948' in Rouse R. and Neill S.C.(eds), *A History of the Ecumenical Movement 1517-1948* (London, 1954)

Tourigny, Y., *So Abundant A Harvest* (London, 1972)

Versteijnen, F., *The Catholic Mission of Bagamoyo* (Bagamoyo, 1968) (typescript)

Waliggo, J.M., *A History of African Priests* (Nairobi, 1988)

Walsh, M., *From Sword to Ploughshare: Sword of the Spirit to Catholic Institute for International Relations 1940-1980* (London, 1980).

———— *The Tablet: A Commemorative History 1840-1990* (London, 1990)

Walsh, J., *The Growth of the Catholic Church in the Diocese of Jos 1907-1978* (Ipero-Remu, 1993)

Warren, M., *The Missionary Movement From Britain in Modern History* (London, 1965)

Watkin, E.I., *Roman Catholicism in England from the Reformation to 1950* (London, 1957)

Waugh, E., *Ronald Knox* (London, 1959)

Weight, R., *Patriots: National Identity In Britain 1940-2000* (London, 2002)

Wheeler-Bennett, J.W., *King George VI* (London, 1958)

Williams, M.E., *The Venerable English College, Rome: A History 1579-1979* (London, 1979; new edition Leominster, 2008)

———— *St Alban's College Valladolid* (London, 1986)

Wilkinson, A., *Dissent or Conform: War, Peace and the English Churches 1900-1945* (London, 1986)

Wilson, H.S., *The Imperial Experience in Sub-Saharan Africa Since 1870* (Oxford, 1977)

Wolfe, K.M., *The Churches and the British Broadcasting Corporation, 1922-1956* (London, 1984)

(b) Articles

Barnes, A.E., 'Catholic Evangelising in one Colonial Mission: the Institutional Evolution of Jos Prefecture, Nigeria 1907-1954' in *Catholic Historical Review*, vol. lxxxiv, no. 2, 1988

———— 'Evangelising where it is not wanted: Colonial Administrators and Missionaries in Northern Nigeria during the first third of the Twentieth Century' in *Journal of Religion in Africa*, vol. 25, 1995

Beales, A.C.F., 'The Sword of the Spirit' in *The Month*, vol. CLXXVI, no. 916

Bellenger, D.A., 'Cardinal Gasquet (1846-1926): An English Roman' in *Recusant History*, vol. 24, no. 4, Oct. 1999

Davies, J., 'The Catholic Church and Negotiations over the White Paper and Education Bill, 1944' in *Recusant History*, vol. 22, no. 2, Oct. 1994

———— 'Bishop Moriarty, Shrewsbury and World War Two' in *Recusant History*, vol. 25, no. 1, May 2000

Flint, J., 'English Catholics and the Proposed Soviet Alliance, 1939' in *Journal of Ecclesiastical History*, vol. 48, no. 3, July 1997

Gurian, W. and Fitzsimons, M.A. (eds) *The Catholic Church in World Affairs* (Notre Dame, Indiana, 1954)

Hagerty, J.M., 'Hinsley at Ushaw' in *Northern Catholic History*, no. 23, Spring 1986

———— 'Habemus Ducem: The Appointment of Archbishop Hinsley to Westminster, 1935' in *Recusant History*, vol. 29, no. 1, May 2008

Hogan, E.M., 'The Motivation of the Modern Irish Missionary Movement 1912-1939' in *Journal of Religion in Africa*, vol. 10, 1979

Kieran-Hyland, St G., 'Arthur Hinsley – Parish Priest' in *The Venerabile*, vol. xiii, no 1, 1946

Lowry, D., 'The Crown, Empire Loyalism and the Assimilation of Non-British White Subjects in the British World: An Argument Against "Ethnic Determinism" ' in *Journal of Imperial and Commonwealth History*, vol. 31, no. 2, May 2003

Mayne, C., 'Lay Apostles in the Forces' in *The Month*, vol. CLXXIX, no. 932, March–April 1943

Meagher, R.W., 'Early Years As Rector of the English College' in *The Ushaw Magazine*, July 1943

Murray, J., 'Some Successful Experiments in Christian Formation' in *Lumen Vitae*, vol. II, no. 1, 1947

————— 'The C.M.S. and the "Female Circumcision" Issue in Kenya 1929-1932' in *Journal of Religion in Africa*, vol. 8, 1976

Okwu, A.S.O., 'The Beginning of the Maynooth Movement in Southern Nigeria and the Rise of the St Patrick's Missionary Society 1920-1930' in *Journal of Religion in Africa*, vol. 10, 1979

Porter, A, 'Church History, History of Christianity, Religious History: Some Reflections on British Missionary Enterprise Since the late Eighteenth Century', in *Church History*, vol. 71, no. 3, Sept. 2002

Rolls, D., 'A Troubled Transition – The Roman Association and the English College, 1913-1922' in *The Venerabile*, vol. xxix, no. 2, 1988

Smith, R.L., 'Cardinal Hinsley: An Appreciation' in *The Venerabile*, vol. xi, no. 2, May 1943

Walsh, M., 'Ecumenism in Wartime Britain' in *The Heythrop Journal*, no. 23, July 1982

————— 'The Sword of the Spirit and Religion and Life, 1940-1945' in *The Heythrop Journal*, Oct. 1982

INDEX